THIRD EDITION

SOCIAL WELFARE

in Canadian Society

Rosalie Chappell, B.S.W., M.S.W.

THOMSON

NELSON

Australia   Canada   Mexico   Singapore   Spain   United Kingdom   United States

THOMSON

NELSON

**Social Welfare in Canadian Society,
Third Edition**

Rosalie Chappell

Associate Vice-President, Editorial Director:
Evelyn Veitch

Executive Editors:
Anne Williams
Rod Banister

Senior Marketing Manager:
Murray Moman

Developmental Editors:
Sandra de Ruiter
Glen Herbert

Permissions Coordinator:
Kristiina Bowering

Production Editor:
Julie van Veen

Copy Editor:
Matthew Kudelka

Proofreader:
Karen Rolfe

Indexer:
Jin Tan

Production Coordinator:
Ferial Suleman

Creative Director:
Angela Cluer

Interior Design:
Joanne Slouenwhite

Interior Design Modifications:
Sarah Battersby

Cover Design:
Roxanna Bennett

Cover Image:
Steve Lewis/Photographer's
Choice/Getty Images

Compositor:
Janet Zanette

Printer:
Webcom

Library and Archives Canada Cataloguing in Publication

Chappell, Rosalie, 1955–

Social welfare in Canadian society / Rosalie Chappell. — 3rd ed.

Includes bibliographical references and index.
ISBN-13: 978-0-17-641411-5
ISBN-10: 0-17-641411-8

1. Social service—Canada. 2. Public welfare—Canada. I. Title.

HV105.C48 2004   361.971
C2004-904410-9

DEDICATION

This book is dedicated to the women and men who have chosen a career in Canada's social welfare system. Despite its shortcomings, the system is a good one … but you can make it better.

BRIEF TABLE OF CONTENTS

TABLE OF CONTENTS

PREFACE

Canada's social, economic, and political climate has changed a great deal since the publication of the second edition of *Social Welfare in Canadian Society*: terrorism has moved much closer to home, and mad cow disease, softwood lumber disputes, avian flu, and other factors have devastated many Canadian industries and put thousands out of work. Health-related conditions like SARS, and record-breaking fires, storms, and floods have all heightened people's sense of vulnerability. Moreover, Canadian social values, human rights, and freedoms have been challenged by issues such as gay marriage and the detainment of foreign-born Canadians in the name of national security. Throughout all this, the federal and several provincial and territorial governments have managed to eliminate their deficits. Some governments have gone on to amass huge budget surpluses, and Alberta has even rid itself of public debt.

How do these events relate to social welfare? Simply put, they all spark the need for Canada's social welfare system to *change*—to change in response to shifting government priorities; to emerging public attitudes and expectations; to new levels of available resources; and to increasing demands on service delivery systems. As we enter a postdeficit, postindustrial era, our social welfare system must find more innovative and cost-effective ways to respond to an ever-widening range of human needs and social problems. This third edition of *Social Welfare in Canadian Society* explores many aspects of this new era—specifically, the evolving role of our social welfare system, some of the challenges it currently faces, and recent advances made in social welfare programming.

TEXT OBJECTIVES

Remaining true to its original objectives, the third edition of this indigenous Canadian text aims to:

- provide Canadian content, and draw from the wisdom of Canadian scholars and researchers;
- strike a balance between historical and current content;
- explore a wide range of social welfare policies and programs in both the public and private sectors;
- provide real-life examples of social welfare programs from across the country;

- discuss practice issues related to various social welfare fields;
- consider the impact of social welfare programs and policies on social groups; and
- present material in a neutral manner, allowing readers to form their own opinions and conclusions.

It is hoped that this third edition not only meets these objectives, but also gives readers a good sense of Canada's social welfare system and an appreciation of both its strengths and shortcomings.

As with previous editions, this revised text introduces the basic concepts and processes related to social welfare, current issues in the field, and Canadian programs and services. Readers might use the book as a starting point to embark on a more in-depth study of social welfare in Canada. Various resources are available to support readers in this task. Appendix A, for example, offers an expanded chronology of key events in social welfare and related systems over a hundred-year period. This appendix is an excellent resource for readers wishing to learn about a specific period in the development of Canada's social welfare system, or to track important dates in the evolution of particular programs. The reference section at the end of the book is another resource for independent learning; it offers a comprehensive list of Canadian titles, website addresses, and other sources. Finally, readers are encouraged to check out the *Social Welfare in Canadian Society* website at **www.socialwelfare3e.nelson.com** for links to the most current information on issues related to social welfare.

Organization

This edition retains the basic three-part structure of previous editions. Part I introduces readers to some of the fundamental aspects of Canada's social welfare system, including its knowledge and ideological base; its history; its objectives, programs, and services; and its relations to political and economic systems.

Part II is devoted to social welfare's service delivery system. Here readers learn about the various service sectors and the principal activities of social agencies. This section also looks at the range of service providers found in social welfare settings and the approaches they use when helping people.

Part III examines a wide range of social problems and the ways Canada addresses them through social welfare programs and services. It starts with a focus on economic security, the impact of low income on Canadians, and current initiatives that address poverty, unemployment, a housing crisis, and hunger. The remaining chapters explore social welfare issues and programs specific to families with children, seniors, Aboriginal peoples, immigrants and refugees, and people with disabilities.

New to this Edition

The third edition brings the reader up to date on social statistics, policies, initiatives, and issues. A new feature—a glossary of key terms—familiarizes readers with a wide range of words and phrases specific to the social welfare field. The glossary also promises to be especially valuable to students when they are preparing for examinations. In the references section, look for one or more numbers following each citation: these numbers represent the chapter in which the book, article, or webpage has been cited—a useful tool for locating materials quickly and easily in the text.

Readers will be interested in the various themes that are woven throughout this new edition—themes that reflect some of the more significant trends in Canada's social welfare system. These themes include the following:

- *The changing role of government.* Canadian governments are no longer willing to assume the role of a primary provider, and have devolved many of their traditional social welfare responsibilities to lower levels of government, the voluntary sector, First Nations communities, and families. Governments today favour initiatives that will reduce people's dependency on government—that is, programs designed to move working-age citizens into the workforce; strategies to build the capacity of communities and voluntary organizations; and services that support families as caregivers. The third edition explores the consequences of this trend and looks at the challenges some groups face as they assume greater responsibilities for social welfare.

- *An emphasis on partnerships.* As social problems such as poverty and homelessness persist, it becomes clear that no single government, discipline, or service sector has all the tools to eradicate these problems. The third edition explores the trend toward cooperative arrangements for addressing social problems (between different levels of government, between government and the private sector, and between government and First Nations).

- *Regional disparities.* When it devolved many of its responsibilities to the provincial and territorial governments, the federal government also gave them more freedom to set priorities and to design and deliver programs. The provinces and territories are now in a position to tailor their social welfare programs to local needs; however, they also have the right to reduce or eliminate programs and services. The third edition reviews some of the historical, economic, and other factors that have shaped the social agendas of Canada's diverse regions; it also considers the repercussions of increased power at the regional level, the growing disparities in social welfare programs across the nation, and the issue of national standards for social welfare.

- *The shift from a deficit to a postdeficit era.* Many Canadian governments that cut social expenditures and reformed social programs in the 1990s now have balanced budgets, and in some cases budget surpluses. Some governments have begun reinvesting their savings in social welfare programs; others are maintaining tight budgets and offering little relief to people in need. The third edition considers the various approaches taken by the federal and regional governments to restrain, reform, and reinvest in social welfare.

- *Globalization and labour market shifts.* Increasingly, international pressures are influencing Canadian social policy. Globalization has created huge labour-market shifts, which have pushed poor Canadians deeper into poverty and placed new groups at risk of unemployment, underemployment, poverty, and homelessness. At the same time, international organizations, such as the UN, are pressuring Canada to improve conditions for its poor and disadvantaged citizens. The third edition takes a closer look at globalization's impact on Canada's social welfare policies and programs, as well as the impact of international factors on vulnerable groups.

- *Targeted programs for low-income Canadians.* The negative impacts of government cutbacks during the 1990s are being felt mainly by Canada's poorest citizens. Despite recent economic recovery and reinvestment in social programs, many social problems persist. Income inequality is also worsening, creating divisions between rich and poor Canadians and subsequently weakening social cohesion. Universal income-security programs have become a thing of the past as governments target their resources at low-income groups. The third edition considers recent initiatives aimed at improving social and economic conditions for Canada's poorest citizens.

- *Research-based initiatives.* Today, social welfare initiatives are likely to be based on solid research. Social welfare programs no longer exist merely because "they've always been there." Instead, program developers refer to such Canadian studies as the National Longitudinal Survey of Children and Youth, Understanding the Early Years, and the Longitudinal Survey of Immigrants to Canada, to help them design and implement new programs. Programs are being scrutinized through program evaluation and outcome measurement to ensure that they achieve their goals and objectives. This edition considers some of the research findings from Canadian studies and their relationship to social welfare initiatives.

These trends play an important role in social welfare development and underlie many discussions in this edition of *Social Welfare in Canadian Society*.

Pedagogical Features

Reviews of *Social Welfare in Canadian Society* suggested that certain features of the first and second editions be maintained in the third edition. These features, which aim to enhance the reader's comprehension and enjoyment of the book, include:

- a list of objectives at the beginning of each chapter to guide the reader through the content;

- a variety of exhibits to give a visual reference to points made in the text;

- definitions of terms in the main text or in text boxes;

- profiles and examples of social welfare programs, services, and initiatives;

- a section at the end of selected chapters that provides a conceptual link between social welfare and social work practice;

- boldfaced key terms in the text and at the end of each chapter, with their page references; and

- a thorough index to help the reader find information quickly and easily.

Instructor's Resources

An important objective of the third edition of *Social Welfare in Canadian Society* is to create a teaching package that includes a text (to meet the learning needs of students) and an Instructor's Manual (to help educators teach their courses more effectively). The Instructor's Manual has been updated in terms of:

- ideas for in-class activities to facilitate student learning, to stimulate critical thinking and analysis of the text material, and to help students apply social welfare theory;

- suggestions for student assignments to increase students' awareness of social welfare issues, improve research skills, and enhance written and verbal communication;

- recommended readings, which can be used as (a) supplementary readings for the course, (b) sources of information for lecture preparation, and (c) resources for student assignments;

- websites to facilitate further research on social welfare topics; and

- a test bank—which includes true-or-false, multiple-choice, and short-answer questions—to assist students and instructors at course review and examination time.

ACKNOWLEDGMENTS

Although only one name appears on the cover, this book is the result of a team effort. Special thanks go to

- my husband, Paul Wallin, for his unfailing support and encouragement, and for taking on the roles of "in-house" editor, reference manager, and research assistant;

- the team at Thomson Nelson, and especially to my developmental editor, Sandra de Ruiter, and my production editor, Julie van Veen;

- the staff at the Vancouver Island Regional Library, for their patience, and for their efforts to accommodate my deadlines;

- Margaret Wallin, for her technical assistance;

- my sister, Lily Dalley, and friend Margaret Leitner, for all their e-mails during my cloistered year of writing; and

- the many individuals who responded to my requests for information, including Marie Bourassa (Health Canada), Mebrat B. Beyenne (Self-Help Association of B.C.), Gregory Gillespie (Social Development Canada), Sharon Taylor (Central Alberta Refugee Effort), Patricia Living (Government of Yukon), France Audet (Canadian Association of Social Workers), Louise Gunville (National Council of Welfare), Xavier Patry (Statistics Canada), Christian Sauve (Public Service Commission), Michael Cushing (Ontario Social Development Council), and Janice Nelson (HRDC—B.C./Yukon Region).

Before work began on this new edition of *Social Welfare in Canadian Society*, reviewers were selected to critique the previous edition. I would like to thank the review panel participants for providing me with excellent suggestions on how to improve the third edition: Ken Barter of Memorial University of Newfoundland, Les Jerome of the University of Calgary, Neil McMahon of Mohawk College, and Margaret Wright of the University of British Columbia.

I am grateful to the reviewers of the previous editions for their feedback and direction. Reviewers of the second edition include Brian Dwyer, Sheridan College; Luke Fusco, Wilfrid Laurier University; and Paul MacIsaac, Georgian College. Reviewers of the first edition include Phil Durrant, Niagara College; Arvey Hanowski, University of Regina; Emmett Hogan, Mount Royal College; Cheryl Hebert, Memorial University; Mac Davis, Humber College; and Rory Mahood, Cariboo College.

The positive comments I have received from my peers motivate me to work harder to make each new edition better than the last. I hope the recent revisions to this text meet the needs and standards of students and instructors, and that these changes enhance the reader's understanding and appreciation of our social welfare system.

–Rosalie Chappell

ABOUT THE AUTHOR

Rosalie Chappell received her Bachelor of Social Work and Master of Social Work degrees from the University of Calgary. She has taught social work and social service work in British Columbia and Alberta at the University College of the Fraser Valley, Open Learning Agency, Malaspina University-College, and Red Deer College. Besides teaching, Rosalie has worked as a clinical social worker, supervisor, consultant, and program evaluator in a diverse range of public- and private-sector organizations, including family counselling agencies, community corrections agencies, alcohol and drug treatment centres, and extended care. Rosalie currently devotes much of her time to research and writing.

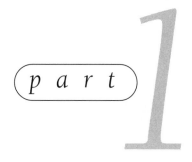

part 1

SOCIAL WELFARE IN CANADA

An Overview

chapter 1

The Nature of Canadian Social Welfare

Objectives

I. To introduce the primary functions and interdisciplinary knowledge base of Canada's social welfare system.

II. To explore the nature and content of income security programs and personal social services, and to consider targeted and universal approaches to service delivery.

III. To examine some of the political and religious ideologies that influence the focus and activities of Canadian social welfare.

INTRODUCTION

The social welfare of citizens is a key consideration in a caring and benevolent society. Social welfare shapes our quality of life, our interactions with one another, and the ways we cope with the negative consequences of unemployment, family breakdown, disability, and other life experiences. Despite its importance, social welfare is a highly abstract term with no single, exhaustive, universally agreed upon definition. The term **social welfare** can nevertheless be understood in various ways. As a *concept*, social welfare embraces the belief that society should provide a minimum level of individual and collective well-being. From the perspective of a *field* or *discipline*, social welfare involves the study of how a society enhances the well-being of its members.

Social welfare can also be understood as a *system* with a specific function in society. In Canada, the social welfare system comprises interconnected organizations and overlapping policies, procedures, and activities designed to

- help individuals, families, and groups meet their basic social and economic needs; and

- prevent, reduce, or alleviate social problems.

In fulfilling its primary functions, the social welfare system plays an important role in maintaining social cohesion and ensuring social justice. **Social cohesion** includes processes that "help instil in individuals the sense of belonging to the same community and the feeling that they are recognized as members of that community" (Maxwell, 2003b, 1). Social welfare is the "glue" that holds society together by preventing poverty, discrimination, and other social conditions that can marginalize certain populations from the mainstream society. **Social justice** holds an equally important place in social welfare since many social welfare activities involve upholding human rights, redistributing wealth from the rich to the poor, and defending people's entitlements to resources.

The boundaries between social welfare and other social programs are not always clear. There is considerable overlap, for example, between the support given by workers in the social welfare field and those in health care. In some communities, social welfare services are provided alongside health services in multiservice centres. It is also common for social welfare and health care providers to have the same clients. Moreover, social welfare and health care programs may be linked administratively, as in the case of Prince Edward Island's Ministry of Health and Social Services. Despite these points of overlap, social welfare has its own distinct mandate, goals, and objectives.

Social welfare is a unique term that is often confused with related concepts and processes and used interchangeably with other terms such as social security, social services, and social policy. Although these concepts are closely linked, there are differences between them (see Exhibit 1.1).

I. THE PRIMARY FUNCTIONS OF SOCIAL WELFARE ACTIVITIES

MEETING HUMAN NEEDS

A primary function of social welfare activities is to identify and respond to basic human needs. In general, a **human need** is a necessary condition or requirement that, if not met, will result in serious physical, mental, or social

Exhibit 1.1

DEFINITIONS OF TERMS

SOCIAL SECURITY

A range of income security programs and personal social services that help people meet their basic human needs from "cradle to grave."

PERSONAL SOCIAL SERVICES

Often referred to as "social services." These provide nonincome and intangible benefits for the purpose of enhancing social functioning and general well-being for individuals, families, and small groups.

SOCIAL ASSISTANCE

An income security program that gives cash to individuals and families who are unable to adequately meet their needs and who have exhausted all other means of support. Generally viewed as the income program of last resort, otherwise known as "welfare."

SOCIAL PROGRAMS

Systems consisting of services, benefits, or activities that are designed to improve human welfare or meet a social need. These include social welfare, health care, and postsecondary education.

SOCIAL POLICY

A plan or blueprint that guides a government's strategies for helping citizens meet a wide range of material and social needs.

SOCIAL WORK

A profession committed to helping people enhance their well-being, develop skills, and utilize resources for the purpose of resolving problems or meeting basic needs.

SOCIAL SAFETY NET

A collection of government-sponsored health, social welfare, and emergency services designed to help people cope with the negative consequences of natural disasters, personal crises, or medical problems.

WELFARE STATE

A country whose government is committed to correcting the problem of unequal distribution of wealth by redistributing income from high- to low-income groups and by ensuring that all citizens have equal access to health, social welfare, and other important resources.

Source: Author.

harm. Human needs—such as the needs for food, water, and affection—are universal in that they do not vary over time or according to a person's culture. What does vary is the way a particular culture chooses to satisfy those needs (Max-Neef, 1991).

Most of our human needs are met by informal support systems (such as family and friends) and by formal institutions (such as the Church and the workplace). When these systems fail to meet the basic needs of individuals and groups, social welfare programs are often called upon to intervene. The diversity of human beings is such that it is impossible to list all possible needs that arise for people over a lifetime. Social welfare programs are primarily concerned with helping people carry out important social roles (such as parent or wage-earner) or obtain sufficient resources to survive, develop, and adequately care for dependants. Some programs also serve a social control function by curbing behaviour that contradicts social norms or that interferes with the safety or development of others (Dobelstein, 1978).

A variety of models have been advanced that outline the range of human needs; Abraham Maslow's *hierarchy of needs* is one of the best known of these models. According to Maslow, a person must first meet basic survival and security needs (for food, water, shelter, and the like) before trying to meet "higher order" needs related to social interaction, self-esteem, and self-actualization. Exhibit 1.2 illustrates the different levels of human needs as identified by Maslow: basic needs are found at the bottom of the pyramid, with higher-order needs listed successively up the hierarchy. Critics of Maslow's theory offer alternative views of how people meet their needs. The Chilean economist Manfred Max-Neef (1991), for example, argues that after basic subsistence needs are satisfied, all other human needs are met simultaneously and not one after another in a linear or hierarchical fashion.

Because there are never enough resources to meet all human needs, social policy-makers must determine which needs should be addressed by government-sponsored programs and which should be left to the resources of individuals, families, the Church, and other nongovernment sources of help. These decisions are influenced most strongly by predominant cultural beliefs and attitudes, economic pressures and priorities, the political mood of the country, and the agendas of various individuals and groups (Johnson et al., 1997; Compton, 1980). During times of economic downturn and tightened government budgets, social welfare tends to focus on the needs of the most vulnerable members of society, such as children in low-income families and elderly people without family support. These shrinking budgets also make it necessary to direct resources to those human needs that are considered "basic," such as the needs for food, shelter, and security; "higher order" needs are left to the resources of individuals and their families.

Exhibit 1.2
MASLOW'S HIERARCHY OF NEEDS

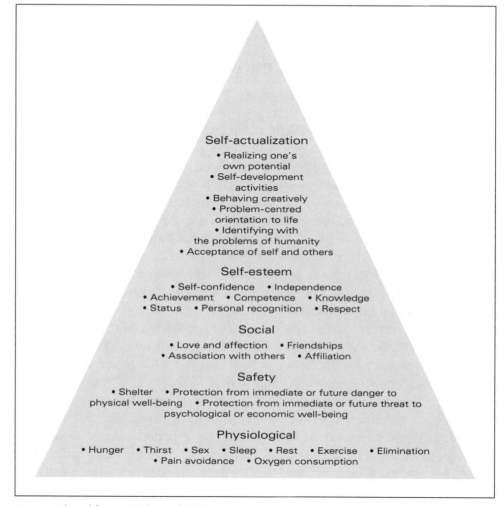

Source: Adapted from A. Harber and R.P. Runyon, *Fundamentals of Psychology*, (McGraw-Hill 1983), 304. Copyright 1983. Reproduced with permission of The McGraw-Hill Companies.

Over time, concerns for certain populations rise to the top of social agendas and demand special attention from government. This happened in 1927 when the Government of Canada, recognizing that seniors required a different level of support than other nonworking Canadians, introduced old age pensions (HRDC, 2002c). During the 1980s, Canadians learned about HIV/AIDS and became aware of the biopsychosocial needs of people who contracted this disease. This led to a variety of social welfare programs and services designed to support people with HIV/AIDS and their families. Canadian governments continue to recognize segments of the population that require more support. Since the late 1990s, for example, the federal and provincial/territorial governments have identified children up to five years old, and people with disabilities, as top social welfare priorities.

ADDRESSING SOCIAL PROBLEMS

People are subject to a number of social conditions that strain their ability to meet personal needs. These conditions include social isolation, poverty, racism, unemployment, and crime. Although social conditions are not problematic in and of themselves, they may produce **social problems**. For example, most people appreciate time alone, but too much social isolation may lead to depression; similarly, a person might initially welcome unemployment, but prolonged idleness may result in stress-related disorders. Thus, for social *conditions* to be considered social *problems,* they must create some measurable degree of economic or social hardship, psychological or physical injury, or other negative consequences. Social problems tend to share other characteristics as well. Usually they are events or behaviours that people are concerned about and want changed, that affect a large segment of the population, and that spark some kind of collective response aimed at correcting the situation (Thompson et al., 2001; Henslin, 2003).

The definition of social problems changes over time. What is currently perceived as a social problem may have been virtually ignored in the past. A case in point is a statement by Sainsbury in 1977 (11–12): "Take ... the situation of women who are severely ill-treated by their husbands; this would not at the present time fulfil the conditions of a social problem, and would be approached by the social worker using the criterion of need rather than problem as justification for his intervention." Perhaps this was a typical response to spousal abuse in 1977; today's attitudes toward domestic violence are strikingly different, as evidenced by the number of women's shelters and by legislation aimed at preventing and treating family violence. It is plain that social welfare policies, programs, and activities tend to reflect what society defines as social problems at any given time.

Canada's social welfare system has long focused on defining, preventing, and alleviating social problems that affect both the individual and general society. For example, child abuse can take an immeasurable toll on children in terms of physical and/or psychological suffering and diminished personal and social functioning. Child abuse is also destructive to society: "It robs all of us of the health, productivity, and contribution of many of its future citizens" (Institute for the Prevention of Child Abuse, 1994, 6). When responding to social problems, those who control social welfare resources must determine to what extent intervention should be directed toward the individual (for example, through child protection services) rather than the broader community (for example, through national child abuse prevention strategies).

Social scientists rely on various "scientific" methods or instruments, such as social indicators, outcome studies, statistics, and indices, to objectively measure the level of social problems in a given geographic area. Thompson and colleagues (2001) have designed a Social Problem Index to measure the "extent of social malaise" in Canada. This study found that social problems are increasing in Canada and that provinces with high rates of one social problem are likely to have high rates of other problems, suggesting a common cause. This finding may have implications for how social problems are treated. As Thompson and colleagues point out, if there is a common cause for various social problems, "this should lead us to question why we then deal with crime, divorce, suicide, and alcoholism in such different ways, with separate and distinct services often being set up for each."

THE KNOWLEDGE BASE OF SOCIAL WELFARE

There are several academic disciplines that help us understand people's needs and society's problems. These disciplines include the following:

- *Sociology* studies human relationships and the rules that guide them, how societies change or resist change, and the roles of social institutions such as churches and schools.

- *Psychology* studies the mind (for example, how people think, feel, imagine, and plan), as well as how mental activities influence what people say and do.

- *Psychiatry* is a branch of medicine that studies disorders of the mind (or mental illnesses) and their associated behaviours.

- *Political science* studies politics (including the workings of government and political events) and areas of power other than government.

- *Economics* studies methods used to allocate resources to meet human needs, distribute income among individuals and groups, and determine national output and employment.

- *Criminology* studies those who commit crimes and a variety of social factors related to crime and victimization.

- *Anthropology* studies past and contemporary cultures, with a focus on customs and the ways in which people live.

- *Statistics* is a science concerned with the collection and analysis of numerical information, often related to the study of a population's characteristics such as age, sex, and marital status (Marsh, 2003).

Each of these disciplines has made important contributions to social welfare's knowledge base, thus making social welfare a highly **interdisciplinary field**. The theories and facts generated by these disciplines are often used by policymakers and program designers to develop or modify social welfare policies and programs.

Much of our understanding of human needs and problems is the result of practice knowledge. This type of knowledge is derived from the work of frontline workers, supervisors, managers, and others who work in the social welfare field. In his study of social inclusion in Canada, Rosenberg (2002, 3) noted: "The front-line workers, generally from non-profit organizations, contribute a lot of practical skill and insights into the implications of different approaches for the populations and communities involved. Their experience is vital."

In recent years, social welfare's knowledge base has expanded as social researchers discover more effective methods of helping people. One nonprofit organization—the Social Research and Demonstration Corporation (SRDC)—was established in 1991 to gather information primarily "to help policymakers and practitioners identify social policies and programs that improve the well-being of all Canadians, with a special concern for the effects on the disadvantaged" (Social Research and Demonstration Corporation, 2004). Through various demonstration projects, experiments, and exploratory and analytical studies, the SRDC has provided valuable insights into which social welfare programs are effective, for whom they are most effective, and why these programs work as well as they do.

II. SOCIAL WELFARE PROGRAMS AND SERVICES

A wide range of programs and services comprise Canada's social welfare system (see Appendix A for a chronological account). Social welfare **programs and services** are often understood as any activity or project that has a specific purpose, goal, and/or objectives. There are nevertheless subtle distinctions between a program and a service. A service involves specific acts of giving assistance to others. A program may or may not have a service component: the federal Social Development Partnerships Program, for example, focuses on disability research and program development rather than the direct provision of help.

Social welfare's programs and services are classified into two categories: (1) income security programs; and (2) personal social services. The importance placed on the provision of each program type depends on the particular economic and social needs people have at any given time. After the Great Depression, for example, the provision of income security programs (such as unemployment insurance) was of utmost concern to Canadians. Today, income security programs are important; however, personal social services are in increasing demand. As Judith Maxwell (2003a) explains, quality childcare is essential for families that have two working parents, more affordable housing is needed for low-income Canadians, and a growing number of elderly people require a full range of support services.

INCOME SECURITY PROGRAMS

Income security programs are government-sponsored initiatives that provide pensions, tax benefits, or other financial aid to individuals and families that are unable to provide for themselves due to old age, sickness, disability, or some other condition deemed beyond personal control. Although the income security system is often criticized for failing to meet the basic needs of Canadians, it attempts to ensure that all citizens live above a reasonable standard of living, otherwise known as a **social minimum**. Most income security programs can be roughly grouped into four categories:

- **Cash transfers** are benefits that are targeted to individuals whose income or assets fall below a certain level. Examples of cash transfers are the Guaranteed Income Supplement, social assistance (welfare), and guaranteed income programs for people with severe disabilities.

- **Social insurance** programs are forced savings plans that require working individuals to contribute to a program, which then compensates them when they are not working. Benefits from these programs are based on the claimant's contributions. Employment Insurance and the Canada and Quebec Pension Plans are examples of social insurance programs.

- **Tax credits** are reductions in the amount of income tax paid by low- or moderate-income earners. Examples of this type of program are the Canada Child Tax Benefit and the Goods and Services Tax/Harmonized Sales Tax Credit. The use of the tax system—as opposed to issuing cheques—is rapidly becoming a preferred method of distributing financial aid to Canadians.

- **Compensation benefits** are awarded to individuals who have suffered a loss as a result of an accident or another person's actions.

Workers' compensation and compensation awarded to victims of crime fit in this category.

There are three types of financial tests used in Canada to determine eligibility for income security programs. **Income tests** determine eligibility based on the applicant's income and generally ignore individual needs or other assets. Since the late 1980s, income testing has been a common method for ensuring that only low- or modest-income earners receive benefits. Old Age Security is an example of an income-tested program; recipients earning over $58 000 a year receive a reduced benefit rate, and those with annual incomes over $95 000 are ineligible for benefits (Government of Canada, 2004f).

Needs tests are used to assess an applicant's personal needs and to determine whether his or her income is sufficient to meet those needs. Provincial social assistance programs tend to use fairly elaborate needs tests: first, there is an inventory of the applicant's fixed and liquid assets; next, all sources of household income are identified; and finally, the total needs of the household are determined. The applicant is then deemed eligible for assistance if the household's needs are greater than its resources (National Council of Welfare, 2003b).

Means tests base eligibility on an applicant's income and assets but virtually ignore personal needs. Although commonly used in the past, means testing is no longer popular since it requires an in-depth—and seemingly intrusive—inquiry into an applicant's finances, living arrangements, and other personal information; also, these tests fail to take the specific needs of applicants into account (Block, 1983). Manitoba's Child Related Income Support Program uses means testing to assess eligibility for financial assistance. Under this program, families are eligible for assistance if they have, among other things, an income under a specified level and no more than $200 000 worth of family assets (Manitoba Family Services and Housing, 2004).

PERSONAL SOCIAL SERVICES

Personal social services are nonincome and intangible benefits that aim to improve social and economic conditions for individuals, families, and communities. In many cases, these services complement or replace the support and care that one's family and other informal support systems might normally provide. The personal social services are sometimes referred to as *transfers-in-kind* since they are distributed to individuals or families in place of cash payments. In some circles, the provision of service is considered more "politically correct" or "nonpaternalistic" than the doling out of cash or charity (World Bank Group, 2001).

In Canada, personal social services can be classified according to six broad categories: (1) socialization programs; (2) personal development programs; (3) therapy and rehabilitation programs; (4) information, referral, and advocacy services; (5) protection services; and (6) prevention services. There is considerable overlap between categories: for example, a therapy program may provide many benefits related to both socialization and personal development. Exhibit 1.3 provides examples of Canada's personal social services.

Socialization Programs

Socialization may be understood as the act of developing or changing behaviours, attitudes, and values to meet society's cultural norms, goals, or expectations. For the most part, children become socialized through their interactions with family members, neighbours, teachers and others in the community and go on to lead fully functioning and productive lives as adults. Besides these natural supports, programs such as childcare and anger management groups are available to facilitate the socialization process. As society becomes more diverse in terms of culture, sexual orientation, and ethnicity, people's expectations of "acceptable behaviour" will continue to evolve.

Personal Development Programs

Personal development programs focus on activities that enhance personal qualities and abilities such as self-esteem, communication, and problem-solving. The objective of these programs is to help individuals develop competence and confidence so that they can reach their full potential as contributing members of society. Among the wide variety of personal development programs available are life skills programs for people with disabilities and employment services for women and youth.

Therapy and Rehabilitation Programs

The goal of therapy and rehabilitation programs is to help people restore certain skills or abilities that have been diminished as a result of marital breakdown, illness, accident, unemployment, or some other life event. Services in this category include family therapy, occupational therapy, alcohol and drug counselling, and transition homes for abused women and their children.

Information, Referral, and Advocacy Services

Information, referral, and advocacy services help the public learn about and gain access to community programs; they also assist people with formal complaints about a service they received. These services are usually provided at information centres, civil rights agencies, human rights commissions, or ombudsman departments.

Exhibit 1.3

EXAMPLES OF PERSONAL SOCIAL SERVICES

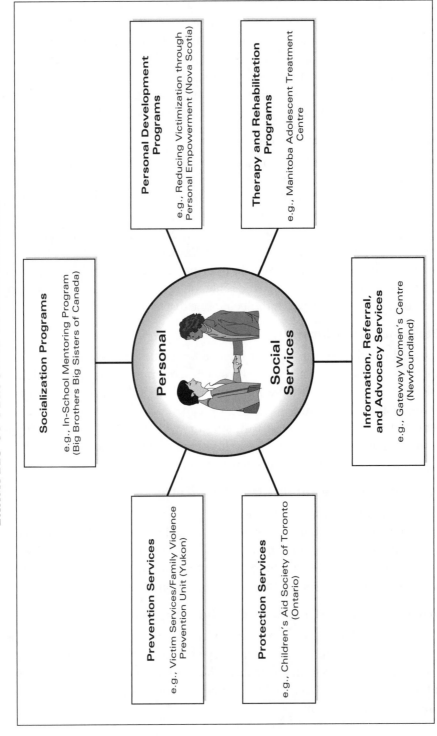

Personal Development Programs

e.g., Reducing Victimization through Personal Empowerment (Nova Scotia)

Therapy and Rehabilitation Programs

e.g., Manitoba Adolescent Treatment Centre

Socialization Programs

e.g., In-School Mentoring Program (Big Brothers Big Sisters of Canada)

Personal **Social Services**

Information, Referral, and Advocacy Services

e.g., Gateway Women's Centre (Newfoundland)

Prevention Services

e.g., Victim Services/Family Violence Prevention Unit (Yukon)

Protection Services

e.g., Children's Aid Society of Toronto (Ontario)

Source: Author

Protection Services

The mandate of protection services is to keep vulnerable individuals from physical or psychological harm. These services are sanctioned by legislation and give designated social agencies the legal authority to stop or prevent people from hurting themselves or others. Child welfare legislation, for example, protects children from abuse and neglect. Some provinces also have adult protection legislation that ensures the safety of elderly people or people with disabilities. There is also legislation allowing the detention of people whose behaviour is violent, sexually inappropriate, suicidal, or otherwise antisocial.

Prevention Services

Prevention services aim to prevent social problems before they occur or to minimize their negative effects once they have developed. A primary function of these services is to educate the public—through the distribution of literature, seminars, and other methods—about potential risks and how to reduce them. There is a wide range of prevention services available across Canada, including drug and alcohol education, suicide prevention programs, and parenting skills groups.

TARGETED AND UNIVERSAL PROGRAMS

In Canada, social welfare programs are either targeted or universal. **Targeted programs** (also called *selective* programs) are restricted to certain populations that can meet some predetermined criteria of being in need. Social assistance, for example, is provided on a short-term or emergency basis, and is restricted to people who can prove their eligibility through needs testing.

Universal programs (formerly called *demogrants*) are available to all Canadians as a matter of right regardless of economic status or need; however, applicants for these benefits must usually meet basic age or residency criteria. Because universal programs provide the same quality of service or amount of benefit to all recipients, they prevent divisions among the "haves" and the "have nots." For example, family allowances, which were introduced in 1945 as Canada's first universal program, provided cash benefits to all Canadian families—rich or poor—that had children.

Originally, all social welfare programs targeted people in need. During the Second World War, the notion of universality in social programs was advanced and generally supported by Canadians. However, as the economy struggled through the 1970s and 1980s, universal programs were criticized for being too expensive and wasteful since they delivered benefits even to individuals who were not in need (Block, 1983). Beginning in the 1980s, the

Exhibit 1.4
THAT AWKWARD AGE

"He's at that awkward age ... too young for old age security, too old for Opportunities for Youth, too late for family allowance, too conventional for Canada Council or local initiative programs, too poor for tax loopholes, too rich for subsidized housing ..."

Source: Len Norris, *That Awkward Age* (1990). Reprinted by permission.

federal government began phasing out universal income security programs that many high income–earning Canadians had become accustomed to receiving. In 1989, for example, the Old Age Security pension lost its universal status when high income–earning pensioners were required to pay back all or part of their pension payments. Similarly, the universal benefits provided under the Family Allowances Act were eliminated in 1993 and replaced by a program that targeted benefits to low-income families. Today, universal income security programs are virtually nonexistent in Canada. There remain a variety of universal personal social services such as crisis intervention, employment counselling, and information, advocacy, and referral services. These are generally open to all citizens.

III. IDEOLOGICAL INFLUENCES ON SOCIAL WELFARE

There are diverse opinions about how people should behave as individuals and with others; however, when widely shared opinions converge, they sometimes create ideologies. An **ideology** is a paradigm or belief system that shapes our perception of the world and guides the ways we interact with that world. Since all ideologies are subjective, they cannot be proven right or wrong by objective measures. Ideologies nevertheless have the power to influence the types of formal institutions we develop in our society, including social welfare. Indeed, our opinions about people in need and the giving of "charity" are largely the result of prevailing ideas, values, and attitudes in society.

Canada's social welfare system is not the product of any one ideology; rather, that system reflects a number of ideologies that have arisen in our history in response to various social, economic, and political developments. This section explores some of the ideologies that have shaped social welfare in Canada.

POLITICAL IDEOLOGY

Political ideologies have considerable influence over social policymakers, who must decide which social conditions will be labelled as social problems and how these problems can best be resolved. In the context of social welfare, political ideologies involve the creation of laws, legislation, or policies to bring about social change.

Three political ideologies have had a particular impact on Canadian social welfare: conservatism, liberalism, and socialism. Each ideology is reflected in the policies of the three main Canadian political parties—the Conservatives, the Liberals, and the New Democrats; that said, their respective platforms rarely reflect any one particular philosophical stance. Each ideology is briefly reviewed below and summarized in Exhibit 1.5.

Conservatism

Although not entirely opposed to change, **conservatism** supports the existing social order, traditional values, and moral (religious) standards. Individualism is important to conservatives in terms of economic advancement—that is, people are encouraged to compete, work hard, and accumulate wealth and property, yet maintain close ties to family, church, and other well-established social institutions.

Exhibit 1.5
COMPARING POLITICAL IDEOLOGIES

	CONSERVATISM	LIBERALISM	SOCIALISM (SOCIAL DEMOCRACY)
Basic values/beliefs	• social traditions • maintenance of status quo • patriarchal • competitive private enterprise • class distinctions • probusiness	• social progress • individual rights and freedoms • competitive private enterprise • equal opportunity • pro-individualism	• cooperation and fellowship • collective participation and responsibility, solidarity • egalitarianism • prosocial
Role of government	• to strengthen traditional institutions (e.g., family, church, government) • to maintain peace and order with as little regulation as possible • to support big business and free trade	• to promote economic growth while ensuring individual rights • to carry out the wishes of the public • to compensate people for problems created by capitalism	• to stabilize society through redistribution of income from rich to poor • to protect the rights of workers by regulating and controlling private enterprise
View of poverty and the poor	• the poor are classified as either deserving or undeserving of public relief • poverty is result of personal failure • the poor lack morals and resourcefulness	• poverty is created by capitalism and economic progress (not the result of personal shortcomings)	• poverty is the consequence of capitalism and power structures in society • the poor are in a subordinate position to the wealthy and powerful

continued

continued

	CONSERVATISM	LIBERALISM	SOCIALISM (SOCIAL DEMOCRACY)
View of social welfare programs	• undermine initiative and weaken moral fibre • interfere with workings of the free market • charity should be given sparingly and only in emergencies	• are necessary to help people reach certain standards of living and self-development • do not provide the extent of security or opportunity that a well-paying job might	• are necessary for protecting and compensating victims of social and economic progress • are a basic institution in modern society and should be available to all citizens as a matter of right

Sources: Adapted from J. Pollard. (1991). "Ideology, Social Policy and Home-Based Child Care," Table 1, pages 104–7. In I. Kyle, M. Friendly, and L. Schmidt, eds., *Proceedings from the Child Care Policy and Research Symposium: Occasional Paper No. 2*, pp. 101–12. Childcare Resource and Research Unit, Centre for Urban and Community Studies, University of Toronto [online]. Available: www.childcarecanada.org/download/2op.doc [March 18, 2004].
Lakewood Public Library. (August 7, 2002). *Lakewood: The Thinking City, Political Identities Discussion Series: Analysis—Conventional Viewpoints* [online]. Available: www.lkwdpl.org/thinkingcity/august7.html [March 4, 2004].

Traditionally, conservatives classified the poor into two groups. The **"deserving" poor** included people who were sick, aged, disabled, or otherwise incapable of supporting themselves and therefore worthy of public aid; in contrast, the **"undeserving" poor** were able-bodied unemployed people who were capable of supporting themselves through paid labour and thus unworthy of public support. According to conservative thought, the undeserving poor were personal failures who lacked morals and resourcefulness and were by nature inferior to the wealthy (Morel, 2002).

For conservatives, the most desirable government is the one that regulates, controls, or intervenes the least. From this perspective, government intervention in the lives of citizens should be restricted to whatever is necessary to maintain peace and order (Wilensky and Lebeaux, 1965). It is for these reasons that conservative governments are often referred to as being

laissez-faire (a French term meaning "to leave alone"). *Laissez-faire* government policies were strongly influenced by Adam Smith, an eighteenth-century Scottish economist who urged the state to allow the process of *natural* laws, such as the law of supply and demand, to take their course without state control, regulation, or intervention.

According to conservative beliefs, social welfare programs and services "undermine initiative, weaken moral fibre, and create imbalance in the workings of the marketplace" (Galper, 1975, 3). Conservatives therefore take a **residual approach** to social welfare—that is, social welfare programs should be used sparingly and only as a last resort, when help from one's family, church, banks, and other private resources has been exhausted. Any help that is given by government should be terminated as soon as the individual being helped can once again be self-reliant (Handel, 1982).

Conservative principles were popular in Canada during the late nineteenth and early twentieth centuries. However, the social and economic hardships created by the Great Depression led many staunch conservatives to adopt a more tolerant view of people and their problems. During the latter half of the twentieth century, many conservatives began to take a fiscally conservative yet socially progressive approach to social welfare. On the fiscal side, these progressive conservatives favoured lower taxes, little or no public debt, and a minimalist government; socially, they promoted a decent standard of living for all citizens but remained reluctant to accept responsibility for ensuring that standard (Prince, 1987; Bracken and Walmsley, 1992). Although many conservatives today generally accept a limited range of targeted (nonuniversal) social welfare programs, they emphasize that such programs should be available only to those who can demonstrate true need, and should be offered for as short a period as possible (Watson, 2001). Progressive conservative governments are also most likely to support social welfare initiatives that strengthen traditional institutions, such as the family. The Progressive Conservatives under Brian Mulroney, for example, introduced the Family Violence Initiative in 1988.

Liberalism

In many respects, **liberalism** is similar to conservatism. Both ideologies emphasize liberty, individualism, and competitive private enterprise. Liberal values are nevertheless tempered by strong humanistic beliefs that promote equality and respect for human rights. Under the liberal banner, people are considered self-determining beings who must be free to express their individuality and develop their full potential (George and Wilding, 1985; Brown, 2004).

Liberals tend to question the ability of the market to meet the full range of human needs in modern society; rather, liberals tend to view economic progress as exacerbating poverty, family breakdown, unemployment, inequality, and other problems. Social problems tend to be viewed as manmade conditions resulting from inherent flaws in the capitalist system and not as a result of individual shortcomings (Frenzel, 1987; Hareven, 1969; Djao, 1983).

Liberals want government to promote economic growth while ensuring individual rights and equal opportunity (Brown, 2004). According to liberals, governments are well suited to the role of enforcer of social justice through legislation, and compensator for the failure of the market to adequately meet human needs (Hareven, 1969; Galper, 1975).

From a liberal standpoint, social welfare programs are necessary to help people reach satisfying standards of health, relationships, and self-development. Liberals traditionally support governments that use their taxing powers to redistribute income and thereby prevent large numbers of people from falling into poverty (Galper, 1975; Wilensky and Lebeaux, 1965).

Liberal governments have introduced several social welfare programs over the years, including Unemployment Insurance in 1940. Since the early 1990s, however, Canadian liberal governments have been criticized for stifling individual development and economic efficiency through their overuse of government regulation and control of market forces. In response to these criticisms, liberal governments have moved toward what political analysts call **neoliberalism**. Day and Brodsky (1998, 9) characterize the neoliberal approach to government as follows: "The private sphere—the home, the market—is considered worthy of enlargement and sanctification, and the public sphere, including the institution of government itself, is considered dangerous and best kept small." Although Canadian liberals have traditionally been *social* liberals who supported social program spending, neoliberals tend to be *economic* liberals who believe that fiscal responsibility (for example, balanced budgets) and a strong economy will provide the necessary resources for meeting many social welfare needs (Pal, 1998). Although neoliberals still promote traditional liberal goals, such as the pursuit of individual freedom and self-development, they favour a businesslike approach to reaching those goals.

Socialism and Social Democracy

Since the term "socialism" was coined in the early nineteenth century, two main camps have evolved: (1) the revolutionary or *communist* camp, which advocates a primarily government-owned and -operated economy; and (2) the evolutionary or *social democratic* camp, which supports an economy in which there is a mix of public and private enterprise. Social democracy, which has gained more support in Canada than its communist counterpart, tends to oppose the extreme of communism. This section therefore discusses socialism from a social democratic point of view.

For the most part, **social democracy** rejects the competitive values of capitalism, individualism, and private enterprise. Instead of personal competition, social democrats advocate fellowship and cooperation among citizens. Solidarity is important to social democrats, who prefer to work toward collective rather than individual goals and who frequently use collective action such as labour strikes to do so. Egalitarianism—that is, equal power and advantage among citizens—is also considered a worthy goal (Spicker, 2004).

Social democrats challenge the conservative notion that poverty is the result of an individual's shortcomings; instead, they see poverty as a consequence of capitalism and the unequal distribution of resources and economic power in society. According to social democratic thought, the inequalities of resources and power trap the poor in a subordinate position to the rich (George and Wilding, 1985).

Social democrats are generally supportive of the state and see government as playing a prominent role in social, economic, and other arenas. Governments are urged to regulate and control private enterprise so that the interests of labour, consumers, and small business are protected. Social democrats also see government as a protector of human rights through labour laws and regulations ("Social Democrat," 2004).

Social democrats see government playing a primary role in compensating those who fall prey to the risks of social and economic progress. This task is best achieved through a welfare state that equally redistributes wealth among citizens and thereby stabilizes society. Needless to say, social democrats accept government taxation as a necessary tool for establishing and maintaining high-quality social programs. In contrast to the residual approach, an **institutional approach** is favoured by social democrats—that is, the social welfare system is viewed as a normal and necessary institution in modern society that provides universal support to all citizens as a matter of right (George and Wilding, 1985; Whitehorn, 2003b).

Social democratic principles motivated many of the social reform movements of the late nineteenth and early twentieth centuries, including the labour reform movement, the workers' compensation movement, and the child welfare movement. Socialist ideals later found expression through the Co-operative Commonwealth Federation (CCF), established in 1932, and the New Democratic Party (NDP), formed in 1961. Although Canada has never elected a social democratic party at the federal level, the social democratic ideals advanced by the CCF and NDP have been instrumental in the passage of major social legislation, including universal health care, old age pensions, workers' compensation, and unemployment insurance (Whitehorn, 2003a).

RELIGIOUS IDEOLOGY

Judeo-Christian Views of Charity

Early Judeo-Christian doctrine considered poverty "a blessed condition which enabled one to be nearer to God, for 'a rich man shall hardly enter into the kingdom of heaven'" (Matthew 19:23) (HRDC, 2002c). While Judeo-Christians believed that human beings were responsible for themselves and accountable to both God and one another, they regarded the giving of charity as an act of selflessness and a reflection of love for one's neighbour. In the Bible, charity is one of the theological virtues—along with faith and hope—indeed, it is considered "the greatest" virtue (Corinthians 13:13). Historically, Judeo-Christians believed that charitable works on earth would yield rewards in the afterlife; thus, compassion and relief were given to the poor in compensation for their lack of material possessions. In turn, wealthy individuals were considered blessed individuals who had a moral obligation to share their riches with the less fortunate.

As in the secular world, Judeo-Christian churches used to discriminate between groups of poor. Charity from the Medieval churches was given unconditionally only to the "deserving" poor. The "undeserving" poor were helped only on the condition that they would work hard to become productive members of society (Olasky, 1995; Johansen, 1996). In 1841, Thomas Chalmers wrote that those giving charity should not only relieve the poor from a life of hardship, but also promote "amongst the poor the habits of industry, providence, frugality, saving and honest desire to rise in the world" (cited in Olasky, 1995, 25).

Social Welfare and the Roman Catholic Church

The Roman Catholic Church has traditionally viewed the provision of social welfare as its moral responsibility. Early Catholics questioned government's ability to achieve social order through state legislation or intervention alone, and families were considered incapable of meeting all their needs on their own. As a consequence, the Catholic church assumed the responsibility for social welfare; its aim was to achieve social order through moral restraint, devotion to God, and the giving of charity (Spicker, 2004).

From the enactment of the Quebec Act in 1774 to the early 1960s, the Roman Catholic Church played a central role in the provision of social welfare services in Quebec. Bellamy (1965, 36) writes that the Roman Catholic Church was well suited to the role of charity provider: "Long experience in ministering to the weak and suffering, backed by a strong administrative organization, dedicated personnel and wealthy patrons, and its own abundant material resources fitted the Church well for meeting the temporal needs of the people no less than the spiritual needs." During the 1960s and Quebec's Quiet Revolution, most of the responsibility for social welfare shifted to the provincial government.

Protestant Influences on Social Welfare

With the Protestant Reformation in sixteenth-century Europe came the belief that success at work, in the form of profits and wealth, was an indication of God's favour. Thus, the Protestant ethic maintained that one must work in this world to be saved in the next. A person's earned prosperity and success were seen as evidence of godly living, virtue, and God's grace. With this new understanding of work and salvation, Protestants began to view poverty as

> an indication of a sinful life and of divine retribution. Therefore, such help as was extended to the poor was often accompanied by unsolicited and largely irrelevant advice on how the poor might regain God's grace through the exercise of those human qualities that he apparently admired and rewarded. The poor were urged to appreciate the values of thrift, hard work, self-help, and self-discipline. (Guest, 1997, 18)

In general, the giving of charity was discouraged by the Protestant ethic, since helping others on earth was not seen as a way to gain entry into heaven.

Until the 1940s, Protestant ideals were the driving force behind many social movements and the introduction of modern social welfare policy in Canada. Protestantism also promoted the development of a largely feminist agenda of government-sponsored social welfare programs, which focused on family policy and the protection of women and children (Christie and Gauvreau, 1996).

Religious Ideologies and the Shaping of Social Welfare

Despite its predominantly secular nature, social welfare continues to be shaped by religious doctrine. Together with social democrats, the Church urged the early twentieth-century governments to take responsibility for the social welfare needs of citizens, and to expand the role of government in areas such as child welfare, unemployment insurance, mothers' pensions, and old age pensions. These efforts eventually led governments, regardless of ideology, to commit a larger share of public funding to social welfare programs (Christie and Gauvreau, 1996; Richards, 1997).

Religious doctrine continues to shape society's perceptions of social welfare and the giving of charity. As one community group notes

> Faith communities and religious institutions help shape our beliefs about what is right and good, such as our responsibility to care for others. Community-based organizations ... call us to serve the common good—things beyond ourselves. As such, they enable us to devote our lives to higher purposes, while working in this world. (Fawcett, 2003)

We can expect that as Canada becomes more culturally diverse, social welfare programs and services will evolve to reflect a rich blend of Christian and non-Christian ideologies.

SUMMARY

■ Introduction

Social welfare can be understood as a concept, as a field or discipline, or as a system with two main purposes: to help individuals and groups meet their basic economic and social needs, and to prevent and reduce social problems. Maintaining social cohesion and ensuring social justice are important functions of the social welfare system.

■ The Primary Functions of Social Welfare Activities

The social welfare system aims to meet a wide range of human needs. Various models identify the range of human needs to which social welfare might respond. Social policymakers decide which needs might best be met by government-sponsored programs and which should be left to individuals. Social problems are conditions that threaten the well-being of large groups and that motivate a collective response to alleviate the problem. Although perceptions of what constitutes a social problem change over time, the social welfare system generally focuses on problems that affect both the individual and general society. A variety of methods are used to measure the existence and extent of social problems. Several academic disciplines and a growing body of practice knowledge contributes to our understanding of human needs and social problems.

■ Social Welfare Programs and Services

Income security programs provide financial assistance to citizens to help them live above a social minimum. Three types of tests are used to determine eligibility for income security programs: income tests, needs tests, and means tests. Personal social services are non-income benefits that aim to improve social and economic conditions. Targeted programs are available to people who can prove their need, whereas universal programs are distributed to all citizens regardless of economic status or need.

■ Ideological Influences on Social Welfare

Canadian politics have shaped social welfare under the banners of three main ideologies. Conservatives promote capitalism and minimal social welfare provision; liberals believe that capitalism should be tempered by moderate government intervention to address human needs; and social democrats maintain that government should play a primary role in meeting human needs. In recent decades, conservatism has become more socially progressive, and neoliberalism has taken a more businesslike approach to social welfare. Religious influences on social welfare stem from the Judeo-Christian concept of charity. Roman Catholic teachings saw the Church as having a primary role to play in social welfare provision; the Protestant reformists had a negative view of poverty and of those who received charity. Religion continues to play a role in shaping perceptions of social welfare and addressing social issues.

▼ KEY TERMS

For definitions of the key terms, consult the Glossary on page 364 at the end of the book.

social welfare p. 3

social cohesion p. 4

social justice p. 4

human need p. 4

social security p. 5

personal social services
  p. 5

social assistance p. 5

social programs p. 5

social policy p. 5

social work p. 5

social safety net p. 5

welfare state p. 5

social problems p. 8

interdisciplinary field
  p. 10

programs and services
  p. 10

income security programs
  p. 11

social minimum p. 11

cash transfers p. 11

social insurance p. 11

tax credits p. 11

compensation benefits
  p. 11

income tests p. 12

needs tests p. 12

means tests p. 12

targeted programs p. 15

universal programs p. 15

ideology p. 17

conservatism p. 17

"deserving" poor p. 19

"undeserving" poor p. 19

laissez-faire p. 20

residual approach p. 20

liberalism p. 20

neoliberalism p. 21

social democracy p. 22

institutional approach
  p. 22

chapter

Social Policy in the Canadian Context

Objectives

I. To review the links between social and economic policy, and to consider the ways in which changes in the economy and labour market affect social policy.

II. To examine sociodemographic shifts such as an aging population, changing family structure and roles, and urbanization, and their implications for social policy.

III. To describe regional differences and how power is divided among the federal, provincial, and territorial governments, as well as the efforts made by various levels of government to share responsibility for social policy.

IV. To consider the procedures by which social policies are created and sanctioned, and the participants in the policy-making process.

INTRODUCTION

Canada's ability to achieve a high standard of living and a better quality of life depends, in large part, on its social policies. Social policy provides choices and options for citizens; it also ensures that Canadians "get the best possible start in life, allows them to capitalize on their talents during their working life and provides security in their later years" (Stewart, 2002).

Social policy refers to a set of guidelines or regulations that provide structure and direction to social welfare programs. Thus, behind every income security program and personal social service is a policy that is used to determine which conditions, needs, or problems are to be addressed; to whom resources will be directed; and how the program or service should be delivered. Because social welfare and social policy are so closely linked, the study of one requires familiarity with the other.

The primary aim of social policies—such as the Employment Insurance Act, the Canada and Quebec Pension Plans, and the National Homelessness Initiative—is to enhance the social and economic well-being and functioning of society. These policies reflect basic principles of affordability, sustainability, and inclusivity (which means that all Canadians benefit), as well as social values such as compassion, collective responsibility, self-sufficiency, and the sharing of resources (O'Hara, 1997).

Social policy objectives are always evolving. Jane Jenson (2003a) notes that social policies introduced after the Second World War focused on economic revitalization and job creation in the belief that increased labour market participation would enhance people's general well-being. More recently, however, people have realized that the challenges created by globalization, shifting demographics, and other socioeconomic changes cannot be "solved" by jobs alone. Jenson (Canadian Policy Research Networks, 2004) believes it is time for Canadians to "make new choices" regarding how they want their social needs to be met; those choices would then form the basis of a "new social architecture" for the twenty-first century. It is clear that governments are already beginning to adopt new social policy models. For example, Canadian governments are introducing more policies that focus on **social investment**—which yield long-term benefits—as opposed to **social amelioration**—which provide only temporary economic relief. As a result of this shift in focus, today's governments are more likely to increase funds to, say, early childhood development (to ensure a more productive future for young people), than to raise welfare rates for single employable adults (to ease the negative consequences of poverty in the short term) (Boychuk, 2004).

Various processes, people, and procedures influence the content and direction of social policy in Canada. These include

- economic, sociodemographic, and political shifts;
- the multiple actors that comprise the policy-making community; and
- the formal procedures by which social policy is developed.

Thus, social policy is the product of several dynamic and interactive components. This chapter looks at some of these.

I. SOCIAL POLICY IN A CHANGING ECONOMY

MERGING SOCIAL AND ECONOMIC POLICY

In the past, economic policy and social policy functioned independently; each had its separate goals. Economic policy aimed to produce a higher standard of living and better quality of life through economic growth; social policy focused on people who were unable to benefit from economic growth or who were faced with particular barriers to independent living (deGroot-Maggetti, 2003a). Today, social and economic policies are interrelated in a variety of ways. For example, social policies influence the amount of taxes spent on social programs and services, whereas economic policies determine the amount of taxes collected and how much is available to meet social goals. Working in tandem, social and economic policies can improve Canadians' quality of life and social cohesion while promoting innovation and productivity (Conference Board of Canada, 2000). Jane Stewart, a past Minister of Human Resources Development, noted in 2002 that an effective and modern social welfare system is possible only if we "create an innovative link between sound economic policy and forward-thinking social policy." The need for such a link is becoming increasingly apparent as Canada adapts to a new economic order.

CANADA'S NEW ECONOMY

Gordon Betcherman (1996) points out that Canada, like other Western countries, is "in the midst of a far-reaching economic transition" that is taking us from an industrial to a postindustrial era. A central feature of postindustrialism is **globalization**, a process that involves "the integration of international markets as a result of advances in communications and transportation, the liberalisation of trade, and the emergence of new competitors in the developing world" (Department of Finance, 2003h, 8).

Although globalization has always been a part of Canada's economic development, the extent of its current influence is unprecedented. For example, it is easier than ever before for non-Canadian corporations and governments to purchase and control large portions of the country's assets; detailed information of high quality can now be transmitted around the world in seconds; advanced knowledge is required in order to produce many goods and services; and international organizations such as the World Bank and the International Monetary Fund are dictating economic practices and reforms (Rankin and Vickers, 2001). Together, these and related phenomena are welding the world into one massive culture, with strong repercussions for social policy (De Long, 1998).

The following section discusses free trade agreements and labour market shifts. Both these economic processes are strongly affecting Canada's economy and social policy and, it follows, the lives of Canadians.

Free Trade Agreements

Canada's economy relies heavily on international trade and the ability to move goods and services freely across international borders. Over the years, Canada has struck numerous free trade agreements with other countries (for example, the North American Free Trade Agreement, or NAFTA). These agreements are touted as having "energized our economy, spurred innovation, attracted foreign investment and created hundreds of thousands of jobs for Canadians" (Department of Foreign Affairs and International Trade, 2003). Nevertheless, there are concerns about the social impact of free trade policies, especially with regard to harmonization, privatization, and social democracy.

Harmonization Free trade agreements usually require member countries to create a "harmonized trading environment" within which to trade (Knutson and Ochoa, 2003, 2). **Harmonization** refers to the establishment of similar programs, services, and/or regulations in all countries in a trading zone. When NAFTA came into effect in 1994, it was feared that the standards of many Canadian social programs would have to be lowered so as to match the more meagre programs in the United States and Mexico. Under NAFTA, however, Canada was able to exempt many of its social programs from trade obligations on the claim that access to such programs (such as health care and old age pensions) should be considered a fundamental right of Canadian citizens regardless of their ability to pay (Jackson and Sanger, 2003; McDougall, 2001; Barlow, 2001). Many experts predicted that under NAFTA, Canada would be forced to reduce its social policies. However, as Andrew Jackson (2001) points out, since the signing of NAFTA, Canada's social welfare expenditures as a share of gross domestic product (GDP) have actually increased.

Despite the exemption clause in NAFTA, there is evidence that harmonization has negatively affected certain social programs. For example, in 1989, 75 percent of Canada's workforce qualified for Unemployment Insurance benefits; by 2000, after the federal government tightened that program's eligibility criteria, only 36 percent of workers qualified for benefits (Anderson and Cavanagh, 2002). The coverage rate of Canada's Employment Insurance program is now close to that of the United States.

Some analysts believe that harmonization is responsible for the sharp reduction in social assistance benefits across Canada. The introduction of the Canada Health and Social Transfer in 1996 significantly reduced the amount of federal cash transfers going to the provinces and territories for social assistance and personal social services. Since then, many provinces and territories have reformed their welfare systems to make it more difficult for people to get on, or stay on, welfare. From 1994 to 2002, the proportion of the population receiving welfare fell from 10.7 percent to 5.9 percent—a level much closer to the American rate of 2 percent (LeRoy and Clemens, 2003).

Privatization Free trade agreements encourage **privatization**—that is, the transfer of most or all assets or services from government to the private sector (Canadian Council for Public-Private Partnerships, 2004). The privatization of social welfare programs and services is becoming more common in Canada; this is reflected in the many programs and services that were once delivered by government and are now contracted out to private agencies (Arai, 1999). Although nonprofit organizations provide most social welfare programs in the private sector, it is becoming more common to find for-profit agencies delivering home support, childcare, and drug and alcohol treatment services.

Canada's negotiations relating to the Free Trade Agreement of the Americas (FTAA) raise particular concerns about the privatization of traditionally nonprofit social programs. According to Maude Barlow (2001), the FTAA—which would expand NAFTA by uniting the economies of thirty-four countries in North, Central, and South America—would allow commercial operations to compete for government dollars that currently go to nonprofit organizations. If a Canadian government does not allow for-profit organizations equal access to those funds, companies would have the right to sue the government for lost potential revenues. Barlow suggests that the threat of such expensive claims could make it impossible for Canadian governments to continue subsidizing many health, education, and social welfare programs.

Social Democracy The political promise behind the expansion of trade and investment is that it will ultimately strengthen democracy. However, as the federal New Democratic Party (2004) points out, "trade rules have been written by, and largely for, large corporations. Instead of expanding democracy they weaken it. They grant powers to multinational corporations that are not available to citizens." Governments have relaxed their controls over big business; at the same time, they have downsized their operations. Rankin and Vickers (2001, 21) suggest that Canadian governments have been "hollowed out" to the point that they no longer have the power or capacity to act on behalf of citizens. This is of particular concern for groups in Canada that are already disadvantaged and that rely on government to protect social rights, ensure the basic necessities of life, preserve wage equity and employment standards, and provide all citizens with equal access to resources.

Labour Market Shifts

The forces of globalization are perhaps most noticeable in the labour market, where the world of work has dramatically changed in the following areas:

- *Knowledge-based economy.* Rapid advances in technology have revolutionized labour by automating many labour-intensive tasks and operations. Changing technologies in practically all fields are demanding highly literate workers with strong computer and other technical skills and a willingness to upgrade as technologies evolve. Although Canada has enough workers to succeed in a knowledge-based economy, its labour force is having difficulty acquiring the skills quickly enough to meet the needs of the economy (Torjman, 2002; Whelan, 2000; OECD, 2001).

- *Growth in service industries.* Producer services, consumer services, and government services now account for over 70 percent of Canada's GDP and employ 75 percent of Canada's labour force. The fastest-growing service sector is producer services, which include communications, wholesale trade, finance, insurance, real estate and business services, and transportation of goods (Industry Canada, 2001a; 2003).

- *Changing face of manufacturing.* As a result of free trade and other economic changes, much of the labour-intensive manufacturing that once took place in Canada is now being outsourced or "offshored" to less-developed countries such as Malaysia and Indonesia, where goods can be produced more cheaply and efficiently (De Long, 1998). The downward trend in Canada's manufacturing sector began in late 2002; by early 2004, a total of 83 000 manufacturing jobs had been lost (Statistics Canada, 2004d).

- *The rise in part-time and temporary work.* Canada's labour market is witnessing a growing split between full-time and part-time workers (defined as 15 to 29 hours a week), and between permanent and temporary work such as seasonal, contract, and self-employed work. The percentage of part-time workers rose from about 13 percent of employed people in 1976 to about 18 percent in 2000 (Pold, 2001).

Social Implications of a Changing Economy

Canada's social policies are struggling to remain relevant and responsive to the rapidly changing economy; meanwhile, a number of social problems persist, especially unemployment, job insecurity and wage inequity, and eroding labour standards. Furthermore, public confidence in Canada's social security system is dwindling.

Unemployment One of the most persistent problems in Canada is high unemployment, a condition largely attributed to declining primary and manufacturing industries, greater competition for well-paying full-time jobs, government layoffs, and technological advances that replace workers with machines. Canada's unemployment rate has increased steadily over the years, from 3 percent or less during the Second World War, to an all-time high of almost 13 percent in 1982; the rate has been over 7 percent since 2001 (Gower, 1992; Statistics Canada, 2004c). Unemployment places heavy demands on a number of social welfare programs such as Employment Insurance and social assistance. Chronic unemployment also poses a problem for federal and provincial governments, which rely on tax revenues to fund the public programs on which many Canadians have come to rely (Battle and Torjman, 2001).

Wage Inequity and Job Insecurity Current labour market shifts are creating a split in Canada's labour force: at one end are those highly skilled, well-educated people who can compete for and secure high-paying jobs with good benefits and opportunities for promotion; at the other end are unskilled, poorly paid, less-educated workers (often older workers, young people, immigrants, and women) in part-time or nonstandard positions with few (if any) benefits and little chance of advancement (Battle and Torjman, 2001). Unskilled workers face the highest risk of unemployment and dependence on income security programs. Similarly, workers in part-time and nonstandard work tend to have limited access to a full range of social welfare programs such as Employment Insurance, pensions, and childcare services (Townson, 2003). Women—who represent almost three-quarters of the part-time workforce—face some of the greatest risks of job insecurity and low pay (Statistics Canada, 2000).

Eroding Labour Standards Under free trade agreements, the countries with the lowest "costs of doing business" typically attract the most trade and investment. Canada has for many decades had fairly high labour, environmental, and other standards; we are now faced with the challenge of maintaining those standards while promoting ourselves internationally as an excellent place to do business. John Peters (2002) observes that in order to become more competitive on the global market, Canadian governments have relaxed labour legislation; in turn, businesses have been able to reduce wages, lay off workers (especially those in unionized positions), and lower working standards. As governments and businesses do whatever they must to attract foreign investment and trade, the ability of unions to influence labour standards weakens. The result, according to Peters (2002, 6), is a "growing disparity between an often-protected organized work-force and an unprotected, unorganized, low-paid, bottom-rung work-force." The groups most likely to bear the brunt of relaxed labour standards are women, people with disabilities, and the **working poor** (that is, people whose earnings from employment are not enough to lift them out of poverty) (Chaykowski, 2003).

Dwindling Confidence In light of the changes taking place in the economic, political, and social arenas, some Canadians are beginning to wonder how much longer governments will be able to provide assistance to those affected by labour market shifts (Chaykowski, 2003). Opinion polls suggest that Canadians are losing confidence in Canada's social security programs. They are questioning whether those programs will be able to adequately support them if their jobs disappear. Exhibit 2.1 shows Canadians' confidence levels over a five-year period.

E x h i b i t   2 . 1

CONFIDENCE IN CANADA'S SOCIAL SAFETY NET: 1998–2002

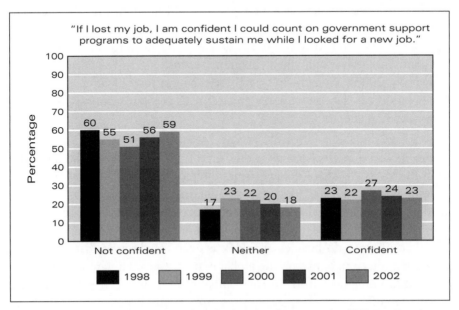

Source: S. Tsoukalas and A. Mackenzie. (2003). *The Personal Security Index, 2003: Five Years Later*, p. 15: Canadian Council on Social Development [online]. Available: www.ccsd.ca/pubs/2003/psi/psi03.pdf [March 4, 2004].

II. SOCIAL CHANGE AND SOCIAL POLICY

Social policies that were designed to meet Canadians' needs in the 1960s will not adequately address Canadians' needs in the twenty-first century for the simple reason that people and their environments keep changing (Courchene, 1987). Thus, social policies must reflect the needs created by an aging population, changes in family structure and roles, urbanization, immigration, and other sociodemographic trends. The following is a brief discussion of selected trends and their implications for social policy.

AN AGING POPULATION

Canada has a declining birth rate and an **aging population**. There are now close to four million Canadians over sixty-five—two-thirds more than the number in 1981. By 2041, seniors are expected to make up almost one-quarter of Canada's total population (Health Canada, 2002d). As more baby boomers enter their senior years, governments will be faced with increased demands for pension benefits, medical and home care, nursing homes, and other social supports.

CHANGING FAMILY STRUCTURE AND ROLES

In 1981, "traditional" families—that is, a mother, a father, and children under twenty-four—represented 55 percent of all families in Canada; by 2001, such families accounted for only 44 percent of Canadian households (Statistics Canada, 2002c). Other types of families are becoming more common in Canada, and this is creating a need for more responsive, appropriate, and diverse social policies and programs. Two of these family types are

- *Lone-parent families.* The number of lone-parent (mostly female-led) families in Canada continues to rise; by 2001, this group represented 16 percent of all families (Statistics Canada, 2002c). Female-led lone-parent families have the highest poverty rate (almost 52 percent of them are poor) of any family type in Canada (National Council of Welfare, 2002a). Besides affordable childcare, this group requires job training programs and strategies to address poverty, hunger, homelessness, and social isolation.

- *Same-sex common law couples.* Just over 34 000 same-sex couples live common law in Canada; that is 0.5 percent of all couples (Statistics Canada, 2002c). Recent changes in the legal status of same-sex couples have implications for a number of social policies and programs, including those relating to separation and divorce, the care and custody of children, pensions, family benefits, and Employment Insurance (Walker, 2003).

In recent decades, a number of trends have redefined family roles and subsequently placed heavier demands on social welfare programs. For example, the dramatic influx of women into the paid labour force since the 1960s has dramatically increased the need for affordable childcare. At the same time, higher rates of marriage breakdown, divorce, separation, and remarriage have demanded a wider range of family support and child protection services (Battle, 2001).

Two groups of Canadians are growing in numbers: the "sandwich generation" (adults with young children and elderly parents) and families with two parents working full-time (CCOHS, 2003). These parallel trends are raising the demand for affordable and accessible programs to assist caregivers of elderly relatives (through adult daycare, home support services, and respite services), as well as programs to assist working parents (through childcare and after-school programs). In addition, flexible working conditions, without fear of losing pay or benefits, are needed so that parents will be able to care for both young and old family members at home (Lapierre-Adamcyk, 2002). According to a review of fifteen countries in the Organization for Economic Co-operation and Development, "the pursuit of 'family-friendly' workplace practices on the part of employers (e.g., emergency leave to care for sick children, on-site child care, flexible working hours) remains in its infancy in Canada" (International Reform Monitor, 2004, 2).

URBANIZATION

Eighty percent of Canadians live in urban areas, up from 58 percent in 1951 (Lewington, 2002). More than half of Canada's urban dwellers are concentrated in four major urban centres: Toronto–Golden Horseshoe; Montreal and environs; Vancouver–Lower Mainland; and the Calgary–Edmonton corridor. More than ever before, Canada's economy "is driven by the urban economy"; experts generally agree that cities are going to play a critical role in "Canada's future prosperity" (Prime Minister's Caucus, 2002, 1–2).

Although there are benefits associated with urban life, there are also social and economic risks. Clutterbuck and Novick (2003) asked 483 people from eleven Canadian cities to name the two most vulnerable populations in their communities. More than one-fifth of the participants thought that poor families and children were most vulnerable (see Exhibit 2.2). Some of the main challenges facing Canadian cities, and the social policies that aim to address them, are described briefly below.

Exhibit 2.2

VERY VULNERABLE POPULATIONS IN CANADIAN CITIES

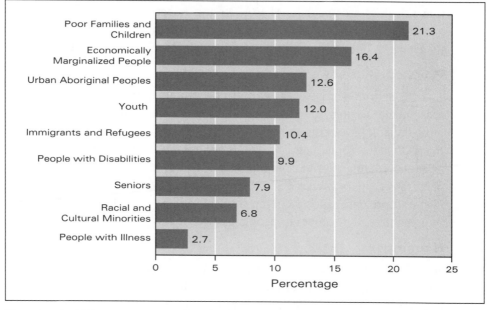

Note: A total of 483 participants privately and independently completed and handed in a written form asking them to identify two "very vulnerable populations in their urban communities."

Source: Adapted from P. Clutterbuck and M. Novick (April 2003), *Building Inclusive Communities: Cross-Canada Perspectives and Strategies*, Table 1, pp. 10–11. Federation of Canadian Municipalities and The Laidlaw Foundation [online]. Available: www.fcm.ca/newfcm/Java/inclusive.pdf [March 4, 2004].

Poverty

Over half of all poor families and unattached Canadians live in cities with populations of 500 000 or more (National Council of Welfare, 2002a). Those at highest risk of urban poverty are lone-parent families, seniors, women, people with disabilities, immigrants, Aboriginal peoples, and the working poor (Prime Minister's Caucus, 2002). To help cities respond better to the social and economic needs of low-income residents, Statistics Canada and the Canadian Council on Social Development have joined forces under the Urban Poverty Project to study urban poverty—in particular, who is affected and how (Canadian Council on Social Development, 2003a). Another initiative is the Urban Aboriginal Strategy, which aims to reduce the high levels of poverty among urban Aboriginal peoples by improving the development and coordination of programs and services, as well as access to both (Privy Council Office, 2003c).

Drug and Alcohol Abuse

A growing problem in Canada's urban centres is alcohol and drug abuse and their associated risks of poverty, homelessness, crime, and the spread of infectious diseases such as HIV/AIDS and hepatitis C. Canada's Renewed National Drug Strategy supports a number of initiatives designed to reduce the demand for and supply of illicit drugs (Health Canada, 2003d).

Physical Access

To benefit from goods, services, and opportunities, people must be able to access them. Seniors, low-income people, and those with disabilities have the most difficulty accessing needed resources (Prime Minister's Caucus, 2002). Many different policies and programs are attempting to improve access. For example, volunteer driver programs and improved transit services (such as para-transit) are now enabling isolated individuals to get around the community; and programs such as home support services and Meals-on-Wheels are bringing needed resources to people in their homes.

Housing

Several large Canadian cities are experiencing a housing crisis because of a severe shortage of affordable housing. Needless to say, adequate or "core" housing "is out of reach for poor families who may spend more than 50 per cent of their income on shelter" (Canadian Council on Social Development, 2002b). Many families, after paying the rent, have little income left for other basics such as food, clothing, and transportation. Homelessness is a particular concern in urban centres: Toronto alone "provides emergency accommodation for approximately 30,000 people a year" (Prime Minister's Caucus, 2002, 18). Canada's National Homelessness Initiative and the Affordable Housing Program aim to reduce and prevent homelessness and provide adequate housing for low-income groups.

Aboriginal Issues

In 1951, only 7 percent of Aboriginal people lived in cities; today, more than half live off a reserve, and most of these have settled in large urban centres. Very often, Aboriginal people move to "cities ill-equipped to face the many challenges that come with adjusting to, and living in, an urban environment" (Prime Minister's Caucus, 2002, 21). Among the Aboriginal people most likely to face poverty, chronic unemployment, and welfare dependency are women—especially lone mothers. Aboriginal urban dwellers have a strong need for affordable housing, youth programs, and training in living and employment skills. In 1998, the Government of Canada introduced the Urban Aboriginal Strategy to make government programs more responsive to the needs of Aboriginal urban dwellers (Privy Council Office, 2003c; Prime Minister's Caucus, 2002).

Ethnic Diversity

About 220 000 immigrants and refugees enter Canada each year, and 85 percent settle in large cities (Prime Minister's Caucus, 2002). Judith Maxwell (2003b, 3) notes: "Diversity of our people greatly enriches our life, but it also introduces different value systems, many more languages, and different ethnic and religious traditions." Language barriers, a lack of affordable housing, and the withholding of recognition for foreign professional and educational qualifications are some of the main challenges facing newcomers to Canada (Prime Minister's Caucus, 2002). Many immigrants prosper in Canada; that said, "too many are stuck in the poor neighbourhoods where their economic and social prospects are severely limited" (Maxwell, 2003b, 3). Refugees face many of the same problems as immigrants but are in particular need of temporary shelter, health care, and social services. Canada's Immigration Settlement and Adaptation Program and the Humanitarian Resettlement Program help newcomers find and connect with social services, language programs, and employment services.

III. DIVISIONS OF POWER: FEDERAL, PROVINCIAL, AND TERRITORIAL RESPONSIBILITIES

FEDERALISM AND CONSTITUTIONAL PROVISIONS

Federalism is a political system that divides legislative power between central (that is, federal) and regional (that is, provincial and territorial) governments. Kathy O'Hara (1997, 6) suggests that each level makes its own contributions to social policy:

> For example, the federal government brings a global and pan-Canadian perspective to issues, and is able to articulate core Canadian values and mobilize Canadians to achieve pan-Canadian objectives. Provincial governments, on the other hand, are better positioned to articulate local needs and priorities and design ways to tailor programs to local circumstances that may be unique.

In Canada, federalism originated with the Constitution Act of 1867 (formerly the British North America Act), which apportioned powers between the federal and provincial governments and gave each level its own sources of revenue and the authority to pass certain laws. Among other things, Section 91 of the Constitution Act gives the federal government jurisdiction over quarantine and marine hospitals, penitentiaries, Status Indians, and reserves; Section 92 makes the provincial governments responsible for such areas as the building and management of hospitals and asylums, charities, and public or reformatory prisons.

SHARED COSTS AND RESPONSIBILITIES

When the Constitution Act was drafted, social welfare matters seemed insignificant and potentially inexpensive, since Canada had a relatively small, rural, and self-sufficient population. Most personal difficulties encountered by citizens were adequately addressed by family, neighbours, churches, charities, or local governments, so it made sense to delegate the less important social welfare functions to the provinces. However, problems created by the Industrial Revolution, urbanization, and immigration changed the way people lived and interacted; this in turn created a need for an expanded social welfare system. As social programs became more important and costly, the provinces realized they could not afford them. This set the stage for the establishment of cost-sharing arrangements between the federal and provincial and territorial governments (Guest, 2003; Wallace, 1950; Irving, 1987).

Since the Great Depression, the federal government has gradually assumed a greater responsibility for social welfare, in part because it has greater taxation powers and a greater ability to redistribute resources. This has ensured a more consistent and equitable provision of social welfare programs across the country. Federal inroads into social welfare matters have blurred the lines separating federal and regional powers, making it difficult to distinguish federal from provincial and territorial programs. Programs for families provide a case in point: the federal government sponsors Nobody's Perfect and Community Action Programs for Children; the provinces and territories sponsor a variety of family support and child protection services.

The regional governments have long viewed federal involvement in social welfare as an unwelcome encroachment in areas that are constitutionally their domain. Regional governments expect to receive federal funding, but they also want to retain their own identities, which are reflected in part in locally developed social welfare policies and programs. A number of factors shape regional identity and create differences in how each region sets its priorities and implements its social policies and programs. Some of these differences are described below.

Heritage. Many regional differences are rooted in the traditions brought to Canada by the early European settlers. Ontario, for example, originally fashioned its approach to social welfare on English civil law, which favoured nongovernmental delivery of social services (Splane, 1965). In contrast, British Columbia was essentially built by government, which naturally led to government's domination in social welfare matters.

Economic capacity. Although the federal government provides the poorer provinces with additional funding through equalization payments, disparities in wealth still exist. One study found that even after equalization payments, "a disparity of 10% remains between the recipient provinces and the average of the 10 Canadian provinces" (Province of Quebec, 2001, 29). Thus, the poorer areas of the country may not be able to provide the same range and quality of social welfare programs as those found in wealthier provinces. This is perhaps most evident in the Atlantic provinces, which have historically lagged behind other provinces in terms of economic development, diversity, and prosperity (Meinhard and Foster, 2002).

Ideological views. Social policies in the various regions of Canada reflect not only the social issues and problems in each region but also general attitudes toward people in need and how to help them. In Quebec, social welfare has traditionally played an important role in preserving the province's unique culture. Even in tough economic times, Quebec has been a staunch supporter of social welfare programs; the result has been one of the most highly developed social welfare systems in the country (Meinhard and Foster, 2002). In contrast, Alberta's approach to social welfare is much more residual. Alberta's wealth and financial ability allow for a wide range of public programs, yet that province is more likely to spend money on business expansion than on social welfare provision (Evans, 2003).

CLARIFYING RESPONSIBILITIES

Federalism is often criticized for inhibiting social policy and the development of social welfare programs and services. The greater the extent to which political power is dispersed across the country and among different levels of government, the less likely it is that a consensus on policy decisions can be reached (Irving, 1987). Over time, the federal and regional governments have made concessions in order to achieve common social objectives. Nevertheless, disagreements and impasses on policy decisions continue to arise, delaying the development of programs that could improve the social and economic lives of Canadians.

The Constitution provides some guidance on the division of responsibilities for social welfare; that said, there are still many grey areas. At the Annual Premiers' Conference in 1995, the provincial premiers (except from Quebec) and the territorial leaders formed a Ministerial Council on Social Policy Reform and Renewal. Among other things, this council set out to clarify "the respective roles and responsibilities of both orders of government" for the purpose of reforming and renewing social policy (Ministerial Council on Social Policy Reform and Renewal, 1996, 1). In one report, the ministers suggested criteria that might be used to clarify federal and provincial roles and responsibilities (see Exhibit 2.3), and that would emphasize more clearly defined program responsibilities and more cooperative intergovernmental working relationships.

Today, the provincial and territorial governments are largely responsible for social welfare. With few exceptions, they are free to set their own social policy priorities. At the same time, the federal government continues to fund a large portion of those programs.

IV. PROCEDURES AND PARTICIPANTS IN THE POLICY-MAKING PROCESS

SOCIAL POLICY-MAKING PROCEDURES

The process of legitimating social policy is largely a government activity, carried out by politicians or legislative bodies at the federal, provincial, and local levels. The two main methods used to create and sanction social policies are agreements and legislation.

Agreements

Social policy is often communicated in written agreements that have been mutually developed by two or more parties. For example, the Social Union Framework Agreement (SUFA) was signed in 1999 by representatives of the federal, provincial (except Quebec), and territorial governments. This document, which is replicated in Appendix B, outlines the mutually agreed upon principles and commitments for future social welfare developments.

Agreements are useful for clarifying the roles, obligations, and intentions of a working relationship, but they are not always legally binding. Moreover, many agreements lack enforceable sanctions if a member does not comply with the conditions laid out in the agreement (Addario, 2001). Thus, written agreements tend to be politically driven documents of good faith. SUFA, for instance, is "more about process—about how governments should relate to one another and to their citizens in the making of social policy—than it is about substantive new social policy commitments" (Lazar, 2000, 7).

Legislation

Social policy is often the product of a complicated process of enacting laws or legislation. At the federal level, social policies are introduced as proposals or **bills** to either the House of Commons (most commonly) or the Senate. There

Exhibit 2.3

CLARIFYING FEDERAL/PROVINCIAL RESPONSIBILITIES FOR SOCIAL PROGRAMS

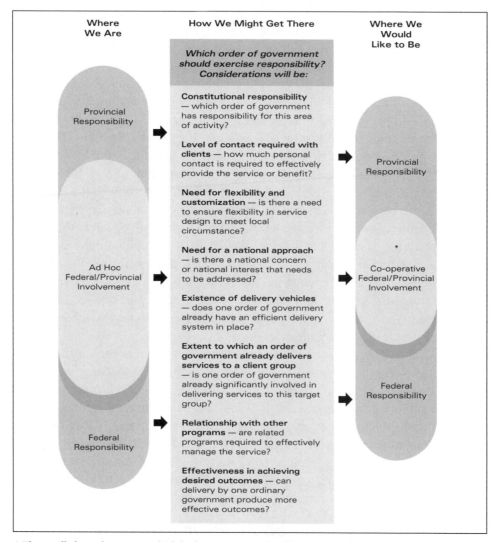

Where We Are	How We Might Get There	Where We Would Like to Be

Which order of government should exercise responsibility? Considerations will be:

Provincial Responsibility

Constitutional responsibility — which order of government has responsibility for this area of activity?

Level of contact required with clients — how much personal contact is required to effectively provide the service or benefit?

Provincial Responsibility

Need for flexibility and customization — is there a need to ensure flexibility in service design to meet local circumstance?

Need for a national approach — is there a national concern or national interest that needs to be addressed?

Ad Hoc Federal/Provincial Involvement

Co-operative Federal/Provincial Involvement

Existence of delivery vehicles — does one order of government already have an efficient delivery system in place?

Extent to which an order of government already delivers services to a client group — is one order of government already significantly involved in delivering services to this target group?

Federal Responsibility

Relationship with other programs — are related programs required to effectively manage the service?

Federal Responsibility

Effectiveness in achieving desired outcomes — can delivery by one ordinary government produce more effective outcomes?

* There will always be areas in which both governments should operate; in these areas, the aim should be effective and respectful cooperation. Cooperation means that major decisions on program design, financing, and delivery should be made through agreement by both levels of government, with delivery of programs by one or the other.

Note: Federal/territorial cooperation should also address the need to clarify responsibilities as proposed in this table, while reflecting the financial arrangements for delivering social programs to native residents of the territories.

Source: Ministerial Council on Social Policy Reform and Renewal. (1996). *Premiers Release Report of the Ministerial Council on Social Policy Reform and Renewal: Report to Premiers*, p. 9. Government of Newfoundland and Labrador [online]. Available: www.gov.nf.ca/exec/premier/social/download/english.pdf [March 4, 2004].

are two types of bills: (1) public bills, which involve "matters of public policy, such as taxes and spending, health and other social programs, defence and the environment"; and (2) private bills, which "propose laws pertaining to the powers and rights of an individual or organization" (Senate of Canada, 2002, 4). All bills are carefully reviewed to ensure that they meet technical and legal requirements and that they can be supported financially if passed into law. Bills are then given three readings by both the House of Commons and the Senate; if the bill passes in both houses, it is approved by the governor general and becomes a law (also called an act or statute). (See Exhibit 2.4 for a more detailed illustration of this process.) At the provincial level, bills are given three readings by the provincial legislature. If approved, the bill is signed by the province's lieutenant-governor and passed as law (Ruff, 2003).

It is not uncommon for several months or years to pass between the proposal of a bill and its enactment. The bill's progress through the legislature may be slowed as a result of opposition by Members of Parliament. (Canadian law provides for several "opposition days" to allow the official Opposition to criticize and debate the details of a proposed bill.) Sometimes the government deliberately delays a bill's enactment so that public and non-governmental lobby groups have adequate time to debate, deliberate, and negotiate the content and direction of the proposed policy. As a result of these types of delays, new social policies and programs may well be outdated by the time they are legally sanctioned.

The passage of an act does not always guarantee its permanency. Some statutes may be amended or repealed altogether. For instance, a series of bills, including Bill C-69, C-14, and C-17, severely amended the Unemployment Insurance Act of 1971. These amendments introduced more restrictive eligibility criteria, shorter benefit periods, and higher premium rates, and terminated the federal government's financial support to the program. Other statutes, such as the Family Allowance Act of 1944 and the Canada Assistance Plan Act of 1966, have been eliminated entirely and replaced with far less generous social legislation.

PARTICIPANTS IN SOCIAL POLICY-MAKING

In a democratic country like Canada, the policy-making process invites the participation of a wide range of groups from both government and non-governmental sectors. The various groups can be viewed as a policy community. This community comprises several concentric rings and overlapping systems (see Exhibit 2.5). At the centre of the action are the government bodies that are ultimately responsible for enacting policy. The next ring includes major interest or pressure groups; government departments and

Exhibit 2.4
OVERVIEW OF THE LEGISLATIVE PROCESS

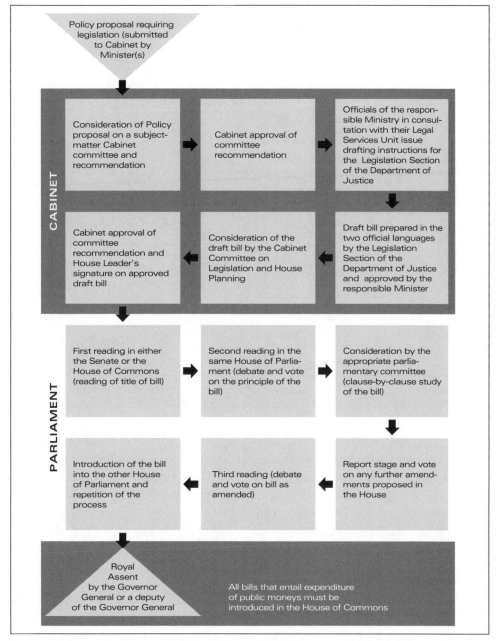

Policy proposal requiring legislation (submitted to Cabinet by Minister(s))

CABINET

Consideration of Policy proposal on a subject-matter Cabinet committee and recommendation

Cabinet approval of committee recommendation

Officials of the responsible Ministry in consultation with their Legal Services Unit issue drafting instructions for the Legislation Section of the Department of Justice

Cabinet approval of committee recommendation and House Leader's signature on approved draft bill

Consideration of the draft bill by the Cabinet Committee on Legislation and House Planning

Draft bill prepared in the two official languages by the Legislation Section of the Department of Justice and approved by the responsible Minister

PARLIAMENT

First reading in either the Senate or the House of Commons (reading of title of bill)

Second reading in the same House of Parliament (debate and vote on the principle of the bill)

Consideration by the appropriate parliamentary committee (clause-by-clause study of the bill)

Introduction of the bill into the other House of Parliament and repetition of the process

Third reading (debate and vote on bill as amended)

Report stage and vote on any further amendments proposed in the House

Royal Assent by the Governor General or a deputy of the Governor General

All bills that entail expenditure of public moneys must be introduced in the House of Commons

Source: Public Service Commission of Canada. (August 2002). *How Government Works: A Primer: What's up on the Hill: Legislative Process: Chart.* © Institute on Governance and Public Service Commission [online]. Available: www.edu.psc-cfp.gc.ca/tdc/learn-apprend/psw/hgw/ legislation_e.htm [March 4, 2004].

Exhibit 2.5
THE POLICY COMMUNITY

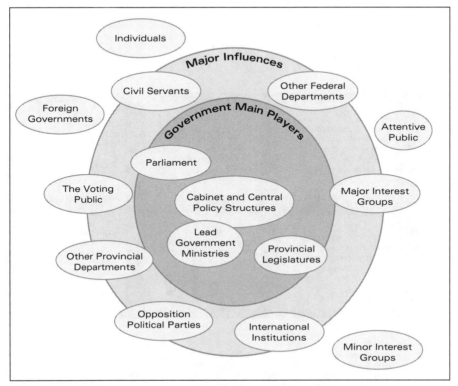

Source: Adapted from A. Paul Pross, *Groups Politics and Public Policy* (Toronto: Oxford University Press, 1986). Copyright © 1986 Oxford University Press Canada. Reprinted by permission of the publisher.

opposition parties whose actions may greatly influence social policy decisions; and foreign bodies that influence Canada's economic policies and therefore affect social policy. In the outermost ring are the individuals and groups (such as the media) that carefully follow the policy process. Each system involved in the policy community constantly interacts with and influences the others. In Canada, no single entity dominates at all times the social policy-making process (Pross, 1995).

Government

During democratic elections at the federal, regional, and municipal levels, Canadians have the opportunity to vote for representatives whom they believe will best serve the public. Each party that campaigns in an election promotes itself as having a commitment to certain aspects of social welfare and suggests ways to improve social policies and programs. Most political parties in Canada support the *concept* of social welfare; however, the extent to which a party supports the public funding and administration of social welfare is influenced by its particular ideology, political aims, and public opinion (Rankin and Vickers, 2001).

Traditionally, each party's platform has reflected conservative, liberal, or social democratic principles (for a discussion of these principles, see Chapter 1). However, in recent years it has become increasingly difficult to distinguish political parties in Canada from one another. All political parties, be they to the right or the left or at the centre of the political spectrum, have gradually moved to the right by favouring balanced government budgets, the reduction of public debt, and a leaner social welfare system (Rankin and Vickers, 2001).

Elected Officials

Policy development, implementation, and evaluation—the key functions in the policy-making process—are primarily the responsibility of elected officials at all levels of government. Federally, it is often the minister of a particular department and his or her staff who identify the need for change in policies or laws, consult with others about the proposed solutions, analyze the resources needed to implement the solutions, and ensure that proposals reach Cabinet for consideration. Members of Parliament play an important role in formulating social policy. Elected officials are expected "to represent the public and make decisions for the common good" and must carefully consider all public interests and present fair compromises to Parliament (Chung Yan, 1998, 39).

Decisions made by politicians relating to publicly sponsored programs are limited by several political and legal factors. For example, rather than making decisions based on whim or personal bias, elected politicians must adhere to the rule of law. This law establishes the limits of the power that can be legally exercised by government officials and requires that these officials account to the public for how public resources are used. The extent of power enjoyed by government officials is also constrained by constitutional provisions such as the Canadian Charter of Rights and Freedoms, by Aboriginal and treaty rights, and by language rights for Quebec and Manitoba (Privy Council Office, 2003a).

Civil Servants

Civil servants (also known as public employees) are found in both front-line and management positions. The most senior ones work closely with elected officials. As nonpartisan government employees, civil servants make a number of contributions to the policy-making process:

- They critique proposed policies in terms of their feasibility.

- They promote new or proposed policies.

- They serve as liaisons between the minister and those who deliver programs, and facilitate communication between the two.

- They write policy proposals, draft bills, and prepare other policy-related documents.

- They design programs, identify consumer needs, keep costs in line with budgets, and translate policy into concrete programs (Mishra, 2001; Wharf, 1986; Splane, 1987).

Because civil servants often hold their jobs longer than elected officials or appointed ministers, they are valuable sources of historical information on policies.

NONGOVERNMENTAL GROUPS

Citizen Participation

Since 1968 and Pierre Trudeau's call for *participatory democracy*, governments have encouraged the Canadian public to speak out about public concerns, voice their opinions about decisions that affect them, and take responsibility for changes in their communities. This **citizen participation** has played an important role in the development of social policy and programs. In 1969, the Canadian Council on Social Development (1969, 16) wrote

> Social policies and programs are intended to meet the needs and serve the interests of the individual citizen, living in community with his fellow man. The citizen therefore has a legitimate interest in the objectives, content and effects of these policies and programs; their planning and their adaptation to changing circumstances will benefit from his active involvement. He himself will also benefit.

Citizen participation is reflected in a variety of activities; that said, most of these involve a "grassroots" or "bottom-up" approach to change whereby people take the initiative to improve conditions in their communities, instead of waiting for plans and interventions to trickle down from professionals or government. Examples of citizen participation include voting in democratic elections, participating in political party activities, and working on behalf of interest groups.

Interest Groups

The social policies that elected government officials eventually pass through legislative channels are often influenced by the efforts of interest groups (also called pressure or lobby groups). **Interest groups** are organized collectives that try to influence government policies for the benefit of their own members or on behalf of the general public. In Canada, there are five broad categories of interest groups (with examples):

- business associations (Canadian Manufacturers and Exporters);
- labour groups (Canadian Labour Congress);
- professional associations (Canadian Association of Social Workers);
- research institutes (Caledon Institute of Social Policy); and
- advocacy groups and advisory councils (National Council on Welfare).

Interest groups generally form to support important causes. In the political arena, they compete with one another for public recognition and government dollars. Although the ideas and opinions of all groups are valuable, the degree to which a given interest group is able to influence social policy decisions often depends on its success at accessing needed resources, setting priorities, devising effective strategies, and forming important alliances (Chung Yan, 1998).

Interest groups use a variety of strategies to pressure governments to change existing policies, create new policies, or give more support to specific causes. Traditional strategies include collective bargaining, polling, holding public information sessions, directly contacting policymakers, participating in government consultation processes (such as "roundtables"), and publicizing issues and concerns through various media. More radical strategies include public rallies, protest fasts or marches, strikes, boycotts, and sit-ins.

Canadian governments have generally encouraged interest groups to promote and facilitate public discussion on a variety of social issues. In the early 1990s, a panel formed by the Conference Board of Canada concluded that interest groups are vital to a democratic society: "The only legitimate way for government to develop policy is by accepting, even seeking, information and views from those affected and the public at large. Lobbyists present competing views, supply otherwise unavailable information, propose solutions, provide unique insight and counsel so government can assess the implications of proposed policy" (cited in Overton, 1991, 18).

Some interest groups are more successful than others at influencing policymakers. Thorburn (2003) observes that successful interest groups are those that are "well financed, cohesive and stable, and their leaders, many of whom are former politicians, tend to represent causes which are favourably regarded by politicians and civil servants"; these groups also "command the ear of Cabinet ministers at will" and "project an air of legitimacy." Joanne Byfield (2003) adds that interest groups that are financially supported by the federal government tend to have far more influence than public opinion in shaping public policy.

INTERNATIONAL GROUPS

International institutions are increasing their influence over Canada's domestic policies. For example, the International Monetary Fund, the World Trade Organization, and the World Bank are promoting the economic integration of nations; this will require countries in the trading zone to have comparable policies. Similarly, Habitat II, the World Summit for Social Development, and other groups are pressuring governments around the world to bring their respective social policies in line with international social standards (Rankin and Vickers, 2001).

International events, and the decisions people make in response to those events, can have a profound impact on Canadian social and economic policy. Canadian pollster Allan Gregg (2003) points out that the terrorist attacks of September 11, 2001, created a significant shift in the way Canadians view themselves, their values, and their governments. He writes that Canadians

> have gone in stages from expecting government to be not just the arbiter but often the provider of the public good, to turning our back on public-sector solutions, to seeking a more focused role for government as a protector of the weak and a facilitator of the strong. Where we once welcomed short-term solutions, we now accept the complexity of the difficulties we confront.

Recent terrorism has, in essence, helped Canada to clarify its social goals and its means for achieving them.

As long as Canada is an active member of the international community, its social policy will be influenced by economic, political, and other forces beyond its borders. Canada, like its Western neighbours, must somehow deal with a rising demand for government programs and services; at the same time, it must adjust its social policy to the needs and demands of a changing global community (Banting, 1995).

SUMMARY

■ Introduction

Social policy aims to enhance Canadians' standard of living, quality of life, and social and economic well-being, while at the same time providing structure and direction to social welfare programs. Social policies are founded on certain principles and values that are important to Canadians. Ideally, social policy reflects the needs of the country; that said, constantly changing environments require that new social policy models be considered and implemented.

■ Social Policy in a Changing Economy

Social and economic policies are interrelated. Canada's economy is changing in response to globalization; we are quickly moving out of the industrial and into the postindustrial era. Free trade agreements, which come tied to harmonization and privatization policies, are doing more than changing how Canada does business; they are also affecting many aspects of social policy and social democracy. An emphasis on knowledge, services, and part-time or nonstandard work, in tandem with a de-emphasis on traditional manufacturing, is changing the labour market, creating many social and economic challenges, and forcing governments to respond with innovative social policies.

■ Social Change and Social Policy

Several trends are shaping the direction of social policy, including an aging population, changing family structure and roles, and urbanization. The fact that 80 percent of Canadians live in cities has called attention to urban living conditions and problems related to poverty, alcohol and drug abuse, housing, Aboriginal peoples, and ethnic diversity.

■ Divisions of Power: Federal, Provincial, and Territorial Responsibilities

Federalism and the Constitution Act assign the larger responsibility for social policy and programs to the provinces; in practice, though, this responsibility is divided among the federal and regional governments. The regions are different from one another in many ways; as a consequence, they tailor their policies and programs to their particular cultures and needs. At times, the federal and regional governments have relaxed their respective constitutional rights to achieve common social goals; however, disagreements on policy decisions continue to arise. One objective of the Ministerial Council on Social Policy Reform and Renewal is to clarify the roles and responsibilities of the two levels of government. The bulk of responsibility for social policy and programs nevertheless rests with the regional governments.

▪ Procedures and Participants in the Policy-making Process

The policy-making process is largely a government activity. Social policies are usually expressed through mutual agreements and legislation. Social policies can take a long time to pass into law; once they have been, they are rarely permanent and can be repealed or changed through the legislative process. Various groups make up the policy community. Political parties, elected officials, and civil servants are key players in the social policy-making process. The Canadian public contributes to the development of social policy through citizen participation. In Canada, a number of interest groups compete for public and government support. International groups are becoming more influential in Canada's domestic social policy-making.

▼ KEY TERMS

For definitions of the key terms, consult the Glossary on page 364 at the end of the book.

social investment p. 28	privatization p. 31	bills p. 42
social amelioration p. 28	working poor p. 34	citizen participation p. 48
globalization p. 29	aging population p. 35	interest groups p. 49
harmonization p. 30	federalism p. 39	

chapter

Social Welfare Developments: An Historical Review

Objectives

I. To introduce the types of social provision available during the colonial era.

II. To examine selected reform movements and socioeconomic issues, from the 1890s to 1940, and to consider their impact on social policy and programs.

III. To review the major developments in social welfare from the early 1940s to the mid-1970s.

INTRODUCTION

Canada's formal social welfare system is not the product of any one period or circumstance in history. Rather, the system's policies, laws, programs, and services were introduced at different times and in response to various human needs and social problems. For the most part, the level of social provision reached at any given time in history has depended on public demand, the political climate of the day, and government priorities.

This chapter looks at the period during which the foundations of Canada's social welfare system were laid. Three main phases comprise this period: the early phase (from colonial times to 1890); the transitional phase (from 1891 to 1940); and the interventionist phase (from 1941 to 1975)

(Moscovitch 2003; Hick, 1998). The period beginning in 1975—known for the "retrenchment" and "dismantlement" of Canada's social welfare system—is discussed separately in Chapter 4.

I. THE EARLY PHASE (COLONIAL ERA TO 1890)

On arriving in their new home, the early immigrants to Canada received food, clothing, work tools, and land grants from government and private sources (Robinson, 1999). For the most part, these settlers obtained basic necessities through self-employment (which mainly meant farming), or by borrowing from neighbours, or by trading. They valued hard work and self-reliance and took pride in their ability to take care of themselves and their dependants. Mutual aid was a primary source of support:

> As the pioneers struggled to adjust to their new way of life, families depended on each other to survive and prosper. People willingly pulled together to help one another in times of need. This spirit of mutual assistance was needed to combat the wilderness and the rigours of the long Canadian winter, as well as to prevent social isolation. (Lautenschlager, 1992, 4)

Direct government aid to the poor was virtually nonexistent until the eighteenth century, when **public relief** (an early term for social assistance or "welfare") was introduced in some settlements. This support was meagre, stigmatizing, and inconsistently provided. Colonial governments took a *laissez-faire* approach to social needs and problems; they expected families to care for their own members, and in the eighteenth century they actually began imposing fines on those who failed to do so (Morel, 2002). The authorities also left the care of the poor, the sick, and needy unattached individuals to Roman Catholic and Protestant charities.

Various unexpected events strained the capacity of private charities to provide for people in need. Thousands of sick and impoverished immigrants began arriving from Europe, and they required far greater levels of care than was readily available. These same immigrants brought several deadly epidemics to Canada with them, which placed additional stress on charities and hospitals. Thousands of settlers died from cholera and typhus, leaving behind large numbers of destitute widows and orphaned children (Lautenschlager, 1992). Despite these and other uncontrollable events, asking for charity in colonial Canada—even from the churches—was generally discouraged, and recipients of "handouts" were often made to feel like personal failures. A residual approach to social welfare was firmly entrenched in Canada's early European settlements (Guest, 2003).

THE FRENCH TRADITION

New France had little tolerance for begging by the able-bodied "undeserving" poor, and passed a Royal Decree that allowed officials to punish anyone helping beggars (Morel, 2002). At the same time, private charitable organizations—many of these associated with the Church—were established in Montreal and Quebec City to care for the "deserving" poor. The Sisters of the Congregation of Notre Dame established themselves in 1653, led by Sister Marguerite Bourgeoys (remembered as Canada's first social worker); they provided care to settlers and their children as they arrived by ship from France. Later, in 1688, Montreal's La Maison de Providence opened, and offered housing and education to young girls from destitute families, as well as care for the sick and the elderly. Quebec City's general hospital, established in 1693, provided refuge to sick, elderly, and impoverished individuals, and, in some cases offered skills training for the able-bodied poor (Lautenschlager, 1992).

Church-sponsored charities predominated in New France, but there were also many secular charities. For instance, the Bureau des Pauvres was founded in 1688 after a fire destroyed much of Quebec City. The volunteers who ran this group, most of them wealthy businessmen, met a wide range of needs, including food, shelter, tools, and help finding work, to those who had lost their homes in the fire (Lautenschlager, 1992).

The number of French charities grew during the nineteenth century. Many volunteers ran soup kitchens and clothing depots, delivered food and fuel, collected and distributed donations of furniture, visited the sick and infirm, and helped out-of-work people find jobs. Many religious societies, such as the Society of Saint Vincent de Paul, were concentrated in the larger centres of Quebec City and Montreal. These societies provided basic necessities to those in need, regardless of religious affiliation, and advocated for improvements in living conditions for disadvantaged people (Lautenschlager, 1992).

THE BRITISH TRADITION

The English Poor Laws

When the British founded Halifax in 1749, they introduced many principles from the **English Poor Laws**, a series of British parliamentary acts that had been established in Elizabethan times. These laws were supposedly intended to address widespread poverty in England; in practice, they were a means to stop the common people from wandering around the countryside begging—an activity the ruling class found highly annoying (Zastrow, 2004).

Some British settlements adopted the Poor Laws more enthusiastically than others. Nova Scotia and New Brunswick enacted Poor Laws in 1763 and 1786 respectively. Prince Edward Island never endorsed these laws to any real extent. Newfoundland encouraged its poor to rely on family, friends, and charities rather than on government (Guest, 2003).

Four basic principles of the English Poor Laws influenced how early Canadian governments addressed the related problems of poverty and public relief:

- Public relief should be *residual*. Only after all private sources of help (friends, family, neighbours, charities) were exhausted did people have the right to seek help from the government.

- Public relief should be *categorical*. Governments generally targeted benefits to specific groups, such as the elderly, the orphaned, and those with disabilities—in other words, at those who could not support themselves through paid employment.

- Public relief should be *conditional*. Recipients of public relief were expected to compensate society for any benefits they received. For example, poverty-stricken parents were given public relief on the condition that they cared for—as opposed to abandoned—their children.

- Public relief amounts should be calculated according to the principle of *less eligibility*. To discourage people from seeking or becoming dependent on government, benefits were to be minimal and less than the wage of the lowest-paid workers in a settlement (Rice and Prince, 2000).

The belief that public relief should be categorical influenced the types of institutions that British settlers built to manage the poor. The "deserving" poor included abandoned or orphaned children, who were to be educated and apprenticed, as well as people who were old, sick, or disabled, who were either extended public relief or herded into large **poorhouses**. Asylums were built to house immigrant women and children who had become widows or orphans during the voyage from Europe (see Exhibit 3.1 for the "Rules for Daily Occupation" used by one of these asylums). The "undeserving" poor included those unemployed who could work; they were often consigned to **workhouses**, where they were expected to learn good work habits and pay for their keep through labour (Guest, 1997; Taylor, 1969; Trattner, 1989).

Exhibit 3.1
RULES FOR DAILY OCCUPATION

"The immigration of 1847 was three times as high as the previous year and plagued with problems. Thousands of Irish were leaving their homes in search of a better life. Many were starving as the potato famine reached its high water mark. From the time they boarded the ships for Canada deaths began to occur. By the time they arrived, thousands had lost their lives and thousands more died at the quarantine station at Grosse Isle …"

In September 1847, the Widows and Orphans Asylum was opened in Toronto to house destitute women and children. Following are the daily rules that the asylum required of its residents.

RULES FOR DAILY OCCUPATION …

Five o'clock, A.M.	Bell to ring for rising.
Five to seven, A.M.	1st. Inmates to wash and dress.
	2nd. Beds to be put in order.
	3rd. Rooms to be cleaned.
Seven to eight, A.M.	1st. Roll to be called.
	2nd. Prayers to be read.
	3rd. Breakfast.
Eight to ten, A.M.	Recreation or work for boys and girls.
Ten, A.M., to half-past twelve, P.M.	School and work.
Half-past twelve to two, P.M.	Dinner, recreation and work.
Two to four, P.M.	School and work.
Four to six, P.M.	Recreation or work.
Six, P.M.	Supper
Seven to eight, P.M.	1st. Roll to be called.
	2nd. Prayers to be read.
	3rd. Prepare for bed.
Half-past eight o'clock, P.M.	Lights to be extinguished.
From 1st of November to 1st of May	Rising hour, six o'clock; breakfast, eight to nine; supper five. Lights to be extinguished at half-past seven o'clock, P.M.

Visitors to be admitted between four and six o'clock.

Sources: Adapted from *Report of the Managing Committee of the Widows and Orphans' Asylum, for the Care and Maintenance of the Destitute Widows and Orphans of the Emigrants of 1847*, Published in Toronto, 1848. © Marjorie P. Kohli, Waterloo, Ontario, Canada, 2000-2002 [online]. Available www.ist.uwaterloo.ca/~marj/genealogy/papers/children1847.html [March 8, 2004]. *Report of the Managing Committee of the Widows and Orphans' Asylum for the Care and Maintenance of the Destitute Widows and Orphans of the Emigrants of 1847: Widows and Orphans' Asylum (Toronto, Ont.)* 1848. Early Canadiana Online: CIHM: 61829. Copyright © Canadian Institute for Historical Microreproductions. Last updated: 2004/3/15 [online]. Available: www.canadiana.org/ECO/PageView/61829/0020?id=645f7476b7d19d55 [March 15, 2004].

Poorhouses and workhouses were unappealing even to the most desperate individuals. Dennis Guest (2003) notes that in the larger towns, the reputation of these establishments "was so fearsome that only those facing starvation would seek such help." In some of the smaller towns, poorhouses or workhouses were too expensive to build or maintain. As an alternative to them, settlement officials, such as those in New Brunswick, auctioned off the poor to work for local families.

Social Welfare in Upper Canada

The Poor Laws were never adopted by Upper Canada (now Ontario). When it incorporated many English civil laws in 1792, Upper Canada favoured the establishment of nongovernmental charities to tend to the poor and needy (Guest, 2003). These charities were financed mainly through the donations of wealthy citizens, many of whom were Loyalists who had fled the United States during the Revolutionary War. Government revenues were rarely used to improve living conditions for the poor in Upper Canada; however, certain institutions, such as orphanages and insane asylums, were eventually deemed worthy of public support and given government grants. Some local governments set up their own publicly funded relief programs; these, however, offered benefits only in cases of extreme emergency, and even then, their "programs" were sporadic, meagre, limited to the truly destitute, and often delivered in a paternalistic manner (Hess, 1993; Lautenschlager, 1992).

CONFEDERATION

The passage of the British North America Act in 1867 had little impact on the amount of government revenue flowing to social welfare programs. Under the new Dominion, the provinces were responsible for most social services, and the federal government showed little or no interest in developing a formal social welfare system. Furthermore, many provinces delegated their social welfare functions to municipal governments or local charities. In some communities, the quality of social welfare services depended "in part on the philanthropic inclinations and concerns of the upper class—in particular of those upper-class women who viewed charitable activities as an extension of their maternal roles and as an acceptable undertaking in society" (Moscovitch, 2003).

II. THE TRANSITIONAL PHASE (1891–1940)

The "transitional period" is characterized by the rapidly changing social welfare needs of Canadians. Industrialization was drawing many rural dwellers into urban centres; at the same time, the farming economy was giving way to one based on cash. As a result of these changes, family roles also shifted: men became the primary wage earners; women and children became their "dependants." If the head of the household fell ill, was injured at work, lost his job, or died, the entire family's financial security was jeopardized (Bellemare, 1993). More and more families slipped into poverty, and crime and social fragmentation threatened the stability of growing cities (Biggs and Bollman, 1991).While maintaining a largely residual approach, Canadian governments assumed a greater role in meeting people's social welfare needs.

SOCIAL MOVEMENTS AND CHANGING ATTITUDES

Industrialization and its associated problems prompted a general increase in social consciousness and a feeling of collective responsibility for one's fellow human beings. As they learned more about the underlying causes of social problems, Canadians began questioning the prevailing belief that poverty and other social ills were the result of individual shortcomings. A number of **social movements**—such as those related to labour reform, child welfare, and women's rights—took firm root during this period. These social movements called attention to the inability of families, charities, churches, and local governments to adequately meet the needs of a modern industrial society. Social movements also played a key role in the decisions of governments to take a more active role in the social and economic lives of citizens (Bellemare, 1993).

The Labour Movement and Workers' Compensation

Industrialization created a number of problems for labourers in the mining, fishing, construction, and manufacturing sectors. These workers were being pressured to put in long hours for low pay, often in unpleasant or dangerous conditions. Mounting dissatisfaction among workers resulted in sporadic protests; eventually, these workers formed unions as a means to demand higher standards of living, income security programs, and better wages with paid overtime. By the 1870s, trade unions were winning collective bargaining power and becoming a powerful political force in Canada (Carniol, 2000; Forsey, 1974).

During the early years of industrialization, primitive and dangerous machines were causing more and more work-related accidents and injuries. At the same time, the compensation system was failing to protect workers and employers alike. For instance, in the late 1800s and early 1900s a worker could sue his employer over an on-the-job injury. The company had the right to dispute his claim by stating, for example, that the injured worker had been negligent. If the company lost, the court made it pay the injured worker. If the damages awarded were considerable, the company was often forced to declare bankruptcy and shut down,which hardly benefited the injured worker (McGilly, 1998).

Many trade unions drew public attention to the increasing number of industrial accidents and the shortcomings of the compensation system, and pressured governments to improve the situation for workers. Canada's first provincial workers' compensation legislation was passed in 1908 by Quebec. However, the country's first comprehensive and compulsory plan came out of Ontario in 1914. Guest (1997, 44) notes: "The Ontario Workmen's Compensation Act of 1914 was hailed as one of the most advanced pieces of compensation legislation in North America." Under the 1914 legislation, all major Ontario employers contributed to the compensation fund; in the event of a work-related accident, instead of directly suing the employer, a worker or his family could apply for compensation. The Ontario act started a workers' compensation movement; by 1920, every province except Prince Edward Island had similar legislation (Moscovitch and Drover, 1987).

Improving Conditions for Women and Children

As the pace of industrialization accelerated, families grew less and less secure in economic terms. Dependent women and children were vulnerable if a male breadwinner was injured at work, or deserted the family, or died. Also, the proportion of lone-parent families was rising as divorce became more common; and women who had to work were often forced to leave their children unattended. These concerns coincided with changing attitudes toward women, children, and the role of government in family life (Strong-Boag, 1979).

The Child Welfare Movement The driving force behind Canada's child welfare movement was John Joseph Kelso, who worked as a reporter for the *Toronto Globe* in the late 1800s. In a series of articles, he stimulated public concern about the neglect and abuse of children in Toronto. Kelso played an important role in the passage of the 1888 Act for the Protection and Reformation of Neglected Children in Ontario (Guest, 1997).

In 1893, Ontario's legislature passed the Act for the Prevention of Cruelty and Better Protection of Children. Considered the first comprehensive piece of legislation in North America to protect children, the new act placed Canada at the forefront of child welfare legislation. The act promoted nonprofit children's aid societies and the placement of dependent children in foster homes rather than institutions. Superintendents were appointed to oversee the care of neglected, abused, and dependent children (Guest, 1997).

The First Wave of the Women's Rights Movement Women have traditionally supported social action endeavours, especially those related to improving social and economic conditions for women and children. During the late nineteenth and early twentieth centuries, it was largely through affiliation with the churches that women's issues and concerns were lent credibility. Christie and Gauvreau (1996, 108) write: "Under the impress of Christian thought, even the most 'radical social teachings', which in any other venue would have been perceived as a threat to the social order, were deemed legitimate forms of social amelioration because they were conducted within the respectable avenues of church reform." By the late 1800s, women's volunteer organizations had expanded to become national in scope. This led to the formation of organizations such as the Young Women's Christian Association (YWCA), the Woman's Christian Temperance Union, and the National Council of Women.

Women were also pushing for extended legal and political rights, such as the right to vote and to run for political office. Although women were not well represented in political parties (which were dominated by men), they exerted considerable influence on social change through pressure groups such as the National Council of Women. By the 1920s, women's groups, and lobbyists like Emily Murphy, Nellie McClung, and other early feminists, were making headway in a number of social causes such as mother's pensions, the minimum wage, prison reform, health policy, and medical care for women and children (Christie and Gauvreau, 1996).

THE FIRST WORLD WAR: CANADA'S FIRST PENSIONS AND ALLOWANCES

The First World War was a stark reminder of the vulnerability of the family unit. The considerable loss of human life on the battlefields led to concerns about the growing number of fatherless families and also about the high infant-mortality rate, which was seen as affecting the ability of families to replenish "the stock of healthy males" (Moscovitch and Drover, 1987, 24).

The federal government established a variety of charities to aid Canadian soldiers overseas and to provide relief to soldiers' families. A more organized system of relief was established when the government introduced two schemes for veterans' pensions: the Soldier Settlement, which provided unemployed soldiers with financial assistance and a parcel of land to farm; and Employment Service of Canada, which helped veterans across the country to find jobs. Also, financial assistance was made available to the families of soldiers who had been lost or killed in combat. Here, the federal government was actively involving itself in pension programs—marking a new direction in social policy. Until this time, it had been held that families, not government, should be responsible for meeting social welfare needs (Struthers, 1983; Guest, 1997).

The war's social and political impact stimulated an interest in legislated income security for mothers and their children. In Canada, the traditional practice of institutionalizing abandoned or poor children was giving way to a more enlightened approach, under which children were kept in the home whenever possible. This change meant that mothers required additional support to raise healthy children. In 1916, Manitoba legislated the first mothers' allowance. This provided a small but certain income to all women with dependants, and established the government's role as the provider of income security and protector of minimum social standards. Soon after Manitoba took the lead, mothers' allowances were established in Saskatchewan (1917), Alberta (1919), Ontario and British Columbia (1920) (Guest, 1997; 1988).

INCOME SECURITY FOR ELDERLY CANADIANS

During the early twentieth century, many Canadians expressed concerns about the ability of the elderly to provide for themselves and about the ability of poor families to care for their aging parents. These concerns were reinforced by the fact that many elderly Canadians were applying for public relief. But it was not until several provinces began complaining about the mounting costs of relief that a federal old-age pension scheme was seriously considered (McGilly, 1998).

The Old Age Pensions Act of 1927, which established pensions as a right to which all older Canadians were entitled, was the first real sign that the federal government was committing itself to social security on an ongoing basis. That said, the pension was highly restrictive. To collect pension benefits, Canadians had to be seventy or older—a remarkably high age requirement compared to what other countries with similar plans were setting. Also, the means test for assessing eligibility was strict and humiliating; clearly, policymakers were reluctant to abandon their "poor law" attitudes (Guest, 2003).

RISING UNEMPLOYMENT IN THE "DIRTY THIRTIES"

The Great Depression in Canada was triggered by various factors, including the 1929 stock market crash in the United States and Europe's slow postwar economic recovery. Severe economic problems in these countries drastically reduced the demand for Canada's primary products. This hurt Canada's entire economy, which relied heavily on exports of raw materials and semi-processed goods (Horn, 1984).

Unemployment rates soared during the Depression years. By 1933, up to 27 percent of Canadians were unemployed, compared to only 2 to 4 percent in 1929. The unemployment rate was especially high among unskilled labourers and workers in the export industries (Horn, 1984).

High unemployment created additional social and health problems. For example, by the time the Depression lifted in 1939, almost one-third of Canadians were too poor to buy adequate amounts of nutritious food. On top of this, slum conditions had developed in the larger cities. In 1934, the Lieutenant-Governor's Committee on Housing Conditions in Toronto reported that "there are thousands of families living in houses which are unsanitary, verminous and grossly overcrowded" (Cassidy, 1943, 57–58). Similar concerns were voiced by investigators in Montreal, Vancouver, Winnipeg, and other Canadian cities.

FORMS OF RELIEF DURING THE GREAT DEPRESSION

At the onset of the Depression, the United States and Britain already had a number of social security measures in place; Canada did not, and was unprepared for the widespread needs the Depression created. Unemployment insurance was nonexistent, which meant that those who lost their jobs sought whatever resources were available. A number of private charitable organizations, such as the Canadian Welfare Council and the Federation of Jewish Philanthropies, were involved in fundraising campaigns to help the unemployed. But these private sources of help had little impact on the problem of mass unemployment and widespread need (Bellamy, 1965).

Most provinces provided some form of public relief for the poor and unemployed. This was usually administered by municipalities, and was available in two forms. **Direct relief** was given out as cash, or as vouchers for groceries, clothing, or fuel, or as tangible goods like food, coal, and clothing. **Indirect relief** was provided through government-funded work projects, which were designed to get the unemployed back to work.

Public work projects tended to be poorly planned and unable to meet demand. Despite provincial and federal grants, they were also too expensive for municipal governments to support. Meanwhile, more and more Canadians were coming to depend on public relief. In 1933, 1.5 million people received public relief; a year later, this figure had risen to 2 million. Many municipal governments soon found it impossible to cover the growing costs of public relief and other social services (Bellamy, 1965; Horn, 1984). The financial strain forced some of the poorer provinces and municipalities into bankruptcy, and ultimately threatened "public confidence in the legitimacy of the institutions of government" (McGilly, 1998, 65).

The federal government grew concerned about the growing number of able-bodied unemployed men, and set up work camps in remote regions of the country where they could work in exchange for food, shelter, and other basic necessities—or for minimal wages—building railway lines, clearing forests, or constructing bridges. The work camps served yet another purpose: they contained the simmering threat of social anarchy and widespread revolt. According to some reports, work camp "recruits" were often transient and homeless men who had broken vagrancy laws and were consequently placed in camps that resembled nineteenth-century workhouses (Yalnizyan, 1994; McGilly, 1998; Guest, 1988). Exhibit 3.2 offers a glimpse into one work project in the B.C. Interior.

While struggling with the financial strain of relief programs, governments at all levels grew increasingly aware of the rising tension among the unemployed. While the government struggled to keep social order, "large numbers of able-bodied unemployed men began to make their discontent and anger unmistakably clear" (McGilly, 1998, 65). Vast numbers of unemployed men organized protests against government and the unemployment crisis. The On-to-Ottawa Trek of 1935 was possibly the largest and most famous protest of the Depression years. Around 4000 men from work camps

E x h i b i t   3 . 2
WORK RELIEF IN B.C.

Road construction at Kimberly–Wasa, May 1934.

Source: Dept. of National Defence collection (Relief Projects-No. 62). Road Construction at Kimberly-Wasa. Library and Archives of Canada/PA-036089.

across the country boarded trains and headed to Ottawa to protest unemployment, poor wages, and unacceptable conditions in the work camps (Carniol, 2000; Yalnizyan, 1994).

A NEW APPROACH TO A GROWING PROBLEM: UNEMPLOYMENT INSURANCE

The federal government eventually began sharing the costs of direct relief programs with the provincial governments; this was highly irregular, since public relief was a provincial responsibility. The federal government's involvement was rationalized on the basis that Ottawa had richer sources of revenue by virtue of its broad taxation powers and greater capacity to borrow. Also, the federal government was in a position to equalize conditions across the provinces, some of which were more severely affected than others by high unemployment. Since the provinces were constitutionally responsible for public relief, the federal government's involvement was intended to be temporary. Nonetheless, by the time the cost-sharing program was terminated in 1941, the federal government had assumed 40 percent of the total costs of public relief, amounting to about $1 billion (Bellamy, 1965; Guest, 1997; McGilly, 1998).

By the end of the Great Depression, Canadians were beginning to question whether unemployment did in fact represent the personal failure of individuals. As Yalnizyan (1994, 31) points out: "The shiver of universal risk had swept over everyone, and people started demanding protections by pooling that risk across society, and not just at the traditional levels of municipalities and provinces." Greater pressure was being placed on governments to provide a minimum of assistance with respect to income, nutrition, health, housing, and education (Mishra, 1981; Friedlander and Apte, 1980).

Although the Second World War ended the mass unemployment created by the Great Depression, government officials worried that unemployment problems would return with demobilization at the war's end. To minimize the threat, Prime Minister Mackenzie King introduced a comprehensive unemployment insurance scheme. Since unemployment was at the time a provincial responsibility, King had to seek a constitutional amendment before the federal government could legislate a national unemployment insurance plan. In July 1940, the British government extended the Canadian government this right. The Unemployment Insurance Act was passed later that year. Except for veterans' pensions during the First World War, Unemployment Insurance was Canada's first large-scale income security program. During the plan's first year, almost 4.6 million Canadians—including dependants—were covered by unemployment insurance (Guest, 1997).

III. THE INTERVENTIONIST PHASE (1941–1975)

From the beginning of the Second World War until the mid-1970s, Canadians encouraged governments to raise living standards through social programs and services. New social attitudes also prompted a growing interest in social equality and human rights; people wanted the social stability that a welfare state might provide. These and other social developments motivated governments to consolidate their social policy ideas and work toward a more comprehensive social welfare system—a move that reflected a continuing shift of public support from a residual to an institutional approach. A number of wartime studies helped lay the foundation for Canada's current social welfare system. Later, during the 1950s and 1960s, strong economic growth, high employment, and rising government revenues enabled governments to spend more on social welfare programs. Canada's social welfare system continued to expand during the early 1970s until economic problems and changing public attitudes ended the expansionary trend. This section explores some of the highlights of the "interventionist phase"—a time during which some of Canada's most revered social welfare policies and programs were established.

THE MARSH REPORT ON SOCIAL SECURITY

A large number of government committees were set up to determine the postwar needs of Canadians, and a series of reports outlining postwar programs were produced. The Marsh Report is perhaps the best known among the documents concerned with social policy; it was influenced by, and contained many principles from, the famous Beveridge Report that came out of Great Britain in 1942. In 1943, Leonard Marsh, a prominent social researcher, professor, and author, released his Report on Social Security, which outlined a comprehensive social security plan for Canada. According to Marsh, this plan was long overdue, considering the progress already made in other countries (see Exhibit 3.3).

The Marsh Report called for a national employment program, social insurance and social assistance measures, and children's allowances. A primary principle underpinning each social security proposal was "the social minimum," which Marsh (1950, 35) defined as "the realization that in a civilized society, there is a certain minimum of conditions without which health, decency, happiness, and a 'chance in life' are impossible." According to Marsh, social security programs were the means by which a social minimum could be established to prevent poverty.

E x h i b i t   3 . 3

MARSH SAYS CANADA'S SOCIAL SERVICES LAG

Leonard Marsh, of Ottawa, research advisor of the advisory committee on reconstruction, in an interview today named Great Britain, New Zealand and Russia as the countries with the most complete social legislation.

Dr. Marsh, author of the Marsh Report on Social Security, said Russia had the most comprehensive training and educational services of any country today.

"As far as English-speaking countries are concerned, Canada seems to be lagging behind. We lack health insurance, widows' and orphans' pensions, and sickness benefits. Our one redeeming quality is our excellent unemployment insurance."

A delegate to the Canadian Conference on Social Work here, Dr. Marsh emphasized the need for a national health insurance scheme and children's allowances.

Source: "Marsh Says Canada's Social Services Lag," *Victoria Daily Colonist*, 17 May 1944, 7. Reprinted by kind permission of the *Times Colonist*, Victoria.

The Marsh Report was hailed as "the single most important document in the development of the post-war social security system in Canada" (Collins, 1976, 5). However, Marsh's recommendation for a comprehensive and coordinated social security system was practically ignored at the time by the Canadian government. Even so, the document provided the structural framework for many of Canada's future social security programs (Guest, 1988; Government of Canada, 1994d).

FAMILY ALLOWANCE ACT OF 1944

According to Marsh (1943, 197), the purpose of family allowance legislation was to ensure a minimum income level for families and, in so doing, make a "direct attack on poverty where it is bound up with the strain imposed by a large family on a small income." Family allowances were also seen as a solution to the growing problems of poor nutrition and high infant mortality revealed by Depression-era and wartime studies.

Even though its passage required a constitutional amendment, the Family Allowances Act was pushed through Parliament and implemented in 1944. This federally administered allowance was Canada's first universal social security program, and was sent to all Canadian families that had dependants under sixteen. In its first year, the program cost taxpayers about $250 million, which was until then the most spent on any social security program in Canada (Bellamy, 1965; Guest, 1988).

SOLIDIFYING CANADA'S RETIREMENT INCOME SYSTEM

The Old Age Pensions Act of 1927 had been criticized for many years because of its stigmatizing means test and inadequate benefits. In 1951, that act was replaced by two new pension plans: Old Age Security, which provided universal benefits and was fully funded and administered by the federal government; and Old Age Assistance, a means-tested scheme that was cost-shared by the provincial and federal governments and administered by the provinces (Guest, 1997; Moscovitch and Drover, 1987; Morgan, 1961).

Introduced in 1965 were the Canada Pension Plan (CPP) and its counterpart, the Quebec Pension Plan (QPP). These provided a first line of defence for paid workers and their families who suffered a loss of income due to retirement, disability, or death. The CPP/QPP was available to 92 percent of the paid labour force when it was first implemented; however, it was expected to be most beneficial to the many workers who did not have access to employer-sponsored pension schemes. The CPP and QPP were different in some ways but had similar eligibility criteria and benefit levels. Also, both plans were compulsory social insurance schemes that required all workers between eighteen and seventy to make contributions as long as they were working.

Although the CPP/QPP has many unique features, its historical significance lies in the fact that it was the first income security program to be fully indexed (in other words, benefits increased automatically as the cost of living rose). Prior to the CPP/QPP, any increases in benefits for income security programs (such as Old Age Security) had to be authorized by Parliament or the provincial legislatures.

The introduction of Old Age Security, Old Age Assistance, and the CPP/QPP underscored the federal government's newly accepted responsibility for the security of elderly Canadians. These plans also took the retirement income system one step closer to ensuring a social minimum for seniors (Guest, 1997; Oderkirk, 1996).

CANADA ASSISTANCE PLAN OF 1966

Before the Canada Assistance Plan (CAP) was introduced in 1966, federal funds to the provinces and territories were highly categorical—that is, the funds were targeted to specific groups such as seniors, people with disabilities, and low-income families. Meanwhile, many other people in need, including abused women, fell through the system's cracks and were often left without adequate support. Existing funding arrangements made the provinces and territories constitutionally responsible for establishing social welfare programs; however, the poorer provinces could not always afford to meet this obligation. To correct these problems, CAP was introduced and federal aid was increased. Under CAP, the provinces and territories would be able to expand, integrate, and improve their respective social welfare programs. In this way, Canada would establish its social safety net, and ensure a minimum standard of living for low-income groups, regardless of why they needed help (Government of Canada, 1994e).

Under CAP, the provinces and territories were required to meet certain national standards but were allowed considerable leeway in designing and administering social welfare programs. Meanwhile, the federal government paid half the costs. Social assistance recipients received financial aid to meet basic living needs, including food, clothing, shelter, and personal needs; in some cases, assistance was also available for transportation, day care, and uninsured health needs such as dental and eye care. Under CAP's original provisions, personal social services were classified as *welfare services*, and were part of an overall strategy to eradicate the causes of poverty, child neglect, and dependence on social assistance, while softening the effects of these problems. Welfare services included protection services for children, rehabilitation programs for people with disabilities, home support for seniors, employment programs, community development services, and childcare (Government of Canada, 1994e).

POVERTY AND THE NOTION OF GUARANTEED INCOME

Several events during the early 1960s motivated Prime Minister Lester B. Pearson to introduce a plan to eliminate poverty in Canada. These events included an increasing awareness of poverty, the American government's declaration of a war on poverty in the United States, and the development of new methods for measuring poverty (Johnson, 1987). The prime minister's announcement paved the way for several studies on poverty. One, by the Economic Council of Canada (1968, 1), concluded

> Poverty in Canada is real. Its numbers are not in the thousands, but the millions. There is more of it than our society can tolerate, more than the economy can afford, and far more than existing measures and efforts can cope with. Its persistence, at a time when the bulk of Canadians enjoy one of the highest standards of living in the world, is a disgrace.

Also in 1968, the Senate Committee on Poverty (chaired by Senator David Croll) was appointed to look into the problem of poverty in Canada and to recommend policy changes. The committee's 1971 report, *Poverty in Canada*, drew public attention to the fact that one in four Canadians were living below the poverty line. Two matters were of particular concern to the committee: the countless numbers of children who were growing up in poverty, and the approximately two million working poor. The committee's report called attention to poverty as a growing social problem and also provided insight into the causes of poverty. The report suggested that a "social minimum" might be a way to raise the living standards of poor Canadians. To establish a social minimum, the entire income security system would probably have to be overhauled; this would involve scrapping a number of existing poverty-oriented programs and introducing a federally funded and administered **guaranteed annual income**, or GAI (Guest, 1997; 2003).

The concept of a GAI has its roots in eighteenth-century England, and was revitalized by the American economists George Stigler and Milton Friedman. According to Djao (1983), a GAI is not a specific income security program as much as it is a social goal. A GAI suggests that all citizens have the right to a minimum income as the result of either paid work or government subsidies (Canadian Council on Social Development, 1969). If all the provinces adopted a GAI scheme, Canadians would be assured a minimum income based on marital status, number of children, financial resources, age, and geographic location.

The Canadian government flirted with the idea of a GAI, but a nationwide plan never materialized in Canada. However, several provinces implemented variations of a GAI for seniors who were already receiving the federally funded Old Age Security and Guaranteed Income Supplement. For example, Ontario in 1974 introduced the Guaranteed Annual Income System (GAINS) to ensure a basic income for residents sixty-five and older; the benefit received depended on how much the recipient needed in order to live above the poverty line.

Manitoba was the only province to implement an extensive, albeit short-lived, GAI program. With over $17 million of federal money, the Manitoba Basic Annual Income Experiment—or MINCOME—provided an income supplement to more than one thousand families from 1975 to 1978. A general loss of public support for GAI programs, and MINCOME's failure to move people into the labour market, led the federal government to cancel its support for MINCOME and scrap plans for any other large-scale GAI programs (Hum, 1985; Government of Canada, 1994d; Djao, 1983).

SOCIAL MOVEMENTS: SHAKING ESTABLISHED FOUNDATIONS

In the early 1960s, Canada and other Western countries witnessed a flurry of new social movements that significantly challenged the *status quo*. These included the "second wave" of the women's movement, the environmental movement, the gay rights movement, and the peace movement. Although concerned with changing government policies and practices, these social movements were perhaps most intent on changing those social values that ultimately oppressed, demoralized, or marginalized people (Smith, 2000; Howlett, 1992).

Among the many social movements of the 1960s, the women's (or feminist) movement was especially effective in influencing social policy. Declaring that "the personal is political," women politicized a variety of issues, such as family violence, that had once been regarded as the exclusive purview of individuals and families (Smith, 2000). Two key goals of the women's movement were to achieve social justice for women in all areas of human endeavour, including the media, law, education, religion, and science; and to break down established patriarchal power structures that oppressed and controlled women (Eichler and Lavigne, 2003; Armitage, 2003). Among the many achievements attributed to the women's movement were reforms in policies and programs relating to sexual assault, family violence, employment, income security, and family law (see Exhibit 3.4).

The Royal Commission on the Status of Women (RCSW), established in 1967, was one of the driving forces behind the women's movement in Canada. The RCSW's research—which included talking to women across the country about their experiences—contributed to "a gigantic national consciousness-raising experience" (Rice and Prince, 2000, 95). The RCSW established an agenda of issues and strategies for improving conditions for women; it also identified government as obviously responsible for addressing equality and equity concerns. As a result of the RCSW's efforts, a number of bureaux for women—including the Canadian Advisory Council on the Status of Women—were established at various levels of government. The RCSW also contributed to the formation or consolidation of women's organizations in the private sector.

CANADA'S WELFARE STATE

Beginning around 1950, Canadian governments steadily assumed much of the responsibility for social welfare that private charitable organizations had long taken on. The years 1963 to 1973 saw the greatest expansion of social

Exhibit 3.4

SELECTED ACHIEVEMENTS OF THE WOMEN'S MOVEMENT, 1969–2000

1969	Women gain legal access to information on birth control and the use of contraceptives.
1971	The Canada Labour Code is amended to give maternity leave to female federal government employees.
1974	Women become eligible for enlistment in the RCMP.
1977	The Canadian Human Rights Act forbids discrimination on the basis of gender and ensures equal pay for equal work.
1982	Women's equality rights are entrenched in the Canadian Charter of Rights and Freedoms.
1985	The Indian Act is amended to restore the status and property rights of First Nations women.
1986	To ensure an equitable participation of women in the workforce, the federal government passes the Employment Equity Act.
1988	The federal government establishes the Women at Risk Program to address the needs of disadvantaged refugee women.
1993	The United Nations World Conference on Human Rights reaffirms that "the fundamental rights of women and girls are inalienable, integral and indissociable from human rights."
1995	Canada releases its Federal Plan for Gender Equality.
1998	Canadian governments release the Iqaluit Declaration, which reaffirms a commitment to end violence against women.
2000	Women mobilize worldwide to launch the World March of Women, an initiative to end poverty and violence against women.

Source: Adapted from Status of Women Canada. (2000). *Key Dates in the History of Canadian Women Throughout the 20th Century:* Commemorative Dates: Women's History Month 2000 [online]. Available www.swc-cfc.gc.ca/dates/whm/2000/dates_e.html [March 8, 2004]. Reproduced with the permission of the Minister of Public Works and Government Services Canada, 2004.

welfare programs; by the early 1980s, these programs represented close to 14 percent of GDP (Drover, 1983). With the introduction of important social security measures such as universal health care, Unemployment Insurance, and the CPP/QPP—and with established funding provided through CAP—

Canada was well on its way to establishing a range of universal "programs that would protect all citizens from the insecurities inherent in an industrial economy and, more generally, assist them in participating effectively in a modern society" (Banting, 1987, 148). The building of a state-provided system of supports represented a move away from residual toward more institutional approaches to social welfare; this is how Canada created what is commonly referred to as its welfare state.

To establish a welfare state, Canadian governments adopted many principles of Keynesian economics. Central to Keynesian economics is the idea of **income redistribution**, whereby the tax system is utilized as a means to shift income away from high- and moderate-income earners toward those with low incomes. As a result of income redistribution, it is possible for all Canadians to enjoy a fair share of this country's opportunities, resources, and benefits. According to Keynesian theory, when government redistributes cash through income security programs, low-income earners are enabled to purchase more goods and services, this spending in turn stimulates the economy. Canada was one of the first countries in the world to embrace Keynesian economics. For almost three decades, these principles were used to justify high levels of government spending and debt accumulation; the goal of this was to stabilize income and stimulate consumerism during recessionary times (Bellemare, 1993; Mishra, 1981).

THE EARLY 1970s: A TIME FOR REVIEW

The Income Security Review of 1970

Increasing concern for rising poverty rates, and a growing uneasiness with the costs of social welfare programs, sparked a renewed interest in reviewing Canada's income security programs. In 1970, the federal government published *Income Security for Canadians*, a report that reviewed Canada's social security system and recommended changes to it that would give Canadians with the lowest incomes "the greatest concentration of available resources" (Canada, 1970, 1). Among its many recommendations, the report called for the elimination of universal family allowances in favour of a program that would target benefits to low-income families; the report also suggested an overhaul of certain aspects of Old Age Security (Guest, 1997; HRDC, 2002d). The report's recommendation to eliminate the universality as it applied to family allowances and OAS drew a mixed reaction in the House of Commons. Owing to the lengthy debates on the proposed reforms and a federal election in 1972, the federal government decided to temporarily shelve its proposed revisions to income security programs.

The Social Security Review (1973–1976)

The provincial and territorial governments had been critical of the 1970 Income Security Review because it excluded them from the review process. At a Constitutional Conference in 1971, the federal, provincial, and territorial governments agreed to launch a joint review and to introduce mutually agreed upon reforms. In January 1973, Prime Minister Trudeau and his Liberal Cabinet called for a Social Security Review that would try to find ways to deal with the problem of low or inconsistent earnings among Canadian workers; a secondary goal was to develop a more universal system of personal social services (Guest, 1997). In 1973, the federal government released its report, *Working Paper on Social Security in Canada*, which outlined a plan to create a more effective social welfare system (HRDC, 2002d).

The oil crisis of 1973, rising unemployment rates, high inflation, and general economic decline placed severe strain on government revenues. Many reforms initiated by the Social Security Review were axed; however, the review paved the way for several income security programs, including Saskatchewan's Family Income Plan (1974), the federal Refundable Child Tax Credit (1978), and Manitoba's Income Support Program (1980). In addition, family allowance benefits tripled (from an average of $7.21 to $20.00 a month per child) and were indexed to the consumer price index.

SHIFTING OF THE TIDE

Despite some positive influence on social welfare programs, the Social Security Review was criticized for (among other things) failing to correct the problem of low or inconsistent earnings among the working poor (Guest, 1980; HRDC, 2002d). Moreover, Canadians raised concerns about the value of social security reforms such as those outlined in the review, given the rising inflation and unemployment rates and a generally unpredictable economy (Johnson, 1987).

The social welfare system was increasingly criticized for being a financial burden; its costs, in fact, started to be seen as "a threat to individuals' economic security" (Heclo, 1981, 400). Many Canadians also denounced social welfare programs for being of poor quality and for doing little to reduce social problems. There were also concerns that more and more Canadians were coming to depend on social assistance (Heclo, 1981; Rice and Prince, 2000).

In the years following the Social Security Review, a more conservative approach to social and economic problems came into fashion. As a result, Canada's social welfare system underwent considerable downsizing as many programs and services were reduced, frozen, or eliminated. Probusiness governments also suppressed the notion that Canada would ever become a full-fledged welfare state. By the mid-1970s, Canada's "welfare state" had become merely a "government system" that provided partial income security to working people, and more extensive support to those outside the labour market, such as seniors and children (Ross, 1987).

SUMMARY

■ Introduction

Canada's formal social welfare system has evolved over several decades in response to public demand, politics, and government priorities. The foundations of Canada's social welfare system were laid over three main phases: early, transitional, and interventionist.

■ The Early Phase (Colonial Era to 1890)

French and British immigrants had their own unique methods of caring for the poor, the sick, and the needy. The early French settlers were helped by both the Roman Catholic Church and by secular charities. Some British settlements adopted the English Poor Laws to guide the treatment of the poor and needy; Upper Canada, however, rejected the poor laws in favour of English civil laws and a network of non-governmental charities. Although the British North America Act assigned responsibility for social welfare to the provincial governments, little was done at this time to develop a social welfare system.

■ The Transitional Phase (1891–1940)

The late nineteenth and early twentieth centuries witnessed a wave of social movements in Canada as governments established a broader range of social programs. Industrialization sparked labour reform, unionization, and workers' compensation legislation. The introduction of veterans' pensions was an early sign that governments would be getting more involved in social welfare provision. Conditions for women, children, and seniors improved as a result of mothers' allowances, child welfare legislation, and old age pensions. Severe economic problems and massive unemployment, along with ineffective public relief and work projects, spurred the federal government to introduce unemployment insurance in 1940.

■ The Interventionist Phase (1941–75)

The Marsh Report of 1943 promoted the concepts of a social minimum and family allowances. Income security for seniors grew more entrenched during this time with the passage of various pension plans. An overall expansion of social welfare programs became possible with the introduction of CAP. The war on poverty was accompanied by calls for income security programs that would provide a minimum income to Canadians. Although the GAI scheme failed, it paved the way for a number of GAI-type programs for seniors. The women's and other social movements were harbingers of the acceptance of collective responsibility. As governments embraced the Keynesian principle of income redistribution, Canada moved closer to becoming a welfare state. The 1970s sparked an interest in social security reviews; by this time, Canadians were concerned more about the economy and the costs of social welfare programs. Conservative approaches were welcomed as possible solutions to the country's problems.

▼ KEY TERMS

For definitions of the key terms, consult the Glossary on page 364 at the end of the book.

public relief p. 54

English Poor Laws p. 55

poorhouses p. 56

workhouses p. 56

social movements p. 59

direct relief p. 63

indirect relief p. 63

guaranteed annual income p. 70

income redistribution p. 73

Social Welfare in an Era of Restraint and Reform

Objectives

I. To review the Progressive Conservatives' approach to governance, the strategies they used to reduce social spending, and the legacy of this government.

II. To explore the fiscal restraint measures introduced by the federal Liberal government, the changes in funding arrangements between the federal and regional governments, and the impact of these changes on national program standards.

III. To examine the various strategies adopted by the provincial and territorial governments to adjust to the new federal/provincial/territorial funding agreement.

IV. To look at Canada's economic advances in recent years and the consequences of fiscal restraint for Canadians, especially with respect to the social deficit, social cohesion, and citizens' rights.

V. To consider the implications of a postdeficit era in terms of budgetary surpluses and reinvestment strategies.

INTRODUCTION

The first half of the 1970s witnessed the ongoing development of social welfare programs. However, by mid-decade this trend had reversed itself. Canada, like other industrial countries, began to experience inflation and stagnating economic growth (stagflation) as the result of a slowdown in wage growth and dropping government revenues. As a consequence, governments found it difficult to balance their annual budgets—that is, to collect enough taxes and other revenues to cover their expenditures.

Throughout the 1970s and 1980s, governments hoped that the economic downturn was only temporary, and chose to borrow money rather than raise taxes or cut costly public programs. As governments continued to spend more than they gathered in revenues, they incurred yearly budget **deficits** (that is, their expenditures exceeded revenues) and a mounting public **debt** (calculated as the total sum of outstanding deficits). By 1993, the federal deficit was close to $42 billion and the combined provincial/territorial deficit totalled $25.2 billion (Standing Committee on Finance, 1997). These accumulated annual deficits, combined with a growing public debt, created a **fiscal crisis** (Government of Canada, 1994c; Swimmer, 1996).

With the public debt soaring, the business community contended that government social spending was hindering economic growth and eating up funds that would otherwise have been used for economic investment (Rice and Prince, 2000). At the same time, governments, business groups, and economists were attacking Keynesian economics and its principle of income redistribution for destabilizing the economy. Economists and politicians warned that annual deficits and growing debt would soon make it harder for governments to finance social programs; eventually, money for social programs would have to be redirected toward servicing the mounting debt. This was an especially disturbing prospect in light of the increased demand that an aging population was already placing on health and social welfare services (Government of Canada, 1999a; 2000a).

What began as a gradual reduction in social expenditures in the late 1970s escalated into a steady erosion of social programs in the 1980s. During this time, Canadian governments terminated programs, repeatedly cut back public spending, and/or redirected funds to other priorities. Drastic reductions in social welfare programs continued through the 1990s, creating a "crisis of the welfare state" (Rice and Prince, 2000, 84). Some critics suggest that Canada's governments exploited the fiscal crisis to rationalize a near dismantling of this country's social welfare system. Linda McQuaig (1995, 9) suggests that the deficit became "a key tool for picking away at what many in the elite consider to be our overly generous social welfare system and government policies dedicated to pampering the undeserving, at the expense of the deserving (such as those in the elite)."

The 1990s opened with a recession, but it ended with an economic boom. By the twenty-first century, Canada was rapidly approaching a post-deficit era, and the focus of social policy was about to shift from how to elim-

Exhibit 4.1

THE NATIONAL DEFICIT

Source: Reprinted courtesy of the artist, Bob Bierman.

inate deficits to how to spend budget surpluses (Rice and Prince, 2000). This chapter looks at the period from 1975 on, a time characterized by two things: fiscal restraint, and social welfare reform.

I. CONSERVATIVE CANADA: TIGHTENING THE PUBLIC PURSE STRINGS

SUPPORT FOR RIGHT-WING GOVERNMENTS

In the 1980s, public debt was rising in tandem with annual deficits. It soon became clear that new policies were required to break the stagflation trend. As in other industrial countries, Canadian voters began leaning to the political right, and electing governments with more conservative approaches to governance and public spending. According to Grady, Howse, and Maxwell (1995, 19), the role of political leaders was redefined during this time: "It became conventional wisdom in the 1980s that governments were too large, too ineffi-cient, and too indebted. The job of political leaders was to shrink govern-ments, reduce taxes, and get out of the way of private investors and citizens."

The election of Brian Mulroney and the Progressive Conservatives (PCs) in 1984 reflected Canadians' shift toward right-wing governments. The PCs broke away from Keynesian economics in favour of monetarism, an eco-nomic philosophy that called for debt reduction, reduced public spending, and a smaller role for government in social provision (HRDC, 2002d). Such an approach, conservatives argued, was necessary to address the economic problems created by "a monstrous government deficit" and to ultimately restore Canada's social and economic systems (Finn, 1985, 1).

THE MACDONALD COMMISSION

In 1982 the federal government appointed the Royal Commission on the Economic Union and Development Prospects for Canada (commonly known as the Macdonald Commission) to examine the challenges facing Canada's economic and political institutions. The commission's three-volume report, released in 1985, criticized Canada's income security system for being unfair, ineffective, and overly complex; for creating disincentives to work; and for being unsustainable in times of unstable economic conditions and changing demographics. The commission recommended that a guaranteed annual income (GAI) scheme be implemented as a means to strengthen the income security system. To free up revenues for this, the commission suggested that various income security programs be eliminated, including the Guaranteed Income Supplement, child tax credits, and family allowances (Royal Commission on the Economic Union, 1985).

The PC government took the commission's advice and scrapped or reduced many social welfare programs; however, it failed to replace these with a GAI. As a result, the income security system was weakened, and many needy Canadians began falling through the system's cracks. The federal gov-ernment also made significant changes to some of Canada's most revered pro-grams: Old Age Security, Unemployment Insurance, the Canada Assistance Plan, and family allowances. These changes are briefly described below.

Clawing Back Old Age Security

In its 1989 budget speech, the PC government announced that benefits from Old Age Security (OAS) would be "clawed back" from high-income earning seniors. This meant that Canadian seniors with high annual incomes would have to repay part or all of the OAS benefits they received each year. At the time, the National Council of Welfare (1990, 18) wrote that the **clawbacks** represented "the most significant backward step in Canadian social policy in a generation, because they end the universal nature of the Old Age Security pension."

Amending the Unemployment Insurance (UI) Act

A common criticism of UI (since renamed Employment Insurance, or EI) was that its benefits provided little incentive for recipients to leave UI and get back to work. In 1990 the federal government stopped financing UI; from now on, it would be funded entirely by employer and worker contributions. Other amendments resulted in more restrictive eligibility criteria, shortened benefit periods, higher premiums, and harsher penalties for those who quit their jobs without just cause (Government of Canada, 1994c; 1994b).

The "Cap" on CAP

Under the Canada Assistance Plan (CAP), the federal government paid half the expenses incurred by the provinces for social assistance and many personal social services. The passage of Bill C-69 in early 1991 enabled the federal government to reduce its CAP contributions to what were then the three wealthiest provinces: Alberta, Ontario, and British Columbia. This "cap" on CAP meant that in those provinces, increases of 5 percent or more in any CAP program would have to be funded solely by the province (Government of Canada, 1994a). In the three provinces affected by Bill C-69, social assistance rates were either cut or frozen, and plans for new social welfare programs were postponed (Canadian Council on Social Development, 1990).

An End to Family Allowances

The family allowance program suffered its first blow in 1989 when benefits were clawed back from high-income earners. The second blow fell in early 1993, when the Family Allowance Act was scrapped altogether and replaced by the Child Tax Benefit. As a targeted program, the income-tested Child Tax Benefit was restricted to low- and moderate-income families (HRDC, 1994). Opponents of the new benefit saw it as a poor replacement for family allowances and as another reminder that universal income benefits in Canada were a thing of the past (Turner, 2001).

THE LEGACY OF THE PROGRESSIVE CONSERVATIVE GOVERNMENT

Throughout their years in power (1984 to 1993), the PCs' approach to social welfare was in stark contrast to what Canadians had generally supported in the postwar era (Rice and Prince, 1993). The PCs were careful not to slash social expenditures too blatantly; instead, they adopted what Grattan Gray (1990, 17) describes as "social policy by stealth," whereby social programs were cut incrementally—in fact, almost invisibly. Sherri Torjman (1995, 1) observes: "The social envelope was reduced by many billions of dollars through direct cuts as well as indirect, hidden cuts in the form of clawbacks and the partial indexation of social programs, transfers to the provinces and the income tax system." Because individual cuts were hard to identify, it was difficult to track the changes in social program funding from year to year. Some analysts maintain that the cuts, however subtle their implementation, had devastating consequences that continued to be felt long after the PCs left office (Mendelson, 1993).

The PCs halted any expansion of the welfare state. But it must be noted that they also introduced a number of positive social reforms during their time in office. For example, they enriched the refundable Child Tax Credit and Spouses' Allowance, increased assistance to people with disabilities, and improved some pension plans (Gray, 1990). Also, they helped pass the Employment Equity Act in 1986 and the Canadian Multiculturalism Act in 1988, and launched the Family Violence Initiative in 1988.

II. NEOLIBERALISM AND FISCAL RESTRAINT

A NEW LIBERAL DIRECTION

The Liberals won the federal election in October 1993, and returned to power with a history behind them of generally supporting welfare state principles. Indeed, Liberal governments had introduced some of Canada's keystone social policies, including the Old Age Pension (in 1927), Unemployment Insurance (in 1940), and CAP (in 1966). In 1993, however, the Liberals recognized the need for new strategies to confront the challenges of a much different political and economic climate from when they last held office in the 1980s.

The Liberals under Jean Chrétien essentially merged economic and social policy to address the country's social and economic problems. In the past, the Liberals had based their public spending on Keynesian principles; in their new term in power, they adopted a form of economic rationalism. This involved cutbacks, support for private-sector service delivery, and targeted expenditures (Spicker, 2004). The Liberals maintained that the market could often do a better job than the government in meeting Canadians' social security needs. In fact, the Liberals believed that the "key to dealing with social insecurity [was] helping people get and keep jobs" (Government of Canada, 1994c, 9).

One task facing the new federal government was to reduce the national debt, which by 1993 had reached about $510 billion (Paquet and Shepherd, 1996). In 1994 it launched a general program review with the goal of finding ways to cut costs and deliver federal programs and services in the most efficient way possible. During the same period, Human Resources Development Canada initiated its Social Security Review.

1995: A TURNING POINT FOR SOCIAL WELFARE

Having completed its program review, the federal government introduced the 1995 budget, which contained plans to drastically downsize most federal departments and cut government spending. This budget slashed the annual operating budget of Human Resources Development Canada by $1.1 billion, bringing the Social Security Review to an abrupt halt (Bakvis, 1997). Sherri Torjman (1995, 1) suggests that although "the Social Security Review could have been a milestone in Canadian history," it was sacrificed for what the Liberals saw as a greater cause—that is, getting its fiscal house in order. The same budget included a reduction of $7 billion in transfer payments to the provinces for health, postsecondary education, and social welfare over a two-year period, as well as additional cuts in subsequent years (Kroeger, 1996; Canada, 1995).

Many economists and financial analysts commended the 1995 budget for taking a hard line on government spending; others, however, expressed concern about the budget's impact on social programs and people's lives. Premier Bob Rae of Ontario, for example, declared that the budget "marks the end of Canada as we know it" (cited in Kroeger, 1996, 21). The National Council of Welfare (1995, 1) maintained that the proposed changes "marked a giant step backward in Canadian social policy. Followed through to its most likely conclusion, it would dismantle a nation-wide system of welfare and social services that took a generation to build. Sadly, the policies of the 1990s would take us back to the 1950s."

Finance Minister Paul Martin defended the budget's position on government spending by insisting that a less drastic budget would negatively affect Canada's economic recovery and ultimately produce higher interest rates, a drop in the value of the dollar, and a loss of confidence in Canada's economy among businesspeople and consumers. Martin also reminded Canadians that the "country simply could not survive the continued build-up of public-sector debt, with an increasing portion of government revenues going to interest payments" (cited in McCarthy, 1995, A10). Martin summed up his position by stating that "there are times in the progress of a people when fundamental challenges must be faced, fundamental choices made—a new course charted. For Canada, this is one of those times" (Canada, 1995, preface).

NEW FUNDING ARRANGEMENTS

Since 1966, CAP had been the vehicle by which the federal government transferred funds for social welfare programs. To receive CAP funding, provincial and territorial governments had to deliver social welfare programs according to set standards; the federal government could withhold CAP funds if those standards were not met. The provinces and territories have always wanted more autonomy in social programming; for them, the conditional nature of CAP was an ongoing "source of annoyance" (Asselin, 2001, 13) and "an assertion of federal 'power' over the provinces to run the show" (Porter, 1998).

In 1995 the Liberal government announced that it planned to eliminate CAP as well as Established Programs Financing (which funded health and postsecondary education). Beginning in 1996, the federal government began rolling its transfers for provincial and territorial programs in health, postsecondary education, and social welfare into one funding arrangement, the Canada Health and Social Transfer (CHST).

The CHST proved to be a far less generous funding arrangement than CAP. Under CAP, the federal government was obligated to pay half the costs of social welfare programs for every province or territory, whatever those costs might be. In contrast, the CHST allowed the federal government to provide the regional governments with a lump sum or **block fund**. Under the CHST, each province and territory received the same amount of federal dollars on a per capita basis, regardless of total program costs. For provinces and territories that had extensive and/or costly programs, the shift to the CHST meant a substantial reduction in federal funding.

Over the years, federal transfers for social welfare have been steadily shrinking (see Exhibit 4.2). A report emanating from the 2003 Canada's Western Premiers Conference points out that the recent boost in health dollars has come out of the budgets for social welfare programs and postsecondary education. Furthermore, this shift of funds from one social program to another is contrary to the recommendations made by the Romanow Commission's report on the future of Canada's health care system. That commission emphasized that when "addressing the apparent deficit in health funding, [the] deficit should not be passed on to post-secondary education and social assistance" (Romanow, 2002, 69).

In 2003 the federal government decided to restructure the CHST to make it easier to account for health spending. This meant splitting the CHST in two. Since April 2004, transfers have been provided along two tracks: the Canada Health Transfer (CHT) supports health care, whereas the Canada Social Transfer (CST) finances postsecondary education and social welfare

Exhibit 4.2

CHANGES IN FEDERAL CASH TRANSFERS: 1992–93 AND 2002–03
(BILLIONS OF DOLLARS)

	1992–93	2002–03	AMOUNT OF CHANGE
Health	10.55	11.84	+ 1.29
Postsecondary education	4.28	2.42	– 1.86
Social welfare	8.83	4.84	– 3.35
TOTAL	23.66	19.10	– 4.12

Source: Adapted from G. deGroot-Maggetti (September 2003). *The Size and Costs of Reduced Social Transfers*, Table 2, p. 4. Public Justice Resource Centre [online]. Available: www.cpj.ca/pjrc/research/03_transfrs.pdf [March 8, 2004].

programs (Department of Finance, 2003d). There are no stipulations under the CST as to how the regional governments should separate the funds between postsecondary education and social welfare. It remains to be seen which program areas—education or social welfare—will be considered funding priorities in each region.

THE EROSION OF NATIONAL STANDARDS

To receive payments under CAP, the provinces and territories had to adhere to certain national standards for social assistance. For example, CAP stipulated that the regional governments would

- provide social assistance to every person in need, regardless of the cause of need;

- take into account a person's basic requirements in setting social assistance rates;

- provide an appeal mechanism so that people would have a legal right to challenge decisions affecting their entitlement to social assistance;

- not deny social assistance to anyone on the basis of how long they had lived in the province (this condition is generally referred to as the **residency requirement**); and

- not require people on welfare to work or volunteer against their will as a condition of receiving assistance (Charter Committee on Poverty Issues, 1998).

The CHST was far less conditional than CAP with respect to social welfare program standards; it required only that the regional governments uphold the residency requirement when providing social assistance. Thus, the CHST allowed the provinces and territories to determine their own standards for social welfare, including which programs should exist and how they should be designed, delivered, and funded. At the same time, the federal government waived its right to sanction any province or territory for having what might be considered substandard programming (Asselin, 2001).

Like the CHST, the new CST comes with few strings attached. The federal government agrees to transfer funds to the provinces and territories for social welfare and postsecondary education; the ways in which those funds are applied within the two program areas are left to the discretion of the provinces and territories. The provinces and territories also agree to uphold the residency requirement with respect to social assistance. Furthermore, both levels of government must support any new, mutually agreed upon principle or objective for any program funded by the CST (Department of Justice Canada, 2004).

III. REFORM AT THE REGIONAL LEVEL

ADJUSTING TO NEW FUNDING ARRANGEMENTS

Although social welfare reform was an ongoing process for the regional governments, the dramatic changes of the mid-1990s presented an entirely new set of challenges. Many regions were struggling with their own deficits and rising debt; others were still trying to recover from the impact of the federal government's cap on CAP; and all were dealing with the reductions in transfer payments under the new CHST. Ideological change was also evident: priorities were shifting "from the welfare state to the private sector, from the collective to the individual, and from public services to the market" (Friendly, 2000, 21).

While the federal government was launching its own program reviews and reforms, the regional governments began to look critically at their own programs. During the mid-1990s, the reasons behind and processes of program reform varied across jurisdictions. For example, reform in New Brunswick was critical to the province's economic survival, whereas reform in wealthy Alberta was sparked mainly by an ideological preference for small government and limited social spending. Ontario, Canada's largest province in population, chose to keep running up annual deficits so that it could cut personal taxes. Quebec was caught up in separatist issues, which meant it began its reforms much later than other provinces. Whatever the route chosen, reforms across Canada during the 1990s virtually redefined the role of government and social welfare provision (Evans, 2003).

DECENTRALIZATION

One of the greatest challenges for the provincial and territorial governments was how to cut social spending (along with other public expenditures) while still retaining a core network of programs and services. Although it wasn't a new strategy, these governments began to decentralize to a far greater extent. **Decentralization** (or devolution) involves one level of government transferring some or all of its functions, authority, and/or assets to another, lower level of government, or to the private sector.

The International Labour Organization (2001) sees four categories of decentralization. All four have been used to some degree by Canadian governments:

- *Political decentralization* refers to the transfer of political power and authority from an upper to a lower level of government (that is, from the federal to the regional governments, or from regional governments to municipal governments).

- *Administrative decentralization* is the transfer from an upper to a lower government of resources, decision-making authority, and responsibilities for delivering specific public services. In this type of transfer, the lower government is accountable to the upper government for how it manages the service.

- *Fiscal decentralization* refers to the partial or full transfer of funds by an upper to a lower level of government for the delivery of a service.

- *Market decentralization* involves the privatization of services. There are varying degrees of privatization. At one end of the privatization continuum is the full sale of an operation by the government to an agency in the private sector. At the other end of the spectrum are public/private partnerships whereby the government contracts out, outsources, or otherwise purchases certain functions from an agency in the private sector for a specified time. The government ultimately owns and is accountable for the contracted program and retains the right to set delivery standards and operating budgets. Many family support and children's aid services delivered by nonprofit societies are the result of public–private partnerships.

The provinces and territories have decentralized social welfare responsibilities to varying degrees. In 1995, for example, the Province of Alberta was able to cut social welfare costs by shifting the responsibility for childcare services to a number of community groups and for-profit enterprises (Hayden, 1997). Between 1995 and 1998, Ontario offloaded several social welfare responsibilities to local governments. The Province of British Columbia is in the process of passing its responsibility for child protection services and supports to people with disabilities to a provincewide network of authorities; these will in turn contract out services to local, nongovernmental agencies providers.

TARGETING WELFARE

In most jurisdictions, social assistance became a principal target for extensive program reform. Cuts to welfare benefits continued throughout the 1990s; by 2002, rates were so low that no welfare recipient in Canada could live at or above the poverty line on welfare alone (National Council of Welfare, 2003b). Besides cutting welfare benefits, many provinces and territories tightened eligibility rules, imposed more stringent conditions on those who were already receiving benefits, cracked down on welfare fraud, and introduced strategies for quickly moving people off welfare and to independence.

The phrase "race to the bottom" has been coined to describe the successive cuts made to welfare benefits across the country: one province slashes its welfare benefits to motivate welfare recipients to seek more generous benefits elsewhere; this places pressure on the more generous provinces to cut their own welfare benefits in order to discourage an influx of welfare recipients (LeRoy and Clemens, 2003). Exhibit 4.3 illustrates the drop in the number of people on welfare between 1993 and 2003. Many provincial leaders are claiming that people are moving off welfare and into gainful employment; such claims, however, have yet to be validated by long-term studies (Prairie Research Associates Inc., 2000).

With most CAP standards having been scratched, the provinces and territories now have the right to require welfare recipients to work or train in exchange for benefits (National Council of Welfare, 2002c). Such initiatives are generically referred to as **welfare-to-work programs** (or "workfare"), and are targeted at able-bodied (that is, employable) welfare recipients. Ontario was the first province to introduce welfare-to-work legislation through its Ontario Works program. There are now several such programs across Canada, including Saskatchewan's Bridges to Employment and Nova Scotia's Employment Support Services. There is every indication that welfare in the twenty-first century will emphasize skill enhancement and work-related activities designed to move people quickly from welfare into the labour force.

E x h i b i t   4 . 3

FALLING NUMBERS ON WELFARE: 1993 TO 2003
(% OF DECREASE IN NUMBER OF PEOPLE ON WELFARE)

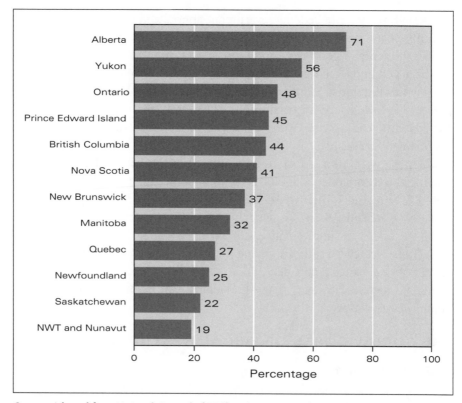

Source: Adapted from National Council of Welfare. (January 2004). *Fact Sheet: Welfare Recipients* [online]. Available: www.ncwcnbes.net/htmdocument/principales/numberwelfare.htm [March 8, 2004]. Reproduced with the permission of the Minister of Public Works and Government Services Canada, 2004.

With the elimination of CAP, the regional governments were free to restrict welfare eligibility. In 2004, British Columbia became the first province in Canada to put a time limit on welfare eligibility; employable recipients were now entitled to collect welfare for a maximum of 24 out of every 60 months. According to the B.C. Public Interest Advocacy Centre (2003), the cutoff rule will prevent people from meeting their basic needs and will not only threaten "their physical and psychological security [but also deny them] their dignity and equal worth as human beings."

IV. THE IMPACT OF FISCAL RESTRAINT

CANADA'S ECONOMIC TURNAROUND

In its 1998 budget, the federal government announced that, for the first time in thirty years, Canada's budget was balanced. By 2000 the federal government had plenty of good news to report: it had just struck its third consecutive balanced budget; strong economic growth had created almost 1.5 million (mostly full-time) jobs in four years; the national unemployment rate was 6.8 percent, its lowest level in twenty-four years; and for the third straight year, Canada was leading the Group of Seven (G-7) countries in job creation (Department of Finance, 2000).

There was also good news from the regions. The combined provincial/territorial deficit in 2001–02 was a more "manageable" $22 billion, down from $58.7 billion in 1993–94. Some provinces, including Saskatchewan and Alberta, had been operating on balanced budgets since 1994–95. (Department of Finance, 2003a).

There was every indication that Canada's prudence in the 1990s was paying off. As Canadians ushered in a new millennium, the fiscal crisis was being laid to rest. However, many Canadians were asking whether the economic victory was worth the social cost.

THE SOCIAL COSTS OF FISCAL RESTRAINT

A Social Deficit

According to the National Anti-Poverty Organization (2003), the country's economic and fiscal success has "not translated into prosperity or even an adequate standard of living" for almost five million Canadians. This **social deficit**—that is, continued hardship and "unmet human potential"—is attributed largely to globalization and heavy cuts in social expenditures (Stutt and Adelberg, 1998, 5). The social deficit is reflected in statistics such as the following:

- From 1990 to 2000, the number of Canadians living in poverty rose from 4.39 to 4.72 million (or 16.2 percent of Canadians).

- In 1999, 18.7 percent of children (1.1 million) lived in poverty compared to 15.2 percent in 1989.

- Between 1989 and 2000, the number of food bank visits doubled (National Council of Welfare, 2003a; National Anti-Poverty Organization, 2003).

The impact on Canadians of social spending cuts has not gone unnoticed in the international community. In 1998, a submission to the United Nations (UN) by the Charter Committee on Poverty Issues reprimanded Canada for its rising poverty rates (especially among children, lone-parent families, and Aboriginal peoples), for the growing number of food banks, and for increasing rates of homelessness. Between 1993 and 2003, Canada fell from first to eighth place on the UN's list of the most desirable places to live in the world, largely because of the poor living standards for Aboriginal peoples, which were persisting despite an annual transfer of $7 billion from the federal government (Fife, 2003).

According to a number of measurement systems—including the UN's Human Development Index and Canada's Personal Security Index and Quality of Life Indicators—Canada's social deficit worsened during the 1990s despite economic growth and balanced budgets. The National Council of Welfare (2003a, 1–2) observes: "It is clear that economic growth by itself cannot safeguard the well-being of economically vulnerable Canadians. Indeed, the significant efforts to eliminate first inflation and then the deficit have left more people in dire straits even in good economic times."

A Challenge to Social Cohesion

Some groups have charged that in their zeal to eradicate deficits, Canadian governments have cut social welfare programs to the point that certain segments of the population (mainly the already poor and disadvantaged) are now marginalized from mainstream society. As more Canadians fall through the cracks of the social welfare system, social cohesion is threatened. Social policy analyst Jane Jenson (1998) recognizes five dimensions of social cohesion:

- A sense of *belonging* to one's community.
- *Inclusion* in and access to important life areas and activities.
- Citizen *participation* and engagement.
- *Recognition* of different needs in society and among social groups.
- *Legitimacy* of public and private organizations that exist to connect individuals and groups.

A lack of social cohesion, then, is characterized by social fragmentation, social conflict, and a threat to the social order. As the Government of Newfoundland and Labrador (2004, 1) points out, these conditions result in society's "failure to act for the common good" and a general "lower level of well-being."

In a report by the Organization for Economic Development and Co-operation (OECD, 1997, 3), OECD countries (including Canada) are urged "to take stock of the longer-term societal implications that are beginning to emerge" from years of deficit fighting and economic restructuring. These implications include increasing income gaps between the rich and the poor; chronic unemployment; and growing public resentment toward government and neoliberal policies—in short, conditions that weaken social cohesion. In response to concerns about social fragmentation and social exclusion, various initiatives have been launched to strengthen social cohesion in Canada. For example, in 1996, the federal government's Policy Research Committee formed the Social Cohesion Network to clarify the policies required to create "an equitable and democratic cohesive society—one in which diversity is understood as a strength and in which an infrastructure of accessible institutions supports the quality of life of all citizens" (Department of Justice Canada/Canada Heritage, 2002, 5). The degree to which these initiatives are making a difference at a "tangible level" is yet to be determined (Government of Newfoundland and Labrador, 2004, 2).

A Threat to Citizens' Rights

Many individuals and advocacy groups have taken exception to the repeal of CAP, the erosion of national standards, cutbacks in social assistance, and other reforms, claiming that these actions have violated citizens' rights by threatening both horizontal and vertical equity.

Horizontal Equity **Horizontal equity** "entitles all persons to be 'counted' equally ... by both the federal and provincial levels of government wherever they reside" (Boadway, 2003, 240). Horizontal equity may be lost because the minimum standards established under CAP do not apply to current federal/provincial/territorial funding arrangements. Because each province and territory is allowed to develop its own standards for social welfare, there are now discrepancies in the programs offered across Canada. For example, provinces differ with respect to their eligibility requirements for welfare recipients; this means that a person may be eligible for assistance in one province but not in another (Collins, 1998; Ross, 1995). Through equalization payments, the federal government attempts to boost the financial capacity of less prosperous regions. However, the poorer provinces, and those with small populations (such as the Atlantic provinces), have modest tax bases or face other economic challenges that limit their capacity to raise sufficient revenues to meet citizens' social needs.

Many governments that have expensive operating costs cannot afford to provide services directly; contracting out those services to smaller and more efficient nongovernmental agencies is a viable alternative. However, when the private sector is more involved in the delivery of social welfare programs, it becomes more difficult to coordinate services, track gaps and overlaps in services, and apply common standards (Rice and Prince, 2000).

Vertical Equity **Vertical equity** refers to governments' use of redistributive powers "to reduce inequalities of income between the wealthiest Canadians and those who are least wealthy, and to enhance equalities of opportunity for those most disadvantaged" (Boadway, 1995, 2). Under current funding arrangements, the provinces and territories are free to distribute incomes across the population in any way they choose. When a jurisdiction cuts funding to welfare and other programs for low-income residents, while cutting taxes to high-income residents, inequalities between rich and poor citizens become more pronounced, and vertical equity is threatened.

Constitutional and International Issues

Some Canadians contend that the repeal of CAP and the resulting hardships for disadvantaged groups have violated citizens' rights—rights protected under the Charter of Rights and Freedoms. Similar claims have been made at the international level; for example, in its submission to the UN, the Charter Committee on Poverty Issues (1998) called the repeal of CAP "a manifestly retrogressive measure in that it is an almost complete abandonment by Canada of a framework which ensured rights for all low-income Canadians." These claims—which are based mainly on sections 7 and 15 of the Charter— maintain that citizens have a *legal right* to an "adequate standard of living" or "minimal social assistance."

Generally, Canadian courts have rejected these claims and have been reluctant to scrutinize social welfare reform in the context of the Charter. Canadian courts have also decreed that under the Constitution, the government has no obligation to eliminate poverty. According to a transcript from one Ontario court, "the plight of welfare recipients, although urgent and serious, relates [not to government activity but] to their inability to provide for themselves"; this same court added: "while poverty is a deeply troubling social problem, it is not unconstitutional" (Charter Committee on Poverty Issues, 1998).

V. CANADA IN A POSTDEFICIT ERA

BUDGETARY SURPLUSES

In 1999, Paul Martin (then Canada's finance minister) announced that the country had entered a new phase, one of **budgetary surpluses**. A surplus is "the amount by which government revenue exceeds budgetary spending" (Department of Finance, 2003i). In 1993–94, the federal government was struggling with an unwieldy deficit of $42 billion; by 2000–01, it had accumulated a surplus of $17.1 billion. Several provinces and territories were also reporting budget surpluses. By 2000–01, the combined federal/provincial/territorial government surplus totalled $29.2 billion (Department of Finance, 2001). However, a number of economic problems in subsequent years—including those related to severe acute respiratory syndrome (SARS), bovine spongiform encephalopathy (BSE, or mad cow disease), floods, storms, blackouts, and forest fires—have slowed the surplus trend.

REINVESTMENT STRATEGIES

Federal Level

At the turn of the twenty-first century, the federal government was expressing an interest in investing its surplus in areas that had been neglected during the deficit-fighting years. One possibility was a **basic income program** (a new name for GAI). This scheme would replace all existing income security programs—such as Employment Insurance, welfare, child benefits, and Old Age Security—with a single assistance program. The basic income program would be federally administered and funded; its aim would be to keep all Canadians, whatever their age or circumstances, above a certain minimum annual income (Charbonneau, 2000; Holcroft, 2000). Other programs were also being considered as possible recipients of surplus funds, including those for drug addiction, urban renewal, early childhood development, and homelessness. According to Shawn McCarthy (2002), the federal government's renewed interest in social spending reflected a return to more "traditional Liberal values."

For some Canadians, the federal government's 2003 budget marked the beginning of a new era for social welfare. Andrew Jackson (2003b) dubbed the budget the "U-Turn Budget" because it represented a sharp reversal in Liberal priorities, from fiscal restraint to social spending. For 2003–04, more than $2 billion was earmarked for child benefits (including childcare and early learning), initiatives to combat homelessness, and affordable housing (Department of Finance, 2003c). John Ibbitson (2003) noted that this sort of federal spending had not been "seen since the heady days of Pearsonian Liberalism and Trudeaumania. This budget represents a massive transfer of wealth from richer to poorer, from private to public, in the interests of a more egalitarian society." Citizens for Public Justice (2003) saw the 2003 budget commitments as having the potential to ameliorate the social deficit: affordable housing would reduce homelessness; child benefits would provide relief for low-income families; and enriched early-childhood programs would strengthen families.

Not all Canadians supported the federal government's 2003–04 plan to increase spending. By March 2003, the national debt stood at $526.5 billion and was requiring an extra $36.2 billion a year for interest payments (Statistics Canada, 2004b; Treasury Board of Canada Secretariat, 2003a). Members of the business community urged the federal government to use its budget surpluses to reduce this debt. Some business groups cautioned the federal government against increased spending. The Canadian Chamber of Commerce (2003, 2), for instance, found the federal government's "aggressive increase in program spending [in 2003 to be] a step in the wrong direction."

Many Canadians support the federal government in its decision to reinvest surpluses in social programs (see Exhibit 4.4). Some social analysts are suggesting specific areas that reinvestment might target. For example, Battle and Torjman (2002) of the Caledon Institute of Social Policy recommend a total restructuring of the social welfare system, while Laurel Rothman (2003), the national coordinator of Campaign 2000, is calling for the elimination of child poverty.

E x h i b i t   4 . 4

WHAT TO DO WITH THE BUDGET SURPLUS?

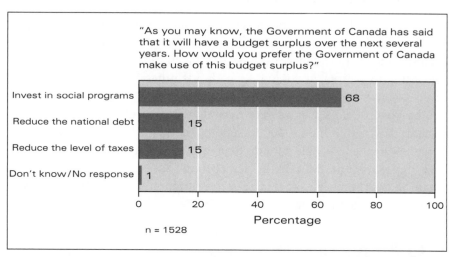

"As you may know, the Government of Canada has said that it will have a budget surplus over the next several years. How would you prefer the Government of Canada make use of this budget surplus?"

Invest in social programs — 68
Reduce the national debt — 15
Reduce the level of taxes — 15
Don't know/No response — 1

Percentage

n = 1528

Source: Adapted from EKOS Research Associates Inc. (March 2003). *Positioning the Voluntary Sector in Canada: What the Elite and General Public Say:* Final Report, page 15. This project was conducted on behalf of the Joint Awareness Table, part of the Voluntary Sector Initiative launched by the Government of Canada in 2001. [online]. Available: www.vsi-isbc.ca/eng/awareness/pdf/ awareness_opinion_report.pdf [March 8, 2004].

Regional Level

Much of the reinvestment activity at the regional level consists of redirecting money that has been saved through cuts to social assistance programs. The National Child Benefit Supplement, for example, is federal money that goes to low-income families with children, many of whom also receive social assistance. Under the National Reinvestment Framework, the provinces and territories are allowed to deduct the amount of the federal supplement from welfare benefits that go to families as long as they reinvest the money in programs for low-income families with children (deGroot-Maggetti, 2003b; National Council of Welfare, 2002b).

There is no guarantee that surpluses at the regional level will translate into improved social welfare programs (Rice and Prince, 2000). Although Alberta and Manitoba, for example, reported surpluses in 2003, both failed to target programs for the poor as an investment priority. Indeed, Alberta cut its spending on social welfare programs by 20 percent in the early 1990s and has kept funding levels low since then (Babin, 2003); Manitoba reduced its personal taxes but has given little relief to its poorest taxpayers (Canadian Centre for Policy Alternatives, 2003). A priority for many other governments is to use surplus money to reduce debt and avoid deficits.

SOCIAL PRIORITIES UNDER A MARTIN GOVERNMENT

The extent to which a Liberal government under Paul Martin will support social welfare programs remains to be seen. However, it is clear that the government intends to remain fiscally responsible in the area of social spending. According to Martin, as long as Canada identifies its priorities, carefully reviews how it spends, and ensures that money is allocated to priorities, it will be possible to "set out a very, very dynamic set of social programs for Canadians" (cited in Elliott, 2003). Among Martin's priorities are early childhood development, people with disabilities, Aboriginal peoples, and community development. Martin hopes to enhance the role of nonprofit organizations (in other words, increase privatization) in the delivery of social services (Office of the Prime Minister, 2004).

SUMMARY

■ Introduction

Stagflation, a burgeoning public debt, and annual deficits created Canada's fiscal crisis. Beginning in the 1970s, governments introduced significant cuts to social expenditures; these triggered a crisis in the welfare state. The social welfare system has been severely retrenched in recent years. However, it seems that a new era of social reinvestment has begun.

■ Conservative Canada: Tightening the Public Purse Strings

In an atmosphere of rising public debt and annual deficits, a more conservative approach to social welfare appealed to many Canadians. In 1985 the Macdonald Commission recommended a restructuring of the income security system. The Progressive Conservatives responded by overhauling many aspects of Old Age Security, Unemployment Insurance (now EI), CAP, and family allowances. The PC government is associated with the term "policy by stealth," but in fairness, it also introduced and enhanced certain social policies and programs.

■ Neoliberalism and Fiscal Restraint

During the 1990s, the Liberal government introduced neoliberal policies and a new brand of fiscal restraint. In 1994, a review of federal programs indicated a need to downsize government; in the 1995 budget, the Liberals announced major spending cuts. In 1996, CAP was replaced by the CHST: this changed how the federal government funded social programs; it also relaxed national standards and, in so doing, gave the regional governments more discretionary power in how they designed and delivered social welfare programs. In 2004, the CHST was divided into the Canada Social Transfer and Canada Health Transfer.

■ Reform at the Regional Level

Besides struggling with their own deficits and debts, Canada's provincial and territorial governments were forced to adjust to reduced federal funding under the CHST. The regional governments reviewed their own programs and devised strategies to cut costs; many of these strategies involved various forms of decentralization. Social assistance became a primary target of cost cutting.

■ The Impact of Fiscal Restraint

The federal government balanced its budget in 1998. Most of the provincial and territorial governments had balanced their budgets by 2001–02. Although Canada's economy seems to be improving, cuts in social welfare spending have left the country with a social deficit. Problems associated with poverty and food bank use are particular concerns. The repeal of CAP, with the subsequent elimination of national standards, has threatened social rights and horizontal and vertical equity.

■ Canada in a Postdeficit Era

By the end of the 1990s, Canada had entered a new phase, one characterized by budgetary surpluses. The federal government under the Liberal Party is showing a renewed interest in social spending; at the same time, business groups are recommending that surplus funds be used to pay down the national debt. Reinvestment activity at the regional level is taking a variety of forms. Some provinces and territories are reinvesting their savings into programs for low-income families; others are using their surplus funds to reduce public debt.

▼ KEY TERMS

For definitions of the key terms, consult the Glossary on page 364 at the end of the book.

deficits p. 78

debt p. 78

fiscal crisis p. 78

clawbacks p. 80

block fund p. 84

residency requirement
  p. 85

decentralization p. 87

welfare-to-work programs
  p. 88

social deficit p. 90

horizontal equity p. 92

vertical equity p. 93

budgetary surpluses p. 93

basic income program
  p. 94

part 2

THE SERVICE DELIVERY SYSTEM

chapter 5

Service Sectors: Public, Commercial, and Voluntary Domains

Objectives

I. To review how public-sector social welfare programs are delivered, legitimated, and funded, and to consider the strengths and limitations of government service delivery.

II. To explore commercial social welfare programs and services, their legitimacy in Canadian society, and their funding patterns and potential strengths and limitations.

III. To examine the range of social welfare programs provided by voluntary agencies, how these programs are legitimated and funded, and their perceived strengths and weaknesses.

IV. To look at the role of competition and cooperation in the service delivery environment and how these forces impact social provision.

INTRODUCTION

Canada's social welfare programs developed at different times, under different administrations, and in response to different needs across the country. As a consequence, there is no single administrative or funding body for all social welfare programs and services. Rather, Canada has a **mixed economy of welfare**—that is, a myriad of service delivery systems, which are organized, funded, and managed in a variety of ways (Rice and Prince, 2000).

The social welfare system comprises two broad service sectors: the public and the private. The **private sector** can be further broken down into the commercial and voluntary sectors. Thus there are three general service sectors:

- The **public sector** includes all programs and services that are funded fully by tax revenues and administered and delivered by government.

- The **commercial sector** delivers services for a profit.

- The **voluntary sector**—also called the charitable, independent, or "third" sector—comprises nongovernmental agencies and organizations that deliver programs on a nonprofit basis.

Because of their many contributions to the development of Canada and its communities, these three sectors are commonly referred to as the "three pillars" of Canadian society (Pillar-Voluntary Sector Network, 2003).

Although the three sectors tend to be viewed as discrete entities, there is considerable overlap between them. As Katherine Scott (2003, 8) notes, the boundaries between the three are "'fuzzy'—if not downright porous." These boundaries lack clear definition for the following main reasons:

- Government and private-sector agencies often work together on, or share the costs of, joint projects.

- The activities, functions, and roles of private and public social agencies are often similar.

- Governments are constantly adjusting their degree of involvement in service delivery; this affects the scope of programs and services delivered by the private sector.

It may be that a mixed economy of welfare offers more effective programs and services, since multiple organizations are in competition to develop and deliver them (Rice and Prince, 2000). Also, separate sectors may provide a broader range of services and offer people a choice as to which type of service they prefer—public or private (Armitage, 2003). However, the mixing of public- and private-sector systems has been criticized for producing a social welfare system that can hardly be called "systematic" and that amounts to a mishmash of fragmented, uncoordinated, and "poorly connected programs that confuses professionals and frustrates consumers" (Wharf, 1992, 43).

This chapter introduces each sector in terms of the nature of its services; legitimation and authority; sources of funding; and strengths and limitations.

I. SOCIAL WELFARE IN THE PUBLIC SECTOR

NATURE OF SERVICES

The responsibility for social welfare programs and services is shared by three levels of government. At the federal level is a broad range of income security programs, including Veterans' Pensions and Old Age Security as well as nonincome programs for families, Status Indians, and other social groups. The federal government does not directly provide as many services as it used to, but it continues to develop, set policy for, and fund a variety of programs that are delivered by lower levels of government or by private-sector agencies. The federal government tends to limit its involvement to social welfare initiatives that promote nation building—in other words, that enhance the well-being of, and equalize opportunities for, all Canadians (Courchene, 2003). The federally funded National Children's Agenda and the Social Cohesion Network reflect a nation-building focus.

Under the Constitution, the provincial and territorial governments are responsible for a wide range of social welfare programs, such as those relating to mental health, child protection, foster care, and social assistance. Over the past decade, decentralization, federal downsizing, and changes in funding arrangements have given the regional governments added responsibility in all aspects of social welfare.

Canada has never had an established pattern for the delivery of social welfare services at the municipal level. However, municipal or local governments played a prominent role early in Canada's history, when the English Poor Laws required that "the management of the poor, the ailing or the indigent [fall] first to local governments and to property tax for their financing" (Melchers, 1999, 36). Since the 1970s—and to a heightened degree in the 1990s—provincial governments have been assigning municipalities greater responsibility for social housing, welfare services, childcare, and other social services (Richmond and Shields, 2003).

LEGITIMATION AND AUTHORITY

Government authority to establish and deliver social welfare programs is rooted in the many policies, legislative acts, and other legal documents that guide the design and implementation of these programs. Public social agencies are legitimated by the Constitution and by the rule of law, and are monitored by various regulatory bodies at the federal, provincial/territorial, and municipal levels.

Much of the government's service provision is also legitimated by professionals and others in the community, who refer clients to public programs, and by citizens, who seek help directly from government agencies.

SOURCES OF FUNDING

For the most part, public social welfare programs are financed by tax revenues. To help cover the costs of social welfare programs, the federal government transfers funds to the provinces and territories by way of three main mechanisms:

- *Canada Social Transfer (CST)*. The CST is the primary funding mechanism used to finance postsecondary education, social assistance, and the personal social services. Because it is a block fund, the regional governments can divide the CST in any way they choose. In the fiscal year 2004–05, the federal government will transfer an estimated $14.55 billion in cash and tax points through the CST to the provincial and territorial governments (Canadian Federation for the Humanities and Social Sciences, 2003).

- *Equalization Program.* This program supplies additional funding to the less prosperous regions so that they can implement social programs that are of similar quality to those in wealthier jurisdictions. In 2003–04, payments provided under this program went to eight provinces and totalled $10.1 billion (Department of Finance, 2003g).

- *Territorial Formula Financing.* This transfer to territorial governments recognizes the higher costs of providing public services in the North. In 2003–04, payments provided under this program totalled nearly $1.7 billion (Department of Finance, 2003g).

Transfers to the provincial and territorial governments may be in the form of cash, or tax points, or a combination of the two. The federal government transfers tax points by reducing its own tax rates to allow provinces and territories to raise their rates by an equivalent amount; this arrangement allows the regional governments to raise additional revenues without increasing the total tax burden for Canadians (Department of Finance Canada, 2003k).

STRENGTHS AND LIMITATIONS

After the Great Depression, Canadians demanded that their governments offer them broader protection during times of need. This acceptance that governments had a role to play in citizens' lives marked a shift from the individualistic, *laissez-faire* approach of earlier decades toward a new "citizenship of entitlement" (Browne, 1996, 13). Canadians have come to expect govern-

Exhibit 5.1

GOVERNMENT ASSISTANCE

Source: Reprinted courtesy of the estate of the artist, Denny Pritchard.

ments to protect them from the risks inherent in modern society—risks such as poverty, unemployment, disability, and illness. Today's broad range of programs and services is the government's response to those expectations.

Yet over time, Canadians have become increasingly critical of how public programs are being delivered and managed. By the 1990s, government departments had evolved into large, bureaucratic systems that were perceived as expensive, rigid, remote, impersonal, and unresponsive to the public's needs (Grady, Howse, and Maxwell, 1995; Rosell, 1999; Wharf, 1992). Over the past decade, federal, provincial, and territorial governments have been restructuring their bureaucracies, reducing staff numbers, devolving many public programs to lower levels of government and the private sector, and, in the process, becoming much smaller operations (Hikel, 1997).

Some municipal governments have been able to accommodate their expanded responsibilities more smoothly than others. Property taxes are the main source of revenue for many cities; unfortunately, they can be "an inadequate and often inappropriate mechanism to address larger urban challenges" (Seidle, 2002, 3). In its 2003 budget, the Government of Canada committed itself to a "new urban strategy," one that would increase funding to municipalities to help them adjust to their expanded role in service delivery, and that would address growing problems such as homelessness, a lack of affordable housing, and aging infrastructures (Department of Finance, 2003b).

Canadians are still committed to social programs, but their views are changing as to which level of government (if *any* level) should deliver these programs (Mendelsohn, 2002). A poll by the Centre for Research and Information on Canada (2003) found that 25 percent of Canadians trusted their provincial government more than the federal or local government to deliver important programs and services. In another poll, 75 percent of 197 respondents thought that their municipal government had a clearer understanding of their community's social needs than either the provincial or the federal government (Clutterbuck and Novick, 2003). Polls and other studies indicate that in general, Canadians are losing their trust in government (Conference Board of Canada, 2000). Indeed, the Centre for Research and Information on Canada (2003) found that almost 25 percent of Canadians do not trust *any* level of government.

Is there still a role for government in social welfare? There is little consensus in Canada on this question: some Canadians favour less government involvement in social welfare; others would like to see government pull out of service delivery but keep funding programs and making policy decisions; still others would prefer a nongovernmental, grassroots approach to social welfare—one that would emphasize self-help, collaboration, and voluntarism (Browne, 1996). Some organizations, such as the National Council of Welfare (2003a) and the Social Planning Council of Ottawa-Carleton (2001), would like government to play a central role in guaranteeing the economic and social rights of all Canadians and in protecting the most vulnerable citizens.

II. SOCIAL WELFARE IN THE COMMERCIAL SECTOR

NATURE OF SERVICES

Although commercial social agencies are common in the United States, they are far from being predominant service providers in Canada. However, these commercial systems are being encouraged in provinces such as Ontario and Alberta, where conservative governments have downsized government, reduced public spending, and opened up traditional government services to the market.

Over the past two decades, Canadian governments have generally been relaxing their monopoly over personal social services such as childcare, eldercare, addiction treatment, and aid to people with disabilities; they have been allowing private, for-profit agencies to deliver these services. As a consequence, certain occupational groups that once relied on jobs in public social services are now branching into commercial enterprise. For example, many social workers have broken away from their traditional roles in government and nonprofit agencies, and are now offering their expertise on a fee-for-service basis (CASW, 2003b).

In Canada, the commercialization of social assistance programs is a relatively new phenomenon. Profit making is gradually infiltrating this area, with governments hiring companies to set up new systems to improve the mechanisms for calculating and distributing welfare. Some provincial governments—including those in Ontario, New Brunswick, and British Columbia—are consulting with profit-making firms in an effort to make their welfare systems more efficient (Klein and Long, 2003; National Union of Public and General Employees, 2000; Daniels and Ewart, 2002). In Exhibit 5.2, three writers from the Fraser Institute urge provincial governments to draw from American examples and include for-profit firms in the provision of social assistance.

LEGITIMATION AND AUTHORITY

Commercial programs are rapidly gaining legitimacy in Canada. As a result of government-issued licences and privatization policies, commercial enterprises are now free to sell services to the general public. Commercial social welfare services are also being legitimated by the growing number of people who question the expense of government-sponsored programs and who welcome the innovative ideas and results-oriented approaches associated with business. The many trade agreements struck between Canada and its international neighbours have served as another means of legitimation. NAFTA and the FTAA, for example, encourage private enterprise and minimal government involvement in the delivery of services, including those related to social welfare.

SOURCES OF FUNDING

Commercial groups obtain funds from a variety of sources. Some entrepreneurs charge the consumer a flat rate for services rendered. Other groups base payments on a sliding fee scale, whereby the fee is adjusted according to the client's financial means; this practice is more common when government subsidizes the costs of services for low-income clients. People who pay for

E x h i b i t   5 . 2
ALLOW PRIVATE, FOR-PROFIT WELFARE PROVIDERS

Since the early 1990s, a diversity of successful approaches to welfare delivery has been developed in the United States and there is also now a wealth of research on the impact of these reforms on former recipients. In these, provincial governments in Canada, which have generally been slow to reform social assistance, will find valuable models and information. There are seven elements that are especially important for the successful reform of social assistance. One of these elements is to allow private, for-profit welfare providers.

During the 1990s, the Canadian non-profit sector has emerged as an important instrument in reforming welfare while the for-profit sector has been left out. This is most likely the result of a Canadian culture that frowns upon profit industries providing health or social services. Consequently, provinces have ignored opportunities to reform social assistance programs and the welfare bureaucracy. Canadian provinces have yet to introduce [commercial]-sector welfare-to-work programs (i.e. America Works) to assist long-time welfare recipients in finding employment. To date, [commercial]-sector involvement in Canadian welfare reform has almost exclusively taken the form of wage subsidies to employers. If provinces are going to move people off welfare, then they must open the door to private for-profit firms like America Works that have proven successful at assisting welfare recipients find employment.

Source: Excerpted and adapted from C. Schafer, J. Emes, and J. Clemens (August 2001). *Surveying US and Canadian Welfare Reform*, p. 55–56. Fraser Institute Critical Issues Bulletin. The Fraser Institute [online]. Available: www.fraserinstitute.ca/admin/books/files/SurveyingWelfare.pdf [March 18, 2004].

services from a commercial agency may be reimbursed for service costs if they are covered under an extended health insurance program or other compensatory program such as workers' compensation. The government is a growing source of funds for commercial organizations: a commercial agency may be contracted to administer and deliver a service, with the government covering the costs of the program and controlling the quality of service by setting standards and regulations.

STRENGTHS AND LIMITATIONS

There is much debate over the pros and cons of commercializing social welfare programs and services. According to Industry Canada (2001b), the commercial sector has the ability to save money through efficient operations, innovations in service delivery, and creativeness in finding new revenue sources. Some Canadians are nevertheless concerned that companies may win government contracts, not on the promise of delivering the highest quality of service, but because they can deliver the service for the lowest cost. Social analysts also question the values on which the commercial sector is founded. Traditionally, social services have been associated with the welfare state and values that centre on "the alleviation of human suffering" (Sauber, 1983, 26). The idea of large companies profiting from people's problems runs counter to these basic values (Klein and Long, 2003). Commercial enterprises are also seen as lacking in social conscience and commitment: as long as the service makes a profit, the company will provide it; once a better rate of return is found elsewhere, the "owners will shift their loyalties" (Quarter, 1992, 3).

Accountability is another concern related to profit-making agencies. Governments are accountable to the public for their expenditures and practices; the same does not necessarily hold true for commercial operations. A lack of accountability may make it difficult to determine whether those receiving services from commercial agencies have been treated fairly (Klein and Long, 2003).

There is a fear that commercial services may be easy for middle- and upper-income groups to purchase, but inaccessible to low-income groups. Peter Clutterbuck (1997) suggests that when commercial services are targeted to those with the ability to pay, services for low-income groups will diminish as a result of government cutbacks. Ben Carniol (2000, 82) observes: "In a twist of irony, the very social services that were supposed to modify the inequalities produced by the system end up by being sold to those most able to afford them." This problem was addressed at the World Summit for Social Development (2000); governments that allowed the commercialization of social services were urged to develop effective strategies for regulating the quality of commercial services and to ensure that such services were equitably distributed.

III. SOCIAL WELFARE IN THE VOLUNTARY SECTOR

NATURE OF SERVICES

The voluntary sector comprises a broad spectrum of voluntary agencies, otherwise known as charitable organizations, nongovernmental organizations (NGOs), or nonprofit societies. Voluntary agencies vary in size from small, community-based groups such as Gamblers Anonymous, to large, national organizations such as the National Action Committee on the Status of

Women. Agencies also vary in their primary activities and functions: some provide direct services to clients through food banks, transition houses, family service agencies, and the like; others play an advocacy or research role and work toward changing social policy or legislation (Scott, 2003). Advocacy/research groups include the National Council of Welfare and the Canadian Council on Social Development. In many respects, voluntary organizations complement the work performed by governments. That is, governments respond to nationwide concerns such as child poverty and homelessness, whereas voluntary agencies apply "their knowledge, expertise and compassion" to their work at the community level (Voluntary Sector Steering Group, 2002, 32).

There is no commonly held definition of a voluntary agency. That said, the International Classification of Nonprofit Organizations describes the majority of them as being

- organized (that is, they have some internal organizational structure);
- nongovernmental (that is, they are structurally separate from government institutions);
- nonprofit (that is, they use any profits to improve the agency, not to benefit the owners or directors);
- self-governing (that is, they are independent from other institutions and regulate their own operations); and
- volunteer-friendly (that is, they engage volunteers to some degree in agency activities or management (Saunders, 2004).

Voluntary social agencies can be divided into two categories: sectarian (religious) and secular (nonreligious). Although secular administrations have dominated in the social welfare community in recent decades, sectarian organizations are playing an increasingly important role in social welfare provision. Ontario's Interfaith Social Assistance Reform Coalition (2001), for example, has been instrumental in educating "members of faith communities on current issues of social justice in Ontario," especially those relating to poverty, homelessness, and hunger.

LEGITIMATION AND AUTHORITY

Voluntary agency operations are usually governed by a volunteer **board of directors** (or board of trustees), whose members represent a cross-section of the community. Boards are accountable to the community, funders, agency members, and other stakeholders for their activities and expenditures. The board also ensures that the agency follows its constitution and operates according to local bylaws and relevant government regulations. As Rose

Marie Jaco (2001, 370) notes: "The board of directors legitimates the activities of the agency in the eyes of the community in the same way that politicians and civil servants legitimate government agencies through their accountability to the public."

Voluntary agencies depend on their clients and the general public to legitimate their role in the community. Studies suggest that except in the 1990s—when the voluntary sector was struggling with the impact of cutbacks and increased responsibilities—Canadians have generally perceived voluntary agencies as competent service providers. A study conducted by Ekos Research Associates (2002b) found that Canadians have twice as much trust in voluntary agencies as they do in commercial or public agencies.

To "prove" they are achieving their goals and operating efficiently, many voluntary agencies seek **accreditation**. If an agency wants to become accredited, it must allow a qualified, external accreditation body (such as Family Service Ontario) to set its performance standards, and then allow that same body to determine whether it is meeting those standards. Once the agency is deemed to be doing so, the accreditation body accredits it. The agency must undergo periodic evaluations to demonstrate that it is continuing to meet minimum standards (Panel on Accountability and Governance in the Voluntary Sector, 1999).

One difficulty the voluntary sector may have in gaining legitimacy is that, despite its prominence in service delivery, there is "surprisingly little information available about the sector and the role that it plays in Canada" (Scott, 2003, 166). Through the work of the Voluntary Sector Roundtable in the late 1990s, and the launching of a Voluntary Sector Initiative in 2000, the voluntary sector is now the subject of many research studies. Ultimately, the voluntary sector's legitimation may depend on the success of these studies in defining the sector and the work that it does.

SOURCES OF FUNDING

Most voluntary agencies have diverse funding sources. Government provides more than 60 percent of income for voluntary agencies; the remainder comes from agency-generated earnings and private donations (Scott, 2003). Exhibit 5.3 provides a breakdown of the various types of income.

In response to government cutbacks, some voluntary agencies have begun engaging in social entrepreneurism—that is, money-making schemes. Some now charge user fees; others hold, for example, bake sales or bingo games. Fundraising is sometimes done by agency staff, but very often it requires considerable time and specialized skills, for which larger agencies hire external professional fundraisers.

Exhibit 5.3

DIVERSE FUNDING SOURCES: VOLUNTARY SECTOR

FUNDING SOURCE	% OF INCOME
GOVERNMENT FUNDING	
Grants	16.8
Contributions	35.8
Contracts	5.4
Public foundations	2.4
Other government funding	.2
Subtotal	60.7
EARNED INCOME	
Fees/dues	6.7
Commercial activities	11.9
Investments	0.5
Other earned income	1.4
Subtotal	20.5
PRIVATE GIVING	
Individual	1.6
Corporate	1.4
Union	0.2
Endowment	0.2
Sponsorship	1.5
United Way	3.0
Private foundations	6.6
Fundraising	2.3
Other private funding	1.9
Subtotal	18.8
Other Income	0.05

Source: Adapted from K. Scott (2003). *Funding Matters: The Impact of Canada's New Funding Regime on Nonprofit and Voluntary Organizations.* Chapter 4, Table 4.14, p. 85 [online]. Available: www.ccsd.ca/pubs/2003/fm/chapter4.pdf [February 9, 2004].

STRENGTHS AND LIMITATIONS

The Government of Canada recognizes the voluntary sector as playing "an increasingly critical and complex role in helping to achieve the goals important to Canadians and ensure a high quality of life. It has become a vital third pillar in Canadian society, working alongside the public and [commercial] sectors to make Canada a more humane, caring and prosperous nation" (Privy Council Office, 1999, 1). There are a number of ways that the voluntary sector enhances and strengthens Canadian society, including

- *The economy*. The 75 000 registered charities in Canada generate more than $90 billion in revenue a year, employ over 1.3 million people, and fill one in every eleven jobs (Picard, 2003).

- *Public policy dialogue*. The sector engages communities in an ongoing dialogue about social issues, gives people an opportunity to voice their issues and concerns, and informs government policymakers about community needs, problems, and priorities (Government of Canada/Voluntary Sector Initiative, 1999).

- *Service and program delivery*. Voluntary agencies provide services to people that public and commercial agencies may have difficulty reaching. They also deliver services in innovative ways, and manage an "enormous breadth and diversity" of programs (Government of Canada/Voluntary Sector Initiative, 1999, 17).

- *Citizen participation*. By engaging citizens in grassroots community development and participation, the sector allows people to contribute to a more "democratic and inclusive society" (Government of Canada/Voluntary Sector Initiative, 1999, 18).

- *Building bridges*. The voluntary sector forges important connections between "communities and cultures, across regions, and between Canada and other nations," and subsequently enhances "understanding, awareness, inclusion, and social justice" at local, regional, national, and international levels (Government of Canada/Voluntary Sector Initiative, 1999, 18).

Despite its many positive attributes, the voluntary sector has been criticized on several counts. Margaret Fietz (2002, 1–2) observes: "Critics of the sector … claim that voluntary-sector organizations are not accountable and not worthy of government or private support. Social service voluntary organizations have been severely criticized as unnecessary, as 'crutches' and handholders, encouraging dependency and laziness among their clients." In one Canadian survey, voluntary-sector workers were concerned that the public held "negative perceptions" of the sector and thought that voluntary agencies were "second-rate" (Hall et. al., 2003a, 17).

Traditionally, voluntary organizations have engaged in activities that match the needs of their own communities. However, with governments cutting back social welfare funding, voluntary agencies are finding themselves competing for fewer government grants and contracts. Contracts, in particular, usually come with specific conditions set by the funder—conditions that may be incompatible with the agency's mission. In such cases, agencies may find themselves having to tailor their programs in order to meet government expectations and, in so doing, inadvertently compromise their mission and goals. According to one Canadian survey, one-third of all voluntary agencies experience "mission drift" when pursuing funding (Canadian Council on Social Development, 2003c). In another study, many voluntary-sector workers reported having to constantly struggle to keep the agency's mission on its intended course (Hall et al., 2003a). Agencies that lose sight of their mission risk losing touch with the needs of their communities; when this happens, agencies also "risk eroding their base of legitimacy and credibility" (Scott, 2003, 11).

Social analysts suggest that the voluntary sector is in a state of crisis. Labour market shifts and other economic changes are increasing the hardships on individuals and families; this in turn is placing more demands on voluntary agencies. At the same time, government downsizing and the devolution of programs to the private sector has increased the responsibilities of voluntary agencies (Richmond and Shields, 2003). All of this is straining the capacity of many voluntary agencies to meet the diverse expectations of funders, clients, and communities. The Panel on Accountability and Governance in the Voluntary Sector (1999, ii) notes that the voluntary sector is being expected "to broaden, deepen and adapt its approaches—and to do all of these at once." In 2000, the voluntary sector and the Government of Canada launched the Voluntary Sector Initiative (VSI) to, among other things, strengthen "the sector's ability to meet the demands placed on it by Canadian society" (Voluntary Sector Initiative, 2004a). Under the VSI, a special Capacity Joint Table was appointed to look specifically at the challenges facing the voluntary sector and how they might be addressed.

IV. COMPETITION AND COOPERATION IN THE SERVICE DELIVERY ENVIRONMENT

COMPETING FOR SURVIVAL

New Funding Arrangements

During the 1990s, the pressure to downsize and reduce social expenditures motivated Canadian governments to not only cut social spending but also change their approaches to distributing public funds to private-sector agencies. Governments tend to favour contracts; service providers generally prefer grants. **Contracts** usually come with restrictions as to how the money can be used; this makes contracted agencies more accountable for their use of public funds. In contrast, **grants** can often be directed to whatever aspect of the organization the agency chooses, be it front-line services, administration, or promotion. As the availability of grants declines, many voluntary agencies are being forced to compete for a dwindling number of short-term, restrictive government contracts (Scott, 2003; Hossli, 2000).

Many voluntary agencies are able to raise funds through marketing and business efforts; others find themselves struggling with the challenges associated with increased competition. A study by Hossli (2000, 6) found that staff in voluntary agencies

- needed to "operate in a continuously competitive mode, defined as rivalry with other service providers";
- felt "pressure to achieve and to be better than their competitors";
- had to increase their administration functions and make their financial and other systems more sophisticated;
- noticed their relationship with funders had changed "because of the need to ... continuously impress them";
- needed more resources to ensure that programs were successful; and
- had to become more "business-like" in terms of increasing professionalism, carefully monitoring expenditures, and generating surplus funds for sustainability.

Some voluntary agencies have found that staff workloads are increasing because of the disproportionate amount of time devoted to finding and securing funds. The bidding procedure for government contracts is especially time-consuming since it so often requires agency staff to complete long and detailed proposals, outlining how they would deliver the service on behalf of government (Scott, 2003; Hossli, 2000).

The competitive funding environment appears to be heightening stress levels in voluntary agencies and raising a general "fear about agency survival" (Hossli, 2000, 7). Ben Carniol (2000, 85) elaborates: "For many non-profit social agencies, if they lose only once in this bidding war they will be forced to close their doors because they have no other source of income." The loss of contracts is becoming more of a fact of life as governments continue to extend the bidding process to commercial agencies. Ironically, even when an agency wins several contracts, the stress of juggling the multitude of contract requirements, and meeting each funder's particular conditions, can be overwhelming (Richmond and Shields, 2003).

Competition and the Role of Advocacy

Advocacy has long been an important activity in the voluntary sector (Canadian Council on Social Development, 2003c). It can be a complex process; generally, however, advocacy often involves speaking or acting on behalf of clients, disseminating information in order to influence the opinions of others, and/or calling for changes in laws, regulations, or government policies.

Advocacy is often viewed as a "political activity" since it typically involves challenging the *status quo* and government policies and practices. Studies suggest that the increasing competition for government funds, and the fear of offending government funders, is discouraging agency workers from advocating (Richmond and Shields, 2003). The Canadian Council on Social Development (2003c) observes that "some groups are speaking out less often on behalf of their constituencies because they are concerned that it may hurt their efforts to cobble together programs and partnerships in this new funding climate." Indeed, a study by the Social Planning Council of Ottawa-Carleton (2001, 24) found that agency workers and volunteers feared that funders might view their advocacy activities as "too aggressive" and withdraw their funding in response to them. According to Richmond and Shields (2003), a reluctance to advocate, or fear of advocating, dulls the political sword that voluntary agencies have long carried when it comes to representing vulnerable groups and bringing about political and social change.

WORKING TOGETHER: THE COOPERATIVE TREND

Government's Urge to Merge

Paradoxically, at the same time that governments are introducing competition into the social welfare arena, they are also emphasizing the importance of interagency cooperation. Various terms—strategic alliances, collaborations, partnerships, and so on—are used to describe different types of working relationships (see Exhibit 5.4). The trend toward cooperative projects reflects a general belief that pervasive and complex social problems can be solved only if several people come together to identify, interpret, and address them. Cooperation also encourages a pooling of money and other resources, and makes joint projects more efficient than individual ones (Government of Canada, 2004e). Interagency communication and positive connections between agencies—or between agencies and the people they serve—may also be strengthened through a joining of forces (Nonprofit Quarterly, 2001).

Exhibit 5.4

LEVELS OF MUTUAL RELATIONSHIPS IN SOCIAL WELFARE

LEVELS	PURPOSE	STRUCTURE	PROCESS
Networking (e.g., Community Homelessness Network in Waterloo, Ontario)	– to foster dialogue and a common understanding – to provide a clearing-house for information – to create a base of support	– nonhierarchical – informal/flexible links – loosely defined roles – community action is primary link among members	– low-key leadership – minimal decision-making – little conflict – informal communication
Alliance (e.g., National Children's Alliance)	– to match needs and coordinate activities – to limit the duplication of services – to ensure tasks are completed	– core group acts as communication hub – semiformal links – roles somewhat defined – members act in advisory capacity – group raises funds	– facilitative leaders – complex decision-making – little conflict – formal communication within core group
Partnership (e.g., Affordable Housing Program)	– to share resources to address common issues – to pool resources to create something new	– clearly defined roles – formal links – group generates new resources and a joint budget	– leadership is autonomous – group decision-making among core members – communication is frequent and clear
Coalition (e.g., Coalition Against Family Violence in Northwest Territories)	– to share ideas – to draw resources from existing systems – to commit to project for at least three years	– roles, time, and commitment are defined – links are formal and clarified in writing – group generates new resources and a joint budget	– shared leadership – formal and group decision-making – communication is frequent and prioritized
Collaboration (e.g., An Accord between the Government of Canada and the Voluntary Sector)	– to achieve a shared vision – to build an interdependent system to address issues and opportunities	– formal roles, time commitment, and evaluation – formal links – written work assignments	– strong leadership – consensus model of decision-making – high trust level among members – high productivity – ideas and decisions equally shared – highly developed communication

Source: Adapted from: Teresa Hogue, The Chandler Center for Community Leadership (1994). *Community Based Collaboration: Community Wellness Multiplied.* National Network for Collaboration [online]. Available: http://crs.uvm.edu/nnco/collab/wellness.html [June 27, 2004].

Intergovernmental Relations: A Social Union

Historically, the three levels of government have formed partnerships to achieve common goals. The seeds for one such partnership were sown in 1995 when, before implementing the Canada Health and Social Transfer, the federal government invited all provincial and territorial governments "to work together on developing, through mutual consent, a set of shared principles and objectives that could underlie the [CHST]" (Canada, 1995, 13). In 1996, representatives from the federal government, along with members of the Ministerial Council on Social Policy Reform and Renewal (see Chapter 2 for more on this council), established the new Federal-Provincial-Territorial Council on Social Policy Renewal. Although the Province of Quebec supported many of the principles of social policy renewal, Premier Lucien Bouchard refused to join the new council because it represented federal intrusion into a provincial jurisdiction ("Quebec Rejects Social Union Deal,"1999).

A **social union** evolved from the council's work. The social union is an umbrella under which Canadian governments at the federal and provincial/territorial levels aim to renew and modernize health and social policy. This renewal would be achieved by meeting three main objectives:

- To promote social cohesion, by promoting, sharing, providing security, and assisting all Canadians to actively participate in economic and social life;

- to support human development, by ensuring that basic needs are met and that individuals' skills and capacities are fully developed throughout their lives; and

- to strengthen the economic union, by sharing risk, ensuring mobility, and providing access to comparable levels of essential public services. (O'Hara, 1997, 6)

Under the social union banner, the governments have agreed to engage in joint planning and consultation, as well as respectful deliberations (Standing Committee on Human Resources, 2000). Appendix B outlines the principles and commitments that will guide union initiatives. The Social Union Framework Agreement is summarized in Appendix B.

Public- and Commercial-Sector Alliances

Governments rely on voluntary agencies—and to some extent on commercial ones—to provide important services, yet they are reluctant to completely or unconditionally relinquish all social welfare responsibilities to the private sector. They prefer to shift certain responsibilities—such as service delivery and day-to-day program management—to nongovernmental agencies while maintaining ultimate control of programs, their budgets, and their standards.

Public–private partnerships (PPPs) are often struck between governments and commercial operations. One type of PPP that is gaining popularity in the social services is called "Advise on Operations and Maintenance for a Fee." In this arrangement, the government hires a for-profit agency to review a public program and make recommendations for improving it. One such contract was struck in 1996 between Ontario's Ministry of Community and Social Services and Accenture (formerly Andersen Consulting) to develop and implement a new social assistance delivery system.

Public- and Voluntary-Sector Relations

Governments have long preferred to work with voluntary rather than commercial agencies in the delivery of publicly funded programs (Richmond and Shields, 2003). Until recently, however, the public–voluntary sector relationship has lacked focus and direction. The establishment of the Voluntary Sector Initiative marked a turning point for the two sectors; it reflected a perceived need to formalize the ways in which they would work together. In 2001, the details of the public–voluntary sector relationship—including the obligations of each party—were articulated in the document *An Accord between the Government of Canada and the Voluntary Sector.*

Some social analysts question the true nature of the federal government/voluntary-sector relationship. This new relationship may have formed in the spirit of building partnerships; however, it has since been criticized as little more than a "top-down, contractual" agreement whereby the government gets to impose complex and burdensome requirements on the voluntary sector in exchange for desperately needed funds (Richmond and Shields, 2003, 2).

Collaboration: A Unique Type of Relationship

Unlike other types of relationships, **collaborations** require the partners to share the benefits and risks *equally*. Collaborations also require the partners to have compatible objectives, to both contribute resources, and to develop "an explicit agreement, contract or other instrument [which] sets out the terms of the arrangement" (Treasury Board of Canada Secretariat, 1995). Most collaborative arrangements between the Government of Canada and voluntary agencies belong to one of these four types:

- *Consultative or advisory arrangements.* These encourage all partners to give their input on policies, program design, service delivery, and other aspects of a specific program.
- *Contributory or support-sharing arrangements.* These make the increase or distribution of resources a shared burden among partners.

- *Operational or work-sharing arrangements.* These ensure that service delivery is a shared responsibility.

- *Decision-making arrangements.* These give all partners a role in directing, administering, or leading the project (Treasury Board of Canada Secretariat, 1995).

Collaborative projects are becoming more popular in the social welfare field. Even so, there are challenges associated with them. For example, a study by Hall and colleagues (2003a) found that voluntary agency staff felt pressured to develop collaborative relationships. Also, staff tended to show little enthusiasm for forming and maintaining collaborations, because they were time consuming and required special skills. On top of this, the success of collaborative projects was jeopardized if one partner did not carry out responsibilities as promised. Some staff thought that increased competition for funding discouraged collaborations between organizations.

SUMMARY

■ Introduction

The public, commercial, and voluntary sectors comprise Canada's mixed economy of welfare. Although these sectors are often viewed as separate entities, there is substantial overlap between them. The dispersal of programs and services across three sectors tends to make the social welfare system fragmented and uncoordinated; however, this arrangement offers choice to people seeking help.

■ Social Welfare in the Public Sector

Each level of government has certain responsibilities for social welfare. As upper levels of government downsize, the municipal level gains more responsibility for delivering social welfare programs and services. Governments are also devolving many programs to the private sector. Public social welfare is supported by tax revenues, which are distributed to the regional governments through three transfer systems. Although governments have been criticized for being bureaucratic and impersonal, they continue to play an important role in social welfare.

■ Social Welfare in the Commercial Sector

As governments' role in direct service provision diminishes, commercial operations step in to deliver services on a profit-making basis. Commercial social welfare services are quickly gaining legitimacy through free trade agreements and other schemes that support free enterprise. These services may be paid for by service recipients, by compensation programs, or by governments. Although commercial enterprises are associated with efficiency and innovation, there are concerns about profit motives, accountability, and the ability to reach low-income clients.

■ Social Welfare in the Voluntary Sector

Voluntary agencies are often referred to as charities, nongovernmental organizations, or nonprofit organizations. These agencies may be secular or sectarian, and they tend to vary in size and function. All voluntary agencies are organized, nongovernmental, nonprofit, self-governing, and volunteer-friendly. Voluntary agencies are legitimated by a board of directors, their clients, and the general public; some agencies are becoming accredited in order to increase their legitimacy. Most voluntary agencies have more than one source of funding. The voluntary sector has long been recognized for contributing to the good of society. Certain areas of the sector (for example, the capacity to assume greater responsibilities) could be strengthened. The Voluntary Sector Initiative was formed to help the voluntary sector adapt to its expanding role in service delivery.

■ Competition and Cooperation in the Service Delivery Environment

Funding cuts and changes in funding arrangements have increased the competition between private-sector agencies and changed the way some agencies obtain funding. Competitiveness is associated with increased stress among voluntary staff and a reluctance to advocate on behalf of clients. As governments encourage competition for funds, they emphasize the importance of cooperation; governments have struck various partnerships with agencies in the commercial and voluntary sectors. Collaboration is a specific type of working relationship—one in which the equal sharing of risks, benefits, and resources is emphasized.

▼ KEY TERMS

For definitions of the key terms, consult the Glossary on page 364 at the end of the book.

mixed economy of welfare p. 101

private sector p. 102

public sector p. 102

commercial sector p. 102

voluntary sector p. 102

board of directors p. 110

accreditation p. 111

contracts p. 115

grants p. 115

advocacy p. 116

social union p. 118

collaborations p. 119

Social Agencies

Objectives

I. To examine the bureaucratic, collectivist-democratic, and learning-based approaches that social agencies may adopt to organize their work, personnel, and processes.

II. To look at the trend toward community-based services and to describe the various types of residential and nonresidential social agencies.

III. To review social agency activities in terms of direct and indirect services.

INTRODUCTION

Once social policies are developed, organizations are needed to translate those policies into social programs and services. Organizations that have this function are commonly called social agencies. Jaco (2001, 364) defines a **social agency** as "a formally structured bureaucratic unit, sanctioned by society, whose goals and activities focus on meeting human need." Examples of social agencies include family service agencies, welfare offices, child protection units, and crisis centres.

Although each social agency has its own unique tasks, administration, organizational structure, goals, and mandate, most social agencies share a number of basic functions and activities. These include the following:

- securing funding, setting and adhering to budgets, and distributing funding to agency programs and services;

- assessing client needs, and providing service and/or material resources to clients who meet the agency's eligibility criteria;

- ensuring the quality of service, and regularly evaluating the effectiveness of programs;

- recognizing and reducing gaps in service, and revising or introducing services to meet client needs;

- being accountable to clients, governing boards, funders, and the community for service delivery and use of resources;

- guiding agency activities by developing and revising policies, procedures, and ethical standards;

- ensuring that the agency follows applicable legislative or licensing requirements;

- recruiting, managing, and supervising staff and volunteers, and ensuring that personnel performance meets agency and legal standards; and

- fostering and maintaining positive relationships with the community, helping clients connect with other community resources, and working with other systems to resolve social problems.

The way that an agency carries out its functions and activities depends largely on *whom* it serves and *what* it intends to accomplish. Many social agencies organize their programs and services around certain populations such as children and families, seniors, women, or people with disabilities. In addition, programs and services are usually designed and implemented to satisfy a specific objective or achieve an intended outcome. For example, a parent support program—one that teaches parents nonviolent methods of child discipline—may prevent child abuse (objective) and ensure children's safety (intended outcome).

The types of goods or services a social agency delivers depends on the identified needs of individuals or families in a community (for example, an isolated rural area may have a high incidence of teen pregnancy and a need for young-parent programs) or across a large geographic area (for example, a general concern for child poverty may spark a national antipoverty campaign). How successful the agency is at meeting people's needs depends on several external factors, including community and political support and funding availability. The effectiveness of programs and services also depends on a number of internal factors, such as the agency's organizational structure, its preferred methods of service delivery, and a solid set of direct and indirect services. This chapter explores some of these factors.

I. ORGANIZATIONAL STRUCTURE: EVOLVING MODELS

All social agencies are **formal systems** in that they operate according to set rules, roles, and procedures. As with any system, social agencies are made up of various parts—typically called departments, units, or program areas. These work together to accomplish an overall goal or mission. Social agencies also have specific *inputs* (resources), *processes* (program activities and administration), and *outputs* (the products or services they provide). All agency systems aim to achieve positive *outcomes* (that is, create benefits for the people they serve).

Social agencies vary in the ways they structure or organize their work tasks, personnel, decision-making processes, resources, and so on. They tend to seek organizational structures that can adapt to the ever-changing needs of service users, funders, and governing bodies. Rarely do social agencies reflect pure forms of any particular organizational model; rather, they tend to borrow principles and methods from a mix of organizational approaches.

SOCIAL AGENCIES AS BUREAUCRATIC SYSTEMS

Until the late 1970s, sociologists praised the **bureaucratic model** as being efficient, reliable, and predictable. A bureaucracy is perhaps best known for its complex hierarchical structure. At the top of the hierarchy is an individual or a board of directors; one or the other oversees and sets policies for the agency's general operations. Below this are the managers, who are responsible for the different divisions of the agency (for example, there may be a division for seniors, another division for children and youth, and so forth). At the next level down are various offices or programs, each with its own department head, who supervises staff and oversees the office's day-to-day operations. At the lowest level of the hierarchy are the front-line workers and support staff, who carry out the program activities, tasks, and services. Agencies with "tall" hierarchies— such as those found in "big" government— have multiple vertical layers; this tends to increase the potential for complex procedures, otherwise known as "bureaucratic red tape."

Support for the bureaucratic model began to decline in the late 1970s, when governments were struggling with economic slowdown, increasing deficits and debt, and the challenge of financing large and expensive government systems. Big bureaucracies were also being criticized for being too slow, inflexible, and inefficient (Bourgon, 1999). With the election of conservative political parties in the early 1980s came a general support for small government, "flatter" hierarchies, and organizational systems that were open and more flexible to change.

COLLECTIVIST-DEMOCRATIC APPROACHES

The **collectivist-democratic model** emerged in the late 1970s and emphasized power-sharing, group consensus, and a team approach to decision-making. This cooperative approach encourages the inclusion of workers and clients in various aspects of the agency's operations. For example, staff may be invited to join the agency's planning or advisory committee, and former clients may serve on the board of directors.

Collectivist-democratic approaches seek to reduce the inequalities inherent in bureaucratic systems, to empower workers and the people who use services, and to promote an environment of inclusion and cooperation. Although these goals are admirable, the model has some shortcomings. For instance, a consensus approach to reaching decisions and negotiating action plans can be time consuming. Also, the level of discussion, sharing, and openness that such an approach requires may be a source of discomfort for those staff who prefer to work with colleagues at a more objective level.

SOCIAL AGENCIES AS LEARNING ORGANIZATIONS

The ways in which organizations structure their work have been influenced by globalization forces, by advanced technologies, and by the shift to a knowledge-based economy. In government, for example, three trends are noticeable:

- There has been a gradual shift in the nature of public service work, from performing clear, well-defined, predictable, largely repetitive tasks to achieving broad results, from a focus on efficiency to a focus on innovation, from vertical structures and top-down communications flows to teams and networks;

- The organization of work is changing from individual responsibility to team responsibility and accountability, from single centres of power to multiple centres of power, from command and control to leaderships and a lessening of central controls in exchange for greater local accountability, creativity, innovation and flexibility; [and]

- The policy and service delivery functions are converging. Services provided by the public sector are more intangible, based on knowledge—requiring skills such as strategic advice, rigorous analysis and judicious

counsel—skills previously regarded as policy skills.
(Canadian Centre for Management Development, 2000,
12–13)

The new context of work demands flexible forms of organization and management, such as those promoted by the **learning organization model**.

The learning organization model has been used in the commercial sector since the late 1980s but is relatively new to the public and voluntary sectors. Peter Senge popularized the concept of the learning organization in his book, *The Fifth Discipline—The Art and Practice of The Learning Organization.* According to Senge (1990, 3), learning organizations are places "where people continually expand their capacity to create the results they truly desire, where new and expansive patterns of thinking are nurtured, where collective aspiration is set free, and where people are continually learning how to learn together." The learning organization model is based on the assumption that change is ongoing and that organizations must learn to develop new goals and ways of reaching them, and to do so constantly—not just at the beginning or planning stages. This model distinguishes between training and learning: training targets skill development or the acquisition of specific knowledge, whereas learning is a continuous lifelong process (Kirkwood and Pangarkar, 2003). All stakeholders in an agency share the responsibility of learning as "a collective undertaking that takes shape in action" (Bourgon, 1999).

The extent to which a group becomes a learning organization will largely depend on its environment, mandate, and capacity to incorporate the model's principles. An agency's transformation to a learning organization also requires that staff and volunteers find effective and creative ways of promoting learning in the workplace, recognizing staff efforts and contributions, translating what one has learned into practice, and evaluating processes and outcomes (Canadian Centre for Management Development, 2001a). Another part of becoming a learning organization involves recognizing and nurturing the connections between society, the organization, teams, and individuals in the continuous learning process. Exhibit 6.1 illustrates these connections.

Canadian governments at all levels are embracing features of the learning organization model. At the federal level, the document *A Proposed Continuous Learning Policy for the Public Service of Canada* articulates the government's commitment to developing a learning culture in federal departments, and to promoting the lifelong learning of civil servants (Canadian Centre for Management Development, 2001b). In 1996, the Government of Alberta (1996) adopted the learning organization model to achieve its busi-

E x h i b i t   6 . 1

LEARNING MODEL: CONNECTIONS AND CONTINUOUS LEARNING

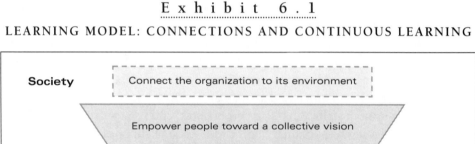

Source: Karen E. Watkins and Victoria J. Marsick (1993). *Sculpting the Learning Organization: Lessons in the Art and Science of Systemic Change.* San Fransisco: Jossey-Bass: page 10. [online]. Available: http://leeds. colorado.edu/faculty/larsenk/learnorg/watkins.html [March 18, 2004]. This material is used by permission of John Wiley & Sons, Inc.

ness plan objectives. This meant restructuring government departments to ensure that the goals of employees, departments, and the government were *aligned*; that processes were in place to strengthen employees' *commitment* to government; that departments had the *competence* to achieve government goals; and, that departments were *versatile* enough to adapt to rapidly changing needs and circumstances.

Social agencies in the private sector are adopting the learning organization model to varying degrees. Because their survival often depends on knowledge acquisition, quick thinking, openness to innovation, and adaptability to a changing market, commercial agencies are already well acquainted with many of the attributes of learning organizations. However, Kirkwood and Pangarkar (2003, 10) suggest that commercial operations may support organizational features that are incompatible with a learning organization model. Some commercial operations, for example, may lack "a clear and functional method of learning, with easy to apply management guidelines." Moreover, many commercial organizations favour hierarchical management models in which company decisions are made by owners or managers with little input from staff (McMullen and Brisbois, 2003).

In many ways, voluntary agencies have long supported various features associated with learning organizations. For example, nonprofits tend to have relatively "flatter" hierarchical structures and to be less bureaucratic than governments. Also, these agencies are likely to accept flexible work schedules and to encourage staff input on matters concerning service delivery and agency management. In these respects, voluntary agencies may be ahead of their public and commercial counterparts in adopting learning organization principles. However, the full adoption of the learning organization model in voluntary agencies may be hindered as long as forces *outside* agencies (for example, funders) are able to dictate staffing levels, service and program development, or other aspects of agency operations (McMullen and Brisbois, 2003).

II. TYPES OF SOCIAL AGENCIES AND THEIR SERVICE ENVIRONMENT

THE SHIFT FROM INSTITUTIONAL TO COMMUNITY-BASED SERVICES

Poorhouses, Workhouses, and Other Institutions

The very first social agencies in this country were relatively uncomplicated operations that served small communities. However, as Canada's population rose during the eighteenth and nineteenth centuries, the number of needy people also increased. Some settlements drew from English and French models, and built large institutions such as poorhouses (or almshouses), workhouses, and insane asylums to house people who could not care for themselves. A number of Canada's earliest institutions were built in Saint John, New Brunswick, a major port and industrial city. Concerns over rising poverty and homelessness rates led city officials to build large poorhouses, workhouses, orphanages, homes for the elderly, and reformatories. Saint John was also the home of Canada's first "lunatic asylum," built in 1801 (Whalen, 2002).

The poorhouses provided food, shelter, and protection to an often indiscriminate mix of individuals, including paupers, criminals, vagrants, the elderly, the sick, abandoned or orphaned children, and people with disabilities (Guest, 1997; Whalen, 2002). Poorhouses gave shelter to the "deserving" poor; workhouses required the "undeserving" poor to earn their keep through forced labour. In the nineteenth century, Canada's best-known workhouse was Toronto's House of Industry, which was privately run and financed (Siena, 2003).

Reform movements in the early eighteenth century called attention to mentally ill residents in the poorhouses and their need for a different level of care than that provided to other residents. Concerns were also raised about the neglect and abuse of poorhouse residents and the fact that few, if any, received rehabilitation services (Sussman, 1998).

The Deinstitutionalization Movement

By the early twentieth century, Canadians were growing intolerant of the overcrowded and unsanitary conditions of large institutions, and the often inhumane, archaic, and countertherapeutic treatment of institutionalized people. This philosophical shift eventually led to the **deinstitutionalization movement** of the 1960s and 1970s and to a general preference for community-based agencies over large, centrally run institutions. This trend coincided with the election of more fiscally conscious governments, which wanted to reduce overall funding to social welfare. To cut the costs of operating large institutions, governments began redirecting funds to smaller residential programs (such as group homes for people with disabilities) and to nonresidential programs.

Community-based agencies have continued to expand in response to government cutbacks in large institutions and the development of more enlightened approaches to service provision. Community-based agencies tend to be nonprofit, "open to the public at large, non-discriminative[,] and have objectives that are in the best interest of the community" (City of Moncton, 2001). Many of these agencies provide a range of programs and services in centrally located facilities. Their staff are usually residents of the community, who are aware of the community's needs and familiar with local services (Tobis, 2000).

The goals of community-based agencies tend to reflect a commitment to helping individuals and families during difficult periods, as well as to ensuring their long-term care and safety. Community-based approaches promote independence and self-sufficiency; they also "try to maximize an individual's chances of reaching his or her full potential and be available before an individual's problems become severe" (Tobis, 2000, 45). People who receive community-based services are encouraged to maintain their ties with friends, family, and other informal support networks—ties that are considered essential for healthy human development and functioning (Tobis, 2000).

RESIDENTIAL AND NONRESIDENTIAL CENTRES

Residential Centres

Residential centres usually provide living quarters, meals, and a comprehensive set of services for people who require round-the-clock care. The type of residential facility that exists in a given community is determined by the needs of its residents. Some common types include

- long-term care facilities or nursing homes for seniors;
- shelters for transient people;
- assessment or treatment centres for children or youth with emotional or behavioural disorders;
- community-based group homes for people who are developmentally delayed;
- rehabilitation centres for children and youth with physical disabilities;
- care centres for people with psychiatric disabilities;
- in-patient treatment centres for people with addictions; and
- transition houses for abused women and their children (Statistics Canada, 2003i).

In 2001, there were 363 230 Canadians living in residential health, social welfare, and correctional settings (Statistics Canada, 2002a).

Not everyone in need or facing a problem requires residential services. This type of intervention is most appropriate when an individual

- requires a type of assessment (such as for psychiatric purposes) that cannot reasonably be done in the person's home;
- exhibits violent or inappropriate behaviour;
- requires supervision or stabilization beyond what family or a nonresidential service provider can give; or
- needs specialized treatment that is unavailable in a nonresidential setting (for example, intensive drug rehabilitation).

An individual in residential care must have a regular review to determine whether that continued level of care is necessary and to ensure that the services are meeting the client's needs and goals (Conceptual Framework Subcommittee, 2002).

There are noticeable trends in the use of residential services in Canada. This country's population is both growing and aging, and the demand for residential services is increasing as a consequence. This in turn has led to long wait lists and delays for those needing intensive care. To cope with this demand, many residential centres have had to tighten their admission criteria; some centres consider new admissions only after all nonresidential services have been exhausted; others admit people on the basis of the greatest need (Sudbury and Rook, 2003).

Nonresidential Centres

Nonresidential centres normally provide services on a drop-in, appointment, or outreach basis. They cater to those who can look after many of their own needs, or who require only short-term help; they are also appropriate for clients that do not pose a threat to themselves or to the rest of society. Although some nonresidential programs (such as child protection agencies) must control or restrain people's socially unacceptable behaviour, it is rarely necessary to institutionalize clients.

Many nonresidential centres provide a continuum of services. This is the case with "one-stop" or multiservice centres, which offer a variety of comprehensive, coordinated, and integrated services under one roof. Services in these centres may be aimed at a particular group. For example, a centre may specialize in programs for children and families, and provide a range of services such as family counselling, parent education, support for teen moms, and child development. Other centres may serve a variety of client groups and provide a mix of services designed to meet a broad spectrum of local needs.

Nonresidential centres generally favour methods of service delivery that are flexible and user-friendly and that provide a variety of options regarding how people can participate. *Drop-in centres*, for example, usually offer loosely scheduled programs that can be accessed at any time during service hours. *Telephone services* offer support and, anonymity, and—in the case of crisis lines—are available around the clock. *Outreach services* are provided "outside the office," in the clients' natural environment. There are various forms of outreach. For example, *in-home services* are provided to people in their homes, whereas *street outreach* seeks out and helps people living on the street, especially in urban centres. *Online support* is offered through a relatively new communication system—the Internet. Chat lines, discussion forums, and e-mail can be used to facilitate services such as information-sharing, peer support, and professional counselling. A Toronto-based online support network is profiled in Exhibit 6.2.

Exhibit 6.2

ABILITY ONLINE

A computer network designed to enhance the lives of children and youth with disabilities or illness by providing an online community of friendship and support.

Ability OnLine is a free Internet community where children/youth with disabilities/illness and their parents can meet others like them, make friends from all over the world, share their hopes and fears, find role-models and mentors, and feel like they belong.

Ability OnLine can be accessed from any computer that is connected to the Internet. Once registered, members can exchange public or private messages on a whole range of subjects, ranging from medical topics to pets and hobbies. Parents, caregivers and other professionals also have conferences that may be of interest to them. We have conference hosts who monitor the public content to make sure it is friendly and appropriate.

What are the benefits of Ability OnLine?

- A nonthreatening and nonjudgmental environment based on mutual respect and friendship breaks down social and emotional barriers.

- The ability to share information, experiences, stories and interests with others of similar backgrounds and life experiences opens doors and minds.

- Online support 24/7 and ongoing monitoring makes this a family-friendly experience.

- Strong family orientation appealing to all ages means everyone is welcome.

- Increased health awareness promotes empowerment and informed decision-making.

- Acceptance and support contribute to enhanced self-esteem and confidence.

- Inspiring role models and mentors create opportunities for personal growth.

Source: Adapted from Ability OnLine (2002). *About Us* [online]. Available: www.ablelink.org/public/aboutus.htm [March 18, 2004].

System of Care

In general, residential and nonresidential centres differ in the range and intensity of services they offer, and in the ways they deliver those services; that said, one type is not inherently more effective than the other. Each has its own strengths to offer the community; working in tandem, these centres can form a solid base of community support and care. The term **system of care** refers to the mix of service components that, when offered in a coordinated and integrated fashion, is responsive to the varying levels and changing needs of clients (Conceptual Framework Subcommittee, 2002). Exhibit 6.3 offers a conceptualization of a system of care for children and youth; this system includes both residential and nonresidential services. The arrows in the diagram indicate the movement the child or youth might make from one type of service to another in order to meet his or her particular needs or circumstances at any given time.

III. SOCIAL AGENCY ACTIVITIES

There are two main classifications of social agency activities. **Direct services** are those that involve face-to-face interactions with clients; these front-line services aim to prevent or reduce problems experienced by individuals, families, and small groups. In contrast, **indirect services** do not usually involve personal contacts with clients; however, they influence the type and quality of direct services. Examples of indirect services are social administration, program development, and program evaluation. Aspects of each type of service are explored below.

DIRECT SERVICES: THREE LEVELS OF PREVENTION

All direct services are preventive in the sense that they either try to prevent the emergence of social problems or try to lessen the negative effects of these problems once they have arisen. A public health prevention model can be adapted to describe most direct services provided by social agencies. This model suggests that programs and services operate at one of the following three levels:

- **Primary prevention** activities aim to prevent the development of personal and social problems by educating people, providing information, or promoting certain practices. They are usually targeted at large segments of the community. Primary prevention programs include alcohol and drug education, AIDS-awareness strategies, antiracism campaigns, marriage-preparation courses, and family-life programs.

Exhibit 6.3

A SYSTEM OF CARE FOR CHILDREN AND YOUTH

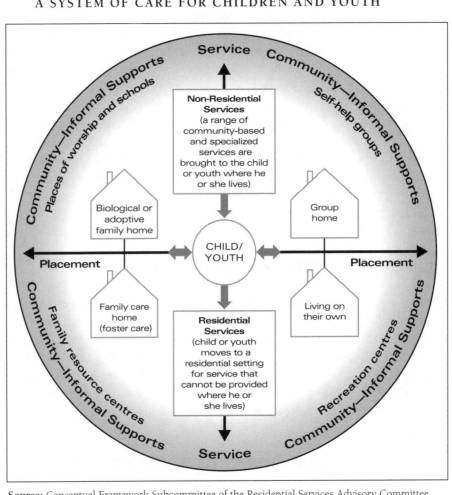

Source: Conceptual Framework Subcommittee of the Residential Services Advisory Committee (January 2000). *Working with Community to Support Children, Youth and Families*, p. 9. [online]. Available: www.mcf.gov.bc.ca/change/pdfs/working_with_community.pdf [March 13, 2004]. Copyright © 2004 Province of British Columbia. All rights reserved. Reprinted with permission of British Columbia. www.ipp.gov.bc.ca.

- **Secondary prevention** activities focus on identifying problems in the early stages of development before they become serious or chronic. This level of prevention involves controlling or changing the conditions that caused the problem. Victim assistance programs, income security programs, support services for children and youth, and respite services for family caregivers fit in this category.

- **Tertiary prevention** activities aim to reduce the negative effects of problems—such as disability and dependence—that have become chronic or complex. Social welfare programs in this category include child protection services, family therapy, residential care for youth with emotional disorders, and in-patient alcohol and drug treatment. Tertiary prevention programs are often mandatory and supported by law. For example, child protection workers have the legal authority to intervene in a family's affairs if child neglect or abuse is suspected.

Tertiary prevention has long been the main focus of direct services. In recent years, however, social programmers have shown a greater interest in primary prevention. The shift from tertiary to primary prevention is being driven by a variety of factors, including the following:

- The cost of treating long-term problems is often prohibitive.

- The direct benefits of treating chronic problems are not easily identified or measured.

- Long-term treatment is not an option under many programs.

- A growing number of studies point to the effectiveness of primary prevention programs.

- Governments are showing more interest in building healthy communities instead of treating individuals.

- It is generally agreed that it is easier, less expensive, and more humane to improve the lives of people before, rather than after, problems develop.

Direct services are undergoing a shift in focus: greater emphasis is being placed on strengthening the natural support systems (for example, friends and extended family) of individuals and on reducing dependence on professional systems. The approach taken by B.C.'s Ministry of Children and Family Development is a case in point. In 2001, the Ministry had close to 11 000 children in foster care. A large proportion of them had been apprehended on the basis of neglect—for example, the parent(s) were failing to provide adequate meals or supervision. To avoid separating so many children from their families—especially in cases that did not involve child abuse—the ministry increased its parent support services so that parents could learn more effective ways of caring for their children in the home (Hogg, 2001).

In recent years, greater emphasis has also been placed on helping people develop problem-solving skills through such methods as coaching, mentoring, and information-sharing. For example, the Edmonton Mennonite Centre for Newcomers (2004) offers a program to help refugee and immigrant children and youth develop conflict resolution and problem-solving skills; the aim of this is to help young people "make thoughtful and informed choices" in their new life in Canada.

INDIRECT SERVICES

Social Administration

Social administration is usually the responsibility of senior employees or a board of directors. It involves developing or interpreting policies and procedures, planning and managing direct service activities, and ensuring that the agency meets its goals and objectives. Social administration is carried out at three different levels: the governance or institutional level, the managerial level, and the work or technical level. The activities found at each level often overlap; that said, each level is distinct with regard to the types of knowledge and skills that are required (Parsons, 1960; Institute on Governance, 2004).

The *governance or institutional level* is "the source of strategic decisions that shape the organization and its work, and ultimate accountability for the work and actions of the organization" (Institute on Governance, 2004). It is at the governance level that the values and goals of society are translated into concrete programs and services. Staff or volunteers at this level must decide what types of social issues the agency will address and to whom the agency's programs and services will be targeted. The administration must also carve out a niche for the agency in the community, develop a positive public image, and ensure that the agency is accountable for its activities.

Activities at the *managerial level* involve the "organization of tasks, people, relationships and technology to get the job done" (Institute on Governance, 2004). At this level, agency managers and supervisors obtain and allocate resources, design programs, recruit staff, and coordinate their duties. A primary activity at this level is finding effective ways to achieve the agency's goals and mandate. This usually involves providing training and professional development opportunities for staff, monitoring the effectiveness of programs, and ensuring that programs are responsive to the changing needs of the community.

The *work or technical level* is concerned with "performing the tasks required to fulfill the [agency's] mission" (Institute on Governance, 2004). This involves the direct provision of materials, services, and/or programs to service users. Important activities at this level include selecting and implementing interventions that are likely to help clients achieve their goals.

Program-Planning and Development

Social agencies are mandated to fulfil a number of societal functions and to uphold essential beliefs, cultural values, and knowledge. Ideally, a social agency's programs reflect its community's broader goals. To ensure that they produce the desired results, programs must be carefully planned. As Ruth Friendship-Keller (1988) notes: "Good programs don't just happen. They are the result of careful consideration as to why the organization exists and what its members want to accomplish." **Program-planning** involves a "series of decisions, from general and strategic decisions to specific operational details, based on the gathering and analysis of a wide range of information" (THCU, 2001, 1).

There are various program-planning models available to social agencies, each with a different focus and set of procedures. However, a generic program-planning process may involve six key steps:

Step 1. Determine how people in the planning process will work together, make decisions, and move through the planning stages.

Step 2. Confirm whether the program development plan should be carried out and, if so, in what manner.

Step 3. Set goals and objectives, and define the target population (that is, the potential client group).

Step 4. Design program strategies and activities.

Step 5. Identify indicators of success (in other words, how will program planners know that the program is achieving its objectives?).

Step 6. Review the viability of the proposed program and determine whether it can be easily evaluated.

These steps do not always progress in a neat, tidy, or chronological order. As new information comes in and and fresh challenges arise, the activities for one step may have to be undertaken earlier or later in the process (THCU, 2001).

Some social agencies implement new programs on a "pilot" basis; a trial period allows the agency to assess the feasibility of a program before a long-term investment is made. Whether a program is implemented as a pilot or on a regular basis, its activities, processes, and expenditures must be monitored. During the monitoring stage, program activities are observed and critiqued to ensure that the program goals and objectives are being achieved. During this stage, the program can be modified to correct any problems.

How do social agencies know which types of programs to develop? Agency personnel usually have a fairly good idea of their community's needs through their day-to-day interactions with clients, other professionals, and the general public. Although this knowledge is valuable, most social agencies try to test these ideas through systematic methods. The methods used to measure community needs and problems include community needs assessments, social indicators, and focus groups. The information gathered through these methods can be useful for planning and developing new programs as well as for rationalizing the use of resources to agency boards, funders, and other stakeholders.

Community Needs Assessments People conducting **community needs assessments** draw from a variety of sources, which when taken together may "paint" a picture of local needs. These sources include community members (including potential program clients), professional groups, health population surveys, community profiles, and local statistics. Community needs assessments are undertaken for a number of reasons:

- to clarify how certain social groups such as youth, seniors, or people with disabilities—are expected to benefit from a new program;

- to identify the types of activities that are likely to achieve a program's goals and objectives;

- to determine the range of services that a certain group needs (for example, women in the community may need a mix of services ranging from health care to self esteem–building to assistance in job searches; or they may need a more focused intervention such as an alcohol or drug abuse program);

- to identify the resources (such as funding or facilities) needed to address a problem; and/or

- to ascertain whether a proposed program will likely be used by the target population (Jill Florence Lackey and Associates, 2004).

Social Indicators **Social indicators** are statistics that are collected over time and then used to measure social conditions or levels of public well-being. Social indicators provide a comprehensive picture of people's real-life situations; they also provide insights into trends affecting overall health. Canada has no single comprehensive system of social indicators; instead, various indices, censuses, surveys, and other tracking mechanisms are used to report on people's levels of well-being. Exhibit 6.4 illustrates the indicators used by one index to measure the social health of Canadians.

Statistics Canada is an especially rich source of information on the health and well-being of Canadians. For instance, during the 2001 population census, this department conducted various surveys on the needs and living conditions of many social groups, such as Aboriginal peoples, seniors, immigrants, and children and youth. A number of community groups, such as Chambers of Commerce and social planning councils, also track or measure local community needs and resources.

E x h i b i t   6 . 4

SOCIAL INDICATORS: THE INDEX OF SOCIAL HEALTH

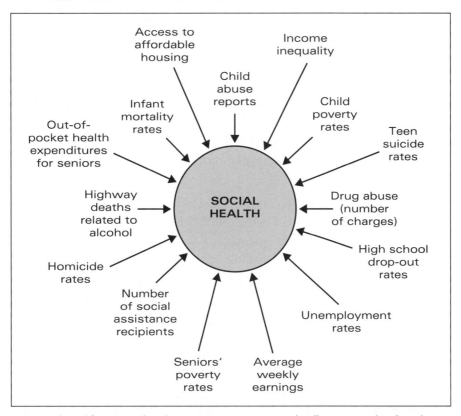

Source: Adapted from S. Brink and A. Zeesman, *Measuring Social Well-Being: An Index of Social Health for Canada* (Hull: Applied Research Branch, Human Resources Development Canada, 1997). Reproduced with the permission of the Minister of Public Works and Government Services Canada, 2004.

Focus Groups Program planners sometimes consult with community members to find out what resources they think the community needs. For example, a program planner for preschoolers might ask parents for their views on childcare and existing programs (Berkowitz, 2003). **Focus groups** are often used to gather this type of information.

A focus group is essentially a group interview, whose purpose is to generate ideas and to clarify people's thoughts and opinions on a particular topic. A typical focus group has ten to twelve participants and is led by a facilitator, who moves the group through a set of predetermined questions. An advantage of focus groups is that they gather information from several people at one sitting, which means they require less time than individual interviews. However, sensitive topics such as addiction or sexual abuse may not be appropriate for group discussion; such subjects are best addressed on a one-to-one basis (Barnsley and Ellis, 1992; Health Canada, 1996b).

Accountability Activities

The 1990s were challenging times for both public- and private-sector agencies. As governments cut social spending, restructured their operations, and devolved many responsibilities to the private sector, accountability or *transparency* became more important than ever. According to Health Canada (2002a), **accountability** means the following:

- understanding and demonstrating the use of resources and achievement of results;
- the obligation of having to render an accounting for the use of resources and results achieved; [and/or]
- the obligation of having to answer for one's responsibilities, to report, to explain, and to give reasons.

The demand for greater accountability is largely a response to the rising costs of social programs. More than ever before, agency stakeholders such as funders, clients, donors, and the general public are demanding to know whether social agency funding is being used in an efficient manner, whether programs are reaching people who need them, and whether the benefits for clients justify the costs (Hall et al., 2000).

The criteria by which social agencies are held accountable have changed over the years. During the 1970s and 1980s, a social agency was deemed accountable if it could provide sufficient information about how funds were spent, who received services, the types of activities offered, and how many people completed programs. Today's accountability requirements of both public and private agencies tend to be more detailed and extensive. For example, government agencies such as the provincial and territorial social services ministries are required to meet the accountability standards of the Social Union Framework Agreement (SUFA). Under SUFA's Accountability Template Guide, government officials must provide details on the nature and scope of program responsibilities, performance expectations, methods used to monitor and report on programs and services, and key outcomes of their efforts (Treasury Board of Canada Secretariat, 2000).

Reports suggest that the pressure to be accountable is felt more by voluntary than by commercial agencies. As Richmond and Shields (2003, 10) point out, "in spite of decades of rapid growth and strong overall public respect for nonprofit organizations an impression remains that the sector is not as efficient as its [commercial] and government sector cousins." Indeed, in its final report on a review of the voluntary sector, the Panel on Accountability and Governance in the Voluntary Sector (PAGVS) emphasized that among other things, voluntary agencies needed to become more accountable for the following:

- developing a relevant mission and set of agency priorities;
- appropriately managing funds they received and spent;
- the structure and processes used to govern the organization; and
- the quality and range of agency programs and services (PAGVS, 1999).

Responses to the current emphasis on accountability have been mixed. On the one hand, increased accountability is considered a good thing: reports can help external stakeholders learn about the status of their "investment" in a social agency, and agency personnel can use accountability methods to identify aspects of the agency that need improvement (PAGVS, 1999). On the other hand, there are concerns about the increased pressure on agencies to be accountable. For example, some voluntary agencies are finding themselves accountable to stakeholders at different levels and often in conflicting ways. Richmond and Shields (2003, 11) explain

> Government demands for 'efficiency and economy of service' may conflict with client desires for 'quality service.' Such tensions are not easily resolvable; they make up an integral component of the politics which nonprofit bodies are engaged. The basic concern is that accountability to the state has increasingly come to trump nonprofit accountability to the community.

In their study of Canada's voluntary sector, Michael Hall and colleagues (2003a, 18) found that accounting requirements by funders tended to be "unduly high and consumed an inordinate amount of staff and board time."

Other concerns have been raised about current accountability requirements in government agencies. Ken Battle (2001) finds that although the regional governments are required to submit annual reports using SUFA's Accountability Template Guide, continued federal funding is not conditional on the content of those reports. In other words, under SUFA, regional governments receive their full share of federal funding regardless of the quality of their social welfare programming—that is, as long as they complete and submit the required reports.

Program Evaluation

Social agencies use various tools to evaluate their programs and services. **Program evaluation** can be understood "as the process in which services and programs are examined to determine whether they are needed and used, how well they are run, whether they meet their stated objective, and whether they are worth the cost" (McDonald, 2001, 435). Whether conducted during or at the end of a program, an evaluation can help agencies identify what is going well, which areas need improvement, and whether the program is running in the way it was originally intended.

There are at least thirty-five different types of program evaluation, including the following:

- process evaluation (examines how program activities are carried out)

- cost–benefit evaluation (looks at the relationship between a program's results and its costs)

- needs assessment (evaluates whether an existing or a new program is needed)

- outcome evaluation (determines whether the program has achieved the desired outcomes or results (McNamera, 1998).

Whichever type of evaluation framework is used, program evaluation is usually conducted by someone outside the program being examined.

In the past, program evaluations were *service*-based—this means that the focus of evaluation was on a program's inputs (for example, the number of dollars spent), activities (including types of service provided), and outputs (perhaps the number of counselling sessions conducted). Owing to pressure on social agencies to prove their effectiveness, social program evaluation has become more *results*-based; it emphasizes how programs have made a difference in the lives of clients. The results of a program are often revealed through an outcome measurement approach.

Outcome Measurement

Outcome measurement is a type of evaluation that (1) assesses what a program actually achieved rather than what it intended to achieve, and (2) identifies any changes in behaviour, skills, attitudes, or knowledge of program participants.

Program funders have taken a particular fancy to outcome measurement since this type of evaluation can tell them whether their dollars are producing expected results. In a 2001 study of Canada's voluntary sector, 89 percent of funders that required program evaluation and 88 percent of those that encouraged evaluation in funded agencies wanted information about client outcomes (Hall et al., 2003b). Outcomes measurement is also required in the public sector. For example, federal government departments that are responsible for programs funded under the Social Union Framework Agreement are required to "measure and monitor the outcomes of programs and report publicly on a regular basis on program performance" (Treasury Board of Canada Secretariat, 2000). The PAGVS (1999, 36) suggests that the recent emphasis on results has made outcome measurement "a preoccupation for private, public and voluntary organizations."

An agency's ability to measure program outcomes may be critical to its survival in the community. Outcomes *in general* can provide the information needed to make programs more responsive to local needs; the discovery of *positive* outcomes may increase the agency's chances of continued funding and also lend credibility to the agency. Unfortunately, as with any type of program evaluation, there are limitations and challenges associated with outcomes measurement. One challenge for evaluators is proving that the increased well-being of program participants is the result of the program and not some other influence in participants' lives (Herman and Renz, 1998). Also, many social agencies are finding that outcome measurement is an expensive, complicated, and time-consuming process that requires a certain expertise not always available in-house (Hall et al., 2003a).

Developing "Best Practices"

While "learning from experience" has always been important to social agencies, it has recently become a critical element in efforts to improve agency services and overall performance. In a knowledge-based economy, there is a greater emphasis on sharing information, solving problems, critiquing program performance, and making informed decisions about future programs and services (Canadian Centre for Management Development, 2001a). The term **best practices** refers to activities or strategies that agency personnel identify as successful or effective in some way. Best practices may be identified through rigorous program evaluation, but they are often discovered by trial and error. Thus, best practices may simply be the ones that people perceive as working. Exhibit 6.5 lists some of the best practices found in a workplace antiviolence program.

Central to best practices is the value of ongoing learning through the accumulation and analysis of knowledge, the application of this knowledge to various contexts and situations, and the sharing of this knowledge with

E x h i b i t   6 . 5
A BEST PRACTICES MODEL: WORKPLACE ANTI-VIOLENCE PROGRAM

Why reinvent the wheel ...

Lots of companies, trade unions and employers have found ways to respond to violence in a workplace setting. Strong responses involve strategies to make sure workplaces are safe from violence, and ensure that they are supportive places for women or men experiencing family violence.

A "best practices model" of an anti-violence program in the workplace could contain the following elements:

- a working environment in which employees are encouraged to use workplace programming to address their situation, with a flexible, supportive and confidential approach to assisting victims or offenders

- a focus on policies supporting safety from personal violence and workplace action to support workers experiencing domestic violence

- program flexibility, to allow each worksite to address the issues at its own pace

- multifaceted awareness, educational and training programs that sensitize both women and men employees to violence prevention, including opportunities for discussion among men and women about the prevalence and consequences of family violence

- using the collective bargaining process to confirm that the workplace is an appropriate venue for preventing violence against women

- strong vocal support for violence prevention from management and union membership.

Source: Adapted and excerpted from Premier's Action Committee for Family Violence Prevention (2001). *Best Practices for Workplace Promotion of Violence Prevention*, pp. 5, 7–8. Interministerial Women's Secretariat, Prince Edward Island [online]. Available: www.gov.pe.ca/photos/original/hss_violprevent.pdf [March 18, 2004].

others so that they too might benefit. The continuous learning and application process within an agency ideally reflects changes in the local community (Arai, 2000).

Best practices can be articulated at all levels of a social agency. At the work level, a list of best practices might guide front-line staff in the assessment of client needs or maintenance of client records; management might refer to best practices for training staff or recruiting volunteers; and those governing an agency might focus on best practices in fundraising strategies or policy development.

SUMMARY

■ Introduction

Social agencies have a number of functions in common, such as securing funding, assessing client needs, and ensuring the quality of services. The mix of services an agency offers is usually directed at a certain segment of the population and reflects the community's needs.

■ Organizational Structure: Evolving Models

Bureaucracies are hierarchal organizational structures with several vertical levels of management and power. In contrast, collectivist-democratic models emphasize power-sharing and the use of group consensus and negotiation in decision-making. Today, the trend in the public and private sectors is toward the adoption of learning organization principles.

■ Types of Social Agencies and Their Service Environment

Since the 1960s, the environment for providing social welfare services has shifted from large institutions to community-based settings. An aging population has increased the demand for residential centres and round-the-clock care. Many nonresidential programs are found in multiservice centres. Some nonresidential services are provided on an appointment basis; others provide support through drop-in centres, telephone, outreach, or the Internet.

■ Social Agency Activities

Direct services are social agency activities that involve face-to-face interactions with clients and are aimed at primary, secondary, and tertiary prevention. In contrast, indirect services do not usually involve personal contact with clients; these services include social administration, program planning and development, accountability activities, and program evaluation. The development of best practices reflects the general shift to a knowledge-based society and economy.

▼ KEY TERMS

For definitions of the key terms, consult the Glossary on page 364 at the end of the book.

social agency p. 122

formal systems p. 124

bureaucratic model p. 124

collectivist-democratic
  model p. 125

learning organization
  model p. 126

deinstitutionalization
  movement p. 129

community-based agencies
  p. 129

residential centres p. 130

nonresidential centres
  p. 131

system of care p. 133

direct services p. 133

indirect services p. 133

primary prevention p. 133

secondary prevention
  p. 134

tertiary prevention p. 135

social administration
  p. 136

program-planning p. 137

community needs assess-
  ments p. 138

social indicators p. 138

focus groups p. 140

accountability p. 140

program evaluation p. 142

outcome measurement
  p. 143

best practices p. 143

Service Providers: A Rich Blend of Formal and Informal Help

O b j e c t i v e s

I. To introduce various aspects of the social work profession and the nature of social service work, and to consider social work's "identity crisis."

II. To review the characteristics and benefits of self-help groups, and the future direction of self-help.

III. To look at the work performed by volunteers in the social welfare context, volunteers' skills and benefits, the changing nature of volunteering, and how Canadian governments support volunteerism.

IV. To explore the trend toward partnerships between formal and informal helpers and the challenges associated with such alliances.

INTRODUCTION

The types of help provided in the social welfare field can be classified as either formal or informal. **Informal help** is provided by volunteer or "natural" helpers. This type of help includes unpaid care and support given through structured social agencies, as well as unstructured help given by family, friends, neighbours, or co-workers. **Formal help** can be divided into professional and self-help:

- **Professional help** is given by paid individuals, who bring a recognized knowledge base, formal training, and relevant experience to their practice. Often, this type of help is guided by a Code of Ethics that is specific to the worker's profession. Professional helpers include social workers, social service workers, psychiatrists, and psychologists.

- **Self-help** refers to mutual aid provided through formally organized yet nonprofessional groups. Self-help groups are run by the members rather than professionals. Even so, they are regarded as formal collectives because they usually have a set procedure for conducting meetings, and because meetings are often coordinated by an organization. Meetings for Overeaters' Anonymous, for example, are coordinated by intergroups, regional offices, and a World Service Office (Pape, 1990).

During the twentieth century, the social welfare system took on many of the supportive roles once played by family and volunteers. The rapid growth of this system in the 1950s and 1960s created a strong demand for the services of professionally trained helpers. Today, the social welfare system includes a mix of occupational groups, all of which share the common goal of helping people. **Social workers** are the largest occupational group in the social welfare system, accounting for about 30 percent of workers. Social workers are found at various levels of the system; they may provide direct services to clients; design, administer, or evaluate programs; or hold policy-making or social-planning positions (Stephenson et al., 2000).

In the 1970s, the deteriorating economic climate prompted Canadian governments to reduce spending on social welfare. At the same time, many social movements and disenfranchised groups began questioning the authority of governments and criticizing their policies and services. All of this led to the recognition of more natural forms of help, such as peer support and mutual aid (Reay-Young, 2001).

Although professional helpers are still in demand, more and more people are seeking assistance from self-help groups, peer support counsellors, and other nonprofessional helpers. This trend can be linked to the cuts in government-funded social welfare programs, to long wait lists for services, and to dissatisfaction with bureaucratic institutions. Also, people are beginning to realize that the care provided by self-help and informal helpers can be as good as or better than that delivered by professionals.

This chapter looks at professional helpers (specifically, social workers and social service workers), self-help groups, and informal helpers (specifically, volunteers). Together, these cover the broad spectrum of helpers in the social welfare system.

I. PROFESSIONAL HELPERS IN THE SOCIAL WELFARE SYSTEM

SOCIAL WORK: A DISTINCT PROFESSION

Social work is similar to other helping **professions** (such as nursing, policing, and psychology) in that it possesses a Code of Ethics, it has the means to regulate and enforce set standards of behaviour among its members, and it has developed a theoretical body of knowledge that guides practice (Cross, 1985). One characteristic that distinguishes social work from other helping professions is its long-standing association with the social welfare system, which influences the development and delivery of many of its programs. Social work is also unique because of its emphasis on *social well-being* (in relation to physical, psychological, and spiritual well-being) and *social functioning* (both the way people carry out their social roles and the extent to which society enables people to perform their roles). Another distinct feature of social work is its *relationship-centred* focus, which recognizes people in the context of their environment (CASW, 2000). Exhibit 7.1 highlights some of the commonalities and distinctions been social work and two other helping professions.

The social work profession is based on altruistic, humanitarian, and egalitarian ideals, all of which shape its philosophy as well as its service goals and interventions. Underlying social work's philosophy are values that promote social justice, acceptance and respect for others, and people's right to self-determination (University of Manitoba, 2004). Social workers believe in "the intrinsic worth and dignity of every human being" and in society's role as the provider of "resources, services and opportunities for the overall benefit of humanity" (CASW, 1994b).

SOCIAL WORK PRACTICE

A Multilevel Approach

As the Canadian Association of Social Workers (CASW) (2000) points out, "the primary focus of social work practice is on the relationship networks between individuals, their natural support resources, the formal structures in their communities, and the societal norms and expectations that shape these relationships." This particular focus demands a multilevel approach to practice. At the *micro* level, social workers aim to help individuals, families, and small groups enhance their social well-being; this may be achieved through a variety of methods, including one-to-one, family, or group counselling. At the

Exhibit 7.1

A COMPARISON OF THREE HELPING PROFESSIONS

	SOCIAL WORK	PSYCHOLOGY	PSYCHIATRY
Focus of attention	Dual focus on individual and environment and interaction between the two	Individual behaviour, which includes internal thoughts, feelings, and emotional responses	Mental illness, wide range of disturbed behaviour and emotional reactions
Assessment/diagnostic tools	Social history; client interviews; observation	Diagnostic tests (IQ, personality, etc.); interviews; observation	Medical exam; use of International Classification of Disease; interviews; observation; tests
Intervention methods	Casework; family and/or group therapy; education/ information; referral to community resources	Behaviour modification; psychotherapy; environmental modification	Prescribe psychotropic medication; psychotherapy; biological treatments
Aim of intervention	To help individuals, families, and communities understand and solve personal and social problems	To solve or prevent behavioural, cognitive, and affective problems	To reduce symptoms, change behaviour, or promote personality growth
Specializations	Counselling, group work, social administration, research and evaluation, community organization, teaching	Clinical, experimental, neurological, developmental, social, counselling, educational, industrial, personality	Child, geriatric, forensic, liaison, behaviour, family, sexual, psychoanalysis, research
Education levels	B.S.W., M.S.W., D.S.W., Ph.D.	B.A. or B.Sc., M.A., Ph.D.	Medical doctor and at least five years' psychiatric training
Professional association (national)	Canadian Association of Social Workers	Canadian Psychological Association	Canadian Psychiatric Association

Source: Author.

mezzo level, social workers seek to improve conditions within and among social welfare organizations; this may involve advocating for or participating in the development of new programs. Broader social problems and political issues are usually addressed at the *macro* level of practice and may involve seeking change in legislation or social policy.

Generalist and Specialist Practice

Some social workers choose to *specialize* in particular areas of practice; others prefer a more *general* approach. A **specialist** is a practitioner who has been trained in a specific area of expertise and who directs his or her attention to a relatively narrow human need or problem. In contrast, a **generalist** is a practitioner who has been trained to apply a wide range of practice skills in a variety of contexts, and with any size of client system, including individuals, families, and small groups (CASW, n.d.). Often, specialists in social work first develop generalist skills and then narrow their focus of practice to a particular area of expertise. Common areas of specialization in social work practice are clinical social work (for example, counselling individuals or families), community organization (as in social planning), and social administration (including social agency management). Because human needs and problems have become more complex, requiring specific types of help, the need for specialization has grown over the years (Stephenson et al., 2000).

A Person-in-Environment Perspective

Social work's **person-in-environment** focus requires social workers to learn about various aspects of a client's life and level of functioning. Learning about the client *system* requires an in-depth assessment of the psychological, social, physical, spiritual, and other human dimensions, and the client's functioning levels on those dimensions. To understand a client's *environment*, a social worker examines how a client's personal functioning may be affected by the general culture, economy, political climate, and other external forces. The way a client interacts with his or her environment must also be understood (McMahon, 1994). The person-in-environment perspective acknowledges the complexity of interactions between people and their environment and recognizes that people both shape and are shaped by their environment (International Federation of Social Workers, 2000).

Scope of Practice

Social work's **scope of practice** is basically a guideline that states which functions and activities are appropriate for social workers to engage in. In 2000, the CASW published a National Scope of Practice Statement for registered social workers in Canada. At the provincial level, Ontario has a scope of practice for social service workers who are members of the Ontario College of Social Workers and Social Service Workers (see Exhibit 7.2).

The scopes of practice for social workers and social service workers often overlap, but there are also fundamental differences. Social service workers tend to have fewer responsibilities and discretionary powers than social workers; in some settings, the former serve as caseworkers under the supervision of the latter. The nature of a client's problems and needs often determines which occupational group will be assigned to a case. This means that social workers tend to have clients who present with more severe, complex, or multilevel problems—ones that require advanced helping skills.

SOCIAL WORK KNOWLEDGE AND EDUCATION

A Knowledge Base

Social work knowledge derives from both inside the social work profession and from other disciplines. Knowledge that is produced indigenously by social workers is based on the shared experience of workers, individual professional experiences, and applied research. Much of the knowledge that is "borrowed" is from other helping disciplines such as psychology, psychiatry, education, and public health; social work also draws extensively from the academic fields of sociology, philosophy, political science, anthropology, economics, and law. This "cross-pollination" of various types of knowledge enhances social work's interdisciplinary nature (Johnson et al., 2000).

Education Levels

Social work requires its practitioners to reach a certain level of educational preparedness—in terms of knowledge, skills, methods, values, and ethics— before they can practise. In 2004, thirty-five universities across Canada offered social work training at the undergraduate (B.S.W.) and graduate (M.S.W.) levels, and seven universities offered postgraduate (doctorate) studies in social work. Changing labour force needs in the late 1960s led to the development of college-level social work programs. Today, close to sixty community colleges and university-colleges across Canada are offering certificate or diploma programs in social work or social services. The various levels of education for social work and social service work are briefly described below.

Certificate and Diploma Programs Training in social service work has not developed uniformly across Canada. That said, most college-level programs combine classroom work with practical experience, focus on a generalist approach to practice, and gear their curricula to the needs of the job

<u>E x h i b i t   7 . 2</u>

SCOPE OF PRACTICE IN ONTARIO: SOCIAL WORK AND SOCIAL SERVICE WORK

According to the Ontario College of Social Workers and Social Service Workers (OCSWSSW), "the scope of practice of the profession of social work [and social service work] means the assessment, ... treatment and evaluation of individual, interpersonal and societal problems through the use of ... knowledge, skills, interventions and strategies, to assist individuals, dyads, families, groups, organizations and communities to achieve optimum psychosocial and social functioning." The scope of practice of social work also includes diagnostic services.

AREA OF FOCUS | TASK OR FUNCTION

Worker and client activities
- assessment
- diagnosis (not applicable to social service workers)
- treatment
- evaluation

(these activities are carried out within a worker/client relationship)

Human service programs
- program development
- management
- administration
- service delivery
- evaluation

(these tasks may be completed in collaboration with other professionals)

Professional supervision of ...
- peers
- students
- other supervisees

Consultation services provided to ...
- peers or professionals from other disciplines in relation to the worker and client activities listed above

Social policy-making
- development
- promotion
- implementation
- evaluation

(these tasks aim to improve social conditions and equality)

Research or educational services related to ...
- worker and client activities
- human service programs
- professional supervision
- consultation services
- social policy-making
- other activities recognized by the OCSWSSW

Source: Excerpted and adapted from Ontario College of Social Workers and Social Service Workers (2000). *Standards of Practice Handbook*, pp. 1–2. [online]. Available: http://206.221.245.198/sections/pdf/1.6B%20code%20of%20ethics%20english.pdf [March 18, 2004].

market (Lecomte, 2001). Graduates of these programs are usually known as **social service workers**, or human service workers. Since people in this group have a lower level of social work education than a bachelor's degree, they are sometimes referred to as **paraprofessionals** in the social work field (Stephenson et al., 2000).

Bachelor of Social Work The first B.S.W. program in Canada began in 1967. Students who want to enter a B.S.W. program are required by most universities to complete two years of undergraduate courses, preferably in the liberal arts. The third and fourth years of study (the B.S.W. program) strongly emphasize social work theory and generalist practice methods.

Master of Social Work An M.S.W. program usually requires one or more years of study following the completion of an undergraduate degree. Students can specialize in specific fields of practice, such as clinical practice, social work administration, or community development.

Postgraduate Degree The first doctorate program in social work was offered by the University of Toronto in 1951. A Doctor of Social Work (D.S.W.) degree usually prepares students for work off the front lines, such as in teaching, administration, or research.

Adapting Social Work Education to a Changing Environment

Ideally, the structure and content of social work education should be shaped by the context in which social work is practised. However, as Gilles Rondeau (2001) suggests, a rapidly changing political, economic, and social climate, the evolving needs of people, and the restructuring of service delivery systems have generated a number of challenges for social work education. One challenge involves keeping social work courses and programs up to date with demographic shifts and changing human needs and problems. Today's field requires workers to have the appropriate skills and knowledge to care for the growing numbers of people who are poor, elderly, or of Aboriginal background, and who have more severe, complex, or chronic problems (Rondeau, 2001; Stephenson et al., 2000).

REGULATIONS AND STANDARDS OF PRACTICE

The "regulation of a profession defines the practice of the profession and describes the boundaries within which it operates, including the requirements and qualifications to practise the profession" (OCSWSSW, 2003). Social work practice is governed by legislation enacted in each province and is regulated by professional associations and/or "colleges." (In this context, colleges are governing bodies, not educational institutions.) Social workers who join the regulatory body in their province become "registered," "certified," or "licensed," and are required to practise according to ethical and/or competency standards (CASW, 2003c; MacDonald and Adachi, 2001).

The CASW was established in 1926 as a national federation of provincial and territorial social work associations. According to its mission statement, the CASW (1994a, 2) "seeks to develop, promote, support and maintain national professional standards of practice of the highest quality." To this end, it sets certain standards and guidelines for social work practice in Canada and participates in the development of social work regulation and legislation. Social workers are expected to practise in accordance with the philosophy, purpose, and standards set by their profession and to be accountable to their clients, their profession, and society.

In 1938, the CASW (1983, 2) developed a social work **code of ethics** "to provide a practical guide for professional behaviour and the maintenance of a reasonable standard of practice within a given cultural context." The CASW code was updated in 1983 and 1994 and is currently under review again. The CASW Code of Ethics is applicable to all practitioners who are registered with their provincial social work association and/or college.

Until recently, there was almost no regulation of social service workers in Canada. Many provinces are currently working on, or have completed, a regulatory process to oversee social service practice. Ontario is one province that has both a provincial association and a college to regulate both social work and social service practice. The two regulatory bodies share many of the same values and principles, and both organizations "are dedicated to ensuring that the [Ontario] public is provided with safe, ethical, competent and high quality service" (OASW, 2000). Despite their shared interests, each body has its own mission, constitution, budget, and organizational structure. Also, the two bodies have distinctly different roles: the main purpose of the Ontario Association of Social Workers is "to represent the interests and concerns of the [social work] profession"; the Ontario College of Social Workers and Social Service Workers seeks "to protect the public by maintaining and improving standards of professional competence and ethics" (OASW, 2000).

EMPLOYMENT

Social Workers

Social workers are employed in a wide range of settings, including school boards, hospitals, voluntary agencies, religious organizations, employee assistance offices, correctional institutions, Indian band councils, and private practice. The number of employed social workers in Canada increased by

46 percent between 1994 and 2001 to a total of 43 000 (Government of Canada, 2003e). However, there was a decline in the number of social workers in government positions—reflecting, in part, the general downsizing of government in service delivery (Stephenson et al., 2000). The Government of Canada (2003e) predicts fair employment opportunities for social workers until 2007. Certain trends, such as an aging population and its need for more services, are expected to drive the demand for social workers.

Social Service Workers

Social service workers are employed by many of the same types of agencies as social workers. Between 1999 and 2001, employment for social service workers rose "at a significantly above-average rate" as government funding increased in the health and social service sectors. Employment for social service workers is expected to remain at fair levels until 2007 (Government of Canada, 2003d).

SOCIAL WORK'S "IDENTITY CRISIS"

For much of the twentieth century, social work was distinguished from other helping professions by "a distinct set of professional skills, based on an identified knowledge base, provided through formal education, and refined through years of practice with others in the profession" (Stephenson et al., 2000, 5). As other occupational groups infiltrated the social welfare system, the boundaries between social work and other occupations blurred. For example, in five provinces, social workers who work in health-related services such as drug addiction and eating disorders are now classified as *health care* professionals (Department of Finance, 2003j). Moreover, programs and services once dominated by social workers—such as family therapy—are increasingly occupied by counsellors with no social work background (Stephenson et al., 2000).

In 2000, the Strategic Human Resources Analysis of the Social Work Sector drew attention to certain trends in the social welfare system. One such trend is that social agencies are trying to maintain high standards of service while keeping costs down. A common approach to this involves employers hiring greater numbers of staff who do not have degrees, and who have little or no social work training. The growing number of social service workers in the social welfare system (57 000 of them by 1991) exemplifies this trend (Stephenson et al., 2000). Many employers consider college-trained workers to be just as prepared as university-trained social workers when it comes to providing intake, referral, advocacy, and other front-line services. Indeed, a Canadian study suggests that graduates of programs in social service work may have more of the necessary skills than B.S.W. graduates. Moreover, social service workers can be paid less (they draw an average hourly wage of $15.84, compared to $22.32 for social workers), and this naturally attracts employers faced with budget cuts and increasing demands for service (Stephenson et al., 2000; Government of Canada, 2003d; 2003e). According to Stephenson and colleagues (2000), the reduced respect for front-line workers (reflected in lower wages) indicates a general shift in social values: poor and disadvantaged people are being seen in a worse light, and by inference so are those who work with them. As a result of all this, social work's identity is being weakened and the service that social workers provide is being devalued. The report *In Critical Demand: Social Work in Canada* concludes that firming up the scope of social work practice and developing "a coherent, clearly defined professional identity" will be key to the overall strengthening of the social welfare field (Stephenson et al., 2000, 195).

Recent developments suggest that social work as a profession is gradually regaining its definition. The clarification of the parameters of social work is, in part, due to the development of "restricted practice activities"—that is, practices that can be carried out only by certain occupational groups or by designated professionals within those groups. Restricted practice activities vary from province to province, but many are likely to become the sole domain of social workers (CASW, 2000). For example, changes in hiring practices in British Columbia are restricting the practice of child protection to those holding a minimum of a B.S.W. degree or an equivalent (HRDC, 2002b).

Other forces are working to retain social work's integrity. For many years in the 1990s, the Alberta College of Social Workers (ACSW) tried to convince other social work regulatory bodies to recognize graduates of college social-service programs "as rightful users of the professional title 'social worker'" (Kuiken, 2001, 8). This attempt was met with resistance across the country, leading to the realization "that other jurisdictions in Canada—and elsewhere—have absolutely no intention of adopting or accepting two-year diploma graduates as 'social workers'" (Kuiken, 2001, 8). As social work's boundaries become clearer through policies and legislation, we can expect the lines between social work and other forms of practice, such as social service work, to become more clear as well.

II. SELF-HELP GROUPS: A VALUABLE SUPPORT

CLASSIFICATIONS AND CHARACTERISTICS

Self-help (or mutual aid) groups are networks of individuals who meet to share common experiences, situations, or problems (Self Help Resource Centre, 2003). There is a self-help group for practically every human issue imaginable, including bereavement, addiction, disability, parenting, physical health, relationships, sexuality, and employment. The quality of support varies among self-help groups; the most effective ones provide their members with opportunities for "shared leadership, open communications, respect, clear boundaries and confidentiality" (Self Help Resource Centre, 2002, 1).

Four types of self-help groups are common in Canada: (1) traditional *face-to-face groups* (such as Alcoholics Anonymous) are voluntary, free, and independent; (2) *support groups* receive assistance from an organization such as free meeting space or the use of agency office equipment, and are facilitated by agency staff or trained volunteers; (3) *transition groups* are initially led by professionals or educators, and later by the members themselves; and (4) *online groups* enable people to connect with others through the Internet (Self Help Resource Centre, 2003; HealthyWay, 1997b). Depending on its purposes, a self-help group may focus on problem-solving (such as Alanon), self-development (for example, Parents Supporting Parents), or consciousness-raising (including Senior Power of Regina).

Self-help groups differ from support groups and professional therapy groups in a number of ways. Some of these ways are outlined in Exhibit 7.3.

BENEFITS OF SELF-HELP GROUPS

Research suggests a strong link between social support (such as that derived from membership in a self-help group) and improvements in physical health. Social support is believed to increase a person's ability to ward off disease, maintain good health, recover from illness, and cope with serious injury. Other evidence suggests a link between social support, mental health, and general well-being. People who play an active role in self-help groups often report improvements in their problem-solving or coping abilities, a greater sense of control over their environment, increased feelings of hope and optimism, and decreased feelings of isolation or loneliness (Self-help groups, 1999).

People can benefit from helping others. One benefit, advanced by self-help expert Frank Riessman, is identified in the helper therapy principle:

> By being the helper as well as the receiver of help, a self-help group participant acquires the enhanced self-esteem and feeling of worth that comes with being important to others. The experiential knowledge, gained from coping with a common problem, is valued, just as credentials and technical expertise are valued in a professional helping situation. (Pape, 1990, 5)

Exhibit 7.3

MAKING DISTINCTIONS: SELF-HELP, SUPPORT, AND THERAPY GROUPS

SELF-HELP/MUTUAL AID	SUPPORT	THERAPY
Primary goal to effect personal change through helper therapy principle.	Primary goal to provide support and information.	Primary goal to effect personal change through therapeutic methods based on human behaviour theory and professional methods.
Interactions among members are de-emphasized and not focused on as a therapeutic device.	Focus on support and comfort.	Focus on the assumption that cure or change is based on reworking relationships in the group.
Helping methods specific to the group ideology. Based on successful strategies developed through shared information, feelings, and experiences among members with a common issue.	Helping methods based on shared information, feelings and experiences among members of a formal agency or organization.	Helping methods based on specific ideology of the therapist. Focus on relationships established among members with the help of a professional therapist. Members often have various issues.
Emphasize that all members are both helpers and helpees.	Support group leader may share personal issues or experiences.	Emphasize psychological distance between professional and members.
No fee or minimal contribution.	Set fee or membership.	Payment for professional service.
Common issue is the reason for the group's existence, and members come from all walks of life.	Members share a common concern.	Members generally have different backgrounds and different issues.
Admit anyone who qualifies.	Membership determined by the organization and/or group leader.	Membership determined by professional.
Rarely depend on outside organizational support except for their own members, and run national federations.	Organizational support for group provided by paid staff.	May meet in agency or private settings. May be dependent on regulations and codes of conduct.
Meetings are structured and task oriented.	Meetings are relatively unstructured.	Meeting structure based on therapeutic technique of psychotherapist or counsellor.

Source: Self-Help Resource Association of B.C. (2004). *Self-Help Mutual Aid and Professionals: A Practical Alliance*, p. 2: Self-Help/Mutual Aid Workshop Series Manuals [online]. Available: www.vcn.bc.ca/shra/publication/ resources/pdf/pdf%20forms/SelfhelpMutualAidProfessionalsAPracticalAlliance-original.pdf [March 18, 2004].

Improvements in self-esteem can in turn have a positive effect on physical and mental health.

Self-help groups are an important support system for thousands of Canadians. In his study of the self-help movement in Canada, Balthazar (1991) suggests that the rising popularity of self-help groups coincided with increasing industrialization and the associated breakdown of the family and other natural social support systems. This need for alternative social support, coupled with the trend toward "do-it-yourself" attitudes, has led to growth in the self-help industry.

SELF-HELP OF THE FUTURE

In the Internet era, more and more Canadians are able to access self-help groups. Online groups have many advantages over face-to-face groups: people can access online self-help groups without having to arrange for meeting space, transportation, or childcare; also, schedules for group meetings are flexible. Online self-help groups are especially appealing to people who live in rural or isolated areas, who reside in small towns where anonymity is difficult to maintain, or who avoid attending face-to-face groups out of embarrassment or fear of stigmatization (Phillips, 1996). There are a number of possible online venues for self-help groups, including newsgroups, e-mail discussion groups, live chat groups, and discussion forums (HealthyWay, 1997b). Some experts see online self-help groups as "the wave of the future" (HealthyWay, 1997a).

III. VOLUNTEERS: CANADA'S GREATEST NATURAL RESOURCE

THE NATURE OF VOLUNTEER WORK

Volunteers are "natural" helpers who donate their time and skills to a community cause or organization. People who volunteer represent all age and ethnic groups and come from all walks of life (Volunteer Canada, 2000a).

In Canada, volunteers are involved in a wide range of activities; most of these activities can be classified as either formal or informal. **Formal volunteer work** usually takes place within or on behalf of an organization and complements the professional services provided by that organization. This type of volunteering may involve working with specific age groups (for example, youth groups or seniors); counselling people in distress, such as on crisis phone lines; giving information and support to women in shelters; or helping recent immigrants settle into Canadian life. **Informal volunteer**

work is help given by relatives, friends, and neighbours. Because this type of assistance is such a normal part of everyday life, it is sometimes overlooked as a valuable part of the social welfare system (Hall et al., 1998; Chappell, 1999). Statistics relating to Canadians who give informal help, and the types of help they offer, are provided in Exhibit 7.4.

Much of what we know about volunteering in Canada comes from the National Survey of Giving, Volunteering and Participating (NSGVP), which was first conducted in 1997 and again in 2000. According to the 2000

Exhibit 7.4

TYPES OF INFORMAL VOLUNTEERING

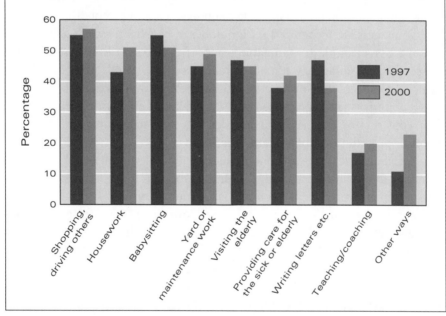

In 2000, the National Survey of Giving, Volunteering and Participating found that 77 percent of Canadians provide unpaid help to others on their own and not through an organization; this rate was up from 71 percent in 1997. The graph indicates the most common types of help given directly to others by Canadians aged 15+ in 1997 and 2000, and the percentage of survey respondents that provide each type of help.

Source: M. Hall, L. McKeown, and K. Roberts (August 2001). *Caring Canadians, Involved Canadians: Highlights from the 2000 National Survey of Giving, Volunteering and Participating,* p. 42. Catalogue no. 71-542-XPE or Catalogue no. 71-542 XIE in electronic format. Ottawa: Statistics Canada. © Minister of Industry, 2001 [online]. Available: www.givingandvolunteering.ca/pdf/n-2000-hr-ca.pdf [February 15, 2004].

NSGVP survey, around 6.5 million Canadians volunteer for charitable or nonprofit organizations, and one-fifth of volunteers devote time to social service organizations. This survey found that the main reason people volunteer is that they believe in the organization's cause. It also found that 77 percent of Canadians help others on an informal basis; of these, 63 percent help relatives not living with them, and 79 percent help people other than relatives (Hall et al., 2001).

SKILLS AND BENEFITS

Volunteers acquire **natural helping skills** through informal personal interactions. In a study by Patterson and colleagues (1992), respondents reported that the most helpful volunteers were the ones who provided humour, physical touching, exchanges of personal experiences, and material resources, who reached out to others, and who followed up after problems were resolved. Emotional support—expressed through listening, encouraging, empathizing, showing concern, and the like—is another important function of natural helping (Gottlieb, 1983). Helping people solve problems by clarifying needs and providing suggestions and information is also central to the natural helping process. According to Romeder (1990), helping efforts are most effective when the person being helped feels understood and accepted.

Volunteers are recognized for a number of benefits they bring to organizations. For example, organizations report that because volunteers have *chosen* to serve an agency for no material gain, they lend credibility to the agency. Volunteers also bring a vitality to their work as well as knowledge, focus, objectivity, and specialized skills. Agencies often rely on volunteers for their constructive feedback and for ideas on how to improve existing programs or procedures (Muegge and Ross, 1996).

Social agencies have become more accepting of volunteers as a result of economic and political factors. As Neena Chappell (1999) points out, volunteers are increasingly being seen as viable sources of help in times of fiscal restraint, budget cuts, withdrawal of direct government services, and the privatization of social welfare. Volunteers supplement the work of paid staff. They are appreciated for reducing the workloads of agency personnel and for making it possible to expand services (Muegge and Ross, 1996).

THE CHANGING NATURE OF VOLUNTEERING

One of the more disturbing trends in volunteerism is the declining number of volunteers in volunteer agencies. In 1997, 31.4 percent of Canadians volunteered for a charitable or nonprofit organization; by 2000, the rate had dropped to 27 percent. This decline is attributed to a variety of factors, including a loss of interest in volunteering among youth, people having less time and energy owing to increased work demands, and changing priorities for women, who have always volunteered at higher rates than men. Community agencies may soon have to limit the range of services they offer because of the decline in the numbers of volunteers (McKeown, 2003; Hall et al., 2003a).

Another disturbing trend is that fewer volunteers are doing more of the work. In 2000, about one-quarter of volunteers contributed three-quarters of all volunteer hours (McKeown, 2003). This situation is of particular concern to voluntary agencies with small budgets, since many of them depend heavily on a core group of volunteers, who may be at risk of burnout (Hall et al., 2003a).

Today's volunteers tend to have clear expectations about what they want out of their volunteer experience. Most volunteers, for instance, favour short-term projects and assignments that do not place them in leadership or administrative roles (Hall et al., 2003a). Volunteers also expect their contributions to be rewarding and "used by the organizations they are helping in a thoughtful and creative way" (Volunteer Canada, 2001).

If they hope to recruit and retain volunteers, agencies will have to find ways to satisfy volunteers' interests and meet their expectations (Volunteer Canada, 2001). Awareness of this has led to new developments in the "science" of volunteering. Increasingly, agencies that utilize volunteers are implementing policies and procedures related to the following:

- *Volunteering by contract.* Volunteer work is negotiated to be mutually beneficial to both the volunteer and the sponsoring agency.

- *Risk management.* Agencies introduce procedures to assess the needs, skills, and other attributes of volunteers so that they can be assigned appropriate activities.

- *Borrowing best practices.* Agencies incorporate certain standards, accountability measures, codes of conduct, and evaluation practices into their operations.

- *Professional volunteer management.* Volunteer coordinators gain equal status with other professionals in the voluntary sector.

- *Board governance.* Volunteers serving on boards are trained to serve in the dual capacities of supervisor and planner.

- *Volunteer development.* Volunteer programs find ways to attract new volunteers while retaining current volunteers (Volunteer Canada, 2004c).

Many voluntary agencies are faced with the challenge of adapting to the needs and expectations of mandatory volunteers. These volunteers—known in some circles as *voluntolds*—account for over 7 percent of Canadian volunteers, and include high school students required to volunteer in order to graduate; people sentenced by the courts to complete community service orders; and recipients of social assistance, who are required to volunteer in exchange for welfare benefits (Volunteer Canada, 2004c; Hall et al., 2001). Richmond and Shields (2003, 8) have found that

> the resources extended by many nonprofits to accommodate the "forced volunteering" programs of provincial governments, such as workfare, has greatly complicated the situation. Many nonprofits are now less capable of taking on genuine volunteers because their volunteering training resources are absorbed in state-driven forced volunteering initiatives.

Mandatory volunteering may be viewed negatively by those who have to do it. Research has found that people required to do volunteer work typically find it unfulfilling; this may reduce the likelihood that they will volunteer willingly in the future (Voluntary Sector Initiative, 2004b).

GOVERNMENT SUPPORT FOR VOLUNTEERISM

Since 1977, Volunteer Canada has been the national promoter of volunteerism. By developing resources, national initiatives, research projects, and training opportunities, and by networking with volunteer centres across the country, Volunteer Canada supports both volunteers and the organizations they serve.

The United Nations proclaimed 2001 the International Year of Volunteers. This underscored the "growing acknowledgement by government and social thinkers of the critical role played by volunteers and voluntary organizations in society" (Volunteer Canada, 2001). This proclamation inspired the Government of Canada to launch the Canada Volunteerism Initiative (CVI), which has the following as its primary goals: "to encourage Canadians to participate in voluntary organizations; improve the capacity of organizations to benefit from the contributions of volunteers; and enhance the experience of volunteers" (Volunteer Canada, 2004a). Under the CVI, volunteer centres have opened in many parts of the country. Also, national centres have been established to focus on various aspects of volunteerism such as capacity-building and community support. The growing support given to volunteerism is no doubt motivated in part by a recognition that volunteerism has economic value. It is estimated that the one billion hours (more or less) of volunteer work performed by Canadians every year is the equivalent of 549 000 full-time year-round jobs (Hall et al., 2001).

IV. FORMAL AND INFORMAL HELPERS: PARTNERSHIPS IN THE MAKING

A GROWING DEMAND FOR INFORMAL HELPERS

During the 1950s and 1960s, the growth of the welfare state encouraged the establishment of formal institutions and the hiring of professional helpers such as social workers and psychologists. By the 1980s, formally trained helpers had largely displaced informal or lay helpers, "who, by implication, could not provide adequate service" (Chappell, 1999). Until recently, professional groups have been reluctant to include informal helpers in the helping process. Increasingly, professionals are now recognizing that the support given by volunteers and self-helpers is a viable supplement to professional service. A service system that makes room for both formal and informal helpers can improve clients' quality of help and give them a wider range of service options. For example, a person suffering from depression may benefit from talking through childhood issues with a social worker, seeing a physician for medical intervention and monitoring, attending a self-help group for mutual support, and enjoying the companionship of a volunteer. Exhibit 7.5 illustrates possible linkages between formal and informal helping systems.

The prevalence of **multidisciplinary teams** in most communities reflects the willingness of professionals and nonprofessional helpers to work together. These teams are vital for coordinating services for clients who have a variety of needs or concerns, or who require assistance from more than one type of helper or agency. What makes these teams *multidisciplinary* is their membership: generally, they include representatives from a variety of social agencies, service sectors, academic disciplines, and backgrounds. In recent years, it has become more common to include nonprofessionals—such as clients' relatives, sponsors (that is, from a twelve-step self-help program), or other close supports—on multidisciplinary teams. Usually, these natural supports are included in the helping team at the request of the client.

SELF-HELP AND PROFESSIONAL GROUPS

As they cut back their social expenditures, government departments are looking to self-help groups to meet many social welfare needs of Canadians and to keep institutional costs down (Roberts, 2001). Health Canada, for example, suggests that the support provided by self-help groups may enhance well-being and subsequently reduce the need for hospitalization and other publicly funded services (Health Systems Research Unit, 1997). Even

Exhibit 7.5

LINKS AMONG VARIOUS FORMAL AND
INFORMAL HELPING SYSTEMS

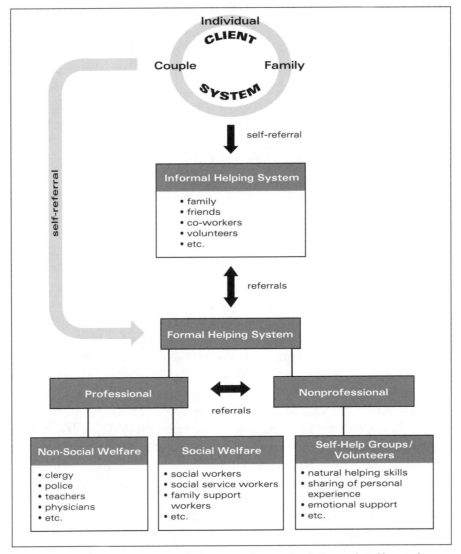

Source: Adapted from Donald Warren, *Helping Networks: How People Cope with Problems in the Urban Community* (Notre Dame: University of Notre Dame Press, 1981), p. 148. Copyright © 1981 by University of Notre Dame Press. Reprinted with permission.

when professional services are available, the "experientially gained knowledge and social support" offered by self-help groups are valuable assets in maintaining health and well-being (Reay-Young, 2001).

Although is not uncommon for professionals to refer their clients to self-help groups, and for self-help group members to also be seeing professional helpers, the two camps have traditionally kept their distance. Today's professionals are more willing to acknowledge that strong self-help groups may complement the services they provide; some may even admit that such groups are more effective than other types of intervention (Pape, 1990).

The recent trend toward collaboration has sparked an interest among professional and self-help groups in considering closer ties. By teaming up in the best interests of people in need, professionals and self-helpers could share their expertise while maintaining their separate identities. Although the two camps share an interest in working together, a common worry among self-helpers is that professional involvement in self-help groups might jeopardize the self-help process. As Pape (1990, 6) observes, some self-helpers are concerned that

> with the participation of professionals, the lay helper ideology is at risk ... Even for most well-meaning professionals, it is difficult to take a back seat at a self-help group. There is an accepted norm in today's society that professionals are the only experts who have the skills to solve our problems. As a result, group members are apt to defer to any professionals who are present.

In short, opening up self-help groups to professionals might result in a loss of the very qualities that make self-help so beneficial.

Professionals have concerns of their own. In critiquing the self-help group approach, they have expressed the following positions:

- Professional and strategic approaches are more effective in promoting change in people than the experiential learning found in self-help.

- Self-help produces only temporary change because it ignores the underlying causes of problems.

- The subjective involvement of some self-help members seems fanatical and is likely to lead to overdependence (Pape, 1990).

In their study of partnerships between health professionals and self-help groups, Banks and colleagues (1997) found several points of agreement and disagreement. The two camps tend to agree with regard to their respective roles and what constitutes a positive working relationship; however, they differ over principles. Professionals, for example, tend to place more importance than self-helpers on group leadership and on clarifying roles and goals.

In contrast, self-helpers place more emphasis on group organization, on providing outreach to group members, and on nurturing "the positive nature of helpful relationships" (Banks et al., 1997, 268).

VOLUNTEERS AND PROFESSIONAL HELPERS

The integration of volunteers in professional settings is becoming increasingly common in Canada. Professionals and volunteers work side by side in a wide range of organizations and on behalf of various groups, including immigrants, refugees, children and families, and victims of crime. In 2004, the federal government reaffirmed the future of volunteerism in nonprofit social agencies when it promised to help the voluntary sector mobilize volunteers (Office of the Prime Minister, 2004). Despite the connections between professional and volunteer helpers, research on professional/volunteer relationships is sadly lacking (Saunders, 2004).

Specken and Geyer (2000) believe that an aging population will expand both the role of volunteers in seniors' services and the role of seniors as volunteers. Furthermore, this anticipated volunteer "boom" is likely to prompt the formation of interorganizational partnerships. It is possible that by pooling their volunteers, social agencies will be able to minimize the bureaucratic red tape for volunteers. Thus, volunteers could move from agency to agency without having to go through a screening process at each one. Also, partnerships could strengthen the system of service for clients. For example, a volunteer matched with a senior could follow the senior from an outreach program, to home care, to the hospital, and finally to palliative care. As Specken and Geyer (2000, 20) point out, the client could move through the separate service delivery systems yet be "a constant and consistent presence throughout."

There is every indication that professionals and volunteers will be working more closely in the future. Government support, in terms of funding, training, and information-sharing, may be a strong incentive for social agencies to encourage volunteer participation and for volunteers to consider donating their time to social service.

SUMMARY

■ Introduction

Service providers in the social welfare system include professional helpers, self-help groups, and informal helpers. Each group brings a unique set of skills and approaches to the helping process, thereby creating a diverse range of supports for people in need. Social workers are the predominant occupational group in the social welfare system. Although professional helpers are still in demand, there is a greater need for the support provided by natural helpers and self-help groups.

■ Professional Helpers in the Social Welfare System

The social work profession is unique in its emphasis on social well-being, relationships, and social functioning. An altruistic, humanitarian, and egalitarian philosophical base guides the profession. Some social workers are generalists, and others are specialists, but all take a multilevel approach to problems and work from a person-in-environment perspective. The profession's knowledge base is interdisciplinary. Various levels of social work education are available in Canada. Codes of ethics, provincial legislation, and regulatory bodies guide the functions of social workers and, in some jurisdictions, of social service workers. Employment opportunities for social workers and social service workers are expected to be fair until 2007. As other occupational groups infiltrated the social welfare system, the social work profession became less defined; the introduction of restricted practices and changes in hiring policy may help strengthen social work's identity.

■ Self-Help Groups: A Valuable Support

Self-help groups promote the mutual exchange of ideas and feelings; this allows people with common problems to support one another. Four types of self-help groups are common in Canada. These groups provide both physical and mental-health benefits to those being helped; the people who are helping others benefit as well. Self-help groups have become popular in recent years as a result of a breakdown in traditional support systems and changing public attitudes. Online self-help groups have extended support to people who have difficulty attending face-to-face groups.

■ Volunteers: Canada's Greatest Natural Resource

Canadians volunteer in both social service organizations and natural settings. Natural helping skills are recognized as a vital component of the helping process. In recent years, there has been greater recognition of the benefits volunteers bring to social agencies. Fewer Canadians are volunteering, and more work is being done by a small core of volunteers. The needs and expectations of volunteers are changing, and this has prompted voluntary agencies to advance the "science" of volunteering. Many agencies are trying to cope with the rising numbers of mandatory volunteers. Government support for volunteerism is strong: Volunteer Canada and the Canada Volunteerism Initiative aim to strengthen the role of volunteers in organizations.

■ Formal and Informal Helpers: Partnerships in the Making

More and more professionals are recognizing that volunteers and self-helpers can supplement professional care. As governments cut back social expenditures, they look more to self-help groups to meet people's needs and reduce the costs of professional care. Despite an interest in forming partnerships, both professionals and self-helpers have concerns about the consequences of such alliances. Professionals and volunteers work side by side in a number of organizations and for various causes. It is expected that the aging population will create a volunteer "boom" and involve greater numbers of seniors in volunteer efforts. Government support for volunteerism is likely to increase in the years to come.

▼ KEY TERMS

For definitions of the key terms, consult the Glossary on page 364 at the end of the book.

informal help p. 147

formal help p. 147

professional help p. 148

self-help p. 148

social workers p. 148

professions p. 149

specialist p. 151

generalist p. 151

person-in-environment p. 151

scope of practice p. 151

social service workers p. 154

paraprofessionals p. 154

code of ethics p. 155

volunteers p. 160

formal volunteer work p. 160

informal volunteer work p. 160

natural helping skills p. 162

multidisciplinary teams p. 165

chapter

8

Promoting Change in Micro, Mezzo, and Macro Systems

Objectives

I. To explore various aspects of micro-level change, and to review programs and services that promote change in individuals, families, and small social groups.

II. To consider mezzo-level change as it applies to organizational restructuring.

III. To examine macro-level change and community organization in terms of community change, social planning, and social action.

INTRODUCTION

The primary goal of all social welfare programs is to change conditions that threaten individual and/or social functioning. To achieve this goal, intervention of some kind must be applied. In the social welfare context, the term **intervention** refers to strategies, techniques, and/or methods that are used to help individuals, families, communities, or other social systems change. Interventions vary with the nature of the problem and the size of the system that needs to be changed. Examples of interventions include coaching parents on techniques for disciplining children, facilitating an antiracism seminar for financial aid workers, and changing social policies that discriminate against the poor.

The change process may involve helping people change how they think, behave, or deal with feelings, or it may involve changing the environment so that it is more conducive to meeting human needs. Many social welfare programs that focus on changing *people* have their origins in the English Poor Laws. In colonial times, most change efforts took the form of imposed work. The able-bodied unemployed were herded into workhouses and put to work in the hope that they would learn to be productive and contributing members of society. Social welfare's interest in changing people's *environments* can be traced back to the social reform movements of the late 1800s and early 1900s. Social activists in the urban reform movement, for example, sought changes in housing and health legislation with the goal of reducing poverty and suffering among urban dwellers. Similarly, supporters of the women's rights movement lobbied for changes in social, political, and economic institutions that would improve living conditions for women and their children.

After the First World War, a growing body of research in the helping professions paved the way for more professional, systematic, and "scientific" approaches to change. It was no longer enough for practitioners to simply "mean well"; social workers were now required to have formal training in the social sciences and to draw from recognized bodies of practice models when helping others. Until the 1930s, these models were based mainly on Freudian principles and the diagnostic school of social work. Accompanying the emergence of these and later models was a recognition that there are three distinct levels of change:

- **Micro-level change** involves face-to-face interactions with individuals, families, and small groups. The primary goal of micro-level change is to help people obtain the resources and skills they require to become self-sufficient. This type of intervention is often referred to as direct service or clinical practice.

- **Mezzo-level change** generally occurs at the organizational level of society and involves little direct contact with service users. The focus is on changing formal systems that directly affect customers, such as social agencies and their programs, policies, and procedures, and service delivery mechanisms.

- **Macro-level change** takes place at the community level and seeks to change social conditions. Collective action is usually required at this level of change, since the conditions identified as requiring change are typically complex and well established in the existing political or cultural systems.

Exhibit 8.1 illustrates how these three levels are linked and gives examples of interventions for each level.

E x h i b i t 8 . 1

LEVELS OF CHANGE AND RELATED INTERVENTIONS

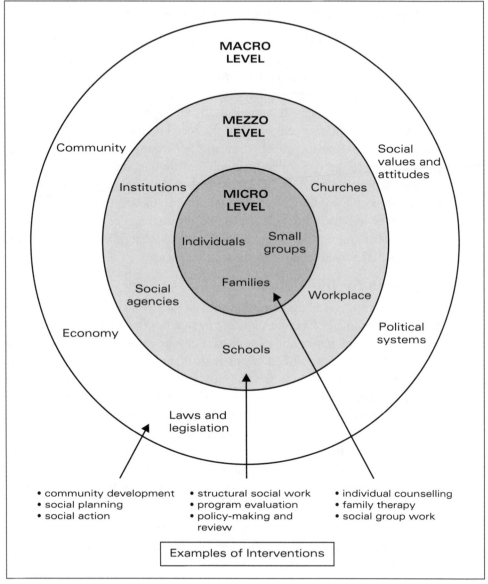

MACRO LEVEL

MEZZO LEVEL

Community

Social values and attitudes

Institutions

MICRO LEVEL

Churches

Individuals

Small groups

Families

Social agencies

Workplace

Economy

Political systems

Schools

Laws and legislation

- community development
- social planning
- social action

- structural social work
- program evaluation
- policy-making and review

- individual counselling
- family therapy
- social group work

Examples of Interventions

Source: Author

I. CHANGE AT THE MICRO LEVEL: CLIENT SERVICES

THE NATURE OF MICRO-LEVEL CHANGE

Social welfare services that focus on micro-level change are aimed at helping individuals, families, or small groups obtain "the basics they need to survive, subsist, develop, and even flourish within society" (Kahn, 1995, 571). An advantage of such programs is that they target relatively small systems, which makes it more likely that identified needs will be met. One disadvantage is that even after a client's needs are met, the social or environmental conditions that created those needs probably remain. For example, a soup kitchen that provides food for hungry individuals will "ensure that, on a given day, a given number of people are fed. But it cannot and does not address the question of why these people are hungry. If the soup kitchen closes, the people it serves will again be hungry" (Kahn, 1995, 571). Despite this type of limitation, programs that attempt to help micro-level systems change are necessary, and they are still the main focus of many social agencies.

Programs for Individuals

These days, most social agencies that provide direct client services have programs for individuals. Examples include mental health counselling, settlement programs for immigrants, and support services for abused women. These programs and services are justified on the basis that communities suffer—as does society as a whole—when individual needs are not met. Social workers and other professional helpers also recognize that providing services on a one-to-one basis can help people change their behaviour, learn new coping strategies, and either change or adapt to their environment (Fischer, 1978).

Every individual who seeks help from a social agency has a unique set of needs, issues, and concerns. That said, most requests for service by individuals relate to one or more of the following areas (adapted from Epstein, 1980, 178–79):

- *Interpersonal conflict*—Disagreement between two or more people who recognize that a problem exists. Examples: marital discord, parent–teen conflict.

- *Dissatisfaction in social relations*—A lack or excess that a person perceives as being damaging to a relationship. Examples: loss of sexual desire in a marriage, spending too much time away from family.

- *Problems with formal organizations*—Tension between an individual and an organization. Examples: getting expelled from school, getting fired.

- *Difficulties in role performance*—Trouble in carrying out a particular social role. Examples: a parent failing to care for a child, a student unable to complete course work.

- *Decision problems*—Uncertainty around taking a particular course of action. Examples: deciding whether to leave a spouse, trying to choose a new career.

- *Reactive emotional distress*—Dealing with difficult feelings. Examples: coping with grief and loss, learning to manage anger.

- *Inadequate resources*—Lacking the basic necessities of life. Examples: living in poverty, living on the streets.

Depending on their particular discipline, service providers may draw from a variety of counselling models (such as cognitive behavioural therapy, feminist therapy, and reality therapy) to help individuals achieve their goals. The recent popularity of brief therapies is compatible with a rapidly changing political and economic environment that values efficiency and outcomes. For example, *solution-focused* brief therapy emphasizes goal-setting, the efficient use of time (which usually means lower costs to agencies), and measurable results or solutions.

Programs that are designed for individuals are rooted in the **social casework** approach, which evolved in the late 1800s as an outgrowth of the organized charity movement. The casework method took a step-by-step approach to counselling and was used by "friendly visitors"—volunteers who visited the poor and provided friendship and support rather than financial relief. Under the influence of the American social worker Mary Richmond, casework eventually became more scientific, requiring practitioners to conduct a thorough and systematic exploration of the individual's social environment, using formal interviewing skills and strict assessment procedures (Johnson et al., 2000).

Today, the scientific approach is used to empower people to "identify and use their own problem solving skills in order to improve their life situations" (CASW, 2000). To this end, social workers apply a generic, formal, and systematic set of procedures. This problem-solving process is commonly referred to as the **planned change process**. It consists of five phases:

1. The *intake phase* involves screening applicants who apply to social welfare programs. Client needs must be considered in light of the agency's eligibility criteria and resources.

2. In the *assessment phase*, information about the client's concerns or needs is gathered and then organized to form an overall picture of the client's situation.

3. During the *planning and contracting phase*, the worker and the client decide together what needs to be changed (perhaps a behaviour, an emotion, a thought pattern, or an environmental condition), the goals and objectives relating to this change, and the strategies that will be used to meet those goals and objectives.

4. The *intervention phase* involves putting the plan into action, monitoring its effectiveness, and modifying strategies as necessary to achieve the goal.

5. The *evaluation and termination phase* concludes the change process. During this stage, the intervention is reviewed to determine its effectiveness. The client–worker relationship is eventually terminated.

The planned change process does not always evolve in a linear fashion; as new client needs or goals arise, certain phases may be repeated or deferred.

Family Services

The needs of and challenges facing modern-day families are diverse and often complex. That said, most families approach social agencies in the wake of one or more of the following events:

- An addition to the family, be it through marriage, remarriage, birth, adoption, fostering, an adult child moving back home, or an elderly relative being taken in.

- The separation or loss of a family member through divorce, marital separation, death (including suicide), incarceration, institutionalization, or a child leaving home.

- Dysfunctional behaviour, such as addiction, delinquency, domestic violence, child abuse, or an eating disorder.

- A change in status or role, which can be the result of job loss, retirement, children growing up and leaving home, or a developmental crisis (Janzen and Harris, 1997).

Not all families seek services voluntarily. In the case of child protection matters, families can be compelled to accept services or risk having their children permanently removed from the home and placed in alternative care.

Family services in Canada can be traced back at least to the Canadian Patriotic Fund (CPF), which was established during the First World War. The CPF's goal was to "maintain the home life." With that purpose in mind, CPF workers offered support and supervision to a large number of families that were temporarily without fathers because of the war. Strong-Boag (1979, 25) comments: "It seems very probable that the good results that the CPF demonstrated in improved school attendance, better housekeeping, lessened mortality and increased family stability helped further other efforts to shore up the nuclear family as the best guarantor of social order."

In the 1920s and 1930s, **family casework** emerged as a more scientific approach to helping families. When providing services, family caseworkers set out "to reinforce and strengthen the endangered family, by drawing in the community's resources, not only in material relief, but in character and spiritual strength as well" (McGill University, 1931).

Today, a number of nonresidential programs are available to support or strengthen individual families. These family services take various approaches and are provided by practitioners from various disciplines, including social work and psychology. Below are some of the types of family services offered in Canada:

- *Family support programs* generally focus on helping families access resources and learn problem-solving skills so that the members can fulfil their respective roles (parent, student, provider, and so on).

- *Family therapy* aims to restructure family dynamics and communication patterns, or to alter dysfunctional behaviour patterns.

- *Family preservation* is intensive intervention that takes place in the family home; it aims to improve family functioning, especially in terms of caring for children.

- *Family reunification* helps separated families reunite and learn new ways of coping so that they can stay together.

- *Family group decision-making* involves the family, its closest supports, and a professional facilitator; these work together on a plan to resolve family problems (such as violence against a spouse or a child) (Conceptual Framework Subcommittee, 2002).

Exhibit 8.2 illustrates the variety of family-oriented services offered by Canadian family-support programs.

Social Group Work

Some social agencies provide group programs as a more affordable and less time-consuming alternative to individual services. Group programs can meet certain client goals—such as the attainment of appropriate social skills—more effectively than one-to-one sessions. These groups usually have three to ten members, who share common goals, needs, or lifestyles. Many social agencies offer group experiences to their clientele in the form of

- socialization groups (such as an anger management group comprising adolescent boys);

E x h i b i t   8 . 2

WHAT IS A FAMILY SUPPORT PROGRAM?

Family support programs are community-based organizations that work with children, families, and caregivers to enhance strengths, build capacities, and promote healthy development. The following are among the many resources and services available to families:

- child development
- community development
- community outreach
- counselling and mediation
- drop-in programs
- early learning and care
- educational upgrading
- employment assistance
- family literacy

- food and nutrition support
- parent and caregiver support
- parent education
- peer contact and mutual support
- play and recreation
- promotion of health and safety
- referrals to other resources
- toy lending

Source: Adapted from Canadian Association of Family Resource Programs (1999–2003). *What Is a Family Support Program?* [online]. Available: www.frp.ca/PDFDocuments/support-e.pdf [March 9, 2004].

- support groups (such as a parent support group that focuses on parent–teen interactions);
- educational skill-enhancement groups (such as a life skills group for people with severe disabilities); and/or
- therapy groups (such as those focused on issues related to schizophrenia, manic depression, or other psychiatric disorders).

Facilitators use a variety of group activities to help members achieve emotional, physical, learning, or social goals.

Social group work originated in the 1800s in settlement houses. These were large, privately run houses located in city slums. Middle-class facilitators attempted to "use the power of group associations to educate, reform, and organize neighborhoods; to preserve religious and cultural identities; and to give emotional support and assistance to newcomers both from the farm and abroad" (Zastrow, 2004, 82–83). The techniques used in early social groups were poorly defined; group leaders claimed that any attempts at definition would interfere with the spontaneous nature of the group process.

Grace Coyle, an American settlement house worker, laid the foundations for modern social group work in the 1930s. The theoretical framework she developed introduced a strategic or scientific approach to working with small groups. Her approach emphasized the development of common group goals and democratic decision-making (Tropp, 1977). Coyle (1959) identified three ways that small groups can meet members' personal and social needs:

- The face-to-face interactions inherent in small groups can increase the emotional maturity of members.

- Relationships formed within the group can be effective supplements to outside relationships.

- Group experience can help members prepare for more active participation in society: individuals can try out new behaviours and interaction skills in a relatively safe and controlled environment, and receive feedback from fellow group members before applying those skills in the "real world."

Under Coyle's approach, the group leader identifies the group's interests and then builds on those interests by providing new opportunities for learning, personal growth, and assuming greater social responsibilities.

II. CHANGE AT THE MEZZO LEVEL: ORGANIZATIONS

THE NATURE OF ORGANIZATIONAL CHANGE

Most social agencies are used to making minor changes in programs, staffing schedules, and other areas to keep their operations running smoothly. **Organizational change** goes beyond these day-to-day adjustments. In most cases, it involves a significant restructuring of one or more aspects of an agency.

Outside influences tend to trigger the need for organizational change. In recent years, much of the change taking place in social agencies has been in response to drastic restructuring at the government level, the subsequent shift of many service delivery responsibilities to private-sector agencies, and, as Michels (1996) puts it, "an unprecedented dismantling of the infrastructure for caring in our society." Substantial cuts in government funding have forced some social agencies to cancel entire programs or to seek funding from alternative sources. In some communities—especially resource-based ones—economic and labour market changes have resulted in local industry downsizing, high unemployment, and increased demands on social welfare resources. To meet increased levels of need in these communities, some social agencies have had to merge in order to share resources and the costs of service provision. The extent of organizational change in Canada's social welfare system has created a "culture of reform" (Hoffart and Cooper, 2002, 6).

LEVELS OF CHANGE

According to Brewster and colleagues (2002), organizational change must take place simultaneously at two levels: (1) at the individual level of change, staff or volunteers learn new skills, attitudes, and/or behaviours; and (2) at the systemic level of change, various aspects of an agency's operations are improved. Each type of change requires help from the other: for individuals to change, the system must provide a supportive environment; for a system to change, the staff must be willing to embrace the agency's new policies or procedures. Thus, for organizational change to succeed, there must be careful and comprehensive planning in which front-line workers, administrators, supervisors, and board members all take part.

Individual Level of Change

There is no universally accepted approach to facilitating individual change, although most experts agree that training is a key element. A variety of training kits have been developed to increase awareness, improve skills, or change behaviour in Canadian workplaces. Some of these kits target workplace discrimination. For example, the Manitoba Civil Service Commission uses the training module Building a Respectful Workplace to help civil servants understand workplace discrimination and harassment, and to suggest what they can do to develop a healthy work environment.

An effective training package will have the following elements:

- a thorough *needs assessment*, to ensure that training is relevant to the needs and expectations of the participants;

- clear *goals and objectives*, to guide the training and to articulate what the training aims to achieve;

- training *information*, which describes the rationale for training, the training schedule, the content and methods of training sessions, and the expectations of the trainers and management; and

- an *evaluation plan*, to measure the outcomes of training and to identify what is required in order to improve future training sessions (Brewster et al., 2002).

It is human nature for people to revert back to old habits even after they have learned new ways of doing things. So it is important for the training package to include a strong follow-up component—one that offers members of the agency post-training support and feedback on their change efforts.

Systemic Level of Change

Systemic change targets an agency's working environment and procedures. This type of change usually begins with a careful and comprehensive review of the agency, including its accounting practices, its policies and procedures, its communication and technological systems, and its programs and services. Various frameworks are available for conducting an agency review. The Diagnostic Framework developed by the Canadian Centre for Management Development provides a generic, step-by-step approach to organizational change:

1. Identify the need for change.

2. Describe the vision or desired outcomes for change.

3. Mobilize the commitment to change by developing the agency's capacity for change and addressing any resistance to change.

4. Plan and implement the change strategies.

5. Monitor the progress of change by measuring the effectiveness of the strategies.

6. Modify the course of change based on stakeholder feedback.

7. Sustain the changes by reinforcing new policies, procedures, or processes adopted by the agency.

This framework, which emphasizes "continuous learning and improvement, flexibility, and anticipation of new opportunities," is compatible with the changing nature of today's environment (Shepherdson, 1995, 7).

TARGETS OF ORGANIZATIONAL CHANGE

As was noted in Chapter 6, many social agencies use program evaluation to identify the strengths and weaknesses of their programs and services. Through evaluation processes, social agencies can determine the extent to which their services are reaching the people who need them, whether there are enough services to meet the demand, and whether those services treat clients in a fair and respectful manner. Evaluations may point to the need for changes in policies, procedures, and/or practices. This section considers certain service issues that often underlie organizational change in social agencies.

Access to Services

Accessibility relates to how easily people can reach and use programs and services. Many people are able to identify a need for professional help, locate the appropriate agency, use the services provided, and resolve the issue that prompted them to seek help; others, however, are unable to get the help they need. Access may become a problem:

- when funding cuts and the trend toward targeted programs results in tighter eligibility criteria for programs;

- when overly complex referral systems require client applications to pass through several agency departments in order to be approved;

- when the demand for services exceeds the supply, so that people's applications must be wait-listed;

- when front-line workers, receptionists, and other staff discourage service usage by not speaking the same language as the clientele, or by not respecting the cultural differences of their clientele;

- when service settings lack comfort, privacy, or cleanliness, subsequently deterring clients from visiting the agency;

- when agency buildings are not located close to a public transportation route;

- when services are poorly distributed across remote or rural areas, making them inaccessible to people with limited mobility or transportation; and/or

- when people (such as new immigrants) do not understand how programs work or are fearful, suspicious, or distrustful of service providers (Jaco, 2001; Canadian Mental Health Association, 2003; Canadian Council on Social Development, 2000a).

When improving access, the first step is to become aware of how people are inhibited from using services, and to understand why. Agencies may identify access problems through various means, including client satisfaction questionnaires, focus groups with members of the community, or discussion groups at interagency meetings. In some cases, governments appoint committees to study problems of service accessibility and to make recommendations for improvement. For example, Alberta's MLA Committee to Review Low-Income Programs studied how access to services for low-income individuals might be improved. After consulting with 6000 Albertans, this committee devised a plan to modify services according to what people said they needed rather than what services were currently offered (Government of Alberta, 2002).

Various technologies are available to help clients connect more easily with services. For example, it isn't always necessary for people to apply for assistance in person; much of the information an intake worker needs can be obtained by telephone or by e-mail, instead of through face-to-face interviews. Also, agencies can modify their service hours or staffing schedules; for instance, by extending their office hours into the evening, they may be able to accommodate clients who work during the day. Agency workers can also take their services—through street outreach or home-based services—to places where their clients are. Some agencies establish satellite programs in homeless shelters, welfare offices, or other locations that are visited regularly by their clients (MLA Committee to Review Low-Income Programs, 2001).

Service Availability

Availability relates to the number of programs or the coordination of programs in a community. A shortage of services occurs "when demand exceeds supply because there are too few services for the size of the population, because existing services do not have the capacity to manage client volume, or because there are gaps in the spectrum of services required" (Hoffart and Cooper, 2002, 2). Poorly coordinated programs are often the result of service fragmentation and/or service duplication. See Exhibit 8.3 for possible indicators of these conditions.

Uncoordinated programs may create unnecessary delays in service—delays that frustrate clients and may even discourage them from seeking help. Changes in traditional funding methods are making it more likely that community services will lack coordination. With funding becoming more categorical—that is, targeted to specific services or groups—programs are apt to function separately and in isolation from others in the community. Also, social agencies are competing more intensely for a shrinking pool of funds and other resources. This may reduce the willingness of agencies to work cooperatively with one another (Hoffart and Cooper, 2002; Hall et al., 2003a).

The first step toward program coordination is to develop an action plan. Hoffart and Cooper (2002) recommend a framework (see Exhibit 8.3) that can be used to "diagnose" problems and generate possible solutions. They suggest that the scope of the diagnostic process will depend on the extent of the problem and on the number of programs or organizations being looked at.

Research suggests that program coordination can be strengthened through better systems of information exchange. There are a number of ways to improve the flow of information between agencies. One possible way is to establish a centralized and up-to-date clearinghouse where workers can learn about programs and services in the community. Workers may also benefit from having an information sheet that summarizes each agency's services. Workers from various agencies who serve on community task forces can discuss common issues and concerns (Cain and Todd, 2002).

Cutbacks in funding and a subsequent loss of available services may prompt social agencies to improve interagency relations and program coordination. Ever since fiscal restraint measures were implemented in the 1990s,

Exhibit 8.3

PROBLEM DIAGNOSIS AND SOLUTIONS FRAMEWORK

DIAGNOSE THE PROBLEMS

MAP PROGRAMS BY AGENCY

Program Description
- Issue and target population addressed
- Best practices identified by research for redressing the issue, program rationale
- Detailed program description including outputs and, if possible, outcomes
- Service delivery items—hours, location, culture/language/disability access, transportation, child care, fees for service
- Referral and any other inter-service protocols

Program/Agency Resources
- Funding breakdown, including sources and detailed allocations, successful and unsuccessful applications
- Staffing—job descriptions, qualifications, salary ranges
- Volunteers, including governance
- Hard assets, including facility, technology

TRACK CLIENTS WITHIN/AMONG PROGRAMS
- Number of discrete clients, demographics, and issues
- Referrals made and followed up, resulting intakes and turnaways
- Reasons for denial of service
- Repeat clients, shared clients, and presenting issue
- Time between application, intake, service start date, service end date

IDENTIFY THE PROBLEM

Indicators of lack of services
- Clients repeatedly apply for and are denied services
- Services are denied due to absence of appropriate programs
- Clients do not access services due to service barriers (language, culture, disability, transportation, location, hours, child care, fees)
- Wait lists preclude prompt access to services
- Service providers identify unmet need(s) or gaps in services in community (issue or population)

Indicators of service duplication
- Same clients receive services for the same issue from multiple programs, simultaneously or in succession
- Service barriers (above) are minimal, but discrete clients from same/similar demographic group receive services for the same/similar issues from multiple programs, simultaneously or in succession

Indicators of service fragmentation
- Same clients receive distinct services from multiple programs for inter-related issues
- Service specialization not reflecting best practices research
- Inter-agency referrals are lacking or inappropriate
- Smaller agencies providing similar or complementary programs do not engage in joint administrative initiatives, such as joint purchases, joint training, shared IT support
- Agencies within the sector do not participate in inter-agency committees, collaborative ventures
- New or established agencies seek funding for discrete, highly specialized programs offering services that may already exist or would be more effective if nested within or linked to other programs

IDENTIFY THE SOLUTIONS

MATCH THE SOLUTIONS TO THE PROBLEMS

Lack of services alone
- Increased funding to expand existing, develop additional services
- Increased coordination at program, agency, and within-sector levels

Services duplication alone
- Limited: Increased specialization or niche marketing/re-allocation of responsibilities with increased coordination; integrations at program, agency, within-sector, or among-sector levels; merged functions at agency level; agency mergers/acquisitions
- Extensive: Agency mergers/acquisitions or, if mergers not possible, de-funding of less effective, efficient programs or agencies

Service fragmentation alone
- Limited (inappropriate referrals, funding applications for discrete programs, absence of inter-agency communication): Increased coordination and targeted integrations at program, agency, within-sector, or among-sector levels; increased funder integration
- Extensive (clients accessing multiple services; lack of joint administration among agencies): then decreased funder fragmentation, integration at program and agency levels, selective merged functions and mergers/acquisitions; increased funder integration

Service duplication and fragmentation
- Will have multiple causes and varying manifestations. Unilateral imposition of any solution will not correct the problems. Precise diagnosis will reveal the correct combinations of solutions at program, agency, within-sector, and among-sector levels.

Source: I. Hoffart and M. Cooper (2002). System Reform: Meeting the Challenges of Service Fragmentation, Duplication and Shortages in the Child and Youth Not For Profit Sector, Figure 2, p. 17. Written for the Calgary Joint Funding Review Initiative of the City of Calgary, United Way of Calgary, and Calgary Rocky View Child and Family Services. (Calgary, Alberta). [online]. Available: www.calgary.ca/docgallery/bu/community/fcss_SERVICE_REFORM_PAPER.PDF [February 12, 2004].

social agencies have shown more interest in interagency coordination and devoted more attention to forming social planning councils, advisory committees, multidisciplinary teams, and interagency management committees.

The Problem of Stigma

The North American values of self-sufficiency, independence, and resourcefulness have influenced the social meaning of "asking for help." Admitting that one needs help from "outsiders" is sometimes viewed as a sign of personal inadequacy or failure. The fear of being negatively labelled or stigmatized can discourage a person from seeking the help he or she needs.

Not all human problems—and not all programs addressing them—carry the same degree of **stigma**. Social assistance is one of the more stigmatizing social welfare programs in Canada, ranking "lowest in terms of adequacy and highest on the scale of intrusiveness and humiliation" (Torjman, 1997, 5). The stigma attached to welfare has its roots in colonial times—an era when distinctions were made between the "deserving" and "undeserving" poor, and poverty was associated with individual failure and "excessive drinking" (Guest, 2003). This perception of people on welfare persists; for example, in the 1990s both Prime Minister Jean Chrétien and Ontario Premier Mike Harris came under attack for linking welfare with beer drinking (*Calgary Herald*, 1994; Philp and Mackie, 1998).

Negative perceptions, attitudes, and treatment in the social welfare system are not restricted to people on welfare. Exhibit 8.4 illustrates the persistence of stereotypes toward people with mental illness.

Public awareness campaigns are often used to educate the public about human conditions such as mental illness and to dispel myths about people with those conditions. For example, one of the main activities of the Schizophrenia Society of Canada (1999, 184) is to educate Canadians "on the realities of [schizophrenia] in hopes of eliminating the stigma and discrimination associated with it."

Perhaps the stigmatizing effects of social welfare programs can be reduced by changing the approaches used to deliver those programs. For instance, a federally funded basic income program (described in Chapter 4) would ensure that Canadians requiring financial assistance receive it automatically through the tax system; in this way, low-income groups would be less visible and identifiable and therefore less likely to be negatively perceived (Lerner, 2003).

Stigmatization might also be reduced by changing the terms used to describe service recipients. Since the 1970s, many service providers have stopped using the term *patient*, which is associated with sickness, disease,

E x h i b i t   8 . 4
BATTLING STIGMA OF MENTAL ILLNESS

For decades, advocates have been trying to open that very stubborn door, to get society to look past the labels and misconceptions that discriminate against those suffering from mental illness.

Last week, interested parties from around the globe came to Kingston for a conference on stigma sponsored by the World Psychiatric Association.

"Stigma has been in the making more than 5,000 years. It is a beast that has to be broken," says Switzerland's Dr. Norman Sartorius, the scientific director of a major international anti-stigma program that the World Psychiatric Association has implemented in more than 20 countries since 1996.

For those struggling with mental disorders, stigma is indeed a beast. Research has shown that the prejudice and discrimination against those with mental illness can cause more problems than the disorders themselves.

[A]nalyses of newspaper content in many countries show a clear pattern of ... misrepresentation [of people with mental illness].

Stories linking mental illness with violence are given more prominence, more space, and more emphasis than stories about violence where the suspect did not have a mental disorder. The overall impression left by such coverage is that people with mental illness are dangerous and the source of a considerable amount of crime. This, despite the fact that people who do *not* have a mental disorder commit more than 95 per cent of violence in the community.

The "axe-wielding psycho" is just one of numerous commonly held myths about mental ill-health. Many still believe that "once crazy, always crazy," despite the fact that the majority of people with mental illness recover. Others cling to the misconception that people with mental disorders are lazy, unpredictable, unreliable. There's us ... and then there's *them*.

One of the troubling aspects of stigma is that large numbers of people suffering from symptoms of mental illness do not seek any assistance—despite the availability of effective treatments—because they are ashamed or concerned about what others might think. Many don't share their thoughts or feelings even with close friends due to similar fears.

And those who do seek help sometimes find their own self-image eroded by what's known as selfstigma, internalizing all of those negative perceptions.

Source: Excerpted from S. Simmie (October 17, 2003). "Battling Stigma of Mental Illness." *Toronto Star*, page 1–2 [online]. Available: www.oacas.org/whatsnew/newsstories/03/oct/17stigma.pdf [March 9, 2004]. Reprinted with permission—Torstar Syndication Services.

and dependence. They have replaced it with the terms *client, service user, customer*, or *consumer*, which suggest the strengths, rights, and capabilities of individuals.

SOCIAL WORK PRACTICE AND ORGANIZATIONAL CHANGE

Front-line workers are often the first to recognize workplace policies or practices that are demeaning, discriminating, or oppressive—in other words, that reflect sexism, racism, classism, ageism, or patriarchy. According to the CASW Code of Ethics, social workers are professionally bound to confront conditions that are not in the best interests of their clients. The code clearly states that a social worker's primary responsibility is to the service user, not the social agency. In the event of a conflict between the needs of clients and those of employers, a social worker's "professional obligations outweigh any obligations to a workplace" (CASW, 1994b, 22).

Structural social work is one among many approaches that social workers can take to change the organizations that employ them. A proponent of the structural model, Robert Mullaly (1997), contends that to change a social agency from within, social workers must radicalize and democratize the agency. *Radicalizing* an agency involves confronting agency policies and procedures (such as intrusive intake procedures) that negatively affect clients, and working to ensure that clients can access the full range of available services. *Democratizing* the agency involves taking steps to make the organization less bureaucratic and hierarchical and more democratic and inclusive. This process may include helping clients become more involved in the agency's decision-making process (for example, by encouraging them to serve on the board of directors); replacing boss–subordinate relationships with relationships that are more equal (perhaps by *consulting with* instead of *reporting to* supervisors); and sharing staff responsibilities, resources, and information.

III. CHANGE AT THE MACRO LEVEL: COMMUNITY ORGANIZATION

WHAT IS COMMUNITY ORGANIZATION?

A pioneer in the study of community change, Murray G. Ross (1967, 40), defines **community organization** as a process by which a community identifies its needs or objectives, orders (or ranks) these needs or objectives, develops the confidence and will to work at these needs or objectives, finds the resources (internal and/or external) to deal with these needs or objectives, takes action in respect to them, and in so doing extends and develops cooperative and collaborative attitudes and practices in the community.

Change at the community level may involve modifying conditions in neighbourhoods, social or political institutions, or other macro systems. Community organization is especially concerned with enhancing social functioning, reducing social problems, and meeting community needs through social or economic policies (Barker, 1991).

According to the classic model of community organization developed by Jack Rothman (1979), community organization involves three main approaches: community (or locality) development, social planning, and social action. These three approaches to community organization are compared in Exhibit 8.5 and explored briefly below.

COMMUNITY DEVELOPMENT

Community development is the process of helping citizens resolve local problems that directly affect them. The aim of community development is not to challenge or reform established social structures, but rather to work with existing structures to increase the community's problem-solving capacity. Building a community's capacity starts with building **human capacity**—that is, "increasing the skills, knowledge, and abilities of residents" (Halseth and Booth, 1998). By providing high-quality training and skills development programs, communities can empower citizens to access the resources, opportunities, and information they need.

Community development originated in settlement houses such as the one Sarah Libby Carson opened in Toronto in 1899. These houses were established with the "aim of bridging the gulf between rich and poor" (Bruce, 1966, 143). Local residents were given an opportunity to learn from their educated middle-class "peers" about social problems and how to resolve them. During the 1950s and 1960s, when Canada's welfare state was expanding, governments took over many community development responsibilities, including decision-making about what communities needed and how those needs might be met. Many communities resisted the bureaucratic, "top-down" approach used by governments, and responded by impeding community improvement

Exhibit 8.5
THREE MODELS OF COMMUNITY ORGANIZATION

CHARACTERISTIC	COMMUNITY DEVELOPMENT MODEL	SOCIAL PLANNING MODEL	SOCIAL ACTION MODEL
1. Goals	Self-help; improving community living; emphasis on process goals	Using problem-solving approach to resolve community problems; emphasis on task goals	Shifting of power relationships and resources to an oppressed group; basic institutional change; emphasis on task and process goals
2. Assumptions concerning community	Everyone wants community living to improve and is willing to contribute to the improvement	Social problems in the community can be resolved through the efforts of planning experts	The community has a power structure and one or more oppressed groups; social injustice is a major problem
3. Basic change strategy	Broad cross-section of people involved in identifying and solving their problems	Experts using fact-gathering and the problem-solving approach	Members of oppressed groups organize to take action against the power structure, which is the enemy
4. Characteristic change tactics and techniques	Consensus: communication among community groups and interests; group discussion	Consensus or conflict	Conflict or contest: confrontation, direct action, negotiation
5. Practitioner roles	Catalyst; facilitator; coordinator; teacher of problem-solving skills	Expert planner; fact gatherer; analyst; program developer and implementer	Activist; advocate; agitator; broker; negotiator; partisan
6. Views about power structure	Members of power structure as collaborators in a common venture	Power structure as employers and sponsors	Power structure as external target of action, oppressors to be coerced or overturned
7. Views about client population	Citizens	Consumers	Victims
8. Views about client role	Participants in a problem-solving process	Consumers or recipients	Employers, constituents

Source: From *Introduction to Social Work and Social Welfare, Empowering People* (with InfoTrac) 8th edition by C. Zastrow. © 2004. Reprinted with permission of Wadsworth, a division of Thomson Learning: www.thomsonrights.com. Fax 800-730-2215.

in some areas. As voluntary-sector agencies became more prominent, so too did a "bottom-up," **grassroots approach** to community development. A grassroots approach relies on citizen participation to drive community development: citizens are encouraged to identify and articulate their goals, design their own methods of change, and pool their resources in the problem-solving process (Halseth and Booth, 1998).

It is not uncommon for top-down and bottom-up approaches to converge. This is often the case in isolated communities, which may be the target of both government intervention and grassroot efforts. For example, the federally sponsored Canadian Rural Partnership (CRP) encourages the formation of networks among community groups, the private sector, and all levels of government. The CRP also supports grassroots initiatives that aim to "enhance the quality of life in rural communities and better equip the communities to compete in a global economy" (Government of Canada, 2002c). Community projects—such as creating opportunities for rural youth, and improving access to government services in remote areas—are the result of joint efforts between community and government.

One form of community development is a revitalization strategy known as **community economic development** (CED). This is "a process by which communities can initiate and generate their own solutions to their common economic problems and thereby build long-term community capacity" (Community Economic Development Centre, 1995). The CED approach was a response to the welfare state's failure to ensure full employment, stabilize and stimulate the economy, and provide adequate social and income support for community members (Boothroyd and Davis, 1991). CED strategies combine economic activities (including local job creation); community cooperation and participation (including local ideas and networking); and social structures (including social welfare, health, and education) to create positive economic and social change in communities (Ameyaw and Simpson, 1994).

SOCIAL PLANNING

Social planning is committed to social development in a variety of areas, including health, safety, economic security, and education, and involves urban renewal by planning new towns, neighbourhoods, or housing projects. A key objective of these initiatives is to improve the general functioning of residents by meeting a wide range of needs. The plan for a new apartment block for seniors, for instance, may include special safety and security options as well as facilities for recreation and social events.

Social planning usually begins with the identification and assessment of community needs. To identify needs, social planners collect facts, statistics, and other objective data as well as the opinions of community members.

Once community needs have been determined, planners set objectives for programs, services, or facilities. After the planning and implementation process, social planners formally evaluate the results of their efforts.

In Canada, social planning originated in the late 1800s with the organized charity movement and subsequent establishment of Charity Organization Societies. These societies set out to coordinate and integrate services so that people could access social services more easily. The social planning movement gained momentum during the 1950s, 1960s, and early 1970s in response to continued economic growth and the rapid expansion of social programs. As a result of the increased demand for planning at several levels, social planning councils emerged to identify social planning issues, needs, and resources; conduct research on social issues; help organizations set up new services; and perform other community planning activities (Social Planning Council of Metropolitan Toronto, 1997; Ginsler, 1988).

In recent years, social planning councils have focused many of their efforts on increasing **social capital**. Whereas human capital refers to the strength of human resources, "social capital refers to social connections and the associated norms and trust that enable community members to act together more effectively to pursue shared objectives" (Torjman, 1998, 9). According to Michael Woolcock (2001), there are three main sources of social capital:

- *bonds* such as close relationships with family, friends, and neighbours;
- *bridges* between acquaintances, business associates, or co-workers; and
- *linkages* created by formal institutions (such as governments) through social policy.

Various community-based initiatives illustrate the role that social planning can play in forming social capital. For example, Halton's Food for Thought program *bridges* all of the separate school-breakfast programs for poor children to a regionally coordinated school-breakfast program that is open to all children; the program also nurtures an important *linkage* with its funder, the Halton Board of Education (Clutterbuck, 2001).

SOCIAL ACTION

Social action refers to collective and coordinated efforts that aim to solve a social problem, correct an injustice, or meet a human need. This approach usually involves efforts to influence those with power (such as politicians) to change certain policies, laws, or procedures, and/or to reform institutions that are considered inadequate. Social activists often act on behalf of people who are perceived as disadvantaged or oppressed. Unlike community development, social action does not require a consensus for change within the community. Indeed, social action may take place even when a majority of the community denies that a problem exists.

While the organized charity movement focused on helping people adjust to existing social conditions and services, reformists from the settlement houses fought for changes in social institutions. Settlement houses were located in the poorest sections of town, which meant that settlement workers quickly became aware of the conditions and problems caused by poverty. These workers rejected the prevailing *laissez-faire* philosophy, and strove to correct social inequities and injustices for disadvantaged groups (Burghardt, 1987). Social movements that arose at the turn of the twentieth century, and later during the 1960s and 1970s, were headed by social activists, and had a considerable impact on Canadian social policies and programs for children, women, labourers, Aboriginal peoples, persons with disabilities, gay men and lesbians, and low-income groups.

Local events that affect a large segment of the population can become catalysts for social action. For instance, during the Winnipeg General Strike of 1919, almost 30 000 workers went on strike. This protest, which called attention to poor wages, deplorable working conditions, and other labour-related problems, sparked various forms of social action. In response to the unrest in Winnipeg, a group of citizens formed the Community Welfare Council—one of Canada's first social action groups devoted to community awareness on social issues. Through carefully planned strategies, the council pressured government into improving many labour-related policies (Social Planning Council of Winnipeg, 2004).

Social activists rely on the collective efforts of "average" citizens to achieve their goals. This grassroots approach is obvious when members of a community come together because of a common concern, and go on to establish an organization or group committed to addressing that concern (Burghardt, 1987; Connaway and Gentry, 1988). Mothers Against Drunk Driving (MADD), for example, was founded by mothers whose children had been killed by impaired drivers.

Social activists use a variety of strategies to promote their cause, gain support, and bring about change. These include *collaboration* strategies (such as lobbying), *campaign* strategies (such as petitions), and *contest* strategies (such as demonstrations).

Social action organizations tend to be independent, community-based operations that are not affiliated with governments. Their members advocate on their own or another group's behalf. An example of such an organization is the National Anti-Poverty Organization (NAPO). Since 1971, members of NAPO—many of whom have had personal experience with poverty—have worked to eliminate poverty in Canada, to reduce social inequality, and to empower local groups. More specifically, NAPO members campaign for changes to laws, policies, and programs that discriminate against the poor, and serve as watchdogs for inequities in the social welfare system. Acting in an advocacy role, NAPO represents low-income groups on a wide range of national issues related to poverty (National Anti-Poverty Organization, 2004).

COMMUNITY SOCIAL WORK

By virtue of their training and knowledge base, social workers can make good community organizers (CASW, 1998). For example, they tend to have good listening and communication skills, understand how systems work, and be comfortable working with both individuals and groups. Social workers who engage in **community practice** stimulate and assist "the local community to evaluate, plan, and coordinate its efforts to provide for the community's health, welfare, and recreation needs" (Zastrow, 2004, 96). Community practice often involves organizing or mobilizing citizens around certain issues, problems, or unmet needs; developing strategies for change; and providing relevant information to community groups.

Depending on the type of community organization being undertaken, social workers fulfil various roles:

- *Community development.* As *brokers*, social workers help individuals and groups connect with needed programs and services in the community. Since a main focus of community development is problem-solving, social workers may also act as *enablers* by teaching community members effective problem-solving skills.

- *Social planning.* In a social-planning capacity, social workers may be employed to develop action plans, collect and analyze data on local issues and concerns, and share research findings with social-planning councils, government departments, and others. Social workers may also be instrumental in connecting with, generating interest among, and motivating local groups to participate in the planning process.

- *Social action.* Until the professionalization of social work in the early twentieth century, all social workers were social activists: "Whether through visits to the poor and homeless, demonstrations in the streets, or surveys to expose shocking conditions, the first social workers were crusaders whose full-time occupation was social action" (Thursz, 1977, 1274). Today's social workers may assume the role of *advocate* (speaks or acts on behalf of a client to achieve certain goals); *agitator* (stirs up or excites others about a specific cause); or *negotiator* (engages two or more opposing parties in a discussion to reach a mutual agreement) (Zastrow, 2004).

The extent of social action a social worker engages in may be restricted by rules imposed by the Canada Revenue Agency (CRA). Under the CRA's "10 Percent Rule," registered charities must not use more than 10 percent of their budgets for "political activity" (which may include social action or advocacy by staff) (IMPACS, 2002). This policy aims to prevent organizations that benefit from public funds from opposing government policies. At the same time, the 10 Percent Rule may hinder social workers who are employed by registered charities from properly representing their clients.

SUMMARY

■ Introduction

The main goal of all social welfare programs is to change conditions that threaten personal or social functioning. A variety of interventions are used to create change at the micro, mezzo, and macro levels. These interventions have become more scientific over the years.

■ Change at the Micro Level: Client Services

Micro-level change is directed at individuals, families, and small groups. Social casework uses the planned change process and a variety of techniques to help individuals address needs, issues, and concerns. Family therapists and family service workers take different approaches to helping families. Social group work is often used to help people with similar goals and concerns work toward better social functioning.

■ Change at the Mezzo Level: Organizations

Organizational change is triggered by outside influences and involves restructuring certain aspects of an organization at the individual and systemic levels. Targets of change in social agencies may be problems related to program access, availability, or stigma. Social workers use various models, including the structural model, to change organizations from within.

■ Change at the Macro Level: Community Organization

There are three basic approaches to community organization. All three aim to bring about change at the macro level: (1) *community development* is the process of helping citizens work with established social structures to resolve the problems that affect them; (2) *social planning* involves the design, development, and coordination of services in a community; and (3) *social action* refers to collective efforts that aim to correct injustices or meet human needs.

▼ KEY TERMS

For definitions of the key terms, consult the Glossary on page 364 at the end of the book.

intervention p. 171

micro-level change p. 172

mezzo-level change p. 172

macro-level change p. 172

social casework p. 175

planned change process
  p. 175

family casework p. 177

social group work p. 178

organizational change
  p. 179

accessibility p. 181

availability p. 183

stigma p. 185

structural social work
  p. 187

community organization
  p. 187

community development
  p. 188

human capacity p. 188

grassroots approach p. 190

community economic
  development p. 190

social planning p. 190

social capital p. 191

social action p. 191

community practice p. 193

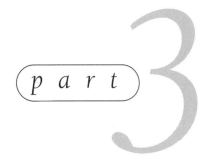

part 3

MEETING THE NEEDS OF CANADIANS THROUGH PROGRAMS AND SERVICES

chapter

Economic Security and the Basic Necessities

O b j e c t i v e s

I. To look at how Canadians are faring economically, and to explore the specific problems of income inequality, unemployment, and poverty.

II. To review governments' shift from a passive to an active approach in the provision of Employment Insurance, social assistance, and child benefits.

III. To consider the growing problems of hunger, the shortage of affordable housing, and homelessness, and some of the Canadian initiatives that are addressing these problems.

IV. To explore social work practice with low-income and marginalized groups.

INTRODUCTION

Economic security is an important component of personal well-being and is therefore a concern of the social welfare system. The Canadian Council on Social Development (2003d, 1) defines **economic security** as "an assured and stable standard of living that provides individuals and families with the level of resources necessary to participate economically, politically, socially, culturally, and with dignity in their communities." Western nations generally agree that economic security is derived from four primary sources:

- *market income,* that is, personal earnings from a job or investments;

- *nonmarket services or benefits* derived from within the family;

- *government-sponsored programs and services,* for which citizens do not pay full market price; and

- *community services and supports*, which are provided through non-profit or volunteer efforts (Jenson, 2003b).

Social welfare policies and programs aim to strengthen each of these sources to some degree. For example, employment services can help Canadians find work and thereby increase their market income; the care of children by parents is a nonmarket service that is bolstered by parent support programs; many mental health services are government-sponsored and are available to all Canadians at little or no cost; and a variety of family services are provided on a nonprofit basis by voluntary organizations.

The average market income of Canadians has been rising since the late 1990s; personal income taxes have fallen, and disposable income per capita has increased at an average annual rate of 2 percent (Treasury Board of Canada Secretariat, 2003c). Despite this economic trend, a significant number of Canadians are unable to earn a living wage or make ends meet. Also, more and more families are finding themselves burdened with heavy debt and on the brink of bankruptcy. Especially disturbing is that Canada's recent economic turnaround has done little to reduce unemployment and poverty (Tsoukalas and MacKenzie, 2003).

With Canadian governments entering an era of budget surpluses, some policy-makers are suggesting it is time to reinvest in social welfare programs that will enhance economic security. Others believe that economic security can be sustained only by investing in business expansion and job creation. This chapter takes a closer look at economic security in Canada and at some of the associated issues, challenges, and approaches.

I. JOBS AND INCOME: HOW ARE CANADIANS FARING?

INCOME INEQUALITY

In Canada, just as in many other capitalist countries, the rich get richer while the poor stay poor: the richest 10 percent of Canadian families receive 28 percent of all available income, whereas the poorest 10 percent receive only 2 percent of all income. In other words, the richest families are earning fourteen times more than the poorest families (Statistics Canada, 2003d). The term **income inequality** refers to the income gap between rich and poor Canadians. Some analysts attribute this gap to the following: government fiscal restraint measures that were introduced in the 1990s; cuts in federal transfers to low-income families; reductions in Employment Insurance and social assistance benefits; persistently low wages in part-time and nonstandard jobs; and generally stagnant wages (Jackson, 2003a).

People need to earn enough money to purchase the basic necessities of life. An adequate income also provides people with "a stable base from which they can participate in their community" (Arundel, 2003, 2). Generally speaking, community participation is a function of having enough money for transportation, recreation, and other activities that connect people and facilitate meaningful experiences. In countries where wealth is poorly distributed, there tends to be a disconnect between the rich and the poor; this weakens social cohesion and marginalizes lower-income groups (Raphael, 2003). Moreover, low incomes tend to segregate the poor into cheaper neighbourhoods or "ghettos" (Arundel, 2003).

A number of reports indicate that many Canadians are slipping into, and getting stuck in, low-income brackets. These people are at risk of being marginalized from the rest of society. The following groups are most likely to be found in the lowest income bracket: recent immigrants, visible minorities, seniors, people with disabilities, lone-parent families, and Aboriginal peoples. Large cities are more likely than rural areas to have wide income gaps; that said, the largest gap in Canada is in Nunavut, where the richest 10 percent of families earn twenty-five times more than the poorest 10 percent (Arundel, 2003; Statistics Canada, 2003e).

UNEMPLOYMENT

Unemployment is a persistent social problem in Canada. Thousands of new jobs are created each year, but many are also lost. In 2000, the unemployment rate dropped to 6.8 percent, its lowest level in nearly twenty-five years (Government of Canada, 2000b); in more recent years, however, the rate has been well over 7 percent (Statistics Canada, 2004f). Unemployment rates are especially high among Aboriginal peoples, recent immigrants, young adults, and people with disabilities. Some parts of the country, such as the Atlantic provinces, have historically higher unemployment rates.

Unemployment has many human costs. Economically, it represents a loss of revenue for Canadian governments and their ability to fund important social programs. Unemployment is also associated with poor health, family breakdown, depression, suicide, crime, and other social problems. The high value our society places on having a job may contribute to the difficulties people experience when they are not working. According to the Canadian Public Health Association (1996), having a job can provide a number of personal benefits such as "a sense of regularity, purpose and identity; social status and social connectedness ('belonging'); and opportunities for personal development and growth"; it follows that many people experience the loss of a job as a significant personal loss.

POVERTY IN CANADA

Canadians cannot agree on a definition of **poverty**. Michaud and colleagues (2004, 6) explain

> At one pole are those who see poverty as a subsistence standard of living with an income that is not sufficient to purchase the bare necessities. At the other pole are those who see poverty as being unable to fully participate in the life of the community ... This is often referred to as a social inclusion definition.

All of this means that Canada does not have an "official" method of measuring poverty. However, government departments and private institutions in this country have developed their own tools for measuring various levels of *deprivation*. Statistics Canada, for example, bases many of its poverty reports on the following measurements:

- The *Low-Income Cut-Offs* (LICOs). These cut-offs represent the income level below which a family spends a disproportionate amount of its income on food, shelter, and other basics (some groups refer to these cut-offs collectively as "the poverty line").

- The *Survey of Labour and Income Dynamics* and the *Survey of Consumer Finances*. These are used to calculate the number of low-income families in Canada.

- The *Low-Income Measure* (LIM). This estimates the proportion of a selected geographic area that has substantially less income than the rest of the area.

- The *Market Basket Measure* (MBM). This estimates the costs of basic necessities such as food, shelter, and transportation, and then compares those costs to a family's disposable income (Michaud et al., 2004).

By any measurement, many Canadians are poor. Furthermore, poverty in Canada is on the rise. In 1999, 16.2 percent of Canadians were poor, compared to 13.6 percent in 1989 (National Council of Welfare, 2002a). Some groups are at higher risk of poverty than others. In 2000, Statistics Canada used LIMs to identify the three poorest groups living in metropolitan areas:

- lone-parent families (46.6 percent were poor, compared to 15.1 percent of other family types);
- Aboriginal peoples (41.6 percent were living in poverty); and
- recent immigrants (35 percent were poor) (Heisz and McLeod, 2004).

Other groups that are likely to be living in poverty are visible minorities and people with disabilities (Arundel, 2003).

Child poverty is of particular concern. Despite an improved economy and government investments in child benefits, child poverty rates remain high: in 2001, 15.6 percent of Canadian children (one out of six) were poor—a percentage that has held steady for thirty years. At the provincial level, Manitoba has the highest rate of child poverty in Canada—over 22 percent (Campaign 2000, 2003).

A disturbing trend in Canada is that more middle-class individuals and families are finding it difficult to make ends meet. Wiley Norvell (2003) writes that "the fastest growing sectors of our economy are non-unionized with low wages and little security." This is especially true in large cities like Toronto, where as a result of high living costs and intense competition for jobs, many white-collar, middle-class workers have been pushed into poverty.

Many working Canadians are **underemployed**—that is, they can find only part-time or nonstandard jobs, or they have work that does not pay enough to lift them out of poverty. One Canadian study found that of 1.7 million low-paid workers in 1996, fewer than half had been able to rise out of poverty by 2001 (Statistics Canada, 2004g). Since 1976, increases in minimum wages (which are set by the provinces) have not kept up with the rising cost of living. This is making it difficult for people working full-time at minimum wage to support themselves and their families (National Council of Welfare, 2001; 2004). People in this group are sometimes referred to as the *working poor*. Saunders (2003) adds that people in this situation are also "vulnerable workers"—in other words, they are active participants in the labour market, but because they have low-paying jobs, their well-being is always at risk. This situation may apply especially to "the working homeless." A study in Calgary found that about half of the people in shelters were employed at minimum wage but could not afford their own housing (Arundel, 2003).

As a result of the National Longitudinal Survey of Children and Youth (NLSCY), the National Population Health Survey, the UN's Human Development Index, and other research tools, we have a better understanding of the effects of poverty. Compared to people in middle- and upper-class families, poor people tend to have more health and developmental problems (a result of poor nutrition, inadequate housing, unsafe neighbourhoods, and limited opportunities). In general, the working-age poor encounter more barriers when trying to enter, re-enter, or stay in the workforce; poor working-age families have limited access to adequate childcare (National Council of Welfare, 2001; Canadian Council on Social Development, 2002c; Urban Poverty Consortium of Waterloo Region, 2000).

Parents who are poor often suffer from psychological problems, such as stress and depression. Jones and colleagues (2002, 3) developed a Family Stress Model (see Exhibit 9.1) to illustrate how chronic poverty, overall family stress (including marital discord), poor parenting, and reduced levels of well-being for children are all linked. Poor parenting practices may include "insufficient surveillance, lack of control over the child's behaviour, lack of warmth and support, inconsistency, and displays of aggression or hostility by parents or older siblings."

II. POLICIES AND PROGRAMS: TAKING AN ACTIVE APPROACH

In the past, Canadian governments have tackled the problems of inadequate income by expanding the economy, creating jobs, and raising wages (Picot et. al, 2003). Governments have also introduced a wide range of policies and programs to help able-bodied working-age citizens find and keep jobs. These actions reflect governments' acceptance that the market cannot meet the basic needs of all citizens, and that some people may need additional help to become self-sufficient. Canadian governments also tend to agree "that increasing labour force participation will not *solve* the problem of low incomes. Cash and other [government] transfers are needed if large numbers of individuals and families are not to live in poverty" (Jenson, 2003b, vi). Thus, Canadian governments have from time to time assumed the roles of "economic stabilizer" and "interventionist" and provided short-term assistance to those who need it (Reichwein, 2002, 8).

In the years when Canada's welfare state was expanding, Keynesian economics encouraged governments to develop extensive income security systems that gave "unconditional" cash to nonworking adults. This system was essentially passive in that it provided financial benefits while leaving it up to able-bodied recipients to find their way into—or back into—the workforce. Since the mid-1980s, industrialized countries have been moving away from passive income security programs toward active ones. Canadian governments generally view **passive programs** as encouraging dependency on income security programs; they see **active programs** as a way to foster self-sufficiency (Melchers,

Exhibit 9.1
FAMILY STRESS MODEL

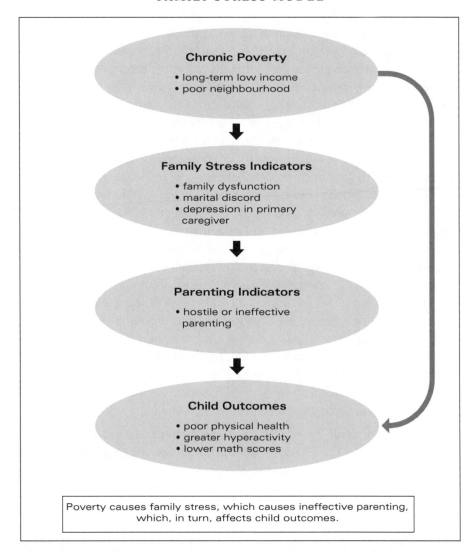

Chronic Poverty
- long-term low income
- poor neighbourhood

Family Stress Indicators
- family dysfunction
- marital discord
- depression in primary caregiver

Parenting Indicators
- hostile or ineffective parenting

Child Outcomes
- poor physical health
- greater hyperactivity
- lower math scores

Poverty causes family stress, which causes ineffective parenting, which, in turn, affects child outcomes.

Source: Author adapted graphic from C. Jones, L. Clark, J. Grusec, R. Hart, G. Plickert, and L. Tepperman, (2002 March). *Poverty, Social Capital, Parenting and Child Outcomes in Canada: Final Report.* Applied Research Branch: Strategic Policy: Human Resources Development Canada, p. 4. Cat. No.: RH63-1/557-01-03E-IN [online]. Available: http://www11.sdc.gc.ca/en/cs/sp/arb/publications/research/2002-002357/SP-557-01-03.pdf [May 13 2004]. Reproduced with the permission of the Minister of Public Works and Government Services Canada, 2004.

1999). Recent changes have made Employment Insurance, social assistance, and child benefit programs more active; as a result, beneficiaries now have more incentives to move off income security systems and into the workforce.

EMPLOYMENT INSURANCE AND SERVICES

In 1996, the Unemployment Insurance Act was replaced by the Employment Insurance (EI) Act. (The name change was intended to emphasize employment and de-emphasize unemployment.) The new EI Act tightened the criteria for determining eligibility; it also reduced the number of weeks that workers could draw benefits. All of this led to a sharp drop in the proportion of unemployed people eligible for benefits: in 2002, only 38 percent of Canadian workers were eligible, compared to 57 percent in 1993 (Bailey, 2004b). Women have been especially hard hit by this particular reform. In 2004, only 33 percent of women (compared to 44 percent of men) were eligible for EI, mainly because women are concentrated in part-time or nonstandard jobs that are not covered by benefits (Fraser, 2003).

The dramatic decline in the number of people eligible for EI has saved the federal government a huge amount of money. By early 2004, the EI account had a surplus of almost $44 billion (Bailey, 2004b). This surplus is the result of more working Canadians making contributions to the EI fund and fewer contributors being eligible for benefits once they become unemployed. The federal government manages the EI surplus and is using some of the windfall to fund a wider range of social benefits for employed Canadians. These benefits in a sense "reward" people for working and include paid leave for compassionate family care, sickness, and maternity/paternity, and early childhood development services through the parental benefits program.

The active nature of EI is reflected in the variety of employment programs that have been set up to help Canadians enter or re-enter the workforce. Examples of these programs include the following:

- Under federal-provincial-territorial Labour Market Development Agreements, the regional governments are helping people reduce their dependency on EI through job creation partnerships, targeted wage subsidies, skills development, and self-employment opportunities.

- Employment assistance programs are available across Canada to provide job search workshops, employment counselling, and/or work experience opportunities to people who want to improve their job prospects.

- Some federal initiatives—such as the Opportunities Fund for Persons with Disabilities, the Aboriginal Human Resources Development Strategy Renewal, and the Youth Employment Strategy—are tailoring employment assistance services to groups that face specific barriers in the labour market (Nicholson, 2001; HRDC, 2004b).

Most people who are receiving EI benefits, training allowances, or other government-sponsored support must demonstrate that they are participating actively in strategies to improve their employment prospects. Those who cannot provide this evidence risk having their benefits cut off.

SUPPORT FOR LOW-INCOME GROUPS

Social Assistance

Social assistance (or "welfare") is considered the income program of last resort because it is reserved for people who have exhausted all other avenues of support and who can prove they are in need. Each province and territory is responsible for developing its own social assistance system, including legislation and procedures for determining welfare eligibility, benefit rates, appeal procedures, and monitoring systems. This means there are thirteen different social assistance programs across Canada, with names such as Ontario Works, BC Employment and Assistance, and Nova Scotia's Employment Support and Income Assistance Program (National Council of Welfare, 2003b).

By capping CAP in 1991, and introducing the CHST in 1996, the federal government was able to reduce its cash transfers to the provinces and territories by several billion dollars. These federal actions compelled many regional governments to take a critical look at the rising costs of their social assistance programs. Other forces besides these, including the ones listed below, also placed pressure on regional governments to at least consider restructuring their welfare systems:

- Canadians were demanding less government spending in general, and disapproved of welfare benefits going to able-bodied employable people.

- Research showed that training opportunities offered to those on welfare did little to move people (especially men and youth) into the workforce.

- Reports from social workers drew attention to the negative effects—such as problems with health and in school—that welfare dependency had on children. There was also the concern that children growing up on welfare would become adults dependent on welfare.

- Welfare systems were criticized for providing disincentives to work. Since welfare recipients lost several welfare-related benefits and services once they found work, they had little incentive to accept part-time or low-paying work (HRDC, 2000).

Most jurisdictions reformed their welfare systems by making substantial cuts to benefit rates. Alberta was the first province to drastically lower its welfare rates, but it was Ontario's actions that were truly revolutionary. Shortly after becoming premier, Mike Harris introduced his Common Sense Revolution, a scheme that cut welfare rates by 21.6 percent in 1995 for all beneficiaries except seniors and people with disabilities (National Council of Welfare, 1997). By 2003, the rates in almost every other province and territory had dropped so sharply that the National Council of Welfare (2003b, 25, 60) described them as "grossly inadequate," as "punitive and cruel," and as a disgrace "in a country often regarded as the best place [to] live in the world." Exhibit 9.2 shows how welfare incomes for four groups compare with low-income cut-offs in each province.

In most Canadian jurisdictions, the concept of welfare has been transformed into welfare-to-work (or "workfare"). Welfare-to-work programs are not a new phenomenon in Canada; compulsory work programs—in which able-bodied men worked in exchange for public relief—were common during the Great Depression. Today's welfare-to-work programs bear little resemblance to the Depression-era work camps; rather they support welfare recipients in the transition to work and self-sufficiency by directing them to volunteer placements in nonprofit organizations, or to subsidized positions in business settings. Also, provincial and territorial governments are using workfare as a strategy for deterring able-bodied people from drawing welfare, for helping chronically unemployed people re-enter the workforce, and for reducing the number of people eligible for welfare (Herd, 2002).

Action plans or contracts between welfare recipients and the government play a central role in welfare-to-work programs. These agreements specify the training program, job search plan, or other work-related activity in which the welfare recipient agrees to participate. A welfare recipient who refuses to follow through on an action plan may be penalized. The penalties vary across jurisdictions; however, most of them involve a cut in welfare benefits or termination from welfare (HRDC, 1999a).

Most workfare programs have built-in incentives to encourage welfare recipients to make the transition to paid employment. In some jurisdictions, welfare benefits are gradually reduced as earnings increase; also, in situations where wages are lower than the welfare rate, participants may receive a combination of wages and a top-up of welfare benefits. One of the most generous incentive programs is in Quebec, where beginning in 2005, welfare recipients will receive a $150-a-month bonus for participating in volunteer work or job training. The province's incentive plan is part of its larger National Strategy to Combat Poverty (Seguin, 2004).

Exhibit 9.2

WELFARE INCOMES AND POVERTY LINES 2002

Note: The poverty lines shown above are based on Statistics Canada 2002 low-income cut-offs (1992 base) for the largest city in each province.

Source: Author generated charts from numbers found in citation: Adapted from National Council of Welfare. (Spring 2003). *Welfare Incomes 2002.* Volume #119, Table 2.1: Adequacy of 2002 Benefits, pp. 27–28. Ottawa: National Council of Welfare [online]. Available: http://www. ncwcnbes.net/htmdocument/reportwelfinc02/WelfareIncomes.pdf [May 14 2004]. Reproduced with the permission of the Minister of Public Works and Government Services Canada, 2004.

There is much debate in Canada over the pros and cons of welfare-to-work programs. Some people support these programs, arguing that passive welfare programs have destroyed the incentive to work and that people should take any job, regardless of pay or conditions (Canadian Council on Social Development, 1999). Proponents of workfare point to the falling number of welfare recipients as a sign that welfare-to-work programs are succeeding. The Government of Ontario, for example, credits its welfare-to-work programs for moving 472 090 people off welfare between 1995 and 2002 (Ontario Ministry of Community and Social Services, 2000).

Opponents of workfare point out that these programs typically offer jobs with poor pay and few if any benefits. Furthermore, many jobs are part-time or nonstandard rather than full-time, and they give workers little opportunity to learn advanced skills. Some question whether these types of jobs can sustain workers, let alone their dependants. The federally funded National Welfare to Work Study concluded that workfare programs have done little more than move people off welfare and into the growing ranks of the working poor, and that in so doing they have drawn a discrete veil over the problem of poverty in Canada (HRDC, 2000).

A study by Human Resources Development Canada (HRDC) (1999a) found that in some parts of the country, workfare had moved well-trained, experienced people off welfare and back to work; however, many people "with poor education, no job experience, and multiple personal and family barriers" were left behind on welfare. Reports also indicate that large numbers of people return to welfare after completing a welfare-to-work program. In their study of welfare-leavers across Canada, Frenette and Picot (2003) found that within a year of getting off welfare, more than one-third had returned; within five years, one-half had returned.

In its assessment of welfare-to-work programs, HRDC (1999a) recommended that strategies be developed to help welfare-to-work participants find and keep long-term jobs; this would reduce the number of people returning to welfare. HRDC also stressed the following needs: to address the income gap between high- and low-paying jobs; to help people access training; and to provide additional support to lone parents and to people with physical or psychological limitations who are trying to move into the labour market.

Child Benefits

According to Battle and Mendelson (1997,7), child benefits—in the form of cash or tax breaks for families with children—are a way for governments "to acknowledge the contribution that all parents make to society in raising future citizens, workers, and taxpayers". These benefits also reflect the general belief that families with children face heavier financial burdens than single or childless couples with similar incomes. A number of child benefit schemes have been introduced, revised, and scrapped over the years. The current scheme is the National Child Benefit (NCB), introduced in 1998. All provinces and territories participate in the NCB except Quebec, which has chosen to develop its own family and child support programs (Government of Canada, 2004i).

At the federal level, the NCB provides support to Canadian families through two main streams:

- *Canada Child Tax Benefit* (CCTB). This is an income-tested monthly payment available to low- and middle-income families with children under eighteen; about 82 percent of Canadian families with children receive this benefit.

- *National Child Benefit Supplement.* This is used to top up the monthly CCTB payments for Canada's lowest-income families with children; about 40 percent of Canadian families with children receive the supplement (Government of Canada, 2004d).

Exhibit 9.3 illustrates the linkages and overlaps between the NCB provincial, territorial, and Aboriginal components.

The primary goals of the NCB are "to help prevent and reduce the depth of child poverty, support parents as they move into the labour market and reduce overlap and duplication of government programs" (Government of Canada, 2004i). The NCB also aims to lower the **welfare wall** for families on social assistance. This "wall" refers to factors that make staying on welfare more financially attractive than employment. Many families find that when they leave welfare for a job (especially a part-time, nonstandard, or low-paying job), they lose access to many subsidized welfare services. At the same time, employment brings work-related expenses such as transportation, work clothes, and childcare, and workers must pay income taxes and contribute to Canada Pension Plan and EI. Thus, some families are financially worse off employed than they are on welfare. The NCB is designed to lower the welfare wall "by providing child benefits outside of welfare and ensuring that enhanced benefits and services continue when parents move from social assistance to paid employment" (Government of Canada, 2004i). By making it easier for parents to support their children while working, the NCB aims to strengthen parents' attachment to the workforce (Jenson, 2003c).

The federal government allows the provincial and territorial governments to reduce or "claw back" welfare payments from families receiving both the CCTB and social assistance. Eight provinces and territories have chosen to deduct the amount of the child benefit supplement from the

Exhibit 9.3

HOW DOES THE NATIONAL CHILD BENEFIT INITIATIVE WORK?

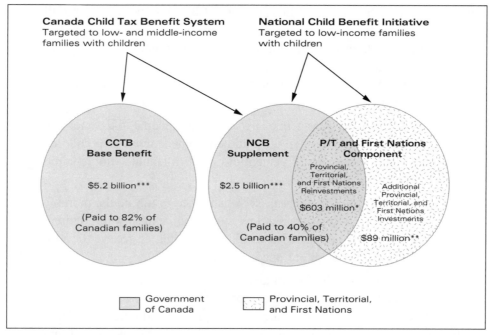

Canada Child Tax Benefit System
Targeted to low- and middle-income families with children

National Child Benefit Initiative
Targeted to low-income families with children

CCTB Base Benefit

$5.2 billion***

(Paid to 82% of Canadian families)

NCB Supplement

$2.5 billion***

(Paid to 40% of Canadian families)

P/T and First Nations Component

Provincial, Territorial, and First Nations Reinvestments

$603 million*

Additional Provincial, Territorial, and First Nations Investments

$89 million**

☐ Government of Canada

☐ Provincial, Territorial, and First Nations

* Reinvestment funds comprise social assistance/child benefit savings and, in some jurisdictions, Children's Special Allowance. (CSA) recoveries

** Investment funds comprise additional funds that some jurisdictions devote to the NCB, over and above the reinvestment funds.

Additional investments for First Nations are provided by Indian and Northern Affairs Canada.

*** Amounts are for the July 2001 to June 2002 period.

Source: *The National Child Benefit Progress Report: 2002–2. What is the National Child Benefit Initiative? How Does the National Child Benefit Initiative Work?* http://www.nationalchildbenefit.ca/ncb/NCB-2003 /ncb-report2002_e.pdf, by Federal-Provincial-Territorial Council. The Council includes representation from nine provinces, both territories and Government of Canada and is co-chaired by Liza Frulla, Minister of Social Services Canada and Tim Sale, Minister of Family Services and Housing, Manitoba. 1997. Reproduced with the permission of the Minister of Public Works and Government Services Canada, 2004.

amount that families receive from social assistance. This ensures that families on welfare do not earn more money (by collecting both social assistance and CCTB) than poor working families. In this way, the clawback creates a built-in incentive for families to obtain money through employment rather than welfare (National Council of Welfare, 2003b). Provinces and territories that claw back social assistance payments are required to reinvest the savings into programs for low-income families. These programs vary across jurisdictions; often, they involve extending additional cash benefits to working parents to offset the costs of employment, increasing the number of government-subsidized childcare spaces, or developing early childhood services for at-risk children (Government of Canada, 2004b).

Not everyone supports the practice of clawing back welfare payments from CCTB recipients. The National Council of Welfare (2003b, 14) argues that clawbacks "discriminate against families on welfare," especially lone-parent female-led families, which consistently receive a smaller proportion of the NCB supplement than two-parent families. The NCB also appears to have done little to raise children and their families out of poverty. Some social analysts suggest that in light of research on the negative impact of poverty on children, welfare and NCB benefits may be "low enough to harm a child's future" (National Council of Welfare, 2003b, 75).

III. THE GROWING PROBLEMS OF HUNGER AND HOMELESSNESS

FOOD INSECURITY

According to the UN Food and Agriculture Organization, a person is hungry or **food insecure** if he or she lives with worries about not having enough money to buy food, is not eating the desired quality or variety of food, or does not have enough to eat. In 2001, the National Population Health Survey found that almost three million Canadians (10 percent of the population) were food insecure (Statistics Canada, 2001). Those most at risk of hunger are homeless people, lone-parent mothers, children, recent immigrants and refugees, Aboriginal peoples, and the unemployed (Agriculture and Agri-Food Canada, 2003).

Child hunger is a serious problem in Canada. In 1998, the NLSCY reported the following:

- Approximately 57 000 Canadian families with children under twelve experience hunger.

- Most hungry families live in large urban centres and are headed by lone mothers.

- About one-third of hungry children live in low-income (that is, working poor) families.

- Aboriginal families living off a reserve are four times more likely than non-Aboriginal families to experience hunger (McIntyre et. al., 1998).

Data from the NLSCY show a correlation between hunger and developmental problems in children: "Nutritionally deprived children experience more health problems than food-secure children including anaemia, weight loss, colds, and infections" (McIntyre et al., 1998, 3). Child hunger has also been linked to problems in school, including absenteeism and poor academic performance. For adults, the main consequence of hunger is poor health. Among women who report experiencing hunger, there is a high incidence of chronic health conditions such as back problems and migraine headaches (McIntyre et al., 1998).

One yardstick for measuring hunger problems is the number of people using emergency food programs. Many of these programs are grassroots community-action food projects, such as soup kitchens, community gardens, and food box programs. Food banks are the most common type of community-based food program in Canada. In 2003, around 778 000 Canadians (39 percent of whom were children) used a food bank every month; this was double the use in 1989. More than half of all food bank users are on social assistance; others are receiving disability pensions or other income security benefits, and almost 13 percent are working. Among the provinces, Newfoundland has the highest rate of food bank use per capita. Canada's first food bank, which opened in Edmonton in 1981, was established as a temporary response to the hardships arising from Canada's economic recession. Since then, the demand for food banks has grown. By 2003, there were 639 food banks across the country (Canadian Association of Food Banks, 2003; 2004). Surveys suggest that over 80 percent of Canadians attribute the need for food banks to government cutbacks and inadequate social welfare programs (Heimann, 2003).

Although the number of food programs is increasing, they are generally considered inadequate for addressing the growing problem of hunger in Canada. Food banks, in particular, cannot be relied on to eradicate hunger. This is because they rarely have enough food to meet the demand, they rely solely on donations (which tend to be inconsistent), and the food itself may be substandard (McIntyre et al., 1998). Food banks are meant to be temporary, yet the federal government has shown an interest in their continued operation: between 1999 and 2003, federal funds were used to enhance or expand 399 food banks and soup kitchens (Government of Canada, 2004a).

In 1998, representatives from 187 countries (including Canada) gathered at the World Food Summit and made a commitment "to reduce the number of undernourished people by half no later than the year 2015" (Agriculture and Agri-Food Canada, 1998, 1). Canada's Action Plan for Food Security was subsequently developed as a national framework to guide public- and private-sector organizations in their efforts to combat hunger. In its second progress report on the implementation of the Canadian plan, Agriculture and Agri-Food Canada (2002) outlined ten areas requiring more work to ensure food security both in Canada and abroad. Among these ten priorities is an effort to reduce poverty so that people will have more money to buy or grow food. With regard to poverty reduction, the federal government has committed itself to strengthening "Canada's social [welfare] system, especially with respect to those programs that target our most vulnerable populations."

HOUSING AND HOMELESSNESS

A Housing Crisis

Along with nutritious food, clean water, clothing, and other basic necessities, housing is an important component of general health, well-being, security, and quality of life. Proper and secure housing is especially important for children because it "anchors them in a community, increases their chances of success at school and provides a base for their parents' participation in the workforce, training or education" (Campaign 2000, 2003, 9).

A lack of affordable or "core" housing is a growing concern for many Canadians. According to the Canada Mortgage and Housing Corporation (CMHC) (2003, 41), "**affordable housing** is adequate and suitable shelter that can be obtained without spending 30 per cent or more of before-tax household income" (to be adequate, housing must be in good repair; to be suitable, it must be uncrowded). A study by the Federation of Canadian Municipalities (2001) found that roughly one household in five spends more than 50 percent of its income on housing. Many of these households are headed by seniors, Aboriginal people, persons with disabilities, and recent immigrants (CMHC, 2003).

Over the decades, the federal government (through the Canada Mortgage and Housing Corporation) has supported a number of **public housing** projects for Canada's poorest citizens. In the 1980s, federal money went to the building of 20 000 public housing units a year. By the mid-1990s, as a result of federal cutbacks in social expenditures, only 4450 public housing units a year were being built (Campaign 2000, 2001). The Canadian Union of Public Employees (2000) argues that the lack of support for public housing "is a main reason for the shortage of affordable housing across Canada" and for the escalating problem of homelessness.

Many municipalities are finding that a wide range of affordable housing and facilities (such as shelters for the homeless) is required in order to meet the diverse needs of local populations (Alberta Urban Municipalities Association, 2004). Exhibit 9.4 presents a continuum of housing and facilities that are in increasing demand in Canada.

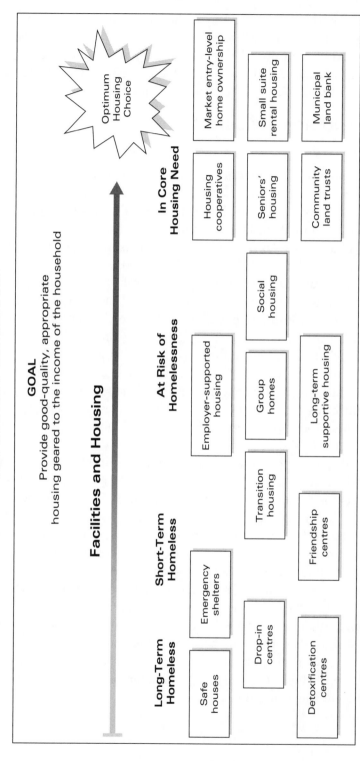

E x h i b i t   9 . 4
THE HOUSING CONTINUUM

GOAL
Provide good-quality, appropriate
housing geared to the income of the household

Facilities and Housing

Optimum Housing Choice

Long-Term Homeless

Safe houses

Emergency shelters

Drop-in centres

Detoxification centres

Short-Term Homeless

Transition housing

Friendship centres

At Risk of Homelessness

Employer-supported housing

Group homes

Social housing

Long-term supportive housing

In Core Housing Need

Housing cooperatives

Market entry-level home ownership

Seniors' housing

Small suite rental housing

Community land trusts

Municipal land bank

Source: *Housing Affordability in the Mountain West: Assessing Housing Needs in Canmore*, prepared by Norm Connolly. All rights reserved. Reproduced with the consent of CMGC. All other uses and reproductions of this material are expressly prohibited.

Populations at Risk

Tenants in large Canadian cities find it especially difficult to access affordable housing. The elimination of rent controls in many parts of the country between 1989 and 1999 resulted in rents rising by about 20 percent; at the same time, household income rose by only 2.7 percent. By 2001, rental vacancy rates were under 3 percent in most of Canada's largest cities. Campaign 2000 (2001; 2002) observes that a continued scarcity of public housing, coupled with rising rents and falling vacancy rates (especially in urban centres), has put affordable housing far out of reach for many of Canada's poorest citizens.

Low-income families with children face additional challenges when affordable rental units are in short supply. In 2002, Toronto social workers said that substandard housing was the reason they removed one out of every five children from their homes and placed them in foster care (Results–Resultats Canada, 2004). Campaign 2000 (2002, 6) outlines further potential risks for low-income families: "Unaffordable housing means parents have fewer resources to direct to children's nutrition, health and education ... Families living in unaffordable housing are at a greater risk of eviction, [which] threatens children's social and educational links to the community."

People with mental health problems and/or addictions have their own difficulties in obtaining affordable housing. According to Rehman and Gahagan (2003, 3), "due to stigma, discrimination, and a variety of complex social issues, access to appropriate housing [for these groups] may be compromised." The challenge of trying to find appropriate housing may actually increase stress and thereby exacerbate physical and mental health problems.

Homelessness

Homelessness—that is, living in emergency shelters or on the street—is becoming an increasingly visible social problem in Canada, especially in the large urban centres of Vancouver, Montreal, and Toronto. The number of homeless people in Canada is unknown, mainly because of the difficulties in tracking this fairly mobile population (HRDC, 2003c). However, the National Anti-Poverty Organization (2002) estimates that at least 500 000 people in Canada are homeless.

The **homeless** population may be understood in terms of three subgroups. The *visible homeless* live on the street, in shelters, or in temporary housing situations. The *hidden homeless* are those who are housed but who are living in substandard conditions or abandoned buildings, or who drift from one friend's house to another. People who are *at risk of homelessness* are living in unstable conditions and may be forced to suddenly leave their home; women living in physically and/or sexually abusive situations are included in this group

(O'Sullivan, 1996). A study by the Federation of Canadian Municipalities (2000) estimates that for every person currently homeless, four families are at risk of eviction and homelessness because they cannot afford their rent.

Homelessness is associated with a variety of health, developmental, and psychological problems. For example, unsanitary, damp, or overcrowded living conditions may contribute to chronic colds or infectious disease. Children who are homeless are prone to behaviour problems; to social, physical, and cognitive delays; and to depression, sleep disturbances, and bed-wetting. Homeless adults are at high risk of mental illness, substance abuse, injury, and physical or sexual assault (Hourston, 2000). A study on homeless women living in Toronto found that the mortality rate of homeless women between eighteen and forty-four was ten times that of other women in the same age group (Cheung and Hwang, 2004).

Government Responses

Affordable Housing Program Canada's economic growth in the late 1990s improved housing conditions for many Canadians. For example, the percentage of Canadian households in "core housing need declined from 17.9 per cent in 1996 to 15.8 per cent in 2001"; the regions that saw the most improvement in affordable housing were New Brunswick, Manitoba, Quebec, and Yukon (CMHC, 2004a). Despite these gains, many Canadians were still in need of core housing. This prompted the federal government in 2001 to launch the Affordable Housing Program (AHP)—an initiative that cost-shares government-subsidized housing projects with the provinces and territories (Privy Council Office, 2003b). Under the AHP, financial aid is available to build new low-cost housing units and to enable low-income groups, landlords, and rooming house owners to bring existing housing up to acceptable living standards. A total of $1 billion of federal money has been earmarked for affordable housing for the period 2001 to 2008 (CMHC, 2004b). One requirement of the AHP is that any contribution made by the federal government be matched by the province or territory. By 2004, affordable housing agreements had been signed between the federal government and every province or territory.

Canada's National Homelessness Initiative In 1999, the federal government launched the National Homelessness Initiative to eradicate homelessness in Canada. Through partnerships between public and private institutions and populations at risk, the initiative is being implemented in two phases:

- Phase I (1999–2003) has been focusing on building and renovating emergency shelters and creating a continuum of services for homeless people, including street outreach, support services, food banks, meal service programs, and furniture and clothing banks (HRDC, 2003b).

- Phase II (2003–06) is providing communities with support to combat homelessness, serve homeless people, and develop long-term housing goals for eliminating homelessness (HRDC, 2004a).

Under the initiative, a special effort is being made to address the disproportionate numbers of homeless youth and Aboriginal people (HRDC, 2003b).

IV. WORKING WITH LOW-INCOME AND MARGINALIZED GROUPS

Social workers have always helped people cope with the effects of poverty and improve their life circumstances. They have also rallied to many poverty-related causes and advocated on behalf of low-income individuals and groups. With the emergence of new fields of social work, many social workers have been turning their attention toward populations that are not poor. That said, a substantial number of social workers continue to help people meet their financial and other basic needs through welfare, employment, housing, and food programs.

Only recently have attitudinal factors been considered as an influence on social welfare reform. This has led to a closer examination of the role that attitudes play in the approaches that social workers and other professionals take when helping clients on welfare and EI move toward independence. Research suggests that some front-line workers resist the trend toward active programming. One Canadian study found that welfare workers failed to engage clients in discussions about work opportunities, provide clients with information about employment support services, or raise other issues relating to increased independence. This study concluded that workers who continue to emphasize passive rather than active measures—and who as a result keep their clients on welfare—make it appear as if welfare reforms have not worked (HRDC, 1999a).

One of the challenges in working with poor and disadvantaged groups is learning to appreciate the complexities of living in hardship. Poverty represents a lack of income, but it is also a condition characterized by social isolation, discrimination, poor housing, and limited access to recreation, transportation, and childcare. The Family Stress Model (see Exhibit 9.1) illustrates the problems faced by many low-income people. Jones and colleagues (2002, 3) suggest that some of these problems may be exacerbated by well-meaning social workers and other professionals. For example, welfare workers may feel pressured by their employer to move their clients into work or training and, in so doing, create "a complex juggling of work and domestic responsibilities for those with children." In turn, clients may experience stress, marital discord, and difficulties in parenting. Through careful observation and active listening and by maintaining a person-in-environment perspective, practitioners may help families identify, describe, and address the various pressures they feel.

Charles Zastrow (2004) points out that to leave welfare, one must be motivated to take the necessary steps to improve one's circumstances. However, ongoing economic pressures and past failures to leave welfare may be discouraging and sap an individual's motivation to change. To help discouraged or unmotivated people, practitioners must be encouraging—that is, they must be accepting, sensitive, empathic, nonjudgmental, and genuinely interested in their clients. Workers also need to help their clients find creative ways to learn new skills, behaviours, and roles. Finally, workers should recognize and call attention to signs of progress and convey a sense of confidence in the client's ability to succeed.

SUMMARY

▪ Introduction

People need economic security in order to participate fully in society. Canada's social welfare system helps Canadians access the four sources of economic security. Although Canadians' market incomes have risen in recent years, unemployment and poverty are persistent problems. In this postdeficit era, no one is sure which approach to economic security will work best: strengthened social welfare programs, or investment in business and job creation.

▪ Jobs and Income: How are Canadians Faring?

Income inequality is a growing problem in Canada and has many negative consequences. Groups likely to be found in the lowest income bracket include lone-parent families and Aboriginal peoples. High unemployment is common among certain groups such as youth and recent immigrants, and is associated with social problems ranging from family breakdown to crime. More and more Canadians are living in poverty; two particular concerns are the persistently high rate of child poverty and the growing ranks of the working poor. People living in poverty are more likely to encounter health and developmental problems, difficulties in the parenting role, barriers to employment, and limited access to resources.

▪ Policies and Programs: Taking an Active Approach

Today, income security programs are designed to be more active than passive and aim to increase labour market participation by providing incentives to work. EI and social assistance have been reformed to make it more difficult for people to receive benefits. EI's programs, which include wage subsidies and self-employment assistance, attempt to get people back to work; there are also federal initiatives aimed at reducing employment barriers for identified groups. Many jurisdictions have introduced welfare-to-work programs in order to move people off welfare. Through the National Child Benefit, the federal government financially assists families with children. Some provinces and territories "claw back" welfare benefits from families receiving the CCTB and reinvest the savings in programs for low-income families.

■ The Growing Problems of Hunger and Homelessness

About three million Canadians are believed to be food insecure. Studies associate hunger with long-term negative effects on children and adults. A growing number of Canadians are relying on emergency food programs such as food banks. Canada's Action Plan for Food Security is a guide for public- and private-sector initiatives to combat hunger. Many Canadians have limited access to affordable housing and are either living on the streets or at risk of homelessness. Canada's housing crisis has prompted government-sponsored measures such as the Affordable Housing Program and the National Homelessness Initiative.

■ Working with Low-Income and Marginalized Groups

Traditionally, social workers have focused on helping people cope with poverty conditions. To be effective, practitioners must try to understand people's experiences of poverty and make a better effort to help people become self-sufficient. It is important for professionals to understand the pressures people face when moving from income security programs to independence, and to encourage and support clients in their efforts to change.

▼ KEY TERMS

For definitions of the key terms, consult the Glossary on page 364 at the end of the book.

economic security p. 199	passive programs p. 204	affordable housing p. 215
income inequality p. 201	active programs p. 204	public housing p. 215
poverty p. 202	welfare wall p. 211	homelessness p. 217
underemployed p. 203	food insecure p. 213	(the) homeless p. 217

Social Welfare and Families with Children

Objectives

I. To look at trends in family formation and their implications for social welfare programs and services.

II. To explore a variety of needs, issues, and programs relating to Canadian children and youth.

III. To examine various forms of family violence as well as initiatives aimed at eradicating this problem.

IV. To consider aspects of social work practice with families with children.

INTRODUCTION

In proclaiming 1994 the International Year of the Family, the United Nations was calling attention to the importance of families and their changing needs and responsibilities. Yet in spite of this recognition, there is no single, universally accepted definition of "family." However, for the purpose of collecting data, Statistics Canada (2003c) defines a **census family** as a

> married couple (with or without children of either or both spouses), a couple living common law (with or without children of either or both partners) or a lone parent of any marital status, with at least one child living in the same dwelling. A couple living common law may be of opposite or same sex."

This chapter focuses on Canadian families with children.

Some organizations prefer to define *family* in terms of the roles that families play in society. The Vanier Institute of the Family (1992, 34–35), for instance, offers the following functional definition of family:

> Any combination of two or more persons who are bound together by ties of mutual consent, birth and/or adoption/placement and which serves the interest of individuals and societies by ensuring the
>
> - physical maintenance and care of its members; and/or
> - addition of new societal members through procreation or adoption and their relinquishment when mature; and/or
> - socialization of children for adult roles, such as those of spouse, parent, worker, neighbour, voter and community member; and/or
> - social control of members (the maintenance or order within the family and groups external to it); and/or
> - production and consumption of goods and services needed to support and maintain the family unit; and/or
> - maintenance of family morale and motivation to ensure task performance both within the family and the other social groups.

This definition of family is highly inclusive and emphasizes the diversity of family activities and tasks; also, this definition does not limit itself to any particular cultural environment. Note, however, that the roles and functions of families change in tandem with changes in society.

Families are recognized for the economic contributions they make: "Families are a basic social unit of production and consumption and, as such, are at the heart of the economic process. Their needs must be intimately connected with the objectives of economic and social development, as a minimum standard of progress" (United Nations, 1999). To strengthen families and foster self-sufficiency, Canadian governments create and support a number of family policies and programs.

Unlike many European countries, Canada has no national **family policy** that supports a full range of universal family services. Rather, each province and territory is responsible for setting its own priorities for family programs. The result has been considerable disparity in services across the country.

Moreover, within each province and territory, family services tend to be poorly coordinated. Quebec is the only province that has developed a comprehensive approach to serving families. In 1997, while other provincial governments were *narrowing* the focus of their family programs to concentrate on low-income families, the Government of Quebec was *broadening* its focus by integrating child allowances, early childhood education, child development services, and parental leave programs and making all of these universally available to all families regardless of income level. Quebec also coordinated its separate public- and private-sector family programs and services so as to establish a cohesive network (Standing Committee, 2000; Canadian Policy Research Networks, 2003b).

There are a number of reasons Canada has not yet developed a national family policy. Katherine Scott (1996) suggests that Canadian governments have generally been reluctant to introduce "public policies and programs that infringe on the privacy rights of individuals or families, or to curtail what is viewed as the parents' responsibilities to their children." According to Baker (1997), attempts to develop a coordinated system of family services have been frustrated by the lack of agreement among Canadians regarding what family policy and programs should encompass. In fact, Canadians cannot even agree on a definition of "family." Politicians and social policy-makers tend to avoid making family policy decisions when the issues involved (a) are controversial or (b) are not part of traditional party agendas. Issues such as abortion, same-sex legislation, and wages for homemakers are examples of sensitive policy issues. However, Canadian governments have made some progress with regard to policy development in these areas.

I. FAMILY FORMATION AND SOCIAL WELFARE PROGRAMS

Family formation refers to the founding of the family unit through marriage, cohabitation, procreation, or adoption. The term is also used in reference to the re-formation of the family following marital separation, divorce, or the loss of a family member. Census data reveal certain trends in family formation that have implications for social policy and programs. Some of these trends are considered below.

DECLINE IN "TRADITIONAL" FAMILIES

"Traditional" families—those with a mother, father, and children—are becoming less common in Canada: in 2001, married or common-law couples with children living at home constituted 44 percent of Canadian families, down from 55 percent in 1981. Another trend is the rising proportion of common-law couples with children—from 2.1 percent in 1981 to 7.4 percent in 2001. Over the same years, the proportion of married couples with children fell from 60 percent in 1981 to 44 percent in 2001 (Statistics Canada, 2002e).

People who marry or live common law encounter a number of responsibilities, roles, rights, obligations, and challenges. These apply to the partners themselves and also to any children they have together or bring into the relationship. A wide range of programs and services are available to help couples strengthen their relationship and deal effectively with problems that arise. Some of these are listed below:

- legal services related to marriage or common-law relationships;
- group workshops in marriage preparation and enhancement;
- marital therapy;
- online marriage enhancement programs;
- education services relating to relationships and marriage; and
- group sessions on how to resolve marital problems and improve relationship skills (B.C. Council for Families, 2001b).

DIVORCE AND SEPARATION

Even though changes in social attitudes have made divorce more acceptable for people in unhappy marriages, Canada's divorce rate has been declining since 1988. Social analysts attribute this trend to an increase in the number of couples remaining married, to a rise in the number of unmarried couples, and to the growing number of married couples who have separated without obtaining a divorce (Milan, 2000).

Findings from the National Longitudinal Survey of Children and Youth (NLSCY) indicate that "children are experiencing parental separation at increasingly younger ages. Furthermore, children born into common law unions are more apt to see the separation of their parents" (Statistics Canada, 2002e, 7). Research tells us that parental conflict related to a relationship breakdown is potentially more harmful to children than the actual separation. In many cases, the negative effects of marriage breakdown can be reduced if conflict between partners is kept to a minimum and there is a concerted effort to ensure that the child's relationship with both parents is close and secure (Horner, 2002). A range of services—such as Giving Children Hope in Manitoba, and Parenting After Separation Workshops in Alberta—support parents through the separation process and help children adjust to family breakdown.

LONE PARENTHOOD

In 2001, around 1.3 million Canadian families were **lone-parent families.** That number represented 16 percent of all families. Most lone-parent families are headed by women—a phenomenon often attributed to a general increase in women's economic independence and to a decrease in the stigma attached to having children outside marriage (Statistics Canada, 2002e). Among lone-parent families, young mothers are especially vulnerable to economic challenges. These women often lack education, job skills, work experience, affordable childcare, and child support; as a consequence, it is often difficult for them to keep themselves and their families out of poverty (Milan, 2000).

The rising number of lone-parent families is creating a demand for specialized services. Single-parent resource centres, for example, are becoming more common in Canada. These centres offer support, information, and parenting courses to lone mothers and fathers. Some programs for lone-parent families focus on finances. Newfoundland's Single Parent Employment Program, for instance, helps lone parents on welfare gain financial independence through full-time employment programs (Government of Newfoundland, 2000).

SAME-SEX UNIONS

In 2001, for the first time in Canadian history, the national census collected data on **same-sex unions**. There are 34 000 same-sex couples in Canada, representing 0.5 percent of all couples. There are slightly more male than female same-sex unions (55 percent versus 45 percent), and female couples are more likely to have children living with them (Statistics Canada, 2002e). One of the greatest challenges for the gay rights movement has been in the area of family status and law. Only recently have Canadian governments considered same-sex couples in the context of "family," and as having the same rights and responsibilities as heterosexual couples.

Same-sex unions are having and will continue to have an impact on various aspects of law and social policy. At the regional level, same-sex laws are affecting adoption laws, health insurance, and matrimonial property. At the federal level, same-sex laws are having an impact on Old Age Security, the Canada Pension Plan, the Income Tax Act, EI, and the Immigration Act (Government of Canada, 2000d; Lawton, 2000). Some people are worried that same-sex legislation will raise the costs of social programs, in that more people will have access to pensions, tax exemptions, and other spousal benefits. The federal government has responded to this concern by pointing out that although same-sex couples will have greater access to services and benefits under the legislation, they will also have additional financial and social obligations ("Same-Sex Bill Passes," 2000; Ayed, 2000).

ADOPTION

Many families choose to increase their membership by adopting one or more children. **Adoption** is a legal process that transfers the rights and duties of birth parents to adoptive parents. Social trends are changing some aspects of adoption in Canada. For example, more single women are choosing to keep their babies instead of putting them up for adoption; this means there are fewer infants available for families wishing to adopt a baby (Sobol, 2000).

The federal government is responsible for international adoptions; each province and territory has its own laws for domestic adoption. Depending on the jurisdiction, domestic adoptions may be arranged through provincial or territorial child-welfare authorities, children's aid societies, private licensed adoption agencies, or the courts. Many adoptions in First Nations communities follow Aboriginal peoples' customs (Tyjnych, 2003).

Some provinces—such as Newfoundland and British Columbia—have recently amended or replaced their adoption laws to better reflect modern needs and trends. Although adoption laws vary across the country, the following trends are visible:

- Children are being given more say in their adoptions.

- More information is being made available to help adult adoptees and birth parents reunite.

- Open adoptions are being allowed so that children can maintain contact with their birth family.

- Eligibility criteria are being expanded to allow unmarried couples, individuals, and same-sex couples to adopt.

A number of children in Canada are considered "hard to place" because they have behavioural or psychological disorders, or have developmental, medical, or physical disabilities. Some provinces and territories are making a special effort to find permanent homes for these children. For instance, New Brunswick in 2002 launched its Kids Can't Wait to Have a Family campaign to find adoptive families for children under the care of child welfare agencies. This initiative established Canada's first adoption foundation, which raises public awareness of adoption and promotes the efforts of the provincial adoption campaign. In its first twenty months, the adoption campaign matched 265 children in care with adoptive families; prior to this initiative, New Brunswick was placing only thirty or so children a year (Government of New Brunswick, 2003a; 2003b).

II. CHILDREN AND YOUTH:
A NATIONAL PRIORITY

Research helps us understand the needs of children and discover the factors that contribute to healthy child development. For example, Understanding the Early Years was a five-year federal initiative launched in 1999 to assess how children are faring in Canada and to determine how communities influence child development. In Canada, child well-being is measured in terms of "physical health and motor development; emotional health; social knowledge and competence; cognitive learning; and language communication" (Government of Canada, 2002d, 4).

Although most Canadian children are physically, emotionally, and socially healthy, a substantial number experience problems. For example, more and more children are going hungry, and child poverty remains at high levels (Canadian Council on Social Development, 2002a). Child development experts emphasize the importance of addressing these problems early in order to minimize the health, academic, social, and/or labour market difficulties that children may encounter as they grow older (Ross et al., 1996). This section looks at some Canadian approaches to addressing the needs of children and youth.

AN INTERNATIONAL COMMITMENT TO CHILDREN AT HOME AND ABROAD

Canada has a long history of providing families with both income security programs and personal social services. Yet it was not until the United Nations declared 1979 the International Year of the Child that Canada formally committed itself to improving the welfare of children. At the time it signed the UN Convention on the Rights of the Child in 1991, the Government of Canada agreed to introduce legislation and policies to protect children and their rights. A further commitment followed in 2002, when Canada and other nations adopted the UN's plan, A World Fit for Children. This strategy aims to eradicate child poverty, provide care to all children, and generally improve conditions for children around the world (Health Canada, 2002c).

In response to A World Fit for Children, Canada developed a national action plan for children. The document, A Canada Fit for Children, released in 2004, has committed the federal government to actions that support three primary conditions, all of which are known to facilitate healthy child development:

- adequate income for families with children;

- effective parenting within strong and cohesive families; and

- supportive and inclusive communities (Government of Canada, 2004a, 42).

Initiatives under this national plan are expected to be child centred, to focus on long-term results, and to involve representatives from academic disciplines and service sectors when it comes to planning and implementing activities. Exhibit 10.1 summarizes the main components of Canada's national plan for children, and provides examples of child-centred federal initiatives that have been introduced in recent years.

CHILD AND FAMILY INITIATIVES UNDER THE SOCIAL UNION

Many of Canada's present initiatives for children and families have been the result of the social union, a framework used by the federal, provincial (except Quebec), and territorial governments to guide a renewal of Canada's social welfare system. One of the union's earliest policy priorities was to address the needs of young children living in poverty (Government of Canada, 2004g). This decision was based in large part on the understanding that

> what happens to children when they are very young shapes their health and well-being throughout their lifetime [and that] children in low-income families experiencing abuse and/or neglect, physical or mental health problems or family difficulties need particular attention to ensure they get a good start in life (Government of Canada, 1997a).

In 1997, the federal and provincial/territorial governments agreed to work on a National Children's Agenda, a comprehensive and long-term plan to improve the quality of life for Canadian children.

National Children's Agenda

The National Children's Agenda (NCA) (1999) reflects a cooperative working arrangement across the various levels of government, a shared vision for children, and a nationwide commitment "to ensure that all Canadian children have the best possible opportunity to realize their full potential." Initiatives under the NCA aim to improve children's physical, emotional, and spiritual

Exhibit 10.1

WHAT ARE WE DOING TO MAKE CANADA FIT FOR CHILDREN?

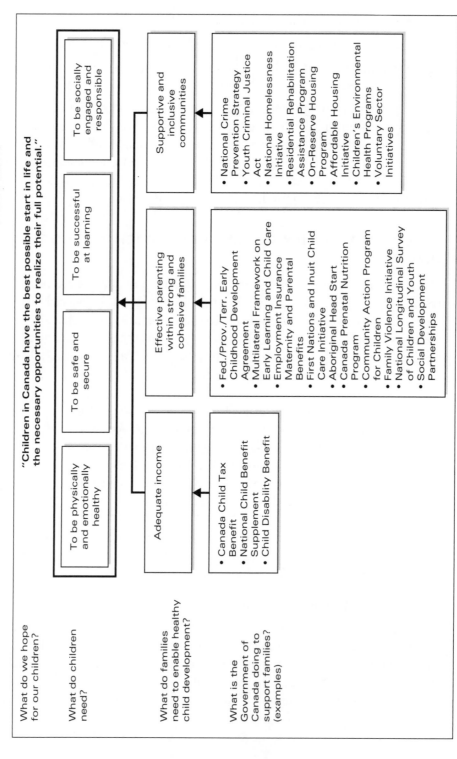

Source: Author generated chart, information derived from Government of Canada (April 2004). *A Canada Fit For Children: Canada's Plan of Action in Response to the May 2002 United Nations Special Session on Children* (quotation p. 7) [online]. Available: www11.sdc.gc.ca/en/cs/sp/socpol/publications/2002-002483/canadafite.pdf [May 17, 2004].

health; ensure their safety and security; enhance learning opportunities for them; and promote social engagement and responsibility among all Canadians. Federal funding for NCA initiatives is transferred to the provinces, territories, and First Nations through the National Child Benefit program (see Chapter 9 for a description of this program), the Early Childhood Development Agreement, and the Multilateral Framework on Early Learning and Child Care.

In 2000, the Early Childhood Development Agreement was introduced under the NCA to "improve and expand early childhood development programs and services across the country." The federal government agreed to transfer $2.2 billion to the provinces and territories for early childhood development over a five-year period. In turn, the regional governments agreed to use the funds for parent and family programs, pre- and post-natal care, infancy programs, early childhood learning and development, and childcare (Government of Canada, 2002a).

When the federal, provincial, and territorial governments agreed on a Multilateral Framework on Early Learning and Child Care in 2003, they all promised to help parents work or attend school by improving early learning and childcare programs for young children. Under the agreement, the provinces and territories are receiving federal funding to design, implement, and regulate these programs. The provinces and territories can set their own program standards; however, they must make those programs available, accessible, affordable, of high quality, inclusive (that is, responsive to the needs of all children), and flexible to a broad range of family and employment situations (Government of Canada, 2003g).

A National Childcare Program

Despite new and enriched programs under the Early Childhood Development Agreement and the Multilateral Framework on Early Learning and Child Care, many social analysts maintain that Canada still needs a national childcare system. A national system would standardize childcare services across the country and, in so doing, ensure that all young Canadian children have equal access to affordable, high-quality care. This type of system would also reduce disparities in childcare programs among the provinces and territories: up until now, for example, the different provinces and territories have not been required to offer learning opportunities in publicly funded childcare programs; the level of training required of childcare workers has also varied widely across jurisdictions (Liberal Party of Canada, 2004a). A national childcare system is expected to increase the number of government-subsidized childcare spaces. While initiatives under the NCA are allowing the provinces and territories to expand the number of publicly funded spaces, these spaces are still limited. Because of this, most Canadian families have had to rely on private, unlicensed, and informal childcare services (International Reform Monitor, 2004).

The federal and regional governments tried to implement a national childcare program in the early 1990s but could not agree on the terms of a national system; also, many provinces and territories were in the throes of deficit reduction, which made the introduction of any new social welfare initiative a low priority (Canadian Policy Research Networks, 2003a). Canadian governments also lacked an "agreed-upon process to guide federal investment in the provinces' domain of social policy"; this process was finally negotiated and then formalized in 1999 when governments signed the Social Union Framework Agreement (Liberal Party of Canada, 2004a).

In the 2004 federal election, Paul Martin promised to commit $5 billion toward a national childcare program if elected prime minister. This program would build on the foundations already laid by the NCA, and would be based on four primary principles or "QUAD":

- *Quality*. Each facility must be regulated by the province or territory to ensure safety and an appropriate complement of professionally-qualified child development staff.

- *Universality*. The program will be open, without discrimination, to pre-school children, including children with special needs.

- *Accessibility*. The program will be affordable for parents.

- *Developmental*. The program must include a component of development/learning that is integrated with the care component. (Liberal Party of Canada, 2004a)

To receive federal funding under the new childcare system, the provinces and territories would be required to pass legislation that embodied the QUAD principles. As long as childcare programs met the QUAD standards, the provinces and territories would be free to design their own childcare services based on local needs and circumstances.

SCHOOL-AGED CHILDREN AND YOUTH

In the present day, the needs of young children are dominating political agendas; yet many older children also need support. Children in middle childhood (age six to twelve) face challenges relating to entering the school system, choosing friends, and taking greater risks (Hanvey, 2002b). And as children enter adolescence (age thirteen to eighteen), they must deal with issues relating to rapid growth and development while learning the life skills they will need as adults. Today's youth must also make decisions about drug and alcohol use, sexual relations, and other activities that are potentially dangerous and that often have long-term consequences (Health Canada, 1999c).

The levels of support that school-aged children need to become happy, healthy, contributing members of society may exceed what is available in the home. This is why a number of social welfare programs and services have been designed to meet the needs of older children, youth, and their families. Child and youth services vary across Canada but are also similar in many ways. For example, child and youth mental health services, and programs that focus on youth engagement, are offered in most parts of the country.

Child and Youth Mental Health Services

Among the most important factors influencing a child's mental health are quality of relationships with parents and siblings, level of stability in the home environment, and disciplining style used by the parents (Ross et al., 1996). Mental health problems in young people often manifest themselves in the following behaviours: physical aggression, sexual acting out, criminal activity, alcohol and drug abuse, and/or suicide attempts. In 2001, the Ontario Student Drug Use Survey found that a significant number of Ontario youth had emotional problems. During the year leading up to the survey, about one-third of young people experienced psychological distress, one-quarter were bullied at school, and one in ten had suicidal thoughts (Centre for Addiction and Mental Health, 2004).

It is important to recognize and treat mental health problems in children and youth as early as possible. Many treatment programs are offered in non-residential settings. These include the following services:

- *Assessment*. To diagnose developmental disorders or delays, learning disabilities, attention deficit disorders, and other functional difficulties.

- *Individual and family counselling*. To address grief and loss, anxiety, depression, eating disorders, and other issues.

- *Support and educational groups*. For children or teens to meet, share experiences, and learn about such topics as anger management, self-esteem, and parental divorce or separation.

- *Creative therapy*. To help young people deal with sexual abuse or other traumatic experiences through art, play, dance, or other expression.

- *Crisis intervention*. To respond to children and youth in distress or emergency situations.

Residential mental health programs are available for children and youth who are experiencing more severe emotional, social, and/or behavioural problems. One such program is the Benjamin Road Residential Treatment Centre in Kitchener, Ontario, which provides a wide range of services for twelve- to sixteen-year-olds, including anger management, life skills training, and peer relationship-building (Lutherwood, 2004).

Youth Engagement

A popular method used to reduce risk-taking behaviours among youth is to get them engaged in meaningful activities. The Centre of Excellence for Youth Engagement (2004) explains

> Through engagement, youth gain a sense of empowerment as individuals and make healthy connections to others, which result in the reduction of risk behaviours and increases in positive activities. In addition to the social benefits of these behavioural changes the community gains through the energy and ideas that youth bring to organizations, activities, and their relationships with adults.

A number of organizations, such as the two profiled below, focus on **youth engagement**.

- HeartWood Institute (2004) in Nova Scotia relies on volunteer mentors to help youth discover their "personal best." Many of HeartWood's efforts to support youth development are the result of collaborative initiatives with local citizens, community leaders, other groups and organizations, and governments.

- Building Organizational Capacity for Youth Engagement is a Toronto-based initiative sponsored by the Council of Agencies Serving South Asians and funded by the Laidlaw Foundation. This initiative encourages the participation of Chinese-Canadian youth in decision-making and leadership roles, and in projects that promote social justice and change (Laidlaw Foundation, 2002).

PARENT SUPPORT PROGRAMS

The nature of parent–child interaction is a key factor in the way a child develops physically, socially, and cognitively. Findings from the NLSCY suggest that although a child's development may be hindered by factors such as poverty, parental depression, and prenatal problems, parenting is "a much more significant contributor than risk factors to a child's development" (Statistics Canada, 1997, 7).

Poor parenting is closely linked to a range of child behaviour problems, but especially to conduct disorders such as bullying, threatening, and physical fighting (Statistics Canada, 1997). According to Stevenson (1999, 3–4), children who exhibit conduct disorders are thirty-six times more likely to have parents who use "ineffective, aversive, inconsistent or negative disciplining most of the time." Research has also found that "inconsistent, non-positive parenting can lead to signs of vulnerability such as poorer school outcomes" (Government of Canada, 2003h, 24). **Vulnerable children** tend to experience learning or behaviour problems and developmental delays that make it difficult for them to meet challenges, control their emotions, learn new skills, and get along with others. According to a vulnerability index developed by J. Douglas Willms of the University of New Brunswick, roughly 28 percent of Canadian children may be vulnerable (HRDC, 2001).

A number of factors can affect the ability of parents to meet their children's needs. According to policy analyst Michael Prince (2001), recent changes in the labour market, shifts in family structure, roles, and practices, and government cutbacks to family services are making it more difficult for today's parents to raise their children effectively. Female-headed lone-parent families face particular challenges; children in these families are at greater risk for emotional, behavioural, academic, and social problems than are children living in two-parent families (Statistics Canada, 1997). While lone parenthood does not in itself cause behavioural and other problems among children, there is a strong correlation between such problems and factors associated with lone parenthood, such as stress, fatigue, and depression (Lipman et al., 1998; Stevenson, 1999).

Parents and families are ultimately responsible for nurturing and caring for children, but there is also a role for government. The Government of Canada (2004a, 5) articulates its own obligations to families:

> The role of government and society with respect to children is to provide the legislative and policy framework, the institutional and organizational structures, the fiscal and other supports and services to enable families to ensure their children's healthy development. However, if families are unable to care for their children, then governments and society have a responsibility to provide support and ensure that they are cared for and protected.

Governments' commitments to families with children are reflected in a variety of parent support programs across Canada. The mandates of these programs vary; however, most provide parents with skills, information, and resources they can use to raise happy and healthy children.

Health Canada's Nobody's Perfect Parenting Program is an example of a federal parent-support program. This program, which is offered in many communities across Canada, helps parents understand their children and relate to them in more positive ways; it also enhances parents' self-confidence and coping skills (B.C. Council for Families, 2001a). Many other programs are offered by voluntary organizations. For example, the following three programs are available in Saskatchewan:

- TEAM (Together Everybody Achieves More), in Prince Albert, helps parents help children develop social skills.

- Parent Support Groups, in Regina, offers support services to parents of children with attention deficit disorder.

- Parent Talk, in Saskatoon, hosts weekly afternoon meetings for parents (Saskatchewan Education, 1999).

Many parent-support programs are designed specifically for parents of teenagers. British Columbia's Parents Together (2004), for example, is a self-help support program for parents experiencing conflict with their teens.

III. FAMILY VIOLENCE IN CANADA

According to the National Clearinghouse on Family Violence, "**family violence** is abuse of power within relationships of family, trust or dependency" (Health Canada, 1993, 1). Family violence includes a wide range of behaviours such as physical assault, emotional abuse, neglect, sexual assault, financial exploitation, and stalking. People's perceptions of family violence continue to change, and this has resulted in a broader definition of family violence. For example, over the past twenty years, elder abuse, the emotional abuse of children, and children witnessing violence have all been recognized as forms of family violence.

Public perceptions of family violence shape our attitudes toward the perpetrators and victims of family violence. Exhibit 10.2 gives the results of a 2002 Canadian poll that measured Canadians' attitudes toward spousal violence. Canadian law also plays a role in people's perceptions of—and attitudes toward—family violence. Over time, these laws have been amended to reflect how seriously Canadians take family violence. Bringing domestic violence out of the private domain of the family and into the public realm has had a strong impact on how police, justice, social welfare, health, and other systems respond to victims and perpetrators (Ad Hoc Federal-Provincial-Territorial Working Group, 2003).

A growing body of research focuses on the potential consequences of family violence. One report notes

> Family violence is a problem that can have lasting impacts on both the individual and the larger society. Along with the physical, psychological, social and economic consequences on individuals directly affected, family violence can have significant social and economic costs on health care systems, civil and criminal justice systems, housing and shelter services and community services. (Trainor, 2003, 4)

E x h i b i t   1 0 . 2

ATTITUDE TO SPOUSAL VIOLENCE

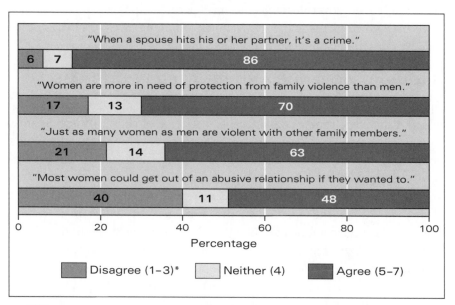

n = 2052

* Survey respondents were asked to rate each statement according to a scale where 1 is "strongly disagree," 7 is "strongly agree," and the midpoint 4 is neither agree nor disagree.

Source: EKOS Research Associates Inc. (May 2002). *Public Attitudes Towards Family Violence: A Syndicated Study: Final Report*, p. 20, Exhibit 3.3 [online]. Available: www.ekos.com/media/files/family31may02.pdf [May 17, 2004].

The following section looks at Canada's Family Violence Initiative and some of the ways in which programs and services address spousal violence and child abuse. (The topic of elder abuse is discussed in Chapter 11.)

THE FAMILY VIOLENCE INITIATIVE

Although family violence is not a new phenomenon in Canada, only in the past twenty years have Canadian governments committed themselves to eradicating it. When it launched the Family Violence Initiative in 1988, the federal government acknowledged that the growing problem of family violence required a more comprehensive and integrated approach. Over the years, this initiative has concentrated on expanding the number of shelters for abused women and their children; addressing the needs of groups at high risk of domestic violence (such as those living in remote or rural areas, visible minorities, Aboriginal peoples, and people with disabilities); and strengthening systems whose job it is to respond to family violence, such as the housing, health, and criminal justice systems (Health Canada, 1998a). Twelve federal departments, agencies, and Crown corporations are responsible for various aspects of the Family Violence Initiative at the federal level. In addition, the federal government has formed partnerships with provincial and territorial governments and First Nations communities to ensure a coordinated approach to family violence across Canada.

SPOUSAL VIOLENCE AND RELATED PROGRAMS

Spousal violence (or partner violence) is a widespread social problem that affects Canadians from all walks of life. This type of abuse includes a broad range of behaviours, from verbal threats to physical and sexual assaults, committed by one partner against the other. In Canada, two-thirds of all family violence crimes reported to police are committed by a spouse or ex-spouse, and most of these (85 percent) are committed against women (Patterson, 2003). The extent of spousal abuse against men is unclear; however, the 1999 General Social Survey on Victimization suggests that 7 percent of men experience spousal violence. The evidence indicates that woman abuse by a male partner is the most frequent and severe form of spousal abuse; furthermore, female victims tend to incur "more serious physical injury and psychological harm" than male victims (Federal-Provincial-Territorial Ministers Responsible for the Status of Women, 2002, 2). Although both sexes report a number of emotional consequences of spousal violence, female victims are more likely to experience fear, lowered self-esteem, sleeping disorders, depression, and anxiety as a result of the violence (Trainor, 2003; Patterson, 2003).

Women use resources available to victims of spousal violence more than men, and the vast majority of these resources cater to women's rather than men's needs. In 1999, 48 percent of female victims (compared to 17 percent of male victims) turned to health, criminal, or social services following incidents of spousal violence (Trainor, 2003; Patterson, 2003). Support services for victims of spousal abuse are found in communities across Canada, and include shelters and transition houses; specialized counselling, information, and referral services; and self-help and support groups. Shelters and transition houses are the primary sources of help for female victims of violence and their children. Between 1975 and 1999, the number of shelters in Canada rose from 18 to 508 (Federal-Provincial-Territorial Ministers Responsible for the Status of Women, 2002). In 2001–02, more than 101 000 women and their children used shelters in Canada, up from 90 000 women in 1997–98 (Code, 2003).

CHILD ABUSE AND PROTECTION SERVICES

A survey by EKOS (2002c) found that of all forms of family violence, Canadians are most concerned about child abuse. Most child welfare experts define **child abuse** (or maltreatment) as "physical assault, sexual assault, emotional/psychological abuse, neglect and witnessing family violence" (Au Coin, 2003b, 33). Child abuse occurs in the context of families, but the problem can also be found in schools, childcare and health centres, and other community settings (Wachtel, 1997).

The 1998 Canadian Incidence Study of Reported Child Abuse and Neglect was the first national study to look into reports of child abuse. Trocmé and colleagues (2001) found that in the 135 000 child welfare investigations conducted in Canada in 1998, 61 000 children were deemed to have been abused. The most likely form of abuse to be investigated was neglect (40 percent of all cases), followed by physical abuse (31 percent), emotional abuse (19 percent), and sexual assault (10 percent).

The same study called attention to the potential discrepancy between actual incidents of child abuse and incidents that are *substantiated* by child welfare authorities. As Exhibit 10.3 illustrates, it is likely that many incidents of child maltreatment go undetected; furthermore, even after detection, some incidents are not reported to the police or the child welfare authorities. Of the incidents reported, not all are investigated, and even when incidents are investigated, not all can be substantiated. These factors make it difficult to determine with any accuracy the rate of child abuse in Canada. However, most professionals would agree that the reported incidence of child abuse is far below actual numbers.

E x h i b i t   1 0 . 3

STAGES OF IDENTIFICATION OF INCIDENTS OF CHILD MALTREATMENT

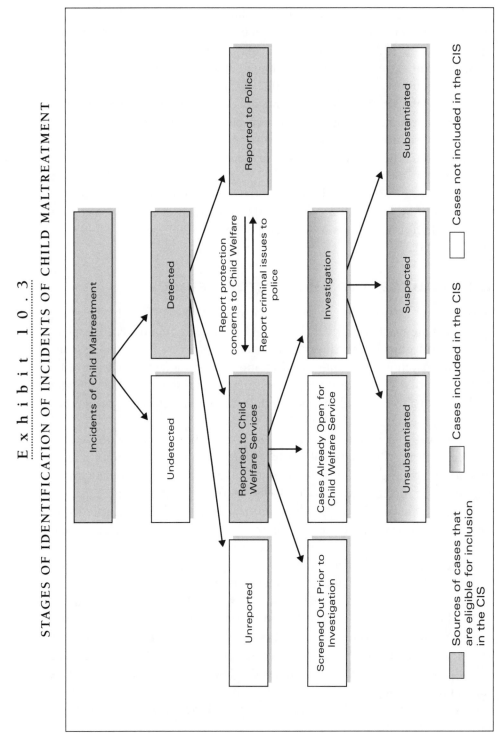

Note: CIS = Canadian Incidence Study

Source: N. Trocmé, B. MacLaurin, B. Fallon, J. Daciuk, D. Billingsley, M. Tourigny, M. Mayer, J. Wright, K. Barter, G. Burford, J. Hornick, R. Sullivan, and B. McKenzie (2001). *Canadian Incidence Study of Reported Child Abuse and Neglect: Final Report*, p. 9, Figure 1-2. Ottawa: Minister of Public Works and Government Services Canada [online]. Available: www.hc-sc.gc.ca/pphb-dgspsp/publicat/cisfr-ecirf/pdf/cis_e.pdf [May 17 2004].Reproduced with the permission of the Minister of Public Works and Government Services Canada, 2004.

The effects of abuse on children depend on such factors as the length of time over which the abuse occurs, the child's developmental level, and the relationship between the child and the abuser (Meston, 1993). However, any problems created by abuse are likely to manifest themselves in one or more of the following areas (with examples):

- psychological (nightmares, depression, anxiety);
- physical (failure to thrive, psychosomatic complaints, overall poor health);
- behavioural (poor socialization, eating disorders, drug abuse, self-destructive or suicidal behaviour);
- academic (poor grades, suspensions, grade repetition);
- sexual (promiscuity, dissatisfaction with sex in adulthood);
- interpersonal (insecure attachments to caregivers, difficulty in making friends, fear of intimacy);
- self-perceptual (low self-esteem, inaccurate body image, confused sense of identity);
- spiritual (general loss of faith, lack of spirit or enthusiasm for life); and/or
- subsequent violence in adulthood (abuse of own children, perpetration of violence against partner) (Latimer, 1998).

Canada addresses the problem of child abuse at three different levels. *Primary prevention* includes raising public awareness about child abuse and neglect and helping people develop the knowledge and skills to reduce the incidence of maltreatment. These programs include public education campaigns, community safety programs, marriage-preparation courses, and parent education. *Secondary prevention* programs attempt to interrupt abuse or neglect at the earliest stage possible. These target high-risk populations, and focus on prenatal nutrition, infant development programs, family support services, and crisis intervention. *Tertiary prevention* focuses on intervention and treatment for both child victims and their abusers and includes child welfare and protection services, family preservation programs, and support for children who witness violence (Wachtel, 1997). Although primary prevention strategies are seen as a wise investment in the future of children and society in general, most resources are targeted at tertiary prevention programs.

Since child welfare is a provincial/territorial responsibility, there is considerable variation in how child welfare services are delivered in Canada. For example, some governments provide direct services, whereas others contract them out to a children's aid society or similar agency. There is also disparity regarding the types of abuse that child welfare workers must investigate, their investigation procedures, and the criteria they apply when deciding whether to remove a child from the home. Further variation is found in First Nations communities, where child welfare services are provided either by self-governed Indian bands, or by First Nations family service agencies that work within regional legislation (Trocmé et al., 2001).

CHILDREN IN CARE

Children who come under the protection of a provincial or territorial child welfare system are referred to as **children in care**. In 2003, there were an estimated 76 000 children in care in Canada. The number of children placed in care continues to rise; this has been attributed to the higher number of reported incidences of neglect and abuse as well as to a general trend toward more aggressive approaches to eradicating child abuse (Farris-Manning and Zandstra, 2003).

Families who become involved in the child welfare system are expected to comply with court orders that stipulate the level of response necessary to protect the child. In Ontario, for example, a *supervision order* gives a children's aid worker the legal right to intervene in and assess the family's situation while the child continues to live in the home. If the child is at greater risk, a *temporary care/voluntary agreement* may be required. In this case, the child may be placed in care while the family works on either resolving its problems or finding a more permanent home for the child (National Youth in Care Network, 1998).

In cases of abuse or extreme neglect, the child may be removed from the family home and placed in alternative care. Depending on the resources available in the community, placements can be made in

- a foster home (the home of a family other than the child's own);
- a group home (a private or government community-based facility run by professional staff);
- an institutional home (a facility that provides more structure, supervision, and support than foster homes or group homes);
- a mental health centre (a residential facility for youth at risk of harming themselves or others); or
- a custody facility (residential care for a child or youth at risk of running away or physically harming someone) (National Youth in Care Network, 1998).

Research suggests that the benefits for children living in foster or family-based care are greater than those offered by group or institutional care. This has led to a trend toward kinship care (which places the child in a foster home with relatives) and guardianship care (which places the child with a family who is known to the child) (Farris-Manning and Zandstra, 2003).

IV. WORKING WITH FAMILIES

Working with families is an important activity in social welfare programs and a primary focus for many social workers. There are a number of rewards associated with helping families meet their basic needs, deal effectively with problems, and reach their goals. There are also many challenges. Social workers, for example, must constantly hone their assessment and intervention skills in order to help families deal with the rapidly changing social, economic, and political environment. As cuts to social welfare programs make services unavailable, unaffordable, or unsuitable, more families may need to provide care for their children and elderly relatives in the home. This will require front-line workers to help families discover their own *internal* strategies for meeting needs and resolving problems, as opposed to relying on *external*, government-sponsored supports.

The term **empowerment** is often used to describe the goal of many family services. When social workers engage in empowering activities with families, they are essentially helping family members help themselves and—ultimately—manage their own lives. Empowerment can be observed when a family is able to (1) identify its needs and know where to go to get those needs met; (2) advocate on its own behalf so that necessary resources can be accessed; and (3) have input into the programs and policies that directly affect the family. To become empowered, families need to know about the services that are available to them. Social workers can provide these services directly, or they can help families connect with appropriate community resources.

Some areas of family practice are more challenging than others. A study by the Canadian Association of Social Workers found that child welfare workers often suffer from low staff morale, huge caseloads, poor pay, a shortage of qualified workers, and high attrition rates. This study concluded that if child welfare workers are to make a positive difference in families' lives, certain personal and environmental conditions must be met. Workers, for instance, have to be personally committed to serving children and families, use social work knowledge and skills in a responsible manner, and adhere to a professional code of ethics. In turn, organizations that serve families must create "a work environment that fosters good practice," encourage a common vision of child protection and a team approach, provide adequate clinical supervision, and set appropriate caseloads (CASW, 2003a, 10).

Most family service agencies have discovered, and drawn from, best practices for serving families. Exhibit 10.4 gives examples of some of these methods.

Exhibit 10.4

SERVING CHILDREN AND FAMILIES: EXAMPLES OF WHAT WORKS BEST

WORKING WITH FAMILIES (GENERAL):

- "Focus on the entire family."

- "Change as a family's needs, roles, and ages change."

- "Encourage families to express their own needs and decide how their needs will be met."

- Respect individual members' choices and preferences.

- "Respect cultural, economic, social, and spiritual differences." [1]

WORKING WITH PARENTS AND YOUNG CHILDREN:

- Reinforce the parent's role as primary caregiver.

- Support parents in their own personal learning and growth.

- Provide information to parents about healthy child development and age-appropriate skills. [2]

WORKING WITH PARENTS AND OLDER CHILDREN:

- Help parents learn how to set clear expectations for child behaviour, monitor children's behaviour, reinforce positive behaviour, provide consequences for inappropriate behaviour, develop and use effective communication skills, and nurture children. [3]

- "Assist parents in the development of parenting skills that support the quality of their relationships with their adolescent (e.g., warmth, acceptance of individuality, active listening, behaviour monitoring, limit setting and negotiation)."

- Help parents learn to *connect* with (attach to) rather than *control* their teen.

- Help parents demonstrate a willingness to understand and relate to their teen despite the teen's behaviour, yet set clear limits regarding unacceptable behaviour. [4]

continued

continued

> WORKING WITH COMMUNITIES TO SUPPORT FAMILIES WITH
> CHILDREN:
>
> - Engage other agencies to facilitate the parent–child relationship
>   (for example, encourage employers to consider flexible workplace
>   hours).[2]
>
> - Engage community organizations and groups in "fostering
>   healthy social development in children and youth."[3]
>
> - Work with other groups in the community to develop a compre-
>   hensive and coordinated response to family violence.[5]
>
> - Provide a combination of family intervention (tertiary prevention)
>   and early childhood programs (community-based primary and
>   secondary prevention) to treat existing problems and prevent the
>   emergence of new problems.[3]

Sources: Adapted from
[1] Family Support Network of Illinois (April 2003). *Family Support Best Practices* [online]. Available: www.familysupportnetwork.org/FamilySupportBestPractices.htm [May 17, 2004].
[2] Adolescent's Family Support Services of Niagara (2004). *Guiding Principles and Best Practices* [online]. Available: www.afssn.org/principles.php [May 17, 2004].
[3] Centre for Addiction and Mental Health (2002). *Youth and Violence: What's the Story?* Youth Scoop, Sheet #3 (quotation p. 2) [online]. Available: www.camh.net/pdf/scoop_sheet_youth_violence.pdf [May 17, 2004].
[4] A.B. Doyle, M.M. Moretti, M. Brendgen, and W. Bukowski (2003). *Parent–Child Relationships and Adjustment in Adolescence: Findings from the HBSC Cycle 3 and NLSCY Cycle 2 Studies* (quotation p. v). Division of Childhood and Adolescence. Ottawa: Health Canada [online]. Available: www.hc-sc.gc.ca/dca-dea/publications/pdf/pcr-rpe_e.pdf [May 17, 2004].
[5] A. Cunningham and L. Barker (March 31, 2003). *Children Who Live with Violence: Best Evidence to Inform Better Practice: Recommendations for Intervention.* National Crime Prevention Centre. Public Safety and Emergency Preparedness Canada [online]. Available: www.prevention.gc.ca/en/library/publications/children/violence/children_who_live_with_violence/recommendations_for_intervention.html [May 17, 2004].

SUMMARY

■ Introduction

Statistics Canada's definition of a census family encompasses a broad range of family types. Families are also defined by the roles they play in society. In recognition of the importance of families, Canadian governments support the provision of family services; however, there is considerable disparity in the types and range of these services across the country. For a variety of reasons, politicians have been reluctant to establish a national family policy.

■ Family Formation and Social Welfare Programs

The proportion of traditional families is on the decline. Many social agencies tailor their services to meet the specific needs of common law, divorced, separated, or lone-parent families. Canada's legitimation of same-sex unions has several implications for social welfare legislation, benefits, and services. Adoption takes place at both domestic and international levels. The provinces are continuing to amend their adoption legislation and strategies to reflect modern needs and trends.

■ Children and Youth: A National Priority

Through research, we have gained a better understanding of the needs of children and the problems they face. Canada has committed itself to improving conditions for children. Under Canada's social union, governments have agreed to work together to improve child well-being. The National Children's Agenda supports initiatives for young children such as early childhood development, early learning, and childcare. Resources for older children include mental health services and programs to engage youth. Parent support programs aim to help parents raise their children and provide a stable environment for children.

■ Family Violence in Canada

The definition of family violence continues to expand as people's perceptions of this problem change. Canada's Family Violence Initiative aims to eradicate all forms of family violence. Spousal violence is widespread in Canada; shelters and transition houses are the primary resources for abused women and their children. The effects of abuse on children can be far-reaching. Canada addresses child abuse at three levels; however, tertiary prevention programs receive the most government support. Child welfare legislation is a regional responsibility, and this has resulted in variation in policies, procedures, and services across Canada.

■ Working with Families

Family practice is the focus for many social agencies and workers. It is important for workers to refine their skills if they hope to help families deal with a rapidly changing environment and with the consequences of government cutbacks to services. To help families cope with fewer services, social workers engage families in activities that promote internal and empowering solutions. Studies suggest that working in child welfare agencies is becoming more challenging; this line of work requires practitioners with particular skills and attitudes, and agencies that can provide a good working environment.

▼ KEY TERMS

For definitions of the key terms, consult the Glossary on page 364 at the end of the book.

census family p. 222

family policy p. 223

traditional families p. 224

lone-parent families p. 226

same-sex unions p. 226

adoption p. 227

youth engagement p. 234

vulnerable children p. 235

family violence p. 236

spousal violence p. 238

child abuse p. 239

children in care p. 242

empowerment p. 243

Social Welfare and Older Canadians

O b j e c t i v e s

I. *To look at current international and domestic approaches to an aging population.*

II. *To consider the security needs of seniors as they relate to finances, housing, and protection from abuse, and the initiatives in place to address these issues.*

III. *To explore aspects of physical and mental health and the various levels of caregiving services available to Canadian seniors.*

IV. *To review the social support needs of seniors, and the types of services and opportunities available to enhance social connections in the later years.*

V. *To consider the nature of social work practice with elderly populations.*

INTRODUCTION

Canada, like other Western industrialized countries, has an **aging population**—that is, a population in which over 10 percent of the population is sixty or older. In 1921, 5 percent of Canadians were sixty-five or older; this had increased to 13 percent by 2001, and is expected to reach 25 percent by 2041 (see Exhibit 11.1) (Health Canada, 2002b; Government of Canada/Government of Mexico, 2003).

Population aging is the result of a combination of factors, including lower fertility rates and increased longevity. From the end of the Second World War to the mid-1960s, it was common for Canadian women to have three or more children. Since that time, families have been getting smaller; on average, women now have 1.5 children. Meanwhile, Canada's baby boom generation (that is, people born between 1947 and 1966) continues to age, and this is pushing the average age of the population higher (Health Canada, 2002b). Also, people are living longer, which means there are more elderly people in absolute numbers. With medical technology advancing, with health care and nutrition both improving, with many infectious diseases under control, and with people making healthier lifestyle choices, we can expect that by 2041, the average Canadian man will be living to eighty-one, and the average Canadian woman to eighty-six (United Nations, 2003b).

Over the last twenty years, population aging has captured the attention of governments, social researchers, financial analysts, and others, especially in relation to the problems (rather than the benefits) of aging. Those who see population aging as a problem tend to make two broad assumptions: (1) a greater proportion of resources (such as health care, social services, public

Exhibit 11.1
CANADA'S AGING POPULATION

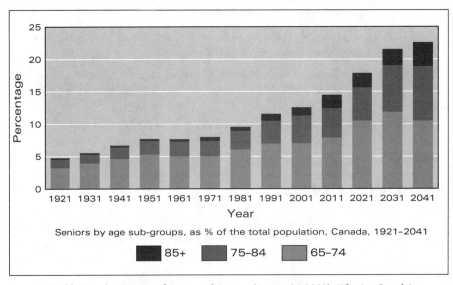

Seniors by age sub-groups, as % of the total population, Canada, 1921–2041

85+   75–84   65–74

Source: Health Canada, Division of Aging and Seniors (August 20 2002). *Who Are Canada's Seniors*, Chart 1 [online]. Available: www.hc-sc.gc.ca/seniors-aines/pubs/fed_paper/fedreport1_01_e.htm [May 18, 2004]. Reproduced with the permission of the Minister of Public Works and Government Services Canada, 2004.

pensions, and housing) will be consumed by a growing number of retired or "noncontributing" members of society; and (2) people in the workforce will have to support the retired population—a burden that is both unreasonable and unsustainable. Although population aging will undoubtedly create challenges, many groups point to the potential advantages of the aging trend. The United Nations (2003a), for example, sees the aging phenomenon as having "far-reaching benefits" arising from the contributions older citizens can make.

Through the combined efforts of seniors, governments, and private-sector groups, the quality of life of elderly people has improved steadily over the years. Health Canada (2002b) is urging Canadians to continue building on these efforts so that the needs of an aging society will be adequately met. Areas identified as requiring ongoing attention include the following:

- the health, well-being, and independence of older persons;
- seniors' participation in economic and social activities;
- support systems within communities; and
- the sustainability of government programs that benefit all Canadians.

Seniors are a highly diverse group. For example, they live in every region of Canada; some were born here, others immigrated here; they have different interests and participate at different levels; some are gay or lesbian, most are heterosexual; some live alone, others with a partner or adult child. With this diversity in mind, this chapter looks at some of the needs and challenges relating to aging and explores some of the ways that international groups, Canadian governments, and nongovernment organizations are responding to those needs. In the discussion that follows, the terms *senior*, *older person*, and *elderly person* are used interchangeably to refer to those aged sixty-five or over.

I. AN AGING POPULATION: GLOBAL AND DOMESTIC RESPONSES

AT THE INTERNATIONAL LEVEL

The global aging trend prompted the United Nations (2003b) to declare 1999 as the International Year of Older Persons (IYOP). This was an attempt to raise international awareness of aging and of seniors' contributions to global society. During the IYOP, various groups promoted certain concepts related to aging. The World Health Organization (2001a), for example, advanced the notion of **active aging** as "the process of optimising opportunities for physical, social and mental wellbeing throughout the life course in order to extend healthy life expectancy and the quality of life in older age." Similarly, Kofi Annan (1998), the UN Secretary-General, called for "a society for all ages"—that is, a world "that does not caricature older persons as patients or pensioners" but rather respects elderly people as being both contributors to and recipients of social development.

In 1982, the United Nations introduced the first international strategy— the Vienna International Plan of Action on Ageing—for governments around the world to use as a guide when developing policies and programs related to aging. By the turn of the millennium, new strategies were needed. In 2002, the UN released its revised International Plan of Action on Ageing (also known as the Madrid Plan) to help governments develop and revise aging-related policies and programs, protect the human rights of older people, and end age discrimination. The Madrid Plan encourages the inclusion of seniors in policy and program development through the forging of partnerships among governments, seniors' organizations, private-sector groups, and international agencies. Since endorsing the Madrid Plan, Canada has been working with other levels of government and with nonprofit groups to tailor that plan for the Canadian context (HelpAge International, 2002; Health Canada, 2003e).

In response to the Madrid Plan, the Pan-American Health Organization (PAHO) is encouraging its member states to work together on a plan for the Americas. Canada and Mexico, with technical help from PAHO, collaborated on the development of A Guide for the Development of a Comprehensive System of Support to Promote Active Ageing. This guide will be used in the Americas to develop policies and programs that promote active aging, strengthen health care, support family caregivers, and develop community alternatives to institutionalization (Government of Canada/Government of Mexico, 2003).

AT THE NATIONAL LEVEL

A number of federal departments participate in strategies for meeting the needs of Canada's aging population. For example, Human Resources Development Canada administers the public retirement income system; Statistics Canada collects social and demographic data, which are then used to develop age-specific policies and programs; and Health Canada's Division of Aging and Seniors works with government departments on research as well as on policy and program development, and shares information on matters of concern to seniors (Health Canada, 2003a).

The National Advisory Council on Aging (NACA), founded by the federal government in 1980, advises the health minister on matters relating to Canada's aging population and the quality of life of seniors. NACA also consults on seniors' issues with seniors, businesses, voluntary organizations, governments, and others. It recommends improvements to public policy or programs, engages the public in discussions on aging issues, and shares information about aging (Health Canada, 2003b).

Aging is not the responsibility of any single government department or service sector. As a consequence, many programs for seniors are the result of partnerships between the federal and regional governments, or between governments and voluntary organizations. These programs are highly varied, but most are based on one or more of the following concepts:

- *Inclusivity*. Programs tend to target all seniors, including those who are at risk and those who are healthy and active.

- *Healthy aging*. Programs are likely to promote behaviours, habits, and choices that enhance the quality of life for people of any age.

- **Population health model**. Programs reflect the belief that factors such as income, housing, social support, education, and transportation are powerful determinants of health.

In 1996, the Federal-Provincial-Territorial Ministers Responsible for Seniors released the National Framework on Aging (NFA) as a policy guide for meeting the needs of Canada's aging society. At the core of the NFA are a shared vision statement and five principles (see Exhibit 11.2). An important contribution made by the NFA has been the development of the Seniors Policies and Programs Database, which is available to all Canadians as a resource for planning and improving policies and programs. Although it supports the NFA's principles, Quebec has chosen not to participate in NFA activities. Instead, Quebec addresses the needs of seniors through its own health and social service programs (Health Canada, 1999a; 1999b).

Every provincial and territorial government has a department that provides information on seniors' services and whose general purpose is to improve the policies, programs, and processes that affect seniors. Two examples are the Manitoba Seniors Directorate and the Ontario Seniors' Secretariat. Many governments also have appointed councils to advise on seniors' issues. An example is New Brunswick's Advisory Council on Seniors.

At the voluntary level, a large number of regional organizations, councils, associations, networks, and committees are working on behalf of seniors. The mandates of these nongovernmental groups are diverse; that said, most of them support seniors in their efforts to live independently, to carry out daily activities in a normal community context, and to make decisions about

<u>E x h i b i t   1 1 . 2</u>

THE NATIONAL FRAMEWORK ON AGING

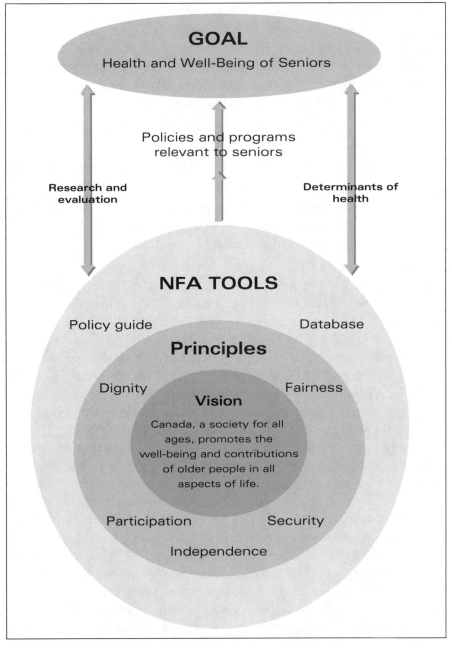

Source: Health Canada, Division of Aging and Seniors (March 1998). *Principles of the National Framework on Aging: A Policy Guide*, p. 7 [online]. Available: www.hc-sc.gc.ca/seniors-aines/ nfa-cnv/pdf/aging_e.pdf [May 18, 2004]. Reproduced with the permission of the Minister of Public Works and Government Services Canada, 2004.

their own lives. Organizations that provide seniors' programs usually focus on specific aspects of seniors' independence, such as physical or mental health, income, housing, or personal security.

II. MEETING SECURITY NEEDS: INCOME, HOUSING, AND PROTECTION

INCOME SECURITY

Most older Canadians rely on the **retirement income system** for financial support. This system was established with two goals in mind: "to ensure that elderly people have incomes high enough to allow them to live in dignity no matter what their circumstances were during their working years; [and] to maintain a reasonable relationship between income before and after retirement so that old age does not bring a drastic reduction in a person's standard of living" (National Council of Welfare, 1999b, 1). Canada's retirement income system has three "pillars":

- *Old Age Security* (OAS). This is funded by general tax revenues to provide a modest monthly pension to anyone sixty-five or older who meets basic residency requirements. Low-income seniors receiving OAS benefits may also be eligible for the Guaranteed Income Supplement, Spouse's Allowance, and Survivor's Allowance. Many provinces and territories provide cash supplements to augment these federal pensions.

- *Canada Pension Plan* (CPP). This is a self-supporting social insurance scheme that requires employed people and their employers to make regular contributions during the working years. A pension can then be drawn on retirement. Quebec residents draw from their own plan, the Quebec Pension Plan (QPP).

- *Private pension plans and savings*. These include both self-administered and employer-sponsored registered pension plans (RPPs), registered retirement savings plans (RRSPs), and other private pension plans (Social Development Canada, 2004a).

In anticipation of a large number of Canadians retiring and drawing pensions in the coming decades, the federal government has had to take certain measures to ensure that the retirement income system will be sustainable over the long term. For example, the federal government is reducing the national debt so that money that would normally go toward interest payments can be used to fund the OAS. The CPP underwent drastic changes in

1998, when its contribution rates were raised to make the system more sustainable. To strengthen the private pension component, the federal government has recently increased and indexed the RPP and RRSP contribution limits (Battle, 2001; Department of Finance, 2003f).

According to the Liberal Party of Canada (2004b), the number of low-income seniors fell from 11 percent in 1993 to 7.3 percent in 2001. Although Canada's retirement income system has received most of the credit for raising seniors' income levels, it has also been criticized for failing to provide benefits high enough to keep many seniors out of poverty. Seniors who have no sources of income other than government pensions run the greatest risk of falling below the poverty line. Many older women fit into this group; in 2000, they made up 71 percent of all poor seniors (Statistics Canada, 2004a). Statistics such as this prompted the Task Force on Active Living and Dignity for Seniors—appointed by Prime Minister Paul Martin in 2003—to recommend an increase in base funding for seniors. In 2004, the federal government responded by increasing the Guaranteed Income Supplement by almost 7 percent (Liberal Party of Canada, 2004b).

SENIORS' HOUSING

Adequate and affordable housing is central to everyone's quality of life, but as Montgomery (1977, 253) states: "The quality of the housing environment becomes increasingly significant in the lives of many aged families and individuals. And the quality of this [environment] largely determines the extent to which they will retain their independence."

Owing to government cuts to institutional care, and to new technologies that allow seniors to maintain their independence, fewer seniors are living in institutions than in past decades. Also, there has been a philosophical shift toward the concept of **aging in place**—that is, the right to grow old in one's own home. These developments are reflected in the variety of housing options now available to seniors. Three of these options are described below:

- *Supportive housing.* This is available in multifamily dwellings; it offers independent living space and a range of services. Many supportive housing complexes include a cafeteria, a recreation area, on-site personal care (such as daily visits or routine hygiene), and support services (perhaps cooking and transportation).

- *Retirement homes.* These are privately owned, operated, and regulated, and cater to relatively independent seniors who have minimal care needs and who seek to balance privacy with independence and with opportunities for socialization.

- *Private homes*. These may be improved through housing adaptation programs, which modify the homes of low-income seniors with physical limitations. For example, the Home Adaptation for Seniors' Independence program may subsidize the cost of installing grab bars in the bathroom or building a wheelchair ramp.

The growing shortage of affordable housing has led to concerns about homelessness among seniors. Although little research has been done regarding the extent of this problem, the evidence suggests that some seniors on fixed incomes have difficulty paying their rent on top of other basic living expenses. Hightower and colleagues (2003) suggest that seniors at risk of homelessness include women with histories of being abused, alcohol- and/or drug-abusers, and Aboriginal survivors of the residential school system. Seniors with physical and/or mental health problems that diminish the capacity to function independently are believed to be most vulnerable to homelessness. Current government initiatives (such as the Affordable Housing Program) have made it their goal to increase the number of low-cost housing units and thereby reduce the risk of homelessness among low-income seniors (National Advisory Council on Aging, 2003).

ELDER ABUSE AND THE NEED FOR PROTECTION

Elder abuse was first recognized as a social problem in the 1980s. The World Health Organization (2002) defines **elder abuse** as "a single or repeated act, or lack of appropriate action—occurring in any relationship where there is an expectation of trust—that causes harm or distress to an older person." Abuse against an elderly person can take the following forms:

- *Physical*. Includes inflicting pain, discomfort, or injury, using unnecessary physical restraints, and over- or under-medicating.

- *Psychological*. Includes insulting, threatening, isolating, or other behaviour that results in diminished dignity, loss of self-worth, or social exclusion.

- *Financial*. Includes stealing or misusing money or property, or forcing or defrauding an elderly person into giving away or selling property.

- *Neglect*. Includes withholding medication, food, water, care, or other basic necessities, or a caregiver's general failure to meet an elderly person's basic needs (Swanson, 1999).

With respect to family violence against seniors, the majority (71 percent) of abusers are spouses or adult children (Poulin, 2003).

It is difficult to determine the extent of elder abuse. Canada has no consistent method of collecting data on the incidence of this problem. The only comprehensive survey on elder abuse in Canada took place in 1989; the National Survey on Elder Abuse concluded that roughly 4 percent of seniors experience some form of abuse or neglect (Podnieks et al., 1990). Police statistics show that less than 1 percent of seniors are victims of criminal abuse; however, most experts would agree that elder abuse tends to be underreported to police or other authorities (Au Coin, 2003a). Some independent, small-scale studies on elder abuse suggest that the problem is greater in institutional settings. In Montreal, for example, researchers in a geriatric psychiatry centre found that elder abuse was either confirmed or suspected in almost 16 percent of patients; financial abuse was the most frequently reported type of abuse (Vida et al., 2002).

In 1998, a number of regional governments began introducing adult protection legislation. These laws vary from region to region, but most support prevention programs and public education related to elder abuse; the development of protocols and investigative procedures for responding to complaints; and regular reviews of relevant legislation and programs (Legislative Review Committee, 2003). In 2002, the UN recognized elder abuse as a global problem and its eradication as a collective, international responsibility; since then, Canadian governments have taken further steps to combat elder abuse. One of the country's most comprehensive plans in this area is the Toronto Declaration on the Global Prevention of Elder Abuse, which Ontario introduced in 2002 (World Health Organization, 2002).

Many communities coordinate and deliver elder abuse programs through multidisciplinary teams. Edmonton's Elder Abuse Intervention Team, for instance, includes a social worker, a police detective, and a representative from community services; these three work together to assess seniors' living situations and to develop safety and service plans for seniors at risk (Poulin, 2003). Other communities rely on interagency committees to advise on how local systems should respond to abuse, and to provide abuse-related information and support to seniors (Health Canada, 1998b).

III. SENIORS' HEALTH AND CAREGIVING NEEDS

PHYSICAL HEALTH ISSUES

According to one Health Canada study (2002b, 9), "more than three quarters of seniors living at home view their health as being good, very good, or excellent." Another study found that about half of all seniors are physically active

(National Advisory Council on Aging, 2003). Even so, one senior Canadian in four reports a long-term health problem—such as high blood pressure, arthritis, rheumatism, or diabetes—that restricts daily activities (Health Canada, 2002b).

Older people are at higher risk of disability than younger ones. Mobility disabilities (such as difficulty walking or standing for long periods) are the most common type of disability among seniors; in 2001, mobility problems limited the daily activities of 23 percent of seniors between sixty-five and seventy-four, and 43 percent of seniors seventy-five and over (Cossette and Duclos, 2002). Women are more likely than men to have mobility problems. Mobility and other types of disabilities increase the need for caregivers and for technical aids such as walkers and wheelchairs.

MENTAL HEALTH ISSUES

The Canadian Mental Health Association (2002, 8) defines **mental health** as "the capacity of individuals to interact with each other and their environment in ways that enhance or promote their sense of well-being, sense of control and choice with their life, optimal use of mental abilities, achievement of their own goals (both personal and collective) and quality of life." For many seniors, mental health problems—such as depression—are associated with the stress of change and a sense of loss brought on by forced retirement, reduced physical activity, separation from loved ones, and/or the death of a spouse. Seniors who experience mental distress tend to be in poor physical health and are likely to be living with chronic pain (Crompton and Kemeny, 1999; Prasil, 1993; Thompson, n.d.).

A national study on mental health conducted in 2002 found a correlation between seniors' mental health and a combination of personal and external factors. Exhibit 11.3 provides a conceptual framework that highlights the links between personal factors (spiritual, emotional, and so on) and external factors (such as transportation and income) and mental health. According to this model, good mental health is likely when an individual's personal needs are met and when resources are readily available through either the private sector or government-funded programs. In some cases, seniors may need encouragement or assistance to connect with the resources they need in order to enhance their mental health (Canadian Mental Health Association, 2002).

Among older seniors, Alzheimer's disease and related dementias are the most common and debilitating mental health problems (National Advisory Council on Aging, 1993). Burke and colleagues (1997, 24) define **dementia** as "a clinical syndrome characterized by severe losses of cognitive and emotional abilities, [which] interferes with daily functioning and the quality of

Exhibit 11.3

CONCEPTUAL FRAMEWORK: FACTORS CONTRIBUTING TO SENIORS' MENTAL HEALTH

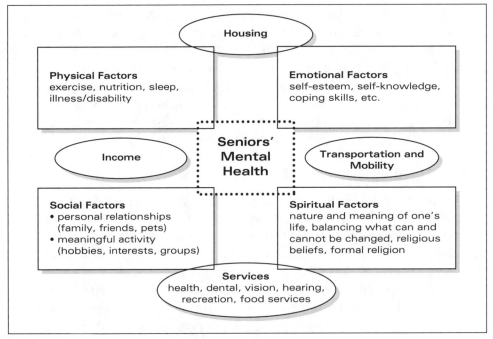

Source: Canadian Mental Health Association (January 2002). *Senior's Mental Health and Home Care: A National Study.* A Report Prepared for the Canadian Mental Health Association [online]. Available: www.cmha.ca/english/shmcare/national_report.pdf [May 18, 2004].

life." The Canadian Study of Health and Aging (2002) estimates that 250 000 or 8 percent of seniors suffer from some form of dementia; this figure is expected to rise to 592 000 by 2021 (Conn, 2003).

CARING FOR SENIORS: ADDRESSING PHYSICAL AND MENTAL HEALTH NEEDS

According to the 2002 General Social Survey, roughly one million Canadian seniors receive care for a long-term health problem. Most seniors receive informal care from family, friends, or neighbours; formal care from public- or private-sector health care providers; or a combination of informal and formal services. The proportion of seniors receiving care rose from 21 percent of women and 17 percent of men in 1996, to 32 percent of women and 26 percent of men in 2002 (Cranswick, 2002).

Of the total number of Canadians eighty-five and over who receive care, 62 percent of women and 24 percent of men live alone. According to Kelly Cranswick (2002), this population represents "a potentially vulnerable group who must rely on sources outside their own homes to help them maintain their independence. Such help often entails the organization of family and friends as well as formal care."

Institutional versus Community-based Care

Most seniors live independently. Institutional or long-term care (such as in a nursing home) is an option for seniors who require high levels of assistance because of a serious physical or mental impairment. These institutions usually provide food, shelter, round-the-clock nursing services, assistance with daily living activities, administration of medications, and therapeutic or rehabilitative services (Caregiver Resource Centre, 2004). In 2001, 4.9 percent of senior men, and 9.2 percent of senior women, were living in health care institutions (Statistics Canada, 2002b).

A growing older population, health care reform in Canada, and a general trend away from institutionalization are combining to generate a huge demand for home and community care services (Canadian Mental Health Association, 2002). The Premiers' Council on Canadian Health Awareness (2002, 4) defines **home and community care** as "programs that enable individuals to receive care at home and/or live as independently as possible in the community." Home and community care programs vary across the country; most, however, have three main functions:

- to provide a substitute for care given in hospitals or nursing homes;
- to help people remain independent in a natural environment; and
- to prevent chronic health problems by regularly checking on care recipients living in the community.

A variety of home and community care services are available in Canada. These include personal support (for example, homemaking), personal care (such as dressing or bathing), social support, seniors-oriented housing programs, transportation services, and a range of professional services (including grief counselling and physiotherapy) (National Advisory Council on Aging, 1995). These services allow many seniors to live independently; they are also less expensive than institutional care. In 2002, home and community care represented 4.25 percent of all provincial and territorial health care budgets, compared to 1.25 percent of health budgets in the early 1980s (Premiers' Council on Canadian Health Awareness, 2002).

A Canadian study on seniors' mental health found that most home and community care services are restricted to those with physical rather than mental health problems. The Canadian Mental Health Association (2002) has observed that physical health concerns are assigned more importance as people age; at the same time, the mental health needs of seniors are largely ignored. Yet a failure to provide mental health services to aging people may lead to a deterioration in seniors' general health. The demand for mental health–related home and community care is expected to rise as the population ages. Noninstitutional programs most in demand are likely to include geriatric daycare, rehabilitation services, support groups, outpatient mental-health counselling, and crisis intervention. Other resources—such as meal, exercise, and volunteer programs—will also be needed for their indirect benefits to mental health.

Home Care

A study by the Liberal Task Force on Seniors (2004, 13) found a "critical absence of adequate home care" for seniors in Canada. In response to this finding, the federal government, in its 2003 budget, enriched its contribution to the provinces and territories to expand home care services (Department of Finance, 2003c). Expanded home care budgets, however, did little to address the quality of service people received. Because it is primarily a provincial and territorial responsibility, home care services have been developed in accordance with each government's priorities and service standards—some being more supportive of quality care than others.

Many reports on Canada's health care system—including the ones by the Standing Senate Committee on Social Affairs, Science and Technology (the Kirby Report) and by the Commission on the Future of Health Care in Canada (the Romanow Report)—have stressed the need for a national home care system. The argument is that such a system would standardize the quality of services and establish a minimum level of care across Canada. Following its own investigation on home care, in 2004 the Liberal Task Force on Seniors called on governments at all levels to begin developing a national home care system. Later that year, the federal government laid out its ten-year plan—that is, to fully develop the home care system and bring it "into the centre of the publicly-funded health system" (Liberal Party of Canada, 2004a).

Canada's proposed national home care program would be supported by federal money amounting to $2 billion over a five-year period. These funds would be distributed on a per capita basis to those provinces and territories "that have passed legislation governing the provision of at least an agreed-upon, minimum basket of home care services." These services may include the following:

- home care services for post-acute patients, including coverage for medication and rehabilitation services;

- home mental health case management and intervention services; and

- palliative home care services to support people at the end of life.

Such services are expected to shorten people's hospital stays and to take the strain off severely limited hospital resources (Liberal Party of Canada, 2004a).

Informal Caregiving

There is a growing trend to shift responsibility for seniors' care away from formal, publicly funded home care toward informal caregivers. This shift is largely in response to the growing number of seniors living in the community, coupled with an insufficient number of home support programs. Publicly funded home care is coming to be restricted to seniors in greatest need; as a consequence, many seniors are being left to hire their own professional caregivers, or they are relying on informal caregivers, or they are doing without the help they need (Canadian Mental Health Association, 2002).

Half of all seniors between sixty-five and seventy-four who require care rely entirely on informal or volunteer care. Typically, the primary caregiver is a spouse or an adult child, *and* a woman. These caregivers provide a wide range of services, including friendly visiting, personal care, transportation to medical or other appointments, housekeeping, and yard work (Cranswick, 2002; Phillips et al., 2002).

In recent years, a phenomenon called **caregiver burden** has gained attention as a negative consequence of caring for another person for an extended period of time. Caregiver burden can have objective consequences. For example, a caregiver might experience physical health problems, or suffer financial loss if caregiving duties require that time be taken off work. There may also be subjective consequences for caregivers, including depression, psychological distress, reduced life satisfaction, and interpersonal conflict (Health Canada, 1998b). Caregiver burden is associated with government cutbacks to formal caregiving services, which lead to overreliance on family members (Reay-Young, 2001).

Little attention has been paid to the negative consequences for people who *receive* care. As Baines and colleagues (1998) point out, some care recipients feel guilty for becoming a burden to loved ones. Furthermore, the emphasis placed on caregiver burden has inadvertently cast many a care recipient in the undesirable role of dependant or "social problem." Seniors who depend on others for their care are also at higher risk of elder abuse (Poulin, 2003).

Many communities have programs to support informal helpers who have taken on the responsibilities of caregiving. **Respite services**, for example, give caregivers a break from their caregiving duties by providing daycare to elderly people, by temporarily placing seniors in residential settings, or by assigning home support workers to help with housework, meal preparation, and other household tasks. Rebecca Reay-Young (2001) calls attention to the changing needs of caregivers over time: the support needs of "beginner" caregivers tend to be quite different from those of "advanced" caregivers. Beginners may require structured courses to learn the basics of care provision; advanced caregivers—after years of providing care—may be ready to set up support groups for other caregivers.

It is generally accepted that a continuation of the current system of community care—with its overreliance on informal caregiving—is unrealistic, given the aging population. A number of reports suggest that more organized and coordinated strategies are needed, ones that will involve various levels of government, the private sector, families, and community groups. Although a comprehensive, nationwide system of elder care has yet to be implemented in Canada, the federal government has already recognized the value of informal caregiving: in 2004, it committed $1 billion over five years to assist family caregivers of seniors and people with disabilities (Liberal Party of Canada, 2004b).

IV. ENHANCING SOCIAL WELL-BEING IN THE LATER YEARS

SOCIAL SUPPORT

Social support or "connectedness" is essential to good physical and mental health in the senior years. Crompton and Kemeny (1999, 24) point out that

> some of the health-related effects of aging are buffered when people have someone they can confide in and can count on, and who can give them advice and make them feel loved. Conversely, lack of such support is a powerful risk factor for poor health, perhaps because people have no one to help shield them from the effects of various stressors.

In 1999, researchers in Health Canada's Seniors' Quality of Life project asked seniors what factors they thought influenced their health. Social networks and connections—derived from having family, friends, or acquaintances close by—and belonging to a community were identified as being primary health determinants (Bryant et al., 2002).

Many seniors live with a spouse, a partner, or an adult child; however, more than one-quarter of seniors live alone (see Exhibit 11.4). Those living alone are more likely to be women. Living alone is becoming a more common living arrangement for Canada's oldest seniors. In 1981, 25 percent of women and 16 percent of men over eighty-five were living alone; by 2001, the figures were over 38 percent for women, and almost 23 percent for men (Statistics Canada, 2002b). Many seniors choose to live alone, yet this particular living arrangement "can be associated with more loneliness, unmet daily needs, increased personal safety risks," and a greater need for social support services (National Advisory Council on Aging, 2003, 17).

A variety of social support programs provide seniors with opportunities for social interaction and mental stimulation. Socializing with others gives seniors a chance to think, reason, solve problems, reminisce, and otherwise exercise their mental capacities. According to Crompton and Kemeny (1999, 25), "seniors who are involved in a variety of activities appear to have strong cognitive capacity, while those with very little social involvement report having trouble concentrating, solving problems and remembering events."

Some voluntary organizations address the need for social support through **intergenerational programs**. These programs match seniors with younger people and encourage the two groups to interact with and learn from each other. One such program is provided by the Volunteer Grandparents Society of Canada, which connects seniors with families that do not have a biological grandparent living nearby. In another program— offered by the Canadian Association of the Deaf (2002)—deaf seniors and deaf youth are matched "so that the seniors can teach sign language and deaf culture to the youth, while the youth can assist the seniors with their everyday chores and needs." Some intergenerational programs focus on meeting the social needs of institutionalized seniors. For example, in Calgary, through the Friends of Seniors program (2003), teen volunteers visit and share activities with seniors living in care centres.

Until it lost its funding in 1996, the federally sponsored New Horizons program supported thousands of projects across Canada—projects that aimed to reduce isolation and loneliness among seniors by keeping them connected to and active within their communities. Following a recommendation by the Liberal Task Force on Seniors to reinstate this program, the federal government revived it in 2004. With an annual budget of $10 million, the program will "enable seniors to participate in social activities, pursue an active life and contribute to their community" (Canadian Association on Gerontology, 2004).

Exhibit 11.4

LIVING ARRANGEMENTS OF SENIORS IN 2001

SEX	AGE GROUP	LIVING ALONE	LIVING WITH SPOUSE OR PARTNER (NO CHILDREN)	LIVING WITH CHILDREN	LIVING IN HEALTH CARE INSTITUTION	OTHER LIVING ARRANGEMENTS[1]	TOTAL (NUMBERS)
Males	Total 65+	16.0	61.4	13.3	4.9	4.4	1 666 400
	65–74	14.0	64.4	15.4	2.1	4.0	1 008 735
	75–84	18.3	60.7	10.2	6.2	4.6	533 705
	85+	22.7	39.5	8.5	22.6	6.7	123 960
Females	Total 65+	34.8	35.4	12.1	9.2	8.4	2 224 395
	65–74	28.2	48.1	14.1	2.3	7.3	1 135 475
	75–84	42.8	27.7	10.8	9.6	9.2	798 300
	85+	38.5	7.2	8.4	35.4	10.6	290 620

1. Includes living with other relatives, such as a niece or nephew, or with nonrelatives, such as a lodger.

Source: Statistics Canada, Census, 2001.
Source: K. Cranswick (September 2, 2002). *General Social Survey Cycle 16: Caring for an Aging Society.* Statistics Canada, Catalogue No. 89-582-X1E, Table 1: Living arrangements of seniors aged 65 and over by sex and age group, 2001, p. 11 Ottawa: Statistics Canada. © Minister of Industry, 2002. [online]. Available: www.statcan.ca/english/freepub/89-582-XIE/pdf/89-582-XIE03001.pdf [May 22, 2004].

SENIORS AT WORK

Most Canadian seniors are retired, but about 6 percent (mostly men) hold down jobs, and about 40 percent work part-time (Canadian Centre for Justice, 2001). Many people over sixty-five remain in the workforce because they are physically and mentally capable of working. There is also evidence that some Canadians—many of them recent immigrants or single women— need to keep working into old age for financial reasons, especially if they are ineligible for CPP or private pension benefits (Liberal Task Force on Seniors, 2004; National Advisory Council on Aging, 2003).

Mandatory retirement policies still exist in some parts of Canada; these require people to stop working when they turn sixty-five. Some groups, such as human rights advocates, denounce mandatory retirement as a form of age discrimination. Other groups point to the advantages of allowing people to work for as long as they choose. The Liberal Task Force on Seniors (2004, 19) points out that "the current employment environment, characterized by a shortage of skilled workers and a rapidly aging workforce, would benefit from the continued participation of older workers able and willing to remain employed." This task force urges the federal government to "sponsor an open and informed national debate on the issue of mandatory retirement and on its possible alternatives."

VOLUNTEERING

Eighteen percent of seniors volunteer in formal organizations. While seniors get involved with organizations for various reasons, the majority (97 percent) do so because they believe in the organization's cause (Volunteer Canada, 2000b).

Volunteering has many potential benefits for seniors. Some find that volunteering helps them make a smooth transition from work to retirement "by providing opportunities to create and maintain relationships, to use their valuable skills, to give back to their communities and to mentor others" (Volunteer Canada, 2004b). A number of studies have associated volunteering with good health. Neena Chappell (2000, 5), Director of the Centre on Aging at the University of Victoria, concludes that "people who give their time to a volunteer activity, especially if it involves helping others, are happier and healthier in their later years ... A lot of benefit [from volunteering] comes from being in touch with others and having an impact on their lives."

Shrinking government funding, and the increasing demand for services, may lead some social agencies to recruit more volunteer service providers. Older people in general, and baby-boomers in particular, are being targeted as prime candidates to provide many of the services once delivered by professional helpers. Bowen and McKechnie (2001, 5) point out that "we need to keep our eyes firmly fixed on the future aspirations and abilities of the country's Baby Boomers so that as they begin to think about retirement and leave the workforce, volunteering and community service will be a real and viable option on their menu of possibilities."

POLITICAL ACTIVISM AND CONSULTATION

A number of organizations employ professionals to advocate on behalf of seniors. Toronto's Advocacy Centre for the Elderly (2003) is Canada's first legal clinic to specialize in seniors' issues. There are also many grassroots organizations established by seniors and run *by* seniors *for* seniors. Two examples are the Manitoba Society of Seniors and the Saskatchewan Seniors Mechanism. These two groups represent seniors in their respective provinces, advise local and provincial governments on matters that concern seniors, and work to enhance the image of seniors as well as their quality of life.

Seniors quite often voice their dissatisfaction with government policy. In 1985, the largest seniors' protest in Canadian history took place in response to the federal government's proposal to deindex pension payments. The collective action of seniors and others forced the government to scrap the deindexation plan. Another seniors' protest, in 1996, ultimately convinced the federal government to cancel its plans to replace existing pensions with the Seniors Benefit—a scheme that would have clawed back benefits from a greater percentage of pensioners (National Council of Welfare, 1999a). The political clout of seniors is expected to grow as the baby boom generation enters its senior years.

Canadian governments are making greater efforts to include seniors in public consultations and policy-making processes. In 1998, for example, the federal government established the Canada Coordinating Committee to consult with seniors on a variety of issues, including seniors' housing and health and the role of seniors in society. The members of the Liberal Task Force on Seniors (2004) considered it critical to include seniors in their 2003 study of social and economic issues related to aging.

Seniors want to be consulted on matters that affect them and future generations; they also want "to make significant and lasting contributions to their communities and to Canadian society" (Government of Canada, 2000c). Yet a study of seniors' quality of life by Bryant and colleagues (2002, 87) found that **ageism** (discrimination based on age) may be inhibiting seniors' participation in society. In this study, ageism was identified as a reason "wisdom derived life experience" is generally devalued in our society; why older seniors lack a strong political voice; why governments don't seem interested in hearing the views of older people; and why governments seem to treat seniors as "a problem and contributing to fiscal difficulties." To give Canadian seniors a stronger voice in the issues, decisions, and policies that affect them, the federal government appointed a Secretariat for Seniors in 2004.

V. SOCIAL WORK PRACTICE WITH ELDERLY POPULATIONS

In many ways, social work practice is the same with elderly clients as with other populations. However, as Steven Hick (2004) points out, **gerontological social work** requires "specialized knowledge of health care issues, poverty, housing and mental health, including knowledge of the ageing process and the issues surrounding Alzheimer's disease."

Gerontological social workers use a variety of methods to help their clients. During the assessment phase, workers must pay particular attention to biopsychosocial functioning; this involves assessing how certain biological changes associated with aging may affect the individual's emotional well-being and social interaction (Watt and Soifer, 1996). Working with older people usually requires a multidisciplinary approach to provide a broad range of services for elderly people and their families. Professionals with expertise in both social welfare and health services can assist in specialized areas such as elder abuse, substance abuse, and grief and loss.

There are many ways that social workers can work with the families of elderly clients. For example, during the assessment phase, family members can provide valuable information about the client's history, needs, and preferences. In turn, social workers can offer emotional support to family members who are finding it difficult to cope with an elderly relative's declining abilities, change in life situation, or institutional placement. Social workers can also provide hands-on assistance with caregiving tasks or help family caregivers connect with community resources such as respite services and support groups (Osterkamp, 1991).

Gerontological social workers who work from a population health model are likely to serve in one or more of the following service areas:

- *Individual and family counselling.* Assessing the needs and strengths of elderly clients and their families, and linking clients with resources to meet those needs.

- *Adult day programs*. Providing outreach, supportive services, group work, and care-planning services in structured day program settings.

- *Adult protective services*. Assessing factors that may put elderly clients at risk of abuse or neglect, and developing, implementing, and monitoring plans to ensure clients' safety and security.

- *Respite care*. Recruiting and training respite care workers and identifying families in need of this service.

- *Transportation and housing assistance*. Helping elderly clients find appropriate housing and safe and reliable transportation services.

- *Hospital or nursing home care*. Assessing social needs, providing counselling and support services, advocating on behalf of elderly clients and their families, and participating in program, care, and/or discharge-planning (Zastrow, 2004).

Working with elderly people "in an age of belt-tightening and economic constraint" can create challenges; however, the opportunity to work with a population that is becoming healthier, more active, better educated, and more politically involved with each generation can bring its own rewards (Holosko et al., 1996, 402). The demand for gerontological social work and social services is expected to increase as the population ages, as the number and proportion of seniors grows, and as health care services continue to face funding restraints (Stephenson et al., 2000).

SUMMARY

■ Introduction

Like other industrialized countries, Canada has an aging population. Some people see aging as a problem; others see it as an opportunity. To meet the future service demands an aging population may bring, Canada must continue working on improving seniors' health, independence, and quality of life.

■ An Aging Population: Global and Domestic Responses

The International Year of Older Persons promoted an awareness of active aging and called attention to the contributions of seniors. International plans of action on aging are guiding governments in the task of developing aging-related policies and programs. Several federal government departments address concerns relating to an aging population; in addition, the National Framework on Aging is helping governments respond to the needs of an aging society. At the regional level, provincial and territorial departments and voluntary organizations are addressing seniors' issues and needs.

■ Meeting Security Needs: Income, Housing, and Protection

Canada's retirement income system consists of OAS, CPP/QPP, and private pension plans and savings. The federal government is taking steps to ensure that the retirement income system is sustainable and adequate. A variety of housing options are available to help seniors "age in place" and remain independent for as long as possible. There is a growing concern about homelessness among seniors. The problem of elder abuse is being addressed by adult protection legislation and a variety of community services.

■ Seniors' Health and Caregiving Needs

Although most seniors are healthy and active, many have a chronic disease or disability. Mental health problems are associated with aging-related stress and personal losses. Dementia is a growing concern among the elderly. Seniors may be cared for in institutions or by community-based service providers. There is a growing demand for home care and a need to address mental health issues through home-based services. More and more seniors who need care are getting it from informal sources. Respite and other services support the efforts of informal caregivers and reduce the risk of caregiver burden.

■ Enhancing Social Well-Being in the Later Years

Social support is essential for maintaining good physical and mental health. Seniors living alone may be in greatest need of social support services. Various programs provide seniors with opportunities for social interaction, connection, and mental stimulation. Canadian seniors also keep active through paid employment, volunteering, and political activism/consultation.

■ Social Work Practice with Elderly Populations

Gerontological social work requires advanced assessment and intervention skills on the part of social workers. Social workers can form mutually beneficial relationships with the families of elderly clients. Through an emphasis on a population health model, social workers may work with seniors in a wide range of services.

▼ KEY TERMS

For definitions of the key terms, consult the Glossary on page 364 at the end of the book.

aging population p. 247

active aging p. 249

population health model p. 251

retirement income system p. 253

aging in place p. 254

supportive housing p. 254

elder abuse p. 255

mental health p. 257

dementia p. 257

home and community care p. 259

caregiver burden p. 261

respite services p. 262

intergenerational programs p. 263

mandatory retirement p. 265

ageism p. 266

gerontological social work p. 267

Aboriginal Canadians and the Social Welfare System

O b j e c t i v e s

I. To look at the evolving relationship between Aboriginal peoples and Canadian governments, and the legislation governing Aboriginal activities.

II. To review the colonization process and Aboriginal approaches to healing and wellness.

III. To consider the needs of Aboriginal children, and some of the initiatives and programs that aim to meet those needs.

IV. To study various issues relating to social work practice and education in an Aboriginal context.

INTRODUCTION

Long before the arrival of European settlers, the Aboriginal population comprised several separate nations, each with its own culture, language, and system of government (RCAP, 1996a). Canada's Aboriginal population is still far from homogeneous: in this population are the Inuit, Métis, and First Nations, and each group has its own needs, issues, and practices. The number of Aboriginal people in Canada is unknown; however, Statistics Canada estimates that at least 1.3 million people (4.4 percent of Canadians) have an ethnic origin of North American Indian, Métis, or Inuit. About 681 000 Aboriginal people are registered under Canada's Indian Act (Statistics Canada, 2003a).

Not everyone with Aboriginal ancestry identifies with an Aboriginal group. Of the 976 000 individuals who identify with at least one Aboriginal group, 62 percent identify with North American Indians, 30 percent with Métis, 5 percent with Inuit, and 3 percent with another Aboriginal group. Unless otherwise stated, the statistics in this chapter are based on Aboriginal *identity* rather than *ethnicity*; this is consistent with Government of Canada reports (Statistics Canada, 2003a).

Improved health practices, lower rates of infant mortality, and other factors have combined to create an Aboriginal "baby boom." While Canada's non-Aboriginal population doubled between 1951 and 2001, the Aboriginal population grew seven times over. One consequence of this population growth is that the Aboriginal population is much younger than the general population—in 2001, half of all Aboriginal peoples were under twenty-five (Statistics Canada, 2003a).

Over the past decade, Aboriginal people have witnessed social, economic, legal, and political reforms, many of which have their roots in international developments. For instance, after the United Nations proclaimed 1993 the International Year of the World's Indigenous People, Canada could no longer ignore the deplorable conditions in which many Aboriginal peoples were living. Toward the end of 1993, the UN declared an International Decade of the World's Indigenous People, and countries from around the world responded with commitments "to solve the problems faced by Indigenous people in such areas as human rights, the environment, development, education and health" (INAC, 1998, 2).

Recent studies suggest that Aboriginal peoples are beginning to see progress in certain life areas. For example, in the Aboriginal Peoples Survey 2001, 56 percent of Aboriginal adults (including Status and Non-Status Indians) living off a reserve reported having excellent or very good health. This survey also found that 9 percent of Aboriginal peoples between twenty and sixty-four living off a reserve were full-time students, compared to only 7 percent of non-Aboriginals (O'Donnell and Tait, 2003). In 2002, the Survey of First Nations People Living On-Reserve found that four out of ten Status Indians, compared to 2 out of 10 non-Aboriginal people, expected their economic prospects to improve in the coming year (EKOS, 2002a).

Despite progress in certain areas, a growing body of research indicates that Aboriginal peoples continue to face serious challenges. A report by the Canadian Institute for Health Information (2004, 19) confirms that "in general, the social, economic and environmental conditions of Aboriginal Peoples are worse than those of non-Aboriginal people." In its 2004 Speech from the Throne, the federal government acknowledged that "Aboriginal Canadians have not fully shared in our nation's good fortune. While some progress has been made, the conditions in far too many Aboriginal communities can only be described as shameful" (Government of Canada, 2004h). Some social analysts attribute the social, health, and economic problems experienced by Aboriginal groups to a history of repressive control by governments, the ineffectiveness of mainstream social welfare programs, and a loss of social and economic autonomy (Carniol, 2000).

I. ABORIGINAL/GOVERNMENT RELATIONS

EARLY GOVERNMENT CONTROL OF ABORIGINAL AFFAIRS

By the turn of the nineteenth century, the Canadian government had assumed a paternal role in Aboriginal affairs and looked upon Aboriginal peoples as "children of the state" (RCAP, 1996c). Duncan Campbell Scott, who served as deputy superintendent in the federal Department of Indian Affairs from 1913 to 1932, described this role:

> The apparent duty was to raise [the Indian] from the debased condition into which he had fallen due to the loose and pampering policy of former days. Protection from vices which were not his own, and instruction in peaceful occupations, foreign to his natural bent, were to be substituted for necessary generosity. (Patterson, 1987, 178–79)

Years later, a Royal Commission on Aboriginal Peoples would describe the apparent "protection" of Aboriginal peoples as a form of domination and "a code word implying encouragement to stop being Aboriginal and merge into the settler society" (RCAP, 1996a).

The British North America Act of 1867 allowed the new Dominion government to divide the responsibility for Aboriginal peoples between two levels of government: the federal government took responsibility for Status Indians and reserves; responsibility for all Non-Status Indians was assigned to the provinces. (For definitions of Status Indian and other terms, see Exhibit 12.1.) Canada's first prime minister, Sir John A. Macdonald, set out to eliminate the tribal system and completely assimilate Aboriginal peoples into the country's Christian and Eurocentric society (INAC, 2003; RCAP, 1996a).

Exhibit 12.1
DEFINITION OF TERMS

ABORIGINAL PEOPLES

Aboriginal peoples are the descendants of the original inhabitants of North America. The Canadian Constitution recognizes three groups of Aboriginal people: Indians, Métis, and Inuit.

BAND

A band is a group of First Nations people for whom lands have been set apart or whose money is held by the Crown. Many bands prefer to be known as First Nations.

FIRST NATIONS PEOPLES

First Nations peoples—a term often used in place of "Indians"—refers to both Status and Non-Status Indian peoples in Canada.

INDIAN

The term "Indian" collectively describes all the Indigenous people in Canada who are not Inuit or Métis. Indian peoples are one of three peoples recognized as Aboriginal in the Constitution Act, 1982. It specifies that Aboriginal people in Canada consist of the Indian, Inuit, and Métis peoples.

There are three categories of Indians in Canada: Status Indians, Non-Status Indians, and Treaty Indians.

- **Status Indians** Status Indians are people who are entitled to have their names included on the Indian Register, an official list maintained by the federal government. Certain criteria determine who can be registered as a Status Indian. Only Status Indians are recognized as Indians under the Indian Act, which defines an Indian as "a person who, pursuant to this Act, is registered as an Indian or is entitled to be registered as an Indian." Status Indians are entitled to certain rights and benefits under the law.

- **Non-Status Indians** Non-Status Indians are people who consider themselves Indians or members of a First Nation but whom the Government of Canada does not recognize as Indians under the Indian Act, either because they are unable to prove their status or have lost their status rights. Many Indian people in Canada, especially women, lost their Indian status through discriminatory practices in the past. Non-Status Indians are not entitled to the same rights and benefits available to Status Indians.

- **Treaty Indian** A Status Indian who belongs to a First Nation that signed a treaty with the Crown.

continued

continued

INUIT

The Inuit are Aboriginal people who inhabit the northern regions of Canada, principally Nunavut, the Northwest Territories, and the northern parts of Labrador and Quebec. Inuit are not covered by the Indian Act.

MÉTIS

The Métis are people of mixed First Nations and European ancestry; they identify themselves as distinct from Inuit and First Nations people.

RESERVE

A reserve is a tract of land owned by the Government of Canada, and set apart for the use and benefit of a First Nations band. Many First Nations have replaced the term *reserve* with *First Nation community*. The terms *on-reserve* and *off-reserve* refer respectively to people or things (such as services) that are part of, or separate from, a First Nation community. Inuit and Métis have never lived on reserves.

Source: Adapted from Indian and Northern Affairs Canada: Communications Branch (October 2002). *Words First: An Evolving Terminology Relating to Aboriginal Peoples in Canada.* 2002. [online]. Available: www.ainc-inac.gc.ca/pr/pub/wf/wofi_e.pdf [May 25, 2004]. Reproduced with the permission of the Minister of Public Works and Government Services Canada, 2004.

THE INDIAN ACT

The Indian Act of 1876 provided the federal government with both a framework for administering Aboriginal affairs and a mechanism for controlling the lives of people living on reserves. Like the Aboriginal policies that came before it, the Indian Act was "based unashamedly on the notion that Indian cultures and societies were clearly inferior to settler society" (RCAP, 1996c). In effect, this philosophical base empowered the federal government to deny the rights of many Status Indians. For example, a Status Indian woman who married a Non-Status man lost her status; in contrast, a Status Indian who married a Non-Status woman was allowed to keep his status (INAC, 1990).

Under the Indian Act, the federal government introduced a national system of reserves, on which only registered Indians were allowed to live. This system reflected many Poor Law principles and European values. Foucault (1965, 45) observes: "A parallel can be made between reserves and 'places of confinement' established in Europe during the mid-seventeenth century to isolate and contain the poor, vagabonds, the mentally ill, and delinquents." The "civilizing" and "normalizing" experiments conducted on people living on reserves in Upper Canada served to separate those people from the rest of society and "encouraged Europeans to consider them as having 'something wrong with them'" (Foucault, 1965, 7). Many of these attitudes and practices would persist for another hundred years.

A key purpose of the Indian Act was to increase **enfranchisement**—that is, to persuade Aboriginal peoples to reject their own heritage and fully assimilate into non-Aboriginal culture. Few Aboriginal people chose to be enfranchised. This resistance was met with laws and policies whose intent was to force enfranchisement on Aboriginal peoples. For example, Aboriginal lands and resources were confiscated, traditional languages and customs were banned, and First Nations communities (that is, bands) were severely disrupted by the relocation of adults to other communities and by the placement of children in residential schools (Patterson, 1987; INAC, 1990).

ATTEMPTS AT REFORM

By the Second World War, the federal government controlled most aspects of life on reserves. However, efforts to enfranchise Aboriginal peoples had largely failed. The Indian Act had not assimilated Aboriginal peoples into mainstream society; it had only deprived them of power and kept them in a state of dependency. As poverty, other social problems, and social disorganization worsened on reserves, Aboriginal leaders came forward to demand change and to defend their people's rights. In particular, Aboriginal peoples wanted the federal government to end its enfranchisement policies, relax its grip on Aboriginal affairs, and honour its own treaties. The Indian Act was amended in 1951 to lift the ban on potlatches, pow wows, and other traditional ceremonies. However, the clauses in the act relating to enfranchisement and Indian status remained intact (INAC, 1990; Ward 2002).

In 1969, in its Statement of the Government of Canada on Indian Policy, the federal government agreed to abolish the Indian Act, relinquish its responsibility for Status Indians, and give First Nations communities more control over their lands. In return, Status Indians would abandon their special status and be treated more like other Canadians. Most First Nations rejected the government's proposal on the basis that the loss of special status would jeopardize both their rights and their land claims (Patterson, 1987; INAC, 1990).

The 1969 statement on Indian policy was not a total failure since it helped spark "a worldwide human rights movement of Indigenous peoples" (RCAP, 1996a). In the early 1970s, Canada's Aboriginal peoples began organizing themselves. The resulting groups would eventually become known as the Assembly of First Nations (representing Status Indians living on a reserve); the Native Council of Canada (representing Non-Status Indians, newly registered Indians, nonband members living off a reserve, and Métis living outside the Prairie provinces); the Métis National Council (representing

Métis living on the Prairies); and the Inuit Tapirisat of Canada (representing Inuit people living in northern Canada) (Dunn, 1992).

The proclamation of the Constitution Act of 1982, and the passage of the Canadian Charter of Rights and Freedoms into law, brought native rights to the forefront of Canadian political agendas and paved the way for further reforms in Aboriginal policy. In 1985, the Government of Canada amended the Indian Act to guarantee the equal treatment of Aboriginal men and women, and to restore status and membership rights to First Nations. Amendments also abolished enfranchisement policies (Canadian Institute for Historical Microreproductions, 2004).

NEW PARTNERSHIPS IN THE 1990S

A Royal Commission on Aboriginal Peoples

In 1990, Prime Minister Brian Mulroney proposed a Native Agenda to settle land claims, improve social and economic conditions on reserves, enhance Aboriginal/government relations, and address other issues of concern to Aboriginal peoples (INAC, 1993). Progress was hindered by the inability of the federal government and Aboriginal leaders to reach an agreement on several constitutional issues; Aboriginal/government relations also deteriorated as a result of a violent confrontation at Oka between members of the Mohawk nation and the Quebec Provincial Police. The need to improve these relations prompted the federal government to appoint a Royal Commission on Aboriginal Peoples (RCAP) in 1991. The RCAP was given a broad mandate, including a review of "the relationship among aboriginal peoples (Indian, Inuit and Métis), the Canadian government, and Canadian society as a whole" (RCAP, 1996b). In 1996, the commission released its final report, which made 440 recommendations for resolving a broad range of Aboriginal issues. According to the commission's report (RCAP, 1996a, 11), any new partnership between Aboriginal peoples, governments, and non-Aboriginal people would have to be "much more than a political or institutional one. It must be a heartfelt commitment among peoples to live together in peace, harmony and mutual support."

Self-Government

Although Aboriginal peoples had their own forms of government centuries before the European settlers arrived in Canada, it was Section 35 of the Constitution Act of 1982 that formally recognized the right of Aboriginal peoples to self-government. Indian and Northern Affairs Canada (INAC, 2002c) defines **self-governments** as "governments designed, established and administered by Aboriginal peoples under the Canadian Constitution through a process of negotiation with Canada and, where applicable, the provincial government."

In 1995, the Government of Canada released its Inherent Rights Policy, which was to serve as a guide for First Nations self-government. This policy restricted First Nations governments to "matters that are internal to their communities, integral to their unique cultures, identities, traditions, languages and institutions, and with respect to their special relationship to their land and resources" (INAC, 2002b). The policy recognized the right to self-government, but it also implied that First Nations peoples would remain citizens of Canada, have the same rights and freedoms as other Canadians, and work within the existing Canadian political and parliamentary structures.

By the end of the 1990s, three self-government agreements had been reached: with the Kativik regional government in northern Quebec, with the Sechelt Indian Band of British Columbia, and with Nunavut, an Inuit government in the eastern Arctic. In addition, more than ninety other self-government agreements between the Government of Canada and First Nations were being negotiated (Pratt, 2002).

Gathering Strength: Canada's Aboriginal Action Plan

In 1998, the Liberal government under Jean Chrétien made a commitment to work with Aboriginal peoples, other levels of government, and the private sector to improve the living conditions of Canada's Indigenous people. To formalize this commitment, the federal government launched Gathering Strength: Canada's Aboriginal Action Plan. This scheme sought to renew the federal government's partnership with Aboriginal peoples and to improve the ways that social and economic programs for Aboriginal groups were structured and implemented. An important first step in the reform process was the Government of Canada's acknowledgment of its unjust treatment of Aboriginal peoples in the past. In 1998, the federal government made a formal apology to Aboriginal peoples in the form of a Statement of Reconciliation.

Canada's Social Union

The Social Union Framework Agreement (SUFA) (see Appendix B) ensures that Canadian "governments will work with the Aboriginal peoples of Canada to find practical solutions to address their pressing needs" (Government of Canada, 1999b). By the time SUFA was adopted, the federal government had already devolved many responsibilities for Aboriginal affairs to First Nations communities and to regional governments; it made sense that both levels of government and Aboriginal peoples would continue working together on social union priorities. In late 1999, the Federal-Provincial-Territorial Council on Social Policy Renewal met with the Ministers Responsible for

Aboriginal Affairs and the leaders of five national Aboriginal organizations to discuss ways in which those organizations might implement the principles and obligations underlying SUFA (Government of Canada, 1999c). Before long, Aboriginal organizations would begin developing new early-childhood development programs and other initiatives supported by the social union.

REVISITING THE INDIAN ACT

In its 2001 Speech from the Throne, the federal government committed itself to improving "its relationship with Aboriginal people" and to supporting "First Nations communities in strengthening governance." It also acknowledged that the 125-year old Indian Act severely hindered First Nations' progress toward effective self-government as well as their capacity to build healthy economies and communities (Ward, 2002). To remedy this problem, in 2002 the federal government introduced the First Nations Governance Act (otherwise known as Bill C-7) to the House of Commons. The Liberal government touted the proposed act as a strategy to reform the Indian Act and to give First Nations "the modern tools they need to operate effective, responsible and accountable governance structures, [and] the solid basis needed for future development" (INAC, 2002a).

For a number of reasons, First Nations peoples rejected Bill C-7. For example, the Assembly of First Nations criticized the bill for imposing several standardized, "one-size fits all" electoral and fiscal codes on more than 600 reserves across Canada and, in so doing, ignoring the diverse needs and circumstances of First Nations communities (Hurley, 2002). When Paul Martin became prime minister in 2003, he too rejected Bill C-7 and proposed that both the Indian Act and Indian and Northern Affairs Canada be eventually eliminated. However, before that step could be taken, Martin explained, a system was needed to identify First Nations goals, create action plans, and evaluate the progress of those plans on a regular basis. In 2004, the federal government—in cooperation with Aboriginal organizations—introduced such a system (Bailey, 2004a).

II. HEALING AND WELLNESS IN ABORIGINAL COMMUNITIES

COLONIZATION AND THE RESIDENTIAL SCHOOL SYSTEM

The high rates of unemployment, poverty, addiction, mental health disorders, and other social problems that exist among Aboriginal peoples are often attributed to **colonization**. Emma D. LaRoque (1994) defines colonization as a "process of encroachment and subsequent subjugation of Aboriginal peoples since the arrival of Europeans. From the Aboriginal perspective, it refers to loss of lands, resources, and self-direction and to the severe disturbance of cultural ways and values."

One of the key mechanisms used to colonize Aboriginal peoples was the **residential school system**, which began operations in 1883. This system attempted to assimilate Aboriginal peoples into mainstream society by separating Aboriginal children from their parents and placing them in distant schools, where they were taught Euro-Canadian values and customs (Jacobs et al., 1992). Residential schools were home to many generations of Aboriginal children until the last school closed in 1996. An estimated 92 000 people alive today attended a residential school. Over the past few years, thousands of former residential school students have come forward with claims that they were physically and/or sexually abused while in the system (Government of Canada, 2003c).

TRADITIONAL VERSUS MAINSTREAM APPROACHES

McKenzie and Morrissette (2003) observe that "colonization is the source of historical trauma and unresolved grief among many Aboriginal people: it resulted in personal and collective losses including family connections, and a way of life." In their efforts to cope with the impact of loss, many Aboriginal people have turned to social welfare programs and services. But mainstream, Euro-Canadian programs are not always sensitive to Aboriginal values, culture, or needs (First Nations Child and Family Caring Society of Canada, 2002). Over the past two decades, a number of Aboriginal healing programs have emerged across Canada—programs developed, delivered, and managed by Aboriginal groups. These programs are tailored to the needs of Aboriginal clients, and are based on "Aboriginal theory" and traditional practices; they are also seen as being outside the mainstream social welfare system although they are sometimes used in conjunction with mainstream services. Thus, Aboriginal peoples can now choose between mainstream programs (such as psychotherapy) and programs based on traditional practices (such as the Medicine Wheel)—or utilize both.

A fundamental difference between a **traditional approach** and a **mainstream approach** relates to world view, which can be defined as "a set of related ideas or views to which members of a distinct culture subscribe" (McKenzie and Morrissette, 2003). The mainstream world view tends to isolate human problems (such as mental disorders) and to treat them as discrete entities that can be "fixed" through medication or psychotherapy. According to this view, individuals are generally separate from—albeit interacting with—their environment. In contrast, people who hold a traditional world view usually see **healing** as a process of restoring balance. They focus on the larger context of a person's relationships with their family, community, the environment, and the spiritual world. They consider physical, emotional, social and spiritual aspects, and tend to emphasize the person's role in their own healing. (Assembly of First Nations, 1999)

Much of the recent literature on Aboriginal issues focuses on how First Nations communities are approaching the process of healing and, in turn, breaking free from their oppressive past and progressing toward a better future. Exhibit 12.2 illustrates how First Nations peoples view the past before European contact, how they experience the consequences of contact, and how they look to the present and future as an opportunity for learning and healing.

HEALING STRATEGIES

Healing initiatives during the 1980s focused on the pervasive problems of alcoholism and drug abuse in First Nations communities. However, it was not long before people realized that substance abuse "was only the 'tip' of a very large and complex 'iceberg,' the bulk of which remained hidden beneath the surface of community life" (Lane et al., 2002). It was soon recognized that other social problems, such as those relating to residential schools, family relationships, and mental health, were serious and widespread in First Nations communities and needed to be made priorities for healing initiatives. This section looks at how some of these social problems are currently being addressed.

Impact of Residential Schools

Recent studies are helping us understand the many impacts that the residential schools had on Aboriginal children. The term "intergenerational impact" refers to the negative effects of residential schools on the offspring of former students. According to Indian Residential Schools Resolution Canada (Government of Canada, 2003c), "former students have indicated that they find it difficult to express love or communicate with their children due to their experience at a residential school." Some Aboriginal professionals describe this particular phenomenon in terms of post-traumatic stress syndrome, which not only affects those who experienced the trauma directly, but also establishes a dysfunctional pattern of response that is expressed within families and passed down to later generations (Castellano, 2002).

Charles R. Brasfield (2001), a psychiatrist for many First Nations people, suggests that although many of the effects of residential schools resemble post-traumatic stress syndrome, they also have a distinct cultural component. For this reason, the term **residential school syndrome** has been coined to

Exhibit 12.2

CYCLE OF HEALING

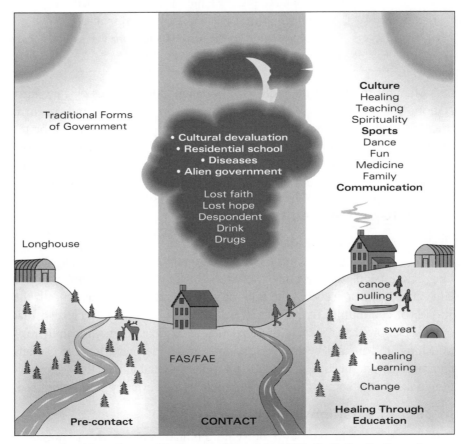

Traditional Forms of Government

Longhouse

• Cultural devaluation
• Residential school
• Diseases
• Alien government

Lost faith
Lost hope
Despondent
Drink
Drugs

Culture
Healing
Teaching
Spirituality
Sports
Dance
Fun
Medicine
Family
Communication

canoe
pulling

sweat

healing
Learning

Change

FAS/FAE

Pre-contact

CONTACT

Healing Through Education

Source: Adaped from Aboriginal Healing Foundation (May 2002). *The Healing Has Begun: An Operational Update from the Aboriginal Healing Foundation*, p. 11[online]. Available: www.ahf.ca/english-pdf/healing_has_begun.pdf [May 25, 2004].

describe the cluster of symptoms specific to Indian residential schools (as opposed to mainstream boarding schools). These symptoms include distressing memories or dreams of life at the school; sleeping disorders; anger management problems; and avoidance of people, places, and events that bring back memories of the school.

To help Aboriginal peoples deal with the adverse effects of the residential school system, three federal departments—the First Nations and Inuit Health Program Directorate, Indian and Northern Affairs Canada, and Aboriginal Affairs of the Privy Council Office—introduced the Aboriginal Healing Strategy in 1997. Part of the healing strategy has been to establish the Aboriginal Healing Foundation, a nonprofit, nongovernmental corporation run by Aboriginal people. Launched in 1998 with an initial $350 million federal grant (to be spent over nine years), the foundation has set out to fund community-based traditional healing projects across Canada. These projects have included the following:

- healing services (healing circles, day treatment centres, sex offender programs);

- community services and life skills (support networks, leadership training for healers);

- prevention and awareness (education and training materials, sexual abuse workshops);

- traditional activities (on the land retreats, support networks for Elders and Healers); and

- training and education (parenting skills, curriculum development). (Aboriginal Healing Foundation, 2002, 12)

The foundation has also supported projects to promote a better understanding of the links between residential school abuse and substance abuse (National Native Addictions Partnership Foundation Inc., 2000).

Family Violence

Family violence has a number of similar attributes across cultures. That said, some social analysts consider violence in Aboriginal families to be distinct in the following ways:

- It affects entire "communities and cannot be considered a problem of a particular couple or an individual household."

- It is directly associated with government policies intended "to disrupt or displace the Aboriginal family."

- It "is fostered and sustained by a racist social environment that promulgates demeaning stereotypes of Aboriginal women and men" (RCAP, 1996d).

Rates of family violence tend to be higher among Aboriginal peoples than in the general population. For example, Aboriginal women are roughly three times more likely to experience spousal abuse than non-Aboriginal women. Moreover, 57 percent of Aboriginal women who are assaulted by their husband (compared to 46 percent of non-Aboriginal women) report that their children witnessed the violence (Statistics Canada/Canadian Centre for Justice Statistics, 2001).

As with most Aboriginal programs, family violence is approached from a **holistic perspective**, meaning that the individual is treated "in the context of the family; the family in the context of the community; [and] the community in the context of the larger society" (Health Canada, 1996a, 4). Reflecting this broad and inclusive focus, healing strategies often involve the survivor of abuse as well as spouses, children, and elders (JamiesonHartGraves Consulting, 2002).

One First Nations community that has adopted a holistic approach to family violence is Hollow Water, Manitoba. The Community Holistic Circle Healing (CHCH) program is based on a thirteen-step process that addresses the needs of the survivor of abuse, the abuser, family members, and workers associated with the incident. The steps focus on educating people about the seriousness of family violence, changing attitudes toward violence, preventing further violence in the community, and helping people heal. This process can take several years to complete (Justice as Healing, 1995; Bushie, 1993). A program evaluation conducted in 2003 found that CHCH had reduced the community's reliance on mainstream resources and had the potential to "be a cost-effective alternative to the traditional criminal justice process" (Public Safety and Emergency Preparedness Canada, 2003, 2).

Mental Health Problems

Mental health problems are believed to be disproportionately experienced by Aboriginal peoples. Canadian studies indicate the following:

- The suicide rate is 2.6 times higher among First Nations men, and 4 times higher among First Nations women, than the Canadian averages (Assembly of First Nations, 2000).

- Although actual rates are lacking, the abuse of alcohol, drugs, solvents, and other substances is a serious problem in many First Nations communities (Health Canada, 1998c).

- Among Aboriginal peoples living off reserve, about 13 percent have a problem with depression, compared to 7 percent of non-Aboriginal people (Statistics Canada, 2002d).

According to the traditional Aboriginal view of health, these symptoms point to an imbalance or lack of harmony in a person's overall health and well-being (Smye and Mussell, 2001).

Mainstream programs have generally failed to help Aboriginal peoples with mental health problems, largely because psychotherapy and other conventional interventions are incompatible with traditional cultural values, current realities, and the unique needs of the Aboriginal population (Kirmeyer et al., 2000). Smye and Mussell (2001, 3) add that "the traditions, values and health belief systems of First Nations and other Aboriginal people are poorly understood by many providers and often are not respected or considered." In contrast, mental health programs and services designed by and for Aboriginal peoples are culturally sensitive and are likely to utilize traditional healing practices; furthermore, these programs take a holistic approach, one that focuses on the connections among individuals, family members, culture, community, and nature (Kirmayer et al., 2000).

There are various organizations across Canada that specifically address the mental health needs of Aboriginal peoples. Some of these organizations concentrate on research and policy development relating to Aboriginal mental health, others on the prevention or treatment of mental health problems. Following are some examples of these organizations:

- The Institute of Aboriginal Peoples' Health provides funding to research projects that focus on improving the mental health of First Nations peoples, Inuit, and Métis.

- Nunavut's Addictions and Mental Health Strategy engages in policy development, health promotion, and the prevention of mental health problems among Inuit.

- The Indian Residential Schools Mental Health Support Program provides mental health treatment for First Nations peoples, Inuit, and Métis who suffered abuse while attending residential schools (Information Centre on Aboriginal Health, 2004).

PROGRAMS ON AND OFF RESERVE

First Nations Communities

Central to the concept of self-government and self-determination is the authority and involvement of First Nations in the design, administration, and delivery of on-reserve social welfare programs and services. Several federal departments, including Indian and Northern Affairs Canada, Human Resources Development Canada, and Health Canada, are working alongside First Nations in the management and delivery of on-reserve programs and services. While these communities evolve toward self-government, they share with government many of the responsibilities for Aboriginal programs. For example, under the federally funded First Nations Child and Family Services Program, First Nations agencies deliver child welfare services on reserves, using their respective provincial/territorial child welfare legislation as a guide to practice (First Nations Child and Family Caring Society of Canada, 2002; INAC, 2001).

Just like other Canadian communities, First Nations communities have their own identified needs, issues, and priorities for programs and services. They also have opinions on which areas of social development government should assist. In 2002, a survey was conducted involving more than 1500 First Nations people living on a reserve. The respondents were asked to identify which areas they thought the Government of Canada should treat as its highest priority. Exhibit 12.3 gives the results of this survey.

Urban Settlement

Self-government and related programs and services may benefit First Nations peoples living on reserve, but they do little for those living off reserve. Yet over 68 percent of Canada's Aboriginal population do not live on a reserve or in a settlement, and almost half (49 percent) of all Aboriginal peoples live in urban centres (Statistics Canada, 2003a). Many urban Aboriginal peoples are faced with high rates of poverty, unemployment, and homelessness; they are also likely to experience family violence, victimization, and/or conflict with the law (Hanselmann, 2001).

A number of urban-based resources—such as Native Friendship Centres—provide support to Aboriginal people whose needs are not adequately met by mainstream social agencies. The development of programs for urban Aboriginal peoples has nevertheless been inconsistent and uncoordinated. In recognition of "the serious socio-economic needs of urban Aboriginal people," and the poor coordination among programs for this population, in 1998 the federal government introduced the Urban Aboriginal Strategy (UAS). The main objective of the UAS is to improve the coordination of Aboriginal policies and programs in urban centres and make them more responsive to local Aboriginal needs and priorities (Privy Council Office, 2003c).

III. CARING FOR ABORIGINAL CHILDREN

The Government of Canada recognizes that "Aboriginal children face greater disadvantages and risks in childhood than any other group of children in Canada" (Government of Canada, 1997b). First Nations children and youth, for instance, are more likely than their non-Aboriginal peers "to be born into poverty, to suffer health problems, maltreatment, incarceration, and placement in the child welfare system" (First Nations Child and Family Caring Society of Canada, 2003, 3). Moreover, compared to non-Aboriginal urban youth, Aboriginal youth (aged fifteen to twenty-four) living in cities have higher rates of disability, suicide, mortality, preventable diseases, and unemployment (Standing Senate Committee on Aboriginal Peoples, 2003). Many

Exhibit 12.3

FEDERAL GOVERNMENT PRIORITIES

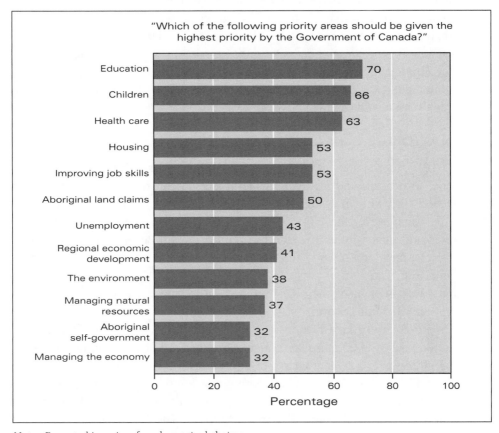

"Which of the following priority areas should be given the highest priority by the Government of Canada?"

Priority	Percentage
Education	70
Children	66
Health care	63
Housing	53
Improving job skills	53
Aboriginal land claims	50
Unemployment	43
Regional economic development	41
The environment	38
Managing natural resources	37
Aboriginal self-government	32
Managing the economy	32

Notes: Presented in series of random paired choices.

Percentage indicates average number of times an option was selected over all others.

INAC Survey October 2002

Number of respondents: 1507

Sample: Respondents were members of an Indian Band or First Nation; a resident (for at least some part of the year) on a reserve in Canada; and sixteen years of age or over.

Source: EKOS Research Associates Inc. (December 17, 2002). *Fall 2002 Survey of First Nations People Living On-Reserve: Final Report.* Indian and Northern Affairs Canada, p. 7 [online]. Available: www.ainc-inac.gc.ca/pr/pub/srv/srv03_e.pdf [May 25, 2004].

problems facing young Aboriginal people are attributed to the weakening of Aboriginal families, an after-effect of the residential school system and place-ment in non-Aboriginal foster care (Castellano, 2002).

Surveys suggest that some conditions for Aboriginal children are beginning to improve. For example, the Aboriginal Peoples Survey 2001 found that most Aboriginal youth living off reserve considered their health to be about as good as that of their non-Aboriginal peers, and were more likely than in previous years to finish high school (O'Donnell and Tait, 2003). Despite this progress, there is an ongoing need to improve the quality of life for Aboriginal children and youth, as well as their families. Some of the programs that aim to meet this need are provided through the National Children's Agenda and child welfare systems.

NATIONAL CHILDREN'S AGENDA

In 1997, representatives of five national Aboriginal organizations and the federal, provincial, and territorial governments began developing a long-term action plan known as the National Children's Agenda (NCA). Since then, Aboriginal peoples have been able to introduce new programs for young children and their families through the National Child Benefit, Early Childhood Development agreements, and the Multilateral Framework on Early Learning and Child Care.

To complement the NCA initiatives, the Government of Canada committed $320 million over five years to a Federal Strategy on Early Childhood Development for First Nations and Other Aboriginal Children. This strategy, introduced in 2002, aims "to enhance existing early childhood development programs[,] … intensify efforts to address fetal alcohol syndrome and fetal alcohol effects in First Nations communities, and support new measures to monitor the well-being of Aboriginal children by enhancing research and knowledge" (Government of Canada, 2001a). The NCA has also enriched several existing programs, such as those described below.

Brighter Futures/Community Action Plan for Children

Health Canada sponsors two initiatives that aim to improve the health and quality of life for Aboriginal children aged six and under, as well as their families:

- Brighter Futures targets families living in First Nations and Inuit communities.
- The Aboriginal component of the Community Action Plan for Children (CAPC) focuses on Métis, Inuit, and off-reserve First Nations families.

Each of these initiatives supports a wide range of culturally sensitive programs and services that are preventative in nature and that focus on enhancing early childhood development, pre- and post-natal care, and parenting skills. These programs encourage parents and other community members to participate in the design and implementation of activities, and in the formation of networks and partnerships within communities (Government of Canada, 2001a; Ontario Métis Aboriginal Association, 2004).

Aboriginal Head Start/First Nations Head Start

Health Canada's Aboriginal Head Start is an early intervention program that prepares "children for school by meeting their spiritual, emotional, intellectual and physical needs." This initiative is delivered through two streams:

- The core program serves First Nations, Inuit, and Métis preschool children and their families living in cities and large northern communities.

- The First Nations Head Start is tailored to the needs of First Nations preschool children and their families who live on a reserve.

Aboriginal Head Start projects are designed, managed, and delivered by Aboriginal groups with the assistance of parents and other community members. Most projects operate out of childcare centres, Native Friendship Centres, or other central facilities. Project activities generally focus on "six areas important to children's healthy development: culture and language; education; health promotion; nutrition; parental involvement; and social support" (Government of Canada, 2001a).

First Nations and Inuit Child Care

The need for Aboriginal childcare has been documented since the 1960s, but it was not until 1995 that the federal government launched the First Nations and Inuit Child Care Initiative. This initiative is allowing on-reserve childcare programs to expand and to better reflect the local and regional needs of Aboriginal and Inuit peoples. A key thrust of this initiative is to create more effective and affordable childcare spaces so that parents of young children can attend work or school. The initiative also offers after-school care for children as old as twelve. By 2004, the initiative had funded more than 7000 childcare spaces in 390 First Nations and Inuit communities across Canada (Government of Canada, 2001b; HRDC, 2004c).

First Nations National Child Benefit Reinvestment

Under the National Child Benefit (NCB), First Nations communities are allowed to claw back social assistance benefits from families with children and use that money to enhance programs and services for low-income families with children. A 2003 review of the First Nations NCB Reinvestment strategy found that children and families, as well as entire communities, had benefited from the NCB reinvestments. Projects under the reinvestment strategy include nutrition programs that provide meals to children and that educate parents on nutrition and meal preparation; and community enrichment projects that connect community members through groups, storytelling, and artistic endeavours (Government of Canada, 2003a).

CHILD WELFARE SERVICES

Until recently, a common practice in child welfare systems was to apprehend Aboriginal children and place them in non-Aboriginal foster care. This practice culminated in what Patrick Johnston (1983) refers to as the "sixties scoop"—a massive apprehension of Aboriginal children beginning in the 1960s. By the early 1980s, Aboriginal children were overrepresented in the child welfare system. In Saskatchewan, for example, 63 percent of all children-in-care were Aboriginal.

The mainstream approach to child welfare contributed to widespread family breakdown and a general lack of cohesion in Aboriginal communities. Anne-Marie Mawhiney (2001, 163) observes that "the values and spiritual base have been seriously eroded in some First Nations because of the lack of continuity from one generation to the next." Furthermore, reports suggest that Aboriginal "graduates of the child welfare system make up a disproportionate number of street kids and commercially exploited youth in the sex trade in Canadian cities" (Castellano, 2002, 19–20).

Today, many First Nations communities and provincial child welfare departments are working together to develop child welfare agencies that meet the specific needs of Aboriginal children and their families. In 1991, Indian and Northern Affairs Canada established the First Nations Child and Family Services program to develop culturally sensitive child welfare services for registered children living on reserve. These services are federally funded and are required to follow provincial/territorial child welfare legislation.

By 2000, there were 105 First Nations Child and Family Service agencies across Canada (INAC, 2001). First Nations child welfare services vary from region to region; all, however, support the following principles:

- native children should not be placed in non-native homes;

- whenever possible substitute care should be located on the reserve or home community;

- follow-up services should be available to the family;

- child welfare workers must assist to prevent crises and not just in times of crises; and

- child welfare workers should be native and familiar with First Nations culture, [and] ideally speak the local language. (Durst, 2002, 9)

Reports suggest that mainstream child welfare regulations are not always supportive of traditional practices; moreover, they do not extend First Nations child protection officers enough decision-making authority (Castellano, 2002). To remedy these problems, some First Nations communities provide child welfare services through their own legislation. The Aboriginal Justice Inquiry/Child Welfare Initiative in Manitoba is one of the more comprehensive efforts to extend child welfare jurisdiction to Aboriginal authorities; this program allows Métis Child and Family Services and First Nations agencies to serve their members, whether they live on or off reserve (Walkem and Bruce, 2002; McKenzie and Morrissette, 2003). Exhibit 12.4 outlines some of the main features of Manitoba's new approach to child and family services.

IV. SOCIAL WORK WITH ABORIGINAL PEOPLES

There is growing evidence that although many Aboriginal people may need help, they avoid seeking it from mainstream agencies or non-Aboriginal professionals. The Standing Senate Committee on Aboriginal Peoples (2003, 40) found this to be the case for many urban Aboriginal youth: "The historical legacy of discrimination and the accompanying feelings of distrust, shame and perceptions of prejudice by non-Aboriginal service providers, make many Aboriginal youth reluctant to access mainstream services."

This trend in seeking help has increased the demand for Aboriginal social agencies and social workers. In their study of social work in Canada, Stephenson and colleagues (2000, 25) conclude that

a variety of policy and actions, ranging from self-government to crime prevention strategies, are creating both greater opportunities and greater demands on delivering social services for Aboriginal peoples. There is an increased emphasis on community delivery models [and on] preventative models of service to increase Aboriginal economic and social well being and

Exhibit 12.4

THE ABORIGINAL-JUSTICE INQUIRY—CHILD WELFARE INITIATIVE (AJI-CWI): A NEW APPROACH TO CHILD AND FAMILY SERVICES IN MANITOBA

WHAT DO CHILD AND FAMILY SERVICES IN MANITOBA DO?

- works to protect children at risk of abuse or neglect
- supports and strengthens the well-being of families, especially those experiencing difficulties in caring for their children

WHAT IS THE AJI-CWI?

- an initiative to restructure the child and family services system
- a joint endeavour of the Manitoba Metis Federation, Assembly of Manitoba Chiefs, Manitoba Keewatinowi Okimakanak, and the Province of Manitoba

HOW WILL THE NEW SYSTEM BE DIFFERENT?

The responsibility for the delivery of child and family services is being transferred from the Province to four new child and family services Authorities, three of which are Aboriginal Authorities. These Authorities are:

- Metis Child and Family Services Authority
- First Nations of Southern Manitoba Child and Family Services Authority
- First Nations of Northern Manitoba Child and Family Services Authority
- General Child and Family Services Authority

When completed, the Authorities and their agencies will provide services across the province. Aboriginal children and families will have access to culturally appropriate child and family services through Aboriginal agencies.

ARE THE CHANGES LEGISLATED?

Changes to the system are sanctioned by *The Child and Family Services Authorities Act* of the Province of Manitoba, proclaimed on November 24, 2003.

WHAT IS AJI-CWI'S VISION?

A child and family services system that recognizes and supports the rights of children to develop within safe and healthy families and communities, and recognizes that First Nations and Metis peoples have unique authority, rights and responsibilities to honour and care for their children.

WHAT IS AJI-CWI'S MISSION?

To have a jointly coordinated child and family services system that

- recognizes the distinct rights and authorities of First Nations and Metis peoples and the general population to control and deliver their own child and family services province-wide;
- is community-based; and
- reflects and incorporates the cultures of First Nations, Metis and the general population respectively.

Source: Adapted from the Aboriginal Justice Inquiry—Child Welfare Initiative (February 2004). *Options for Foster Care Providers* [online]. Available: www.aji-cwi.mb.ca/pdfs/final_eastman_rob.pdf [May 25, 2004].

to reduce rates of violence, substance abuse, and incarceration. These will all require the commitment of further resources, and will increase the demand for Aboriginal social workers and other social service professionals who have considerable experience in Aboriginal issues.

Some experts believe that non-Aboriginal workers may provide effective services if they first receive cross-cultural training. McKenzie and Morrissette (2003, 19) recommend a cross-cultural framework to orient social workers to Aboriginal issues, and to guide social work practice with Aboriginal clients. The core elements of such a framework might include the following:

- an understanding of the world view of Aboriginal people and how this differs from the dominant Euro-Canadian world view;

- recognition of the effects of the colonization process;

- recognition of the importance of Aboriginal identity or consciousness;

- appreciation of the value of cultural knowledge and traditions in promoting healing and empowerment; and

- an understanding of the diversity in Aboriginal self-expression.

The helping and healing process begins with a thorough assessment of a client's needs, strengths, and areas of concern. Assessment should also include a discussion of the types of helping or healing approaches that might be most effective. It cannot be assumed that simply because a client is Aboriginal, he or she will be comfortable with traditional techniques such as storytelling or smudging, just as one cannot assume that a non-Aboriginal client will be comfortable with integrative body psychotherapy or gestalt therapy. Ideally, workers will be familiar with a broad range of traditional and mainstream interventions or know where clients might be referred to get the help they need.

Anne-Marie Mawhiney (2001, 163) points out that at the community development level, social workers may be able to help Aboriginal peoples achieve self-determination and self-government—goals that "are consistent with the profession's ideological position of respecting self-determination and cultural diversity, advocating against oppression and inequity, and promoting non-discriminatory practice." However, for social workers to be effective at this, mainstream social work education programs must change their "dominantly held, middle-class, patriarchal and white values, traditions, assumptions and ways of thinking—ways that are limited in their application to Aboriginal peoples and communities." Many social work schools are currently revising their curricula by adding Aboriginal content relating to culture, past injustices, and current issues and needs (CASW, 1994c).

A growing demand for Aboriginal social workers in self-governed communities and off-reserve Aboriginal organizations has led to an expansion of Aboriginal-controlled social work programs. These programs specifically prepare social workers for service in Aboriginal communities. An example of this type of program is the School of Indian Social Work at the First Nations University of Canada (formerly Saskatchewan Indian Federated College). There, social work courses are "based on a framework of First Nations' culture, values and philosophy" (First Nations University of Canada, 2004). To ensure that training reflects a First Nations approach, the program includes both elders and traditional First Nations educators in curriculum development.

SUMMARY

■ Introduction

The Aboriginal population accounts for 4.4 percent of Canada's total population and is rapidly growing. Ongoing international recognition of Aboriginal peoples has drawn attention to the poor conditions in Aboriginal communities and has led to more positive changes. Despite progress in some areas, Aboriginal peoples face ongoing social and economic challenges.

■ Aboriginal/Government Relations

Colonial governments assumed a paternal role in Aboriginal affairs. At the time of Confederation, responsibility for Aboriginal peoples was divided between the federal government and the provinces. The Indian Act and enfranchisement policies placed the federal government in control of First Nations peoples living on reserves. Attempts to reform the Indian Act have generally not been in the interests of Aboriginal peoples. Rising tensions between Aboriginal peoples and governments led to the formation of Aboriginal organizations to defend native rights; these rights have also been reinforced by the Constitution Act of 1982. Major themes of the 1990s include self-government and new Aboriginal/governmental agreements.

■ Healing and Wellness in Aboriginal Communities

Many of the social and economic problems facing Aboriginal peoples have been attributed to colonization and the residential school system. Mainstream social welfare services are often available to Aboriginal people; however, these services are not always responsive to Aboriginal values, customs, and needs. Many Aboriginal people and communities support traditional approaches to healing, as well as the delivery of services by Aboriginal social agencies. The Aboriginal Healing Strategy was established to help Aboriginal people deal with the negative effects of residential schools. Aboriginal programs take a holistic approach when addressing family violence and mental health problems. Two broad service delivery systems for Aboriginal peoples are evolving: one is tailored to First Nations communities; the other focuses on Aboriginal needs in urban centres.

■ Caring for Aboriginal Children

Aboriginal children tend to face greater challenges than their non-Aboriginal peers. Under the purview of the National Children's Agenda are early childhood development, early learning, and childcare services for Aboriginal children. Other federal programs—such as Brighter Futures, CAPC, Aboriginal/First Nations Head Start, the First Nations and Inuit Child Care Initiative, and First Nations National Child Benefit Reinvestments—aim to meet the needs of Aboriginal children and their families. Many First Nations communities are either developing their own child welfare services or working within provincial child-welfare legislation.

■ Social Work with Aboriginal Peoples

Aboriginal people often avoid the help offered by mainstream social welfare programs and services. At the same time, there is a growing demand for Aboriginal social agencies and social workers. Non-Aboriginal social workers may provide effective services to their Aboriginal clients if they first receive cross-cultural training. Careful assessment is an important component of the helping and healing process. Social workers may be able to help Aboriginal peoples achieve self-determination and self-government if social work education is modified to adequately prepare social workers for this type of practice. Some postsecondary institutions are now developing social work curricula that reflect traditional approaches.

▼ KEY TERMS

For definitions of the key terms, consult the Glossary on page 364 at the end of the book.

Aboriginal peoples p. 274

band p. 274

First Nations peoples
  p. 274

Indian p. 274

Inuit p. 275

Métis p. 275

reserve p. 275

enfranchisement p. 276

self-governments p. 277

colonization p. 279

residential school system
  p. 280

traditional approach
  p. 280

mainstream approach
  p. 280

healing p. 281

residential school syn-
  drome p. 281

holistic perspective p. 284

Social Welfare in a Multicultural Society

Objectives

I. To consider various views of immigration and newcomer groups, as well as historical aspects of Canada's immigration and refugee policy.

II. To examine the concept and stages of settlement; settlement programs and delivery systems; and the issue of geographic dispersion.

III. To explore issues relating to adaptation, and to review strategies used to help newcomers adapt to life in Canada.

IV. To discuss the role of social work practice in a multicultural context.

INTRODUCTION

Canada has always been a multicultural society. The term **multiculturalism** is applied to countries that are ethnically or culturally diverse and that foster equality, mutual respect, and acceptance among various ethnic groups (Burnet, 2004). Canada and the United States can both be described as multicultural nations, but the two have approached the issue of diversity in very different ways. The United States is commonly referred to as a "melting pot"; Americans seem to aim for a melting or assimilation of minority cultures into the established dominant culture. Thus, people who fail to assimilate may have fewer opportunities to participate fully in society (Government of British Columbia, 2000). Canada chose to reject the melting-pot approach and to create a cultural mosaic. This mosaic welcomes and respects "various ethnic and cultural backgrounds, each with its unique perspectives, values, and experiences" (Canadian Council on Social Development, 2003b).

Canada is home to more than 200 **ethnic groups**, whose members share similar racial, political, religious, ancestral, or cultural backgrounds. Census data offer us a better picture of Canadians' **ethnic origins**, which Statistics Canada (2003b, 12) defines as the "ethnic or cultural group(s) to which an individual's ancestors belonged." About half of Canadians report their ethnic origin as Canadian, English, or French; other common ancestries include Scottish, Irish, German, Italian, Chinese, Ukrainian, and North American Indian.

International events, global migration patterns, and changes in Canadian immigration policies continue to shape this country's cultural makeup. For the first sixty years of the twentieth century, most immigrants came to Canada from European nations; in recent decades, those immigrants are more likely to be from Asian countries. According to census data, 58 percent of the 1.8 million immigrants who arrived in Canada between 1991 and 2001 were from Asia. As a result of intermarriage among ethnic groups, more and more Canadians—from 7 million in 1986 to 11.3 million in 2001—report having multiple ethnic origins (Statistics Canada, 2003b).

Over the past few decades, Canadian governments have introduced legislation to promote multiculturalism and to protect the rights and freedoms of all citizens equally. For example, the Canadian Bill of Rights, proclaimed in 1960, prohibited discrimination by the federal government on the basis of race, colour, gender, or ethnic origin. In 1971, Canada's Multicultural Policy paved the way for ethnocultural programs, the purpose of which was to help Canadians from all ethnic backgrounds participate fully in society (Canadian Heritage, 2004a). In 1982, once the Canadian Charter of Rights and Freedoms was entrenched in the Constitution, citizens were guaranteed equal protection under the law "without discrimination based on race, nationality or ethnic origin." The passage of the Canadian Multiculturalism Act in 1988 requires Canadian governments to promote the multicultural heritage of Canadians and the inclusion of all citizens equally in the shaping of Canadian society (Government of Canada, 1988).

Surveys show that the vast majority of Canadians believe "that multiculturalism has contributed positively to the Canadian identity" (Jedwab, 2003) and that multicultural policy fosters "the sharing of common values, helps solve the problems of racism and prejudice, encourages institutions of Canada to reflect and respect cultural diversity, and enhances the value of Canadian citizenship" (Moylum, 2000). The extent to which multiculturalism is promoted in Canada has important implications for social welfare. For example, in a society that promotes multiculturalism, social policies, programs, and services should be inclusive rather than exclusive. To be inclu-

Exhibit 13.1

ETHNIC ORIGIN

Source: Andy Donato. "Duds 'n' Scuds." *Political Cartoons* (Toronto: Key Porter, 1991). Reprinted with permission from the *Toronto Sun*.

sive, social agencies must constantly transform their policies and methods of operation in accordance with the evolving ethnic makeup of the community. In so doing, agencies can respond more readily to the diverse ethnocultural needs of local residents (Carter, 1997).

I. BUILDING A CULTURALLY DIVERSE NATION: PEOPLE AND PROCESSES

CHANGING VIEWS OF IMMIGRATION

Canada's cultural diversity is directly linked to its immigration policies. Although Canada generally considers immigrants and refugees from around the world, its immigration policies have always made it clear which individuals are deemed most worthy of making Canada their home. These same policies have also reflected the country's particular attitudes toward people of various nationalities, races, and colours. Just how far Canada opens its doors to newcomers, and to which newcomers, also depends heavily on the country's current economic needs, resources, and security concerns.

Research suggests that Canadians are becoming more supportive of immigrants and the immigration process. One study shows that in 1996, 46 percent of Canadians thought that Canada accepted too many immigrants; by 2001, this number had fallen to 36 percent (Marcoux, 2002). Many social analysts were sure that the terrorist attacks on the United States of September 11, 2001, would damage Canadians' perceptions of immigrants, refugees, and government-sponsored programs for these groups. Indeed, opinion surveys taken in the wake of September 11 found that the attacks made many Canadians feel "more affinity with Americans" and "more concern about immigration and border security" (Centre for Research and Information on Canada, 2001, 1). Other polls revealed that despite these concerns, Canadians did not feel that the events of September 11 severely affected Canada's social cohesion.

An optimistic view of immigration may be based, in part, on the contributions that immigrants make to Canadian society. A study by Environics in 2001 found that 83 percent of Canadians thought "that people from different racial and cultural groups enrich Canadian culture" (Marcoux, 2002, 14). In economic terms, immigrants are recognized for bringing capital, initiative, and expertise to Canada's labour force (CIC, 1998). Immigrants are also helping to offset Canada's declining birth rate and aging population. Immigrants are increasing the country's population, and as a consequence, Canada will be able to enlarge its workforce and expand its tax base—two conditions needed to strengthen governments' capacity to provide health, social welfare, and other services for a growing number of old people (Trempe et al., 1997).

NEWCOMERS TO CANADA

Canada is a country built on immigration. Sheila Copps (2003), the former heritage minister, noted in 2003 that "immigration continues to redefine the face of the country." People move to a new country for a variety of reasons; many are motivated by a desire "to seek greater economic opportunities; to improve their standard of living; and to experience greater social, religious or political freedom and stability" (Christensen, 2001, 181). Statistics Canada (2003b) defines an **immigrant** as someone who was born in another country and who has, at some time, been granted the legal right to live in Canada. In 2001, more than 5 million people (18 percent of all Canadians) had been born outside the country; this was the highest proportion of foreign-born Canadians since 1931, at which time immigrants represented over 22 percent of the population.

Immigrants move to another country by choice; in contrast, **refugees** are forced by persecution to flee their homeland. Under the UN's Convention Relating to the Status of Refugees (the Geneva Convention) and other international agreements, Canada is obligated to protect legitimate refugees. To qualify as a refugee, people must first meet the criteria for a Convention refugee, a refugee claimant, a protected person, or some other recognized refugee class. Canadian officials investigate the refugee's claim; then, depending on their findings, they accept the person's application for refugee status, reject it, or help the applicant resettle in another country (Canadian Council for Refugees, 2004; CIC, 2004c).

For the past quarter-century, Canada has been admitting a yearly average of 166 000 immigrants and refugees. Since 1967, a larger proportion of immigrants have been coming from non-European countries; as a consequence, Canada's visible-minority population is growing. About two-thirds of recent newcomers to Canada are **visible minorities**—that is, "persons, other than Aboriginal peoples, who are non-Caucasian in race or non-white in colour" (Statistics Canada, 2003b, 10). Between 1996 and 2001, Canada's visible-minority population increased by 25 percent while the total population rose by only 4 percent. The largest single visible-minority group is the Chinese, with one million members (Statistics Canada, 2003b).

IMMIGRATION AND REFUGEE POLICY: HISTORICAL HIGHLIGHTS

During the eighteenth and nineteenth centuries, Canada welcomed newcomers who would develop the vast and sparsely populated land and help build the national railways. By relaxing immigration restrictions and offering free land, the federal government was able to attract large numbers of immigrants to Canada. Immigration peaked between 1904 and 1913, when two and a half million people moved to Canada.

Until 1906, Canada had an "open-door" immigration policy that allowed most white people to move to Canada. The Canadian Immigration Acts of 1906 and 1910 imposed restrictions on immigration that were intended to keep out poor, sick, or "immoral" applicants. Asian immigrants in particular were unwelcome in Canada; the Canadian government kept the entry of Asians into Canada to a minimum by imposing a head tax on Chinese immigrants and by being highly selective with regard to Japanese and East Indian immigrants (CIC, 1995).

A serious labour shortage during the 1940s prompted the Canadian government to revise its immigration policies and accept a greater number of immigrants. Canada also introduced its first refugee policy after thousands of displaced Europeans sought refuge in Canada after the Second World War. Shortly after the war, however, Prime Minister Mackenzie King made it clear that immigration policy would be used as a tool to maintain a predominantly white society. King's position reflected a general attitude among Canadians that non-white people were unsuitable candidates for immigration because of "their presumed inability to adapt to British civilization and democratic political traditions" (Stasiulis and Abu-Laban, 2004, 378).

The new Immigration Act of 1953 opened Canada's doors wider to those from Europe, the United States, and other "white" nations; at the same time, the act made it more difficult for people from less-favoured nations to become Canadian citizens (CIC, 1995). These restrictive policies exacerbated the problem of illegal immigration which in turn motivated the federal government to take a new approach. The Immigration Act was amended in 1967 so that the acceptance of immigrants would no longer be based on discriminatory criteria such as ethnic origin, race, colour, or religion. Instead, applicants would be assessed according to a points system and admitted on the basis of education, occupation, age, knowledge of English or French, employment opportunities in Canada, and other objective criteria (Anderson and Marr, 1987). The lifting of discriminatory immigration criteria drastically altered Canada's ethnic profile. Before the points system was introduced, people from Asia represented just 3 percent of all immigrants; by the 1970s, they made up 33 percent of all immigrants (Statistics Canada, 2003b).

A new Immigration Act, passed in 1976, committed the Government of Canada to do more to help newcomers adapt to Canadian life, to reunite families, and to assist in the resettlement of refugees. This act also required the federal government to project desired immigration levels for one- to three-year periods. Since 1980, when the practice of projecting began, the actual numbers of immigrants admitted to Canada have typically fallen short of annual projections and far below the numbers required to replace the loss of population due to death and emigration (Dirks, 2004). Exhibit 13.2 provides a historical perspective on the numbers of immigrants admitted to Canada between 1860 and 2002.

Exhibit 13.2

CANADIAN IMMIGRATION, 1860–2002

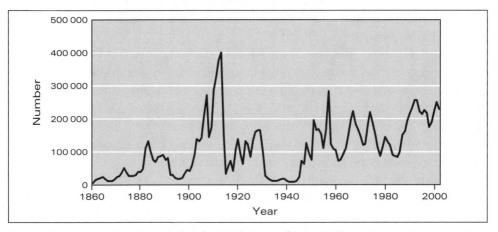

Source: Citizenship and Immigration Canada (2003). *Facts and Figures 2002: Immigration Overview*, p. 3, Immigration—Historical Perspective (1860–2002) [online]. Available: www.cic.gc.ca/english/pdf/ pub/facts2002.pdf [May 28, 2004]. Adapted with the permission of the Minister of Public Works and Government Services Canada, 2004.

By the 1990s, a number of problems with the Immigration Act had become apparent: immigration procedures were complicated and were being applied inconsistently; globalization and changes in the labour market had rendered the selection process outdated; and existing legislation was ill equipped to deal with the growing number of illegal aliens entering Canada. Also, immigration was becoming a burden on social programs: new immigrants were expected to assume responsibility for supporting the family members they sponsored, yet many of these sponsors were reneging on their support agreements, costing taxpayers millions of dollars in welfare costs (CIC, 1995). To address these problems, the federal government amended the Immigration Act in 1997. Immigrants' applications were now divided into three classes: an economic class (which included skilled workers and business immigrants); a family class; and a refugee class. There was now more emphasis on selecting independent immigrants who would bring skills, education, experience, and other assets to Canada's labour force. Another change came in 1998, when the federal government began signing short-term agreements with many of the provincial governments—agreements that gave them more say in selecting immigrants who were destined for their jurisdictions (CIC, 1999a; 1998).

Reform efforts that began in 1997 culminated in 2000 with the Liberal government's proposal to replace the Immigration Act of 1976 with a new act that would "curb criminal abuse of the immigration and refugee systems" and expand "policies to attract the world's best and brightest to Canada" (CIC, 2000). In June 2002, the Immigration and Refugee Protection Act (IRPA) came into force. According to Citizenship and Immigration Canada (CIC, 2002b), the IRPA takes "a balanced approach. It is tough legislation for those who pose a threat to public security while building on the important contributions immigrants and refugees have made in the past and will continue to make in the future."

II. SETTLEMENT IN CANADA: POLICIES, PROGRAMS, AND PROCESS

STAGES OF SETTLEMENT

The process of moving from one country to another can be long, complicated, exciting, and stressful. Herberg and Herberg (2001) suggest that although the settlement period is different for everyone, it commonly takes several years. Researchers suggest that settlement involves three stages:

- *Acclimatization* marks the period "when newcomers make the basic adjustments to life in a new country, including finding somewhere to live, beginning to learn the local language, getting a job, and learning to find their way around an unfamiliar society" (Canadian Council for Refugees, 1998).

- *Adaptation* "is characterized by an immigrant's ability to realize some of the benefits of settlement, that is: being able to access mainstream services independently; understanding Canadian social and cultural norms; improving language skills; developing contacts and building friendships in the community, and reassessing personal goals" (Goss Gilroy Inc., 2000, 9).

- *Integration* "refers to the ultimate goal of the process at which point immigrants demonstrate the ability to be fully functioning members of Canadian society. They, among other things, have found and maintained appropriate employment, participate in mainstream organizations, volunteer their time in the community, associate with Canadian values and participate in the political process (voting, running for office etc.)" (Goss Gilroy Inc., 2000, 9).

During the **acclimatization stage**, newcomers are engaged in a variety of basic settlement tasks, many of which are completed with the assistance of government-sponsored programs and services (CIC, 2004b). Exhibit 13.3 illustrates the types of services most often used by three immigrant groups during their first six months in Canada.

E x h i b i t   1 3 . 3

NEWCOMERS WHO SEEK SERVICES (BY TYPE OF SERVICE AND IMMIGRANT CATEGORY, AT LANDING)

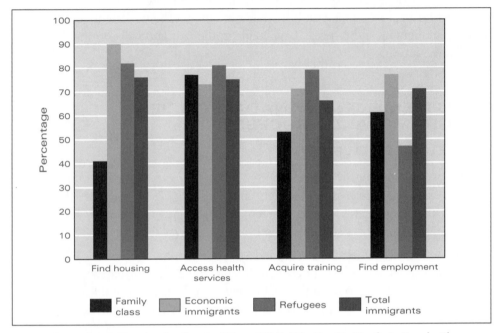

Source: Citizenship and Immigration Canada. (Winter 2004). "The First Six Months in Canada: The Importance of Family and Friends." Feature Article: *The Monitor*, Chart 3: Newcomers who tried to obtain services, by type of service and immigrant category at landing [online]. Available: http://www.cic.gc.ca/ english/monitor/issue04/06-feature.html [May 28 2004]. Adapted with the permission of the Minister of Public Works and Government Services Canada, 2004.

Adapting to a new culture can be a long and extremely complex process. According to Aycan and Berry (1996, 4), the **adaptation stage** has three interrelated levels:

- *Psychological adaptation* includes a sense of well-being and satisfaction with regard to different aspects of one's life.

- *Sociocultural adaptation* emphasizes immigrants' progress in becoming full participants in society and acquiring the skills required to manage everyday situations.

- *Economic adaptation* is conceptualized as the sense of accomplishment and full participation in the economic life in Canada.

A variety of factors influence the extent to which newcomers are able to adapt psychologically, socially, and economically to the Canadian way of life. These factors include the following: "who [the newcomers] are; where they came from; why they left; whether they came alone or with family; what qualifications they bring to the job market; what languages they speak; how long they've been in Canada; where they've settled; which services their community offers; and what reception they're given by other Canadians" (McCloskey, 1998, 2). Because of this wide range of potential influences, the adaptation process is a highly personal and individualistic experience.

A successful economic and social integration of newcomers into Canadian society is essential if Canada is to benefit fully from the assets that immigrants and refugees bring. The **integration stage** requires an effort by both foreign- and native-born individuals: newcomers are encouraged to adapt to Canadian ways without giving up their cultures; at the same time, Canadian-born citizens as well as organizations are urged to respect the cultural gifts that newcomers bring to this country. This mutual obligation is critical to a socially cohesive society where "both the individual and society recognize the value of building a sense of acceptance and belonging among people based on trust, shared values and common experiences that bridge social, cultural, linguistic and religious differences" (Dorais, 2002, 4).

The following discussion explores selected issues and programs relating to the acclimatization stage of settlement; Part III of this chapter focuses on certain challenges and programs relating to adaptation and integration.

SETTLEMENT PROGRAMS: FACILITATING THE ACCLIMATIZATION PROCESS

Since 1948, Canada has offered a variety of **settlement programs** to help immigrants and refugees quickly become self-sufficient, contributing members of Canadian society (CIC, 1999b). Citizenship and Immigration Canada (CIC) is ultimately responsible for settlement policies and programs; however, federal-provincial-territorial agreements determine how settlement programs will be funded, managed, and delivered in each jurisdiction. The first intergovernmental agreement was reached in 1991, when the Canada–Quebec Accord gave Quebec control of its own settlement programs, including language training.

Immigration Settlement and Adaptation Program

The federal government established the Immigration Settlement and Adaptation Program (ISAP) in 1974 to provide a wide range of direct services to immigrants. These services, which are government-funded but usually delivered by private-sector organizations, include the following:

- *Assessment and referral.* Determining newcomers' needs and linking them to community resources and services such as retail stores, banks, health services, and cultural centres.

- *Information and orientation.* Providing newcomers with basic information about their rights and responsibilities as Canadian citizens, assisting them with the tasks of daily living, and helping them learn about their community.

- *Interpretation and translation.* Providing language interpretation as needed, and translating documents and forms required to access medical, legal, education, employment, and other services.

- *Counselling.* Providing support and encouragement to newcomers, and helping them locate more in-depth psychological counselling services if needed.

- *Employment-related services.* Helping newcomers connect with job search services and potential employers (CIC, 2003a).

Host Program

Introduced in 1984, the Host Program helps newcomers cope with the stress of relocation. Under this program, organizations and individuals recruit people who are familiar with Canada, train them as volunteers, and then match them with newcomers to Canada. Host services are often provided on a one-to-one or group basis. The Host Program can benefit both newcomers and volunteers: newcomers learn about Canada, its customs, available services, and possible work opportunities, while volunteers make new friends and learn about other cultures (Treasury Board of Canada, 2003b).

Language Instruction for Newcomers to Canada

The ability to communicate effectively with others is essential to a newcomer's full integration into a country's social, economic, and cultural life. Through Language Instruction for Newcomers to Canada (LINC), adults who are new to Canada receive free basic instruction in English or French. At the same time, the LINC curriculum gives newcomers an opportunity to learn about various aspects of Canadian life. Language instruction is available through colleges, school boards, or local organizations. To encourage attendance in language classes, LINC helps participants cover the costs of childcare and transportation (CIC, 2003c).

Refugee Resettlement Programs

The primary focus of Canada's Refugee and Humanitarian Resettlement Program is to protect refugees and help them settle in their new country. To be eligible for resettlement programs, refugees must be officially sponsored by a government, a nongovernmental organization (such as a church or ethnic association), or a joint public–private partnership. People selected for resettlement must then satisfy officials that they do not have a criminal background, do not pose a public health or security risk, and are likely to integrate successfully into Canadian society (CIC, 2004c). There are various types of refugee settlement programs, including these:

- *Resettlement Assistance Program.* Gives cash for temporary accommodation, household items, transportation, and other basic necessities during the first year in Canada.

- *Immigration Loans Program.* Issues loans to cover the costs of travel documents, airfare, and other items that are needed for the journey to Canada.

- *Federal Health Program.* Pays for emergency and basic health care for refugees who are not yet covered by a provincial medical plan (CIC, 2004a).

Canada also sponsors specialized programs for refugees. The Women at Risk Program, for example, gives refuge to women and their dependants who are experiencing violence or other oppressive treatment in their homeland. Since its inception in 1988, this program has received more than 2250 women and children from around the world (CIC, 2002a).

IMMIGRATION SERVICE AGENCIES

Many mainstream social agencies make efforts to reach the immigrant community—for example, by translating promotional materials into various languages, and by tailoring programs to immigrants' needs. There are also a variety of **immigration service agencies** (ISAs), whose specific purpose is to address the settlement needs of newcomers to Canada. ISAs are voluntary organizations. Usually, they are found in communities with concentrated immigrant populations. The Ottawa Community Immigrant Services Organization (OCISO) is an example of an ISA. In partnership with other community organizations, OCISO (2004) provides a wide range of culturally sensitive services to immigrants and refugees, such as counselling, language instruction, and assistance in finding nonprofit housing.

Various efforts are being made to strengthen ISAs. Under the Voluntary Sector Initiative, for instance, CIC and voluntary settlement organizations are collaborating on the Strengthening Settlement Capacity Project. This comprehensive program examines and improves settlement policy and service delivery methods (Beyene et al., 1996; CIC, 2003b).

THE ISSUE OF GEOGRAPHIC DISPERSION

The phenomenon of **secondary migration** is a growing concern for settlement service providers. Agreements between the Government of Canada and the provinces and territories set the number of immigrants and refugees allowed in each jurisdiction; these numbers are largely determined by each jurisdiction's economic needs, available settlement services, and opportunities for newcomers. People immigrating to Canada are matched to a specific location and connected to local systems. Newcomers who leave their original destination and settle elsewhere in Canada (that is, who make a secondary migration) run the risk of moving to centres that are lacking appropriate reception or settlement services (Simich et al., 2001).

In their study of migration trends among refugees in Canada, Simich and colleagues (2001) found that secondary migration is usually motivated by social and emotional needs. In other words, newcomers move in order to

E x h i b i t   1 3 . 4

IMMIGRATION BY CENSUS METROPOLITAN AREA (PRINCIPAL APPLICANTS AND DEPENDANTS)

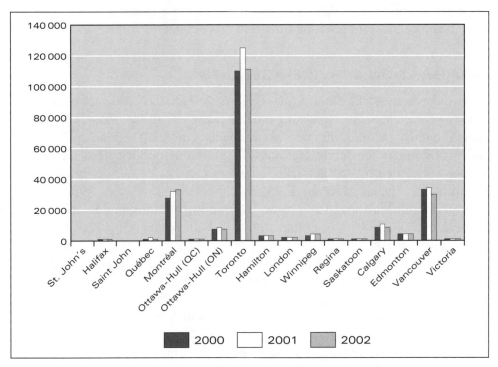

Source: Citizenship and Immigration Canada. (2003). *Facts and Figures 2002: Immigration Overview*, page 6, Immigration by Census Metropolitan Area (Principal Applicants and Dependants) [online]. Available: http://www.cic.gc.ca/english/pdf/pub/facts2002.pdf [May 28 2004]. Adapted with the permission of the Minister of Public Works and Government Services Canada, 2004.

be closer to family and friends already settled in Canada. The Longitudinal Survey of Immigrants to Canada (CIC, 2004b) found that recent immigrants cared more about living near family and friends than about staying where employment prospects were brightest. Most immigrants gravitate to Canada's three largest cities: Toronto, Montreal, and Vancouver (see Exhibit 13.4). As a consequence, the newcomers who follow them to Canada are most likely to settle in those cities as well. According to CIC (2001), the "excessive concentration of immigrants" is placing considerable strain on the resources those three cities can offer newcomers.

To dilute the strong concentrations of immigrants in certain areas, CIC (2001) is developing a dispersion strategy. That is, it is looking for ways to induce immigrants and refugees to stay—for specified periods of time—in selected communities that have the capacity to receive them and that offer the greatest opportunities for successful integration. The inducements being considered include financial incentives and a loosening of entry rules in exchange for living in a designated region.

Immigrant "clusters"—such as Koreatowns and Little Portugals—may be impeding a balanced geographic dispersion of newcomers. In these clusters, large numbers of the same ethnic group have settled, and because the members feel at home, they are less inclined to leave. The concentration of newcomers in ethnic-specific neighbourhoods reduces social isolation for many; however, by segregating themselves from the mainstream society, newcomers may be inadvertently limiting their opportunities to connect with others, learn English or French, seek work, or attend school outside the neighbourhood. To break down this potential barrier to full integration, CIC is encouraging immigrant clustering, not in major cities, but in smaller centres, where ethnic neighbourhoods are not as likely to be so large or isolated from the mainstream community (CIC, 2001; Keung, 2004).

III. ADAPTATION AND INTEGRATION: SELECTED ISSUES AND STRATEGIES

EMPLOYMENT

Employment plays an important role in a newcomer's adaptation and integration. Aycan and Berry (1996, 11) point out that work

> provides purpose to life, it defines status and identity, and enables individuals to establish relationships with others in the society. It is especially the latter function that becomes

> critical for immigrants, because adaptation is facilitated by social interactions. The more one interacts with the groups in the larger society, the faster one acquires skills to manage everyday life.

In Canada, successful economic integration is defined as entering the workforce, achieving financial independence, and eventually being able to advance one's career (Canadian Council for Refugees, 1998).

Most immigrants plan to work once they arrive in Canada; however, they often find it a challenge to land meaningful jobs that provide a living wage, especially if they are lacking skills and education (Canadian Council for Refugees, 2003b). The unemployment rate for recent immigrants fell from 29 percent to just over 12 percent between 1996 and 2001; even so, 12 percent is still almost twice the rate for native-born workers (Badets and Howatson-Leo, 1999; Statistics Canada, 2003f). Even when recent male immigrants do find work, they earn only 63 cents for every dollar earned by Canadian-born workers (Statistics Canada, 2003g). Recent immigrant women face particular challenges in the workforce: these women are less likely than their male counterparts to access job training. Furthermore, among immigrants who do not speak English or French, women are less likely to find work (Rose et al., 2002). The high unemployment rate among recent immigrants to Canada can be attributed in part to the following factors:

- Employers do not understand foreign-acquired credentials and work experience (Canadian Council for Refugees, 2003b).

- The demand for certain labour market skills has declined between the time that people apply to immigrate and the time they actually arrive in Canada.

- Immigrants often must wait years for their occupational credentials to be assessed before they can use their training legally in Canada.

Many of the partnerships that governments have struck with voluntary organizations, employers, and unions focus on helping recent immigrants find the resources they need to succeed in the labour market (CIC, 1994). For example, Human Resources Development Canada is working with other levels of government and with the private sector to offer employment services for new citizens. At their first meeting in 2002, the Federal-Provincial-Territorial Ministers Responsible for Immigration agreed to work together, alongside private-sector organizations, to reduce the barriers to employment for immigrants and to attract more highly skilled immigrants to Canada (Canadian Intergovernmental Conference Secretariat, 2002).

Employment prospects for new Canadians look positive. The aging population is creating a greater demand for skilled immigrants—especially those with a background in information technology—to fill positions vacated by retiring baby-boomers. According to Statistics Canada, if annual immigration rates remain about the same, "it is possible that immigration could account for virtually all labour force growth by 2011" (Statistics Canada, 2003f).

RACISM

Racism plays a central role in the oppression, marginalization, and exclusion of newcomers to Canada, and in their ability to assimilate successfully into Canadian life. Broadly speaking, there are three forms of **racism**:

- *Individual racism* is evident in people's attitudes, beliefs, and behaviours; examples include bigotry, stereotyping, belittling remarks, name-calling, and discrimination based on race.

- *Systemic racism* is organizational in nature, and is reflected in policies and practices that advantage some social groups while disadvantaging others because of their race or ethnicity.

- *Cultural racism*, which underlies individual and systemic racism, reflects the dominant society's values, and supports discrimination "based on perceptions of racial difference, cultural superiority and inferiority" (Roy, n.d.).

Under the International Convention on the Elimination of All Forms of Racial Discrimination, the Canadian Charter of Rights and Freedoms, and the Canadian Multiculturalism Act, Canada has an obligation to eliminate racism in this country (Canadian Heritage, 2004b). However, despite antiracism efforts by the Canadian Race Relations Foundation and other government-sponsored organizations, racism persists in Canada (Stasiulis and Abu-Laban, 2004). Statistic Canada's Ethnic Diversity Survey (2003h) found that 20 percent of visible minorities and 9 percent of nonvisible minorities entering Canada between 1991 and 2001 reported feeling discriminated against because of their race, skin colour, ethnicity, culture, accent, or religion. According to a 2002 poll, 59 percent of Canadians believe that racism is a serious problem in Canada (Centre for Research and Information on Canada, 2002a).

Systemic racism can be found in all types of organizations, including social agencies. By intention or not, some social agencies support policies and practices that discourage members of minority groups from accessing services. Weinfeld and Wilkinson (1999, 71) suggest that newcomers may be discouraged from accessing social welfare services because of "subtle prejudice or stereotypes of the majority group professionals [or] the simple lack of cultural knowledge that could enhance the interaction between immigrant clients and native-born professionals." Surveys suggest that many mainstream social agencies are making stronger efforts to identify and root out their own racist policies and practices so as to better accommodate different cultural norms and practices (Canadian Council on Social Development, 2000b).

ADAPTATION ISSUES FOR YOUNG NEWCOMERS

Research tells us that most young immigrants are adapting well to life in Canada. However, some newly arrived young immigrants experience difficulties. A survey by the Canadian Council on Social Development (2000b) found that many recent immigrant children and youth in Canada:

- cannot speak English or French;
- are less likely than their Canadian-born or more settled immigrant peers "to have someone in whom they could confide";
- find "it difficult to feel totally accepted as Canadians because of their accents and their physical features";
- identify "overcoming social isolation" as one of their greatest challenges; and
- experience "some ostracism, bullying and difficulties with school work."

Some young refugees face additional challenges. Children who have fled war or abuse in their homeland, or who have been separated from their parents, tend to be under considerable stress when they arrive in Canada. The Canadian Council for Refugees (2003a) suggests that refugee children find it hard to feel welcome when people are "blaming refugees for terrorism and other problems; since September 11, Arab and Muslim children particularly have faced prejudice and hostility." In his study of Canada's boat people, Morton Beiser (1999) found that recent refugee youth were twice as likely as adults thirty-five and older to suffer from depression; they were especially at risk of suicide.

Few Canadian studies have focused specifically on the needs and issues of young newcomers; as a consequence, programs and services for this group have yet to be fully developed. Support programs for young immigrants tend to be developed as responses to specific local needs; often, these programs are offered on a casual basis. Examples of "informal supports" for young immigrants in the Waterloo Region (in Ontario) include the following:

- The School Host Program facilitates friendships and support by matching immigrant youth with native-born peers from the same school.

- English-as-a-second-language (ESL) programs occasionally offer peer support programs for immigrant youth.

- The Kitchener–Waterloo Multicultural Centre hosts an orientation program for young newcomers from Kosovo (Centre for Research & Education in Human Services, 2000).

The Central Alberta Refugee Effort (2004) takes a more formal approach. Through regularly scheduled group activities, supportive counselling, and information sessions, this organization's Immigrant Youth Program helps young newcomers adapt to their new life in central Alberta.

Childcare programs sometimes offer play groups, games, and parent–tot programs to enhance young immigrants' emotional well-being and help them deal with the changes they encounter in moving to a new country. Also, young immigrant children are the focus of many projects funded by Health Canada's Community Action Plan for Children (CAPC). One of these programs— Saskatoon's Still Quite New program—"promotes the health, safety and well-being of [immigrant] children, provides their parents with information and support with respect to cross-cultural children's issues, and facilitates access to existing community services for these families" (Health Canada, 2004).

PARTNER VIOLENCE

According to Canadian surveys, police reports, and other data collection systems, about 10 percent of immigrant women experience partner violence. However, recent immigrant women tend to underreport incidents of domestic violence, so the actual rate of abuse is likely higher than reported rates (Federal-Provincial-Territorial Ministers Responsible for the Status of Women, 2002). There are a number of possible reasons many immigrant women fail to report incidents of violence—for example, they may not understand their legal rights, or they may be financially dependent on the husband (who is usually the abuser), or they may be unable to speak French or English (Woodall, 2004). In her survey of front-line service providers, Ekuwa Smith (2004) found that many abused immigrant women are reluctant to seek help because they distrust the police, are unfamiliar with how the justice, social welfare, and other support systems work, and doubt that resources would be culturally sensitive to their needs.

Many programs funded through the Family Violence Initiative are designed specifically for abused immigrant women. For example, through its Multiculturalism Program's Family Violence Strategy, the Department of Canadian Heritage provides information about family violence through ethnic media broadcasts in languages other than English and French, and in ethnic newspapers and other printed materials (Bell-Lowther and Radyo, 2002). Organizations that serve abused immigrant women and their children are funded by a mix of private and public sources, including Immigrant Women Services Ottawa (see Exhibit 13.5).

The federal government is taking a more proactive approach to preventing partner violence in immigrant populations. For instance, government-sponsored orientation programs are providing information about "Canadian values, laws and social expectations, which clearly emphasize that all forms of family violence are illegal in this country" (Health Canada, 2003c, 4). In addition, Canada's new Immigration and Refugee Protection Act recognizes the role that dependency plays in family violence; this act prohibits convicted immigrant abusers from sponsoring any other family members (that is, dependants) for five years after they have completed their jail term.

IV. IMPLICATIONS FOR SOCIAL WORK PRACTICE

During the 1970s, social workers were encouraged to be "colour-blind" when working with racial-minority clients. Proctor and Davis (1994, 316) explain: "Colour-blind practice was assumed to control client–worker racial differences, to foster the conveyance of 'true regard' for minority clients, and to ensure that all clients were treated equally. The acknowledgment of racial difference was seen as akin to racism." The main problem with colour-blind practice was that it failed to recognize obvious and important aspects of a client's identity and social reality; this allowed practitioners to avoid the issue of racial injustice and its impact on the client. Today, **cross-cultural practice models** view racial, cultural, social, and other differences as potentially enriching for both personal relationships and general society. These new practice models are guiding social work practice with minority-group clients and helping workers better understand the experiences of people from different cultures or ethnic backgrounds.

It is becoming more common for social agencies to employ professionals from diverse cultures, the aim being to attract a culturally diverse clientele. Tator (1996, 160) explains

> Minority clients are more likely to use the service if they can communicate and interact with someone of the same or similar cultural background. In the case of racial-minority clients, it is quite likely they will feel more comfortable with a worker of colour, who understands the experience of racism.

Exhibit 13.5

IMMIGRANT WOMEN SERVICES OTTAWA

CRISIS INTERVENTION AND SUPPORT SERVICE

A culturally responsive service to immigrant and visible minority women who are victims/survivors of violence.

SUPPORT GROUPS

A program which provides information, and allows women to express their feelings and to give support to each other.

LANGUAGE INTERPRETATION TRAINING

Language interpretation is a skill which is enhanced through training, and selected candidates participate in approximately 100 hours of an intensive training program in language interpretation as a profession.

CHILDREN WHO WITNESS VIOLENCE PROGRAM

A counselling service for children who are victims of or who witness violence in the home.

CULTURAL AWARENESS TRAINING

A training program for service providers to heighten their awareness of the cultural differences of immigrant and visible minority women and to work towards the provision of appropriate and accessible services.

LONG AND SHORT TERM COUNSELLING

On-going individual counselling to immigrant and visible minority women of all ages.

LANGUAGE INTERPRETATION SERVICE

A FREE 24 hour, 7 days per week service which bridges the communication gap between non-English speaking women who are victims/survivors of violence and legal, social, health, community service providers and other professionals.

EMPLOYMENT SERVICES

A program aimed at helping immigrant women assess their job readiness and acquire the job search techniques required to find employment.

PUBLIC EDUCATION

This program aims to educate immigrant and visible minority women and ethnic communities on the issue of violence against women.

INFORMATION AND REFERRAL SERVICE

Information provided about legal, education, health, medical, government and social services and other community resources. Referrals to other Community services.

WE OFFER FREE ...

- Language interpretation to the Victim Witness Assistance Program–Ottawa Court House, Transition Houses (shelters) for women victims and other agencies serving abused immigrant and visible minority women.
- Childcare for workshops and support groups.
- Transportation to women attending the support group.

Source: Immigrant Women Services Ottawa. (2003). *Services and Programs* [online]. Available: www.immigrantwomenservices.com/Services.htm [May 29, 2004].

Despite these potential benefits, there is little evidence to support claims that matching minority professionals with clients improves services or prevents workers from having racist attitudes and stereotypes (Weinfeld, 1999).

Social workers can increase their cultural sensitivity by engaging in **cross-cultural training**. This type of training often involves some form of cultural immersion: participants are transported into ethnocultural communities, where they become sensitized to the cultural values of others and, at the same time, arrive at a better understanding of their own cultural values (Herberg and Herberg, 2001). Through cross-cultural training, participants may also "become aware of the existence of their prejudices, stereotypes, and racist behaviours, and of the potential impact of these factors on clients" (Christensen, 1996, 148).

To be effective, cross-cultural training must encourage participants to adapt their traditional knowledge frameworks and practice methods to their work with minority clients. For example, social workers might learn to focus less on changing the individual and concentrate more on reducing racist practices in external systems. They might also learn how to refine their assessment skills with regard to clients from different ethnic and cultural backgrounds. This includes recognizing the value that each client places on tradition. Herberg and Herberg (2001, 173) note that although "some [people] cling to their traditional values … others abandon many of their original customs and mores, actively rejecting the 'old ways.'" It is therefore crucial for helpers to develop a clear understanding of the client's cultural values and preferences. Unless they can do this, social workers may find it difficult to establish rapport with minority-group clients and help them stay engaged in the change process.

Although it is widely used in Canada, cross-cultural training has its limitations. Tator (1996, 158) points out that "while [cross-cultural] courses are well intended, the study of the history, values, and norms of minorities often leads to stereotyping and to erroneous generalizations." This type of training may teach workers certain "recipes," such as the proper use of eye contact with certain ethnic groups; however, these guidelines are not always effective for learning how to genuinely connect with people (Hardy and Mawhiney, 2002).

The Canadian Council for Refugees has developed a set of national standards for settlement services in Canada. Among other things, these standards outline the qualities expected from professionals who are working with refugee and immigrant clients. Many of the competencies required for generalist social work practice are compatible with **settlement practice**. These competencies relate to values (such as respect for the individual, client empowerment, and accountability), professional ethics (including respect for client confidentiality and avoidance of conflicts of interest), and skills (for example, interviewing, case management, and advocacy). Nevertheless, the knowledge required of settlement workers is specialized and requires a strong grounding in theories and principles relating to the following:

- settlement (including the adaptation process, influences on integration, and effects of settlement on family);

- the immigrant and refugee experience;

- multiculturalism and cultural change;

- human rights and racism;

- global and Canadian influences that shape immigration and settlement; and

- relevant systems (such as the social welfare, health, education, and justice systems) (Canadian Council for Refugees, 2000).

To be effective, settlement workers must also be personally suited to working with immigrants and refugees; that is, they must be sensitive to racism issues and to the impact that professional helpers can have on clients.

More and more, Canadian institutions are recognizing the role of cultural diversity in social work practice. For example, "the Canadian Association of Schools of Social Work now requires that curriculum address multiculturalism in order for schools to be accredited and the Canadian Association of Social Workers' Code of Ethics requires respect of diversity and autonomy" (Hanley, 2000).

SUMMARY

■ Introduction

One of Canada's most distinguishing characteristics is its ethnic diversity and traditional support of a cultural mosaic. More than 200 ethnic groups live in Canada, and the country's cultural makeup is continuing to shift as immigrants arrive from all over the world. Canadian governments have enacted various laws to promote multiculturalism and to protect the rights of all citizens equally. Most Canadians support multiculturalism, and this support has shaped the country's social welfare policies and programs as they relate to newcomers.

■ Building a Culturally Diverse Nation: People and Processes

Canada's cultural diversity is directly linked to its immigration policies. Polls taken since September 11, 2001, have confirmed that Canadians are still committed to immigration. Immigrants are people who have chosen to move to Canada; refugees come to Canada to escape persecution in their homeland. Most recent immigrants and refugees to Canada are visible minorities. Canada's immigration policy has evolved over the years. It has always been affected by public attitudes, security concerns, available resources, and other factors; that said, Canada has more or less opened its doors to immigrants from non-Caucasian countries. Today's immigration policy reflects an effort to keep people out who pose a threat to public security, but also to embrace newcomers who are likely to enhance Canada's economic, cultural, and social life.

■ Settlement in Canada: Policies, Programs, and Process

The settlement process has three stages: acclimatization, adaptation, and integration. Acclimatization focuses on basic settlement tasks; adaptation takes place at the psychological, sociocultural, and economic levels; integration requires an effort by both foreign- and Canadian-born individuals to achieve social cohesion. The federal government sponsors three main types of settlement programs to help immigrants adjust to Canadian society. A range of resettlement programs are designed to meet the specific needs of refugees. Immigration service agencies are voluntary agencies, and are contracted to serve newcomers to Canada. Secondary migration is a growing concern for settlement service providers.

■ Adaptation and Integration: Selected Issues and Strategies

Unemployment is high among recent immigrants, although job prospects for skilled immigrants are excellent. The federal and provincial governments are working to break down the barriers that have prevented immigrants from gaining access to meaningful employment. Racism in its various forms is a strong barrier to successful adaptation. Surveys suggest that many social agencies are taking steps to better accommodate a culturally diverse clientele. Immigrant children generally adapt well to Canadian life; however, many face challenges during the early stages of settlement. Programs for young newcomers are not well developed in Canada. Women immigrants tend to underreport incidents of partner violence; this places them at even higher risk. Programs under the Family Violence Initiative, as well as orientation resources and immigration policies, aim to address partner violence among immigrant groups.

■ Implications for Social Work Practice

Colour-blind practice has been replaced by cross-cultural practice models, which approach cultural difference as something that enriches relationships and society. One way for social agencies to provide culturally sensitive services is to hire minority social workers; however, this practice does not automatically improve services or reduce racism. Social workers sometimes take cross-cultural training to increase their cultural awareness and sensitivity, to refine their assessment skills, and to adapt their helping strategies to meet the needs of minority clients. Settlement practice is similar to generalist social work practice; however, a sound knowledge of settlement issues is required.

▼ KEY TERMS

For definitions of the key terms, consult the Glossary on page 364 at the end of the book.

multiculturalism p. 296

ethnic groups p. 297

ethnic origins p. 297

immigrant p. 300

refugees p. 300

visible minorities p. 300

acclimatization stage p. 303

adaptation stage p. 304

integration stage p. 305

settlement programs p. 305

immigration service
agencies p. 307

secondary migration
p. 308

racism p. 311

cross-cultural practice
models p. 314

cross-cultural training
p. 316

settlement practice p. 316

14

Social Welfare and People with Disabilities

Objectives

I. To examine various perspectives and classifications of disability, the nature of disability for many Canadians, and disability issues for selected populations.

II. To review the "inclusionary" focus in the context of a community living movement.

III. To explore the highlights in the development of Canada's disability policy since the 1980s.

IV. To look at issues related to income and employment for Canadians with disabilities.

V. To consider social work practice with clients who have disabilities.

INTRODUCTION

People with physical or mental disabilities have always been part of Canadian society, but they have not always had access to the opportunities enjoyed by people without disabilities. Social attitudes have largely determined the extent to which people with disabilities have been included in society. These attitudes have had a major impact on the development of disability-related policies, programs, and services.

Beginning in the mid-1800s, people with mental disabilities were housed in large institutions, where they were educated, trained, and treated for their disabilities. However, because people with mental disabilities were considered inferior to other members of society, they were discouraged from re-entering the community (Roeher Institute, 1996). The popularity of eugenics at the turn of the twentieth century was accompanied by the view that people with mental disabilities were a danger not just to themselves but to others. Institutional programs were redesigned for the purpose of protecting mainstream society from people with mental disabilities. Sterilization became a widely accepted method for controlling the "menace of the feeble-minded" (MacMurchy, 1932, 36) and for preventing mentally "defective" people from "poisoning" the race (Roeher Institute, 1996, 4).

From the 1920s to the 1960s, people with disabilities were considered incompetent, with little or nothing to contribute to society. Most services for this group were provided in institutions, where disability was viewed from a medical perspective and treated as an illness or disease. Treatment was guided by rehabilitation teams consisting of physicians, psychiatrists, medical social workers, and related professionals (Status of Disabled Persons Secretariat, 1994).

A growing awareness of human rights in the 1960s and 1970s fostered the **disability rights movement**, which aimed to eliminate socially imposed restrictions on people with disabilities and give them equal access to mainstream resources and opportunities (New Brunswick Association for Community Living, 1992). In short, "people with disabilities want[ed] to be seen as people first, to be treated as individuals, to have opportunities to participate in and contribute to society. They want[ed] to be seen as persons, not cases or categories of disablement, powerless to shape their own lives" (Rogow, 2002, 1).

The disability rights movement gained momentum when the United Nations declared 1981 the International Year of Disabled Persons, when an International Day of Disabled Persons was established, and when the decade 1983 to 1992 was designated the International Decade of Disabled Persons. Other international developments, such as the World Conference on Human Rights (in Vienna in 1993), and the drafting of the UN Convention on the Human Rights of Disabled People (in 2004), have advanced and protected the rights of people with disabilities. These developments have also contributed to a greater public acceptance of people with disabilities and motivated governments to support the full participation of people with disabilities through policies and legislation.

Exhibit 14.1 provides a historical overview of the evolution of disability rights and responsibilities in Canada. There was a time when people with disabilities were supported by charity; today, they are supported in their right to independent living and full citizenship.

Exhibit 14.1

FIVE HISTORICAL VIEWS OF RIGHTS AND RESPONSIBILITIES

1 Independent Living
Rights and responsibilities are shared, learned, supported, and changed in cooperation with the community with leadership from everyone devoted to the common good from the Federal Government and all others interested in building a country based on inclusion, equity, affordability, and justice.

2 Socio/Political
People have the right to participate in society.
Government has the responsibility to make sure laws and programs facilitate that participation.

3 Rehabilitation
People have the right to work.
Vocational rehabilitation professionals have the responsibility to decide how work can be done and who can do it.

4 Medical
People have the right to medical help. The medical profession has the responsibility to decide if you are sick.

5 Charity
People have the right to hope for help. Those who have been fortunate have the responsibility to give money.

CITIZENSHIP

FUTURE

- Criticizes medical and economical model to excess
- Lacks cohesion
- Conflict
- Rights can be wiped away
- Short-term focus to solve long-term problems

Nevertheless prepares the way for more cooperative models

- Tied to economic policy
- Inefficient
- Disenfranchising
- Dependency
- Hostility and frustration
- Jumping through hoops

Nevertheless connected the individual with social reality

- Passivity
- Isolation
- No attention to social needs
- Sick model

Nevertheless evolves other strategies: chronic and palliative care coping that values individuals

Encourages:
- Isolation
- Prejudice
- Hopelessness
- Helplessness
- People having no voice

Nevertheless individuals and groups supported that would not have flourished otherwise

PAST

Source: Canadian Association of Independent Living Centres (2004). *Five Historical Views of Rights & Responsibilities* [online]. Available: www.cailc.ca/CAILC/graphic/whatisil/diagram1_e.pdf [May 29, 2004].

I. DISABILITY: A CANADIAN PROFILE

DISABILITY PERSPECTIVES

Disability is a complex, multidimensional issue and is therefore difficult to define. This lack of definition is the reason social work, health, education, and other disciplines so often take different approaches to disability; why programs for people with disabilities vary in design and delivery; and why disability-related programs often have different eligibility criteria.

Most social welfare programs for people with disabilities are based on one of three perspectives: an impairment perspective, a functional limitations perspective, or an ecological (or social) perspective. From an **impairment perspective**, disability is a biologically based illness or disease that originates in a person's body or mind and that can be "fixed" or cured. This medical view of disability is often criticized for its general disregard for the role that the physical or social environment can play in the disability experience; for its tendency to focus on the defective element (impairment) of a person's body or mind; and for its traditional practice of labelling people with disabilities as being "defective," "abnormal," and, by implication, "inferior" to nondisabled people.

The **functional limitations perspective** has added social, environmental, and other nonmedical criteria to the definition of disability. From this perspective, disability is defined in terms of how it limits a person's activities and how people with disabilities— and others—perceive and react to those limitations. Notwithstanding its greater reach, the functional limitations perspective supports the notion that disability is biologically based.

The **ecological perspective** emerged in the 1970s, but it was not until the mid-1990s that it gained popularity over the impairment and functional limitations perspectives. Like its predecessors, the ecological perspective assumes that disability is the consequence of an abnormal medical condition and subsequent impairment. However, the ecological perspective places a greater emphasis on the connections between impairment, a person's activity limitations, and his or her participation in specific environments such as home, school, and work. The ecological perspective tends to focus more on a person's dignity and human rights than on physical impairments or limitations (HRDC, 2003a).

DISABILITY CLASSIFICATIONS

In 2001, the World Health Organization introduced the International Classification of Functioning, Disability and Health (ICF)— a new system for classifying a broad range of health-related information. The ICF is significant for its objective descriptions of the "components of health," which can be grouped into two categories:

- *Functioning and disability*. Refers to physiological functions and structures, the anatomical parts of the body, performance tasks or activities, and the extent of participation in life situations.

- *Contextual factors*. Refers to external and internal influences—such as the physical and social environment, and a person's attributes—that either facilitate or hinder a person's functioning.

Within the ICF framework, a disability is the result of interactions among the following: a person's health condition (including any impairments), psychological factors (including attitudes and beliefs), and the physical or social environment. Since each person's living environment is unique, people with similar disabilities may experience those disabilities quite differently. For example, some communities may be more willing than others to make buildings wheelchair accessible; this in turn may either hinder or facilitate access to businesses, social agencies, and other agencies by local residents who use wheelchairs. In recognition of the complex nature and individualistic experience of disability, the ICF integrates principles from the impairment and ecological perspectives to produce a biopsychosocial approach to disability—one that addresses a person's biological, psychological, and social needs (World Health Organization, 2001b).

DISABILITY IN CANADA

In Canada, a person has a **disability** if he or she has "a physical or mental condition or a health problem that restricts their ability to perform activities that are normal for their age in Canadian society" (HRDC, 2003d, 7). According to the 2001 Participation and Activity Limitation Survey (PALS), over 12 percent of Canadians have a disability. Seniors have the highest rate of disability, at 41 percent; children have the lowest rate, at 3 percent. Across all age groups, Nova Scotia reports the highest rates of disability; Quebec reports the lowest rates (HRDC, 2003d).

The term *disability* is often used generically to refer to a broad range of conditions, even though there are many specific forms of disability (see Exhibit 14.2). Over 80 percent of adults with disabilities have more than one disability. For example, an elderly person may have difficulty walking (a mobility impairment) and also be suffering from dementia (a psychological disability) (HRDC, 2002a).

Because a disability may be caused by several factors, its severity can be highly individual. One person with an intellectual disability, for instance, may have no difficulty performing daily tasks of living, whereas another person who has been identified as having the same disability may experience severe functional limitations. The diversity in needs and performance levels of people with the same disability presents policy-makers with the challenge of planning and developing social policies and programs to meet the needs of a group whose needs are anything but homogeneous (Vargo, 2004; Torjman, 1996).

Exhibit 14.2

PREVALENCE OF DISABILITY AMONG ADULTS IN CANADA
(BY TYPE OF DISABILITY AND AGE)

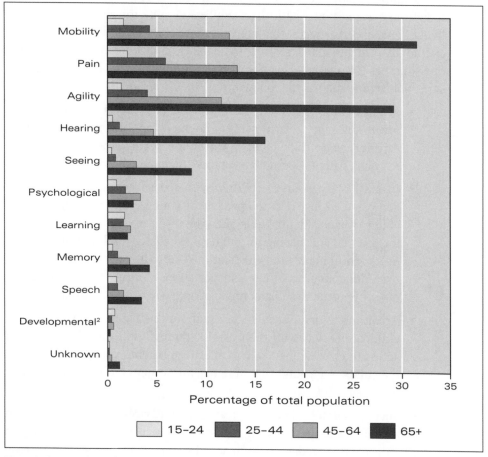

Percentage of total population

15-24   25-44   45-64   65+

Note: 1 The Canada total excludes Yukon, the Northwest Territories, and Nunavut. The sum of the values for each category may differ from the total due to rounding.

2 For "Developmental," the data should be used with caution.

Source: L. Cossette and E. Duclos (2002 December). *A Profile of Disability in Canada, 2001*, p. 18, Chart 5. Ottawa: Statistics Canada. © Minister of Industry 2002. [online]. Available: www.statcan.ca/english/freepub/89-577-XIE/pdf/89-577-XIE01001.pdf [May 22, 2004].

DISABILITY IN SELECTED POPULATIONS

Children with Disabilities

According to the 2001 PALS, the most common disabilities among children up to age fourteen—affecting over 2 percent of all children—are those related to a chronic health condition such as asthma, cerebral palsy, severe allergies, or attention deficit disorder. About half of all children with disabilities have two or more disabilities, and most of these are considered to be mild or moderate (Cossette and Duclos, 2002).

Children with special needs used to be placed in large institutions; today, most live at home with their families. Despite the shift to community living, some experts suggest that many of these children and their families are excluded from full participation in recreational, educational, and other opportunities (Hanvey, 2002a). Social exclusion may be the consequence of a variety of factors, such as the following:

- Studies show that many parents who have a young child with a severe disability turn down employment opportunities in order to care for their child. Limited workforce participation may, in turn, restrict a parent's social connections outside the home.

- In 2001, 27 percent of children with special needs lived in poverty, compared to just over 20 percent of young children without a disability. Financial hardship is often the result of employment restraints for parents, and having to purchase expensive disability-related supports, equipment, and medications. Low-income families tend to have difficulties accessing transportation, recreational activities, and other opportunities that connect people within a community.

- According to one Canadian study, about one parent in five is refused childcare services on the basis of their child's disability. Limited access to childcare is likely to affect the parent's ability to work, and the child's opportunities to interact with other children (Government of Canada, 2003h).

A variety of social welfare, health, and other services aim to help children with disabilities live as normal a life as possible by reducing the stress related to caring for the child, by reducing the financial strain on families, and by keeping families involved in the care and support of their child. Personal social services for children with disabilities and their families are a provincial/territorial responsibility, and so they vary across the country. However, support services for children with disabilities and their families typically include the following:

- counselling, training, and/or the provision of aides to help families care for and meet the specific needs of a child in the home;

- respite services to give primary caregivers a temporary break from caregiving responsibilities; and

- information about and referrals to disability-related health, educational, rehabilitative, and other community services (Government of Manitoba, 2004; Government of Alberta, 2004).

Many of these services are funded through the Canada Social Transfer, the National Children's Agenda, and/or through special arrangements with First Nations and Inuit communities (HRDC, 2002a).

Besides personal social services, income security programs are in place to assist children with disabilities and their families. At the federal level, the Child Disability Benefit is available to children with severe or prolonged disabilities who live in low- or modest-income families (Canada Revenue Agency, 2003). Most provinces and territories also provide financial assistance; these cash supplements may be used to cover the full or partial cost of home modifications, disability-related equipment and supplies, prescription drugs, or special transportation needs.

Disability and Aboriginal Peoples

Studies show that Aboriginal peoples have a higher disability rate than any other group in Canada: almost one in three Aboriginal people has a disability, compared to one in eight in the general population (National Aboriginal Health Organization, 2004). Elias and Demas (2001) surveyed sixty-three First Nations communities in Manitoba; they found that the most common disabilities were related to mobility, and that the main causes of disability were diabetes, injuries or accidents, or birth-related problems.

A general scarcity of disability-related programs and services on reserves has created challenges for First Nations people in general, and for those living in northern or remote areas in particular. For example, poorly maintained roads in rural areas can make it "difficult for wheelchair users to travel about in their communities; having to remain inside their homes can lead to isolation, loneliness and depression" (Federal-Provincial-Territorial Ministers Responsible for Social Services, 2000a). Elias and Demas (2001) found that roughly one-third of Manitoba First Nations people with a disability have to regularly leave the reserve to seek specialist services for their disability.

In response to research findings like these, the Government of Canada and Aboriginal organizations are negotiating agreements aimed at improving conditions for Aboriginal people with disabilities. For example, work for this population might be found through the Aboriginal Human Resources Development Strategy, or the National Aboriginal Clearing/ Connecting House on Disability Issues. Other initiatives—such as the Métis National Council Reference Group on Ability Issues— tailor culturally sensitive services to specific groups of Aboriginal people with disabilities (Federal-Provincial-Territorial Ministers Responsible for Social Services, 2000a).

Women with Disabilities

Women with disabilities face a number of employment and economic barriers. According to Doe and Kimpson (1999, vi), these women "tend to be more prone to cyclical and fluctuating illness that creates difficulty in sustaining employment and basic life activities." Autoimmune conditions, chronic fatigue syndrome, and depression, together with other illnesses to which women with disabilities are prone, are not always easily detected but can severely affect one's ability to participate in social, employment, and other activities.

Women with disabilities are likely to live in poverty: 35 percent of women with disabilities, compared to 16 percent of their male counterparts, have annual incomes of $5000 or less. In addition, women with disabilities are more likely than men to live alone, be socially isolated, and be perceived negatively by others. Women with disabilities also tend to have difficulty accessing rehabilitation and sexual health care services (Alberta Committee of Citizens with Disabilities, n.d.).

Violence against women with disabilities is a growing concern. Research suggests that women with intellectual disabilities living with a husband or partner are at risk of being socially isolated, poor, or dependent on their mate—factors that make it difficult for them to leave an abusive situation. Some of these women "may fear that if they leave their partner, they will be considered incompetent to care for their children and lose custody. For some individuals, an abusive relationship may seem preferable to none at all" (National Clearinghouse on Family Violence, 2002, 4).

Some services in Canada are specifically designed to help women with disabilities address employment, violence, and other issues. However, cuts to health care and government-funded social services have diminished the extent of support for these women. The Canadian Feminist Alliance for International Action (2003, 23) has observed that the shrinkage in home-based services, for example, is leaving women "alone, isolated, and without adequate support for long periods of time." Tightened eligibility rules for provincial and territorial income-support programs have also had a negative impact. Women with disabilities are three times more likely than nondisabled women to rely on government income assistance; however, reduced access to public assistance has left many women with little means of financial support and a greater sense of vulnerability (Federal-Provincial-Territorial Ministers Responsible for Social Services, 2000a).

II. MAKING THE TRANSITION: FROM EXCLUSION TO INCLUSION

INSTITUTIONAL AND COMMUNITY LIVING

By the mid-twentieth century, Canadians were becoming critical of the practice of "warehousing" people with disabilities in large institutions, and of the increasing costs of maintaining those institutions. In the 1960s (and continuing into the 1990s), institutions across Canada began closing, and the residents were returned to their families and communities. By 1995, only 7 percent of people with disabilities were living in institutional settings, and most of these people were adults with severe disabilities or seniors who required long-term care (Statistics Canada, 1995).

As deinstitutionalization progressed, the **community living movement** emerged to help people make a smooth transition back into their communities. This movement has been instrumental in helping Canadians understand "that people [with disabilities] can and do benefit from community services" and that the administration of antipsychotic drugs and other community-based treatments is a more humane, and often more effective, approach to disability than long-term institutionalization (Peters, 2003).

In the early stages of deinstitutionalization, people with disabilities were relocated to community-based settings but continued to be isolated and excluded from mainstream activities. Peters (2003) observes: "Because persons with disabilities were relegated to the margins of society, societal norms only reflected characteristics ascribed to 'able-bodiedness.' For example, [buildings were] only constructed for able-bodied persons who could walk, and not for persons who used assistive devices such as wheelchairs." Over time, this situation began to change. Human rights legislation, public demand for change, and the introduction of government disability policies prompted several reforms that reduced the barriers to full participation. These reforms included changes to the National Building Code of Canada, which made it mandatory for newly constructed public buildings to be barrier free. Also, communication systems were modified to enable people with speech or hearing impairments to use telephones and other devices more effectively. Other changes focused on making it easier for people with disabilities to move around cities—for example, municipalities made their public transit systems wheelchair-accessible, installed visual and auditory traffic control signals, widened sidewalks and gave them curb cuts, and designated handicapped parking slots.

Deinstitutionalization has created a need for alternative housing for people with disabilities. Although health-related institutions are still available for people with severe disabilities, other options have evolved over the years:

- *Community residences or group homes* look like other houses, are located in residential neighbourhoods, and house small groups of people.

- *Room and board* offers a room, meals, laundry, and other services in private residences to those who require minimal support.

- *Supportive housing* consists of individual apartments or housing units for people who are generally independent but who may require assistance with meal preparation, housework, and other activities of daily living.

- *Independent living* refers to a detached home or apartment, where a person with a disability lives either alone or with a spouse or roommate (Roeher Institute, 1996).

Housing reforms have included the development of new housing designs, as well as programs to make independent living a reality for many people with disabilities. Programs such as the federally sponsored Residential Rehabilitation Assistance Program subsidize the costs of modifying residences to make them safer, healthier, and more accessible and adaptable to the changing functional needs of residents.

THE DISABILITY COMMUNITY

The ongoing success of the community living movement is largely due to the efforts of people with disabilities and the organizations that serve them. Together, these individuals and organizations comprise what is commonly referred to as the **disability community**.

Disability-related organizations are highly diverse. Some deliver direct services such as employment assistance; others offer indirect services such as advocacy for improved disability policies; many provide both direct and indirect services. Some organizations are national in scope; others operate at the local or regional level. A number of organizations focus on a single disability, such as intellectual disability; many others, though, are mandated to serve people with any type of disability (HRDC, 2002a). Voluntary disability-related organizations in Canada include the following:

- The Canadian Association for Community Living (CACL) (2004) is a nationwide, private, nonprofit federation with thirteen provincial and territorial chapters. It works on behalf of people with intellectual disabilities. Among other things, the CACL consults with government on disability policy issues and promotes the development of inclusive communities.

- The Council of Canadians with Disabilities (2004) advocates at the national level for the equality and improved status of people with any type of disability. Its activities are based on the principles of self-help and consumer control.

- Independent Living Centres are open to people with any type of disability, are controlled by people with disabilities, and tailor their services to local needs. These centres are based on the philosophy that people with disabilities have a right to access resources and decide how they want to live (CAILC, n.d.).

- The Canadian Mental Health Association (2004) champions the rights and responsibilities of people with mental health challenges (or disabilities) and helps clients find work, housing, and social support. Projects "are based on principles of empowerment, peer and family support, participation in decision-making, citizenship, and inclusion in community life."

III. CANADA'S DISABILITY POLICY AGENDA

Canada's disability community is a highly influential political force that continues to shape the country's disability policy agenda. As Alexander (2001, 169–70) points out: "This community recognizes that the disability policy agenda will not be fully achieved until barriers that exclude individuals from full participation as citizens of Canada are completely eliminated." Although the disability community plays an important role in the policy-making process, it is governments that ultimately create disability policies. This section considers some of the advances made in disability policy since the 1980s.

HUMAN RIGHTS IN THE 1980s

In the 1980s, a number of disability-related committees and government departments were established. For instance, the federal Status of Disabled Persons Secretariat was set up to raise public awareness of disability issues and to support the inclusion of people with disabilities in Canadian society. The federal government also appointed the Standing Committee on Human Rights and the Status of Disabled Persons to consult with people in the disability community and to make policy recommendations to Parliament.

An historic step was taken in 1981, when the federal government established the Parliamentary Special Committee on the Disabled and the Handicapped to assess the needs of people with disabilities and to evaluate existing supports. The committee's 1981 report, *Obstacles*, called attention to a wide range of physical, attitudinal, and other barriers that were preventing people with disabilities from accessing community resources and opportunities. Among its many achievements, the committee provided a catalyst for several disability-related public policies, and "sparked attitudinal change which set a new climate and framework for ensuring that persons with disabilities are treated as full citizens rather than passive recipients of services" (Federal-Provincial-Territorial Ministers Responsible for Social Services, 1999). The committee also ensured that the rights of people with disabilities would be recognized in future human rights legislation—specifically, the Canadian Charter of Rights and Freedoms. By prohibiting discrimination on the basis of physical or mental disability, the Charter "marked the first time that any national Constitution in the world referred specifically to persons with disabilities" (HRDC, 1998b, 1).

THE 1990s: NEW APPROACHES TO DISABILITY ISSUES

The early 1990s were dominated by efforts to deinstitutionalize people with disabilities and to reintegrate them successfully into communities. Canada's five-year National Strategy for the Integration of Persons with Disabilities was introduced in 1991; it funded several hundred projects across Canada that improved access to transportation, education, housing, employment, and communications for people with disabilities. Mainstream 1992 was later introduced as a template to fully integrate Canadians with disabilities into mainstream society.

By the mid-1990s, the federal government realized that stronger efforts would be required to address the personal, day-to-day challenges of living with a disability; to reduce negative attitudes toward disabilities; and to coordinate the confusing array of government policies and programs that were meant to help people with disabilities move successfully to independence (HRDC, 1999b). To gain headway in these areas, in 1996 the federal government appointed a Task Force on Disability Issues. The task force's recommendations would pave the way for increased federal funding to disability-related organizations; they would also bring about the amendment of several pieces of legislation—relating to tax, employment, and justice—to improve the conditions of people with disabilities.

The building of community capacity has always been an important activity in Canada, but it became a dominant theme in the 1990s. In a disability context, community capacity-building focuses on the extent to which people with disabilities participate with other community groups in identifying issues and developing policies and programs (HRDC, 2002a). Various initiatives were introduced in the 1990s to increase community capacity for people with disabilities. For example, the federal Social Development Partnerships program was launched in 1998 to support community-based projects that promote "the full participation of Canadians with disabilities in learning, work, and community life" (Social Development Canada, 2004b).

IN UNISON

In 1996, the Federal-Provincial-Territorial Ministers Responsible for Social Services identified Canadians with disabilities as a national priority. Two years later, the first ministers released the document *In Unison: A Canadian Approach to Disability Issues*, which outlined their shared vision and goals as well as a policy framework for guiding disability reform. *In Unison* intended to build on the achievements of past initiatives, such as Mainstream 1992 and the federal Task Force on Disability Issues.

Initiatives supported under the In Unison framework focus on enabling "persons with disabilities to maximize their independence and enhance their well-being" (Federal-Provincial-Territorial Ministers Responsible for Social Services, 1999). To respond to the changing needs of people with disabilities, In Unison proposes a new approach to disability-related programs and services (see Exhibit 14.3). In addition, In Unison calls attention to those populations that face particular social and economic challenges because of a disability. Those populations include women, Aboriginal peoples, and young people.

Under the In Unison initiative, full citizenship for people with disabilities is to be achieved by means of three "building blocks":

- *Disability supports*. A variety of goods, services, and supports—including technical aids, special equipment, life skills training, and interpreter services—are to be made available to help people with disabilities perform the tasks of daily living and maximize their personal and financial independence.

- *Employment*. Better access to education opportunities, more flexible training programs, and other supports are to be provided to enhance employability and encourage people with disabilities to enter (or re-enter) the workforce.

Exhibit 14.3

A NEW APPROACH TO DISABILITY ISSUES

OLD ...	NEW ...
Recipients	Participants
Passive income support	Active measures to promote employment in addition to providing necessary income support
Dependence	Independence
Government responsibility	Shared responsibility
Labelled as "unemployable"	Identification of work skills
Disincentives to leave income support	Incentives to seek employment and volunteer opportunities
Insufficient employment supports	Opportunities to develop skills and experience
Program-centred approach	Person-centred approach
Insufficient portability of benefits and services	Portable benefits and services
Multiple access requirements	Integrated access requirements

Source: *In Unison: A Canadian Approach to Disability Issues: Next Steps,* http://socialunion.gc.ca/pwd/unison/unison_e.html, by Federal-Provincial-Territorial Council. The Council includes representation from nine provinces, both territories and Government of Canada and is co-chaired by Liza Frulla, Minister of Social Services Canada and Tim Sale, Minister of Family Services and Housing, Manitoba. 1997. Reproduced with the permission of the Minister of Public Works and Government Services Canada, 2004.

- *Income programs.* Independence achieved through employment will be rewarded; however, income security programs will be available to unemployed people with disabilities.

In Unison also requires governments to report their progress in lifting barriers and promoting inclusion on a regular basis (Federal-Provincial-Territorial Ministers Responsible for Social Services, 1999).

INTO THE TWENTY-FIRST CENTURY

In 2000, the Federal-Provincial-Territorial Ministers Responsible for Social Services released *In Unison 2000: Persons with Disabilities in Canada*, to update Canadians on the *In Unison* initiative. The first ministers acknowledged that progress had been made, but they also recognized the need for improvement in certain areas, including the following:

- Stronger partnerships were needed to make disability supports more accessible, portable, and consistent across the country.

- More incentives to work, and more supportive work environments for people with disabilities, were needed.

- The disability income system needed to become more flexible for those depending on a combination of employment earnings and a disability pension.

- The possibility of raising the level of assistance to cover the costs of disability-related aids and supports needed to be explored.

The first ministers recommended that before new policies were implemented in these areas, there be further research, analysis, and consultation with nongovernment groups, including members of the disability community, employers, and Aboriginal peoples' organizations (Federal-Provincial-Territorial Ministers Responsible for Social Services, 2000b).

In its 2002 Speech from the Throne, the federal government outlined an ambitious plan to remove barriers to work and education for people with disabilities, and to create a broader range of opportunities for full participation. Two years later, the federal government expanded the tax credit for people with disabilities and their caregivers, increased its annual contribution to support disability-related employment supports and training needs, and provided postsecondary education grants to students with disabilities (Department of Finance, 2004).

Despite actions like these, some members of the disability community criticize governments for "not doing enough to resolve the many issues faced by Canadians with disabilities" (HRDC, 2002a, 8). Others point out that since the 1980s, over and over, the same disability issues and similar government responses have been raised, and have been addressed by very similar government responses (mainly at the federal level). Policy analyst Michael Prince (2001) suggests that the participants in the disability policy process may be caught in a vicious circle (see Exhibit 14.4).

E x h i b i t   1 4 . 4
THE DISABILITY ISSUES CIRCLE

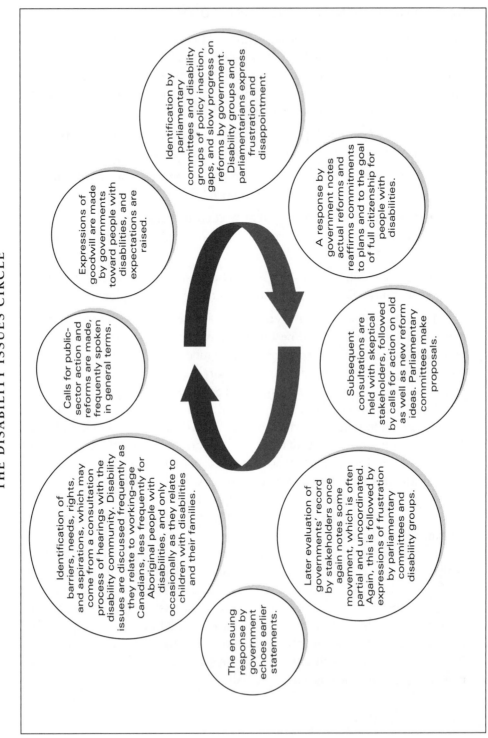

Identification by parliamentary committees and disability groups of policy inaction, gaps, and slow progress on reforms by government. Disability groups and parliamentarians express frustration and disappointment.

Expressions of goodwill are made by governments toward people with disabilities, and expectations are raised.

A response by government notes actual reforms and reaffirms commitments to plans and to the goal of full citizenship for people with disabilities.

Calls for public-sector action and reforms are made, frequently spoken in general terms.

Subsequent consultations are held with skeptical stakeholders, followed by calls for action on old as well as new reform ideas. Parliamentary committees make proposals.

Identification of barriers, needs, rights, and aspirations, which may come from a consultation process of hearings with the disability community. Disability issues are discussed frequently as they relate to working-age Canadians, less frequently for Aboriginal people with disabilities, and only occasionally as they relate to children with disabilities and their families.

The ensuing response by government echoes earlier statements.

Later evaluation of governments' record by stakeholders once again notes some movement, which is often partial and uncoordinated. Again, this is followed by expressions of frustration by parliamentary committees and disability groups.

Source: Michael J. Prince (June 27, 2001). *Governing in an Integrated Fashion: Lessons from the Disability Domain*, p. 63, Box 23. Canadian Policy Research Networks, Inc [online]. Available: www.cprn.com/en/doc.cfm?doc=172# [May 29, 2004].

IV. INCOME AND EMPLOYMENT: KEYS TO FULL PARTICIPATION

THE DISABILITY INCOME SYSTEM

Adequate income—to purchase food, shelter, clothing, transportation, and other basic necesssities—is critical to a person's full participation in society. A variety of factors, including disability, affect a person's ability to earn a living. For people with disabilities who are unable to support themselves, Canadian governments provide "an income safety-net that recognizes individual work efforts as much as possible and that provides financial help if self-support is impossible or insufficient to meet basic needs" (HRDC, 2002a, 44).

Canada's **disability income system** has evolved over several decades and has resulted in what some analysts consider a mix of largely uncoordinated programs. These programs can, however, be grouped into four rough categories:

- *Earnings replacement*. These programs aim to replace income that has been lost as the result of an injury, illness, or disability-related condition (such as AIDS). Included in this category are Employment Insurance, the Canada Pension Plan (CPP) Disability Program, the Veterans Disability Pension, and private disability insurance.

- *Income support programs*. Aimed at people with little or no income, these programs are usually provided through provincial or territorial social assistance departments.

- *Compensation for loss*. This is paid to those who have suffered loss as a result of a disabling injury or accident. These programs include workers' compensation, automobile insurance, and some private insurance programs.

- *Compensation for disability-related costs*. This includes special benefits to offset the costs of having a disability (for example, purchase of a wheelchair or medication). These benefits are usually provided through provincial social assistance or disability insurance programs (Torjman, 1996).

Each type of program has its own system for funding and administering benefits. Depending on the jurisdiction, eligibility for benefits may be determined on the basis of a person's condition or disease, assessed needs, employability, ability to perform basic and/or job-related tasks, and place of residence or status (in the case of Aboriginal peoples). This disparity has resulted in a highly complex disability income system (Federal-Provincial-Territorial Ministers Responsible for Social Services, 1999).

Many people with disabilities are capable of earning their own living through employment. However, Canada's disability income programs have not always provided incentives for people with disabilities to work. For example, in provinces and territories where disability income programs are part of a social assistance program, people receiving disability benefits may be classified as "long-term cases" or "permanently unemployable." These individuals are given more generous benefits than people on welfare, and are offered a variety of additional supports; moreover, they do not have to prove that they are looking for work. As a consequence, they have little incentive to take work that may pay less than their benefits (Federal-Provincial-Territorial Ministers Responsible for Social Services, 1999; Torjman, 1996).

In recent years, Canadian governments have tried to address disincentives to work by reforming their respective disability income systems. For example, in the late 1990s, the federal government revised the CPP Disability Program to make it more difficult for people to collect disability benefits, and to ensure that the system's recipients would be carefully monitored (HRDC, 1998b). The federal government and the provinces and territories also introduced automatic reinstatement policies; under these policies, if an individual starts to work again but cannot continue because of a recurring disability, then income assistance is automatically reinstated (Government of Canada, 2003b). Reinstatement policies are expected to increase the likelihood that people with disabilities will at least try to work, knowing that they will be able to return to benefits if necessary.

According to the Sub-Committee on the Status of Persons with Disabilities, Canada's disability income system continues to be weak in several respects, despite recent reforms. For instance, individuals who rely solely on the CPP disability benefit receive considerably lower rates of benefits than those on workers' compensation or private insurance. Furthermore, people with similar disabilities can end up with vastly different incomes depending on which province or territory they live, and owing to the variations in eligibility among the provincial/territorial disability income programs, some people with disabilities are over-compensated whereas others are living in poverty (Young, 2002). In response to a review of the CPP Disability Program in 2003, the Government of Canada (2003b, 36) acknowledged the inconsistencies in the disability income system and promised—in cooperation with other levels of government—to take a closer look at the various components of the system.

EMPLOYMENT SERVICES AND VOCATIONAL REHABILITATION

Canadian governments have played a central role in the rehabilitation and employment of people with disabilities. During the first half of the twentieth century, the Veterans' Rehabilitation Act and the Workmen's Compensation Act supported the vocational rehabilitation of injured war veterans and industrial workers. In 1961, the passage of the Vocational Rehabilitation of Disabled Persons Act (VRDP) established sheltered workshops and other specialized work opportunities for people with disabilities. Over time, employment and vocational rehabilitation for people with disabilities came to focus on integrating those individuals into mainstream work settings. The replacement of the VRDP with Employability Assistance for People with Disabilities (EAPD) in 1996 was an attempt to increase the labour force participation rate for people with disabilities by helping them prepare for, find, and keep jobs (HRDC, 1998a).

In 2004, a new Multilateral Framework for Labour Market Agreements replaced the EAPD. This framework (not originally endorsed by Quebec and the Territories) is a cost-shared federal/provincial arrangement whereby governments work together to improve the employment situation of people with disabilities (Government of Canada, 2004c). Under the framework, each jurisdiction has agreed to focus on one or more of the following priority areas:

- *Education and training.* Improve the level of basic and postsecondary education and work-related skills for persons with disabilities.

- *Employment participation.* Improve the labour market situation and independence of persons with disabilities through employment-related activities.

- *Employment opportunities.* Expand the availability, accessibility and quality of employment opportunities for persons with disabilities, in partnership with business and labour.

- *Connecting employers and persons with disabilities.* Enhance awareness of the abilities and availability of persons with disabilities and strengthen persons with disabilities' knowledge of labour market opportunities.

- *Building knowledge.* Enhance the knowledge base, which contributes to continuous improvement of labour market policies and programs for persons with disabilities. (Government of Canada, 2003f)

To launch the Multilateral Framework, the 2004 federal budget increased its annual funding for disability-related employment programs from $193 million to $223 million. Prince Edward Island and Ontario were among the first provinces to sign agreements with the federal government under the framework.

Besides mainstream employment services, and employment programs available under the multilateral framework, a number of federal initiatives provide specialized employment assistance to people with disabilities. For example, the Disability Vocational Rehabilitation Program (under the CPP) is designed to help people who receive disability pension benefits return to work. With new technologies, skills training, and medical supports, many people with disabilities who could not before can now join the workforce. Other initiatives, such as the Opportunities Fund for Persons with Disabilities and the Entrepreneurs with Disabilities Program, provide services to help people with disabilities either find work or create their own (Government of Canada, 2002b).

Services to help people with disabilities enter and remain in the workforce are often complex, and can involve a variety of workers such as rehabilitation practitioners, intake workers, and personnel specialists. The key steps and stages for serving clients with disabilities are outlined in Exhibit 14.5.

V. IMPLICATIONS FOR SOCIAL WORK PRACTICE

Professional helpers who serve people with disabilities come with a variety of titles, including community support worker and rehabilitation practitioner. Over the years, social workers, like other helping professionals, have been modifying their approaches to working with people with disabilities. As part of the transition from institution-based treatment to community-based services, social work practice shifted away from traditional medical models; social workers began helping clients adjust to community living through strategies such as sheltered workshops and residential group homes. By the 1990s, the focus of services had shifted again, this time toward helping clients achieve independence in mainstream settings.

In many respects, the evolution of social work practice within the disability community parallels the transition from segregation to mainstreaming (see Exhibit 14.6). The **open house concept** emphasizes the full participation of people with disabilities in school, work, social, and other activities and their enjoyment of the same rights and privileges as Canadians without disabilities. Each component of the open house concept, as it relates to social work practice, is reviewed below.

Exhibit 14.5
CLIENT SERVICE PROCESS

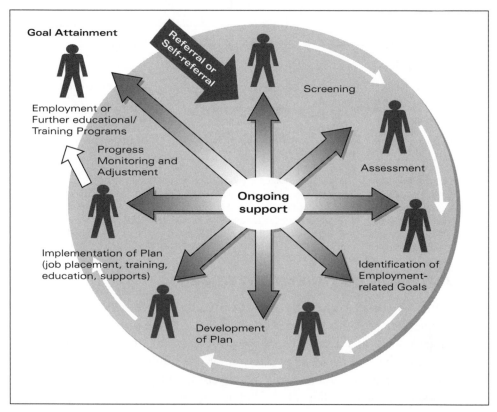

Source: Human Resources Development Canada (August 2002). *Promising Practices in Employability Assistance for People with Disabilities (EAPD) Funded Programs and Services:* Final Report, Figure 4.1. Evaluation and Data Development, Strategic Policy, Human Resources Development Canada, SP-AH-196-08-02E [online]. Available: www11.hrdc-drhc.gc.ca/pls/edd/SP_AH_196_08_02.lhtml [May 29, 2004]. Reproduced with the permission of the Minister of Public Works and Government Services Canada, 2004.

ACCOMMODATION

Accommodation involves modifying the environment so that a person with a disability can participate in activities that take place in that environment. Social workers can promote accommodation in a variety of ways. For instance, a worker may help someone obtain wheelchair access or special computer equipment that is needed for training or employment. Similarly, social workers can help people with disabilities work with government agencies on improving public transportation systems (or other systems) so that they can access work, school, and community activities.

Exhibit 14.6

FROM SEGREGATION TO MAINSTREAMING: A CONCEPTUAL MODEL

WAREHOUSE ⟶	GREENHOUSE ⟶	OPEN HOUSE
Caring for	Enabling	Accommodating
Protection	Support	Autonomy/empowerment
Labelled permanently incapacitated	Adaptation of individual	Adaptation of social and physical environment
Deemed incompetent	Recognition of capacity	Rights/responsibilities

Source: *In Unison: A Canadian Approach to Disability Issues: Next Steps,* http://socialunion.gc.ca/pwd/unison/unison_e.html, by Federal-Provincial-Territorial Council. The Council includes representation from nine provinces, both territories and Government of Canada and is co-chaired by Liza Frulla, Minister of Social Services Canada and Tim Sale, Minister of Family Services and Housing, Manitoba. 1997. Reproduced with the permission of the Minister of Public Works and Government Services Canada, 2004.

AUTONOMY AND EMPOWERMENT

Although social workers do not directly empower others, they can help people acquire the knowledge and skills they need in order to enhance their independence and a sense of empowerment. Social workers facilitate many activities that are personally empowering, including assertiveness training, life skills training, problem-solving exercises, and peer leadership training. Workers can do the following to facilitate the empowering process:

- provide adequate information about possible options so that people can make their own informed choices and decisions;

- encourage people to express their wishes and exercise their right to self-determination;

- acknowledge the capabilities that people have to manage their own lives; and

- help others advocate for themselves, challenge oppressive labels, and regain control of their lives (Roeher Institute, 1996).

ADAPTATION OF THE SOCIAL AND PHYSICAL ENVIRONMENT

Social workers can help staff in social agencies, educational institutions, and other organizations focus on the problems that reside in their own systems rather than viewing the person with the disability as a problem to be solved. In addition, social workers can participate in reviews of agency policies, programs, and practices, as well as in modifications of agency systems to make them more inclusive (that is, free of barriers). Many social workers who serve the disability community find that a community development approach is more effective than traditional counselling approaches: "By promoting community development, the focus is shifted away from individuals and placed on strengthening the capacity of communities to be inclusive" (Panitch, 1998, 10).

RIGHTS AND RESPONSIBILITIES

Social workers have long called called attention to, and demanded changes in, policies and programs that inhibit independent living for people with disabilities. In recent years, however, social workers have shifted much of their attention to helping people with disabilities speak out and assert their rights on their own behalf. One of the underlying themes of the disability movement is the demand for "rights, not charity"; social workers can play an important role in helping people with disabilities gain both control of resources and the right to make decisions that affect their own lives.

SUMMARY

■ Introduction

For much of Canada's history, social attitudes have kept people with disabilities excluded from mainstream society—often through institutionalization. The disability rights movement has sought to remove the barriers to opportunity faced by people with disabilities. That movement, along with international developments and other efforts, has led to greater public acceptance of people with disabilities and more inclusive government policies.

■ Disability: A Canadian Profile

Disability in Canada is commonly defined according to the impairment, functional limitations, and/or ecological (social) perspectives. The International Classification of Functioning, Disability and Health helps us understand the objective components of health and disability. The Participation and Activity Limitation Survey provides information about disability rates, types of disability, and the severity of disability in Canada. Certain groups, including children, Aboriginal peoples, and women suffer particular hardships as a result of disability.

■ Making the Transition: From Exclusion to Inclusion

In the wake of deinstitutionalization, the community living movement emerged to help people make the transition from living in institutions to living in natural settings. To accommodate community living, various reforms were made in building codes, communication and transportation systems, and housing. Individuals who have disabilities, and organizations that serve them, make up the disability community. These organizations have different mandates; all of them, however, focus on removing barriers that exclude individuals with disabilities from fully participating in society.

■ Canada's Disability Policy Agenda

The focus in the 1980s was mainly on raising public awareness of disability issues and advancing the rights of people with disabilities. In the 1990s, Mainstream 1992 was developed, hundreds of disability-related projects were initiated, and building community capacity became a dominant theme. Several legislative reforms were introduced, and the *In Unison* initiative was launched to guide the development of policies and programs for people with disabilities. In the early twenty-first century, the *In Unison* initiative was reviewed and the federal government committed itself to removing the remaining barriers to work and education. Despite these efforts, some analysts believe that progress toward full inclusion for people with disabilities has been slow and inconsistent.

■ Income and Employment: Keys to Full Participation

The disability income system includes programs aimed at providing earnings replacement, income support, and compensation. This system is highly complex, and there is considerable disparity of income benefits across the country. Recent reforms to provincial and territorial disability income programs have included attempts to strengthen work incentives; however, the system is still being criticized for its many shortcomings. Throughout much of the twentieth century, various pieces of federal legislation have supported the rehabilitation and employment of people with disabilities. Under the current Multilateral Framework for Labour Market Agreements, federal and provincial governments work together to improve employment prospects for people with disabilities.

■ Implications for Social Work Practice

Over the years, social workers and other professional helpers have modified their approaches to working with people with disabilities; the focus today is on helping clients achieve independence in mainstream settings. An "open house" approach can be used to help people with disabilities participate fully in society. This approach emphasizes accommodation; autonomy and empowerment; adaptation of the social and physical environment; and rights and responsibilities.

▼ KEY TERMS

For definitions of the key terms, consult the Glossary on page 364 at the end of the book.

disability rights movement
 p. 321

impairment perspective
 p. 323

functional limitations
 perspective p. 323

ecological (or social)
 perspective p. 323

disability p. 324

community living
 movement p. 329

disability community p. 330

disability income system
 p. 337

open house concept p. 340

accommodation p. 341

A CENTURY OF RESPONSE: HISTORICAL HIGHLIGHTS IN SOCIAL WELFARE AND RELATED SYSTEMS

EARLY 1900s

1906 Canada's new Immigration Act restricts entry to several groups of people, especially people from Asia (further restrictions are added in 1910).

1908 The Juvenile Delinquents Act is passed.

   The Annuities Act—precursor of the Old Age Pension Act—is passed.

1914 The First World War begins.

   Parliament creates the Canadian Patriotic Fund to provide financial assistance to the families of soldiers.

   Ontario becomes the first province to enact workers' compensation legislation.

1916 Canada's first mothers' allowances are implemented in Manitoba.

1918 The Canadian Mental Health Association is founded.

   The Canadian National Institute for the Blind opens.

   The First World War ends.

1919 The Soldier Settlement Act is passed.

   The Winnipeg General Strike takes place.

   The Community Welfare Council in Winnipeg becomes one of Canada's first social action groups.

1920 The Returned Soldiers' Insurance Act is passed.

1926   The Canadian Association of Social Workers is founded.

1927   The Old Age Pension Act is passed.

1929   Women become eligible for appointment to the Canadian Senate after they are declared "persons" by the Judicial Committee of the British Privy Council.

1930   The Great Depression begins.

The federal government provides municipalities with unemployment relief.

The War Veterans Allowance Act is passed.

1935   The On-to-Ottawa Trek takes place.

The Employment and Social Insurance Act is passed (and repealed in 1937).

1937   The Royal Commission on Dominion–Provincial Relations (Rowell-Sirois Commission) is appointed by the federal government.

1938   The Canadian Association of Social Workers develops a code of ethics.

1939   The Youth Training Act is passed.

The Second World War begins, putting an end to the Great Depression.

MID-1900s

1940   The Unemployment Insurance Act is passed.

1943   The Marsh Report on Social Security is released by the House of Commons Advisory Committee on Post-War Reconstruction.

1944   The Family Allowances Act is passed (program is implemented in 1945).

The National Housing Act is passed.

The Department of National Health and Welfare is established.

The Department of Veterans Affairs is established.

1945   The Veterans Rehabilitation Act is passed.

The Second World War ends.

1946   The Central Mortgage and Housing Corporation (later renamed Canada Mortgage and Housing Corporation) is established.

The War Veterans Allowance Act is passed (replaces War Veterans Allowance Act of 1930).

1947   Canada's first health insurance program begins in Saskatchewan.

1948   The federal government implements settlement and integration programs for immigrants.

Canada endorses the United Nations' Universal Declaration of Human Rights.

1951   The Indian Act is amended, which lifts a ban on several traditional ceremonies.

The Old Age Assistance Act is passed.

The Old Age Security Act is enacted.

The Blind Persons Act comes into effect.

Canada's first social work doctorate program is offered at the University of Toronto.

The UN adopts the Convention Related to the Status of Refugees (the Geneva Convention).

1953   The Immigration Act is amended, inviting more immigrants from Caucasian countries.

1954   The Rehabilitation of Disabled Persons Act is passed.

1956   The Unemployment Assistance Act is passed (federal government begins sharing cost of provincial social assistance).

1958   The Canadian Association for Community Living is founded.

1960   Status Indians gain the right to vote in federal elections.

The Canadian Bill of Rights is introduced.

1961   The Vocational Rehabilitation of Disabled Persons Act is passed.

The Canadian Bill of Rights becomes law.

1964   The Youth Allowances Act is passed.

1965   The Canada and Quebec Pension Plans are introduced.

The International Convention on the Elimination of All Forms of Racial Discrimination is ratified.

1966   The Canada Assistance Plan is initiated.

The Guaranteed Income Supplement is introduced.

The Medical Care Act is passed.

Canada's first Bachelor of Social Work program is offered.

1967   The Canadian Association of Schools of Social Work is established.

The Royal Commission on the Status of Women is appointed.

Amendments to the Immigration Act eliminate discriminatory criteria for selecting immigrants.

1968   The Senate Committee on Poverty (the Croll Committee) is appointed by the federal government.

The Divorce Act is amended (makes divorce easier to obtain).

1969   The Statement of the Government of Canada on Indian Policy is released.

Homosexual acts between consenting adults are decriminalized.

LATE 1900s

1970   The federal government launches the Income Security Review.

1971   The Unemployment Insurance Act is amended.

       The Senate Committee on Poverty releases its report, *Poverty in Canada*.

       Canada's multicultural policy is introduced.

       The National Council of Welfare is founded.

1973   Newfoundland passes the Neglected Adults Welfare Act—the first adult protection legislation in North America.

       The federal government launches a Social Security Review.

       The Canadian Council on the Status of Women is established.

       The Residential Rehabilitation Assistance Program begins.

1974   Canada's first large-scale guaranteed annual income experiment, MINCOME, is launched in Manitoba.

       The federal government appoints a National Advisory Council on Voluntary Action as a first step to improving Government of Canada/Voluntary Sector relations.

       The Immigration Settlement and Adaptation program begins.

1975   The International Year of Women is declared.

1976   The UN Decade for Women: Equality, Development and Peace begins.

       The Spouse's Allowance is introduced.

       A new Immigration Act is passed (and implemented in 1978) to do more to help newcomers settle in Canada.

1977   Established Programs Financing (EPF)—which puts funding for hospital, medicare, and postsecondary education under one funding formula—is initiated.

       The Canadian Human Rights Act is passed.

       Quebec becomes the first province to forbid discrimination on the basis of sexual orientation.

1978   The federal government establishes a Non-Profit Housing Program.

       The Refundable Child Tax Credit is introduced (first time the Canadian income tax system is used to deliver benefits to families that do not pay income tax).

       An amendment to the Immigration Act allows refugees to apply to Canada as immigrants.

1979   The International Year of the Child is declared.

1980   The International Classification of Impairments, Disabilities, and Handicaps (ICIDH) is released by the World Health Organization.

The Special Committee on the Disabled and the Handicapped is established.

The federal government appoints the National Advisory Council on Aging.

1981   The International Year for Disabled Persons is declared.

The Parliamentary Special Committee on the Disabled and the Handicapped releases its Obstacles report.

Canada's first food bank opens in Edmonton.

Language Instruction for Newcomers to Canada program is introduced.

1982   The Canadian Charter of Rights and Freedoms is entrenched in the Canadian Constitution.

The National Native Alcohol and Drug Abuse Program is established.

The National Clearinghouse on Family Violence is established.

The UN introduces the Vienna International Plan of Action on Ageing.

1983   The UN declares 1983 to 1992 as the International Decade of Disabled Persons.

1984   The federal election is won by the Progressive Conservative Party under Brian Mulroney.

The Canada Health Act is passed.

The Host Program is established to facilitate the resettlement of refugees (services are extended to immigrants in 1991).

1985   The Royal Commission on the Economic Union and Development Prospects for Canada (Macdonald Commission) releases its final report.

The Indian Act is amended, extending several status and property rights to Aboriginal peoples.

The Status of Disabled Persons Secretariat is appointed to raise awareness of disability issues and support the inclusion of persons with disabilities.

The General Social Survey program is initiated, providing information on social trends and issues.

1986   The first Health and Activity Limitation Survey is completed.

The Child Sexual Abuse Initiative is launched.

The National Task Force on Child Care is established.

1987   The Parliamentary Committee on Human Rights and the Status of Disabled Persons is established.

The International Year of Shelter for the Homeless is declared.

1988 The Refundable Child Tax Credit is converted to the Non-Refundable Child Tax Credit.

Phase I of the federal Family Violence Initiative is announced.

The Canada–U.S. Free Trade Agreement is ratified.

The Seniors Independence Program is launched.

The Canadian Multiculturalism Act is passed.

The Women at Risk Program is introduced to assist refugee women and their dependants.

1989 The House of Commons resolves to end child poverty by the year 2000.

Clawbacks are introduced into family allowances and Old Age Security, eliminating these programs' universal status.

The National Survey on Elder Abuse—Canada's first major survey to study elder abuse—is administered.

The Standing Committee on Human Rights and the Status of Disabled Persons is established.

1990 The Unemployment Insurance Act is amended (responsibility for funding shifts to employers and employees).

The Standing Senate Committee on Aboriginal Peoples is formed to review parliamentary bills on native issues.

1991 The Canada–Quebec Accord is signed.

Phase II of the federal Family Violence Initiative is announced.

The Royal Commission on Aboriginal Peoples is appointed by the federal government.

The First Nations Child and Family Services program begins.

A funding "cap" is imposed on Canada's wealthiest provinces under the Canada Assistance Plan (CAP).

Canada ratifies the UN Convention on the Rights of the Child.

The second Health and Activity Limitation Survey is completed.

The National Strategy for the Integration of Persons with Disabilities is introduced.

1992 Mainstream 1992 provides a framework for guiding the full integration of people with disabilities into society.

Canada's Action Plan for Children is released.

The Brighter Futures program is launched.

1993 The Liberal Party under Jean Chrétien defeats the Progressive Conservatives in the federal election.

The International Year of the World's Indigenous People is declared.

The findings of the Violence Against Women Survey—Canada's first national survey of violence against women—are released.

Family allowances are replaced by the Canada Child Tax Benefit.

The Ventures in Independence program for seniors is initiated.

The Unemployment Insurance Act is amended (reduces benefits).

The North American Free Trade Agreement (NAFTA) is ratified (comes into effect in 1994).

The UN begins using the Human Development Index to measure social conditions in member countries.

1994   The federal government conducts a general Program Review (HRDC launches its own Social Security Review).

The International Year of the Family is declared.

Community Action Programs for Children are launched under Health Canada's Child Development Initiative.

The National Longitudinal Survey of Children and Youth is launched.

The National Population Health Survey is introduced.

The Settlement Renewal Initiative is launched.

The International Decade of the World's Indigenous People begins.

1995   The Federal-Provincial-Territorial Council on Social Policy Renewal is formed.

The New Horizons: Partners in Aging initiative is launched (and is terminated in 1996, then reinstated in 2004).

The federal government introduces the Inherent Rights Policy as a guide to First Nations self-government.

Aboriginal Head Start is introduced.

The First Nations and Inuit Child Care Initiative is launched.

Twelve national organizations form a Voluntary Sector Roundtable.

1996   The Federal Task Force on Disability Issues is established and releases its report, Equal Citizenship for Canadians with Disabilities, that same year.

Report on the Royal Commission on Aboriginal Peoples is released.

The Self-Government Negotiations Funding Support program is launched (for First Nations).

The Canada Assistance Plan is replaced by the Canada Health and Social Transfer.

The National Framework on Aging is released.

The new Employment Insurance Act replaces Unemployment Insurance.

Labour Market Development Agreements between the federal and regional governments come into force.

Canada's child poverty rate rises to almost 21 percent.

The Canadian Council on Social Development launches the Urban Poverty Project.

The Federal-Provincial-Territorial Council on Social Policy Renewal meets for the first time, and identifies young children, and people with disabilities, as national priorities.

The Employability Assistance for People with Disabilities replaces the Vocational Rehabilitation of Disabled Persons Act.

1997   Phase III of the Family Violence Initiative begins.

Amendments to the Immigration Act create three categories of immigrant applications.

The Canadian Race Relations Foundation begins operation.

The federal government establishes the Social Cohesion Network.

The Federal-Provincial-Territorial Council on Social Policy Renewal agrees to develop a national children's agenda.

Canada's National Survey of Giving, Volunteering and Participating is administered for the first time.

The implementation of welfare-to-work programs in Ontario is made possible by the enactment of the Social Assistance Reform Act.

Canada's first comprehensive family/child policy is introduced in Quebec.

The Aboriginal Healing Strategy is launched.

The National Reinvestment Framework is developed to guide the reinvestment of social assistance funds into programs for low-income families with children.

The International Decade for the Eradication of Poverty begins.

1998   *Gathering Strength: Canada's Aboriginal Action Plan* is released.

The federal government makes a formal apology to Aboriginal peoples in the form of a Statement of Reconciliation.

The Aboriginal Healing Foundation is established.

The Urban Aboriginal Strategy is introduced.

The Canadian Incidence Study of Reported Child Abuse and Neglect becomes the first national study to examine reported child abuse.

The National Child Benefit is introduced (includes the Canada Child Tax Benefit and the National Child Benefit Supplement).

The federal government achieves a balanced budget for the first time in nearly twenty years.

The Canada Pension Plan undergoes drastic changes to make it more sustainable.

Ontario's Social Work and Social Service Work Act is passed.

The Human Resources Strategic Analysis of the Social Work Sector is launched.

The federal government establishes the Canada Coordinating Committee to consult with seniors.

The document In *Unison: A Canadian Approach to Disability Issues* is released as a guide to the full participation of people with disabilities.

Canada releases its Action Plan for Food Security to guide efforts to combat hunger.

The federal government launches the Social Development Partnerships program to support projects that promote the inclusion of people with disabilities.

1999 The International Year of the Older Person is declared.

Ontario becomes the first province to extend to same-sex couples the same rights as those extended to heterosexual common-law couples.

Members of the Federal-Provincial-Territorial Council on Social Policy Renewal sign the Social Union Framework Agreement (SUFA) and release the document *A National Children's Agenda: Developing a Shared Vision*.

The first report from the National Welfare to Work Study is released.

The federal government launches Understanding the Early Years, a research project that focuses on early childhood development.

The Supporting Communities Partnership Initiative begins, which launches Phase I of the National Homelessness Initiative.

The Panel on Accountability and Governance in the Voluntary Sector releases its report, *Building on Strength: Improving Governance and Accountability in Canada's Voluntary Sector.*

The federal government releases *Future Directions: The Challenges Facing Persons with Disabilities*, a guide to disability policy reform.

The National Improving the Quality of Life of Canadian Seniors Project is launched.

EARLY 2000s

2000 Canada's unemployment rate falls to its lowest level in twenty-five years (6.8 percent).

The Immigration and Refugee Protection Act is tabled in the House of Commons.

Phase I of the Voluntary Sector Initiative begins.

The second National Survey of Giving, Volunteering and Participating is conducted.

The findings of the Strategic Human Resources Analysis of the Social Work Sector are released in the document *In Critical Demand: Social Work in Canada.*

In Unison 2000: Persons with Disabilities in Canada is released as an update on the *In Unison* initiative.

The Early Childhood Development Agreement is introduced.

2001   Canada's Affordable Housing Program is launched.

An Accord between the Government of Canada and the Voluntary Sector is released.

The International Year of the Volunteer is declared.

The Aboriginal Peoples Survey 2001 is administered.

The Office of Indian Residential Schools Resolution of Canada is created to resolve claims related to residential schools.

The 2001 Census finds that "traditional" families represent 44 percent—and lone-parent families account for 16 percent—of all families in Canada.

For the first time in Canadian history, the census collects data on same-sex unions.

The Longitudinal Survey of Immigrants to Canada is launched.

The first National Settlement Conference is held under the Strengthening Settlement Capacity Project.

The World Health Organization introduces its International Classification of Functioning, Disability and Health.

The Participation and Activity Limitation Survey replaces the Health and Limitations Survey.

The Canada Volunteerism Initiative is launched to encourage volunteerism in voluntary organizations.

2002   Phase II of the Voluntary Sector Initiative begins.

Quebec introduces its National Strategy to Combat Poverty and Social Exclusion.

Canada and other nations adopt the United Nations' A World Fit for Children strategy.

New Brunswick establishes Canada's first adoption foundation.

The UN develops an International Plan of Action on Ageing.

The *Toronto Declaration on the Global Prevention of Elder Abuse* is released.

The Survey of First Nations People Living On-Reserve is administered.

The federal government introduces the First Nations Governance Act (Bill C-7) to the House of Commons.

The Federal Strategy on Early Childhood Development for First Nations and Other Aboriginal Children is introduced.

The Immigration and Refugee Protection Act comes into force.

The Federal-Provincial-Territorial Ministers Responsible for Immigration meet for the first time.

The Prime Minister's Caucus Task Force on Urban Issues releases its report, *Canada's Urban Strategy—A Vision for the 21st Century.*

The Standing Senate Committee on Social Affairs, Science and Technology releases its final report (the Kirby Report) on Canada's health care system.

The Romanow Commission releases its final report on the future of health care in Canada.

2003   The federal budget announces substantial reinvestments in social programs.

Canadian governments agree on a Multilateral Framework on Early Learning and Child Care.

Canada and Mexico collaborate on the development of a *Guide for the Development of a Comprehensive System of Support to Promote Active Ageing.*

Prime Minister Chrétien appoints a Liberal Caucus Task Force on Seniors.

Prime Minister Martin appoints a Task Force on Active Living and Dignity for Seniors.

The total number of food banks in Canada reaches 639.

Phase II of the National Homelessness Initiative is launched.

Manitoba passes the Child and Family Services Authorities Act, giving Métis and First Nations the authority to provide child welfare services in that province.

The federal government proposes legislation to legalize same-sex marriages.

2004   The Canada Health and Social Transfer is replaced by the Canada Social Transfer and the Canada Health Transfer.

British Columbia becomes the first province to put a time limit on welfare eligibility.

The United Nations drafts the Convention on the Human Rights of Disabled People.

The Multilateral Framework for Labour Market Agreements replaces the Employability Assistance for People with Disabilities initiative.

The federal Child Disability Benefit is implemented.

The Employment Insurance account reports a surplus of nearly $44 billion.

Canada releases *A Canada Fit for Children*, a plan to improve conditions for children.

The federal government establishes a Secretariat for Seniors.

Newly elected Prime Minister Paul Martin announces plans to establish a national home care program and a national childcare program.

Social Union Framework Agreement

OTTAWA, ONTARIO—FEBRUARY 4, 1999

A Framework to Improve the Social Union for Canadians

An agreement between the Government of Canada and the Governments of the Provinces and Territories

February 4, 1999

The following agreement is based upon a mutual respect between orders of government and a willingness to work more closely together to meet the needs of Canadians.

1. PRINCIPLES

Canada's social union should reflect and give expression to the fundamental values of Canadians—equality, respect for diversity, fairness, individual dignity and responsibility, and mutual aid and our responsibilities for one another.

Within their respective constitutional jurisdictions and powers, governments commit to the following principles:

All Canadians Are Equal

- Treat all Canadians with fairness and equity

- Promote equality of opportunity for all Canadians

- Respect the equality, rights and dignity of all Canadian women and men and their diverse needs

Meeting the Needs of Canadians

- Ensure access for all Canadians, wherever they live or move in Canada, to essential social programs and services of reasonably comparable quality

- Provide appropriate assistance to those in need

- Respect the principles of medicare: comprehensiveness, universality, portability, public administration and accessibility

- Promote the full and active participation of all Canadians in Canada's social and economic life

- Work in partnership with individuals, families, communities, voluntary organizations, business and labour, and ensure appropriate opportunities for Canadians to have meaningful input into social policies and programs

Sustaining Social Programs and Services

- Ensure adequate, affordable, stable and sustainable funding for social programs

Aboriginal Peoples of Canada

- For greater certainty, nothing in this agreement abrogates or derogates from any Aboriginal, treaty or other rights of Aboriginal peoples including self-government

2. MOBILITY WITHIN CANADA

All governments believe that the freedom of movement of Canadians to pursue opportunities anywhere in Canada is an essential element of Canadian citizenship.

Governments will ensure that no new barriers to mobility are created in new social policy initiatives.

Governments will eliminate, within three years, any residency-based policies or practices which constrain access to post-secondary education, training, health and social services and social assistance unless they can be demonstrated to be reasonable and consistent with the principles of the Social Union Framework.

Accordingly, sector Ministers will submit annual reports to the Ministerial Council identifying residency-based barriers to access and providing action plans to eliminate them.

Governments are also committed to ensure, by July 1, 2001, full compliance with the mobility provisions of the Agreement on Internal Trade by all entities subject to those provisions, including the requirements for mutual recognition of occupational qualifications and for eliminating residency requirements for access to employment opportunities.

3. INFORMING CANADIANS—PUBLIC ACCOUNTABILITY AND TRANSPARENCY

Canada's Social Union can be strengthened by enhancing each government's transparency and accountability to its constituents. Each government therefore agrees to:

Achieving and Measuring Results

- Monitor and measure outcomes of its social programs and report regularly to its constituents on the performance of these programs

- Share information and best practices to support the development of outcome measures, and work with other governments to develop, over time, comparable indicators to measure progress on agreed objectives

- Publicly recognize and explain the respective roles and contributions of governments

- Use funds transferred from another order of government for the purposes agreed and pass on increases to its residents

- Use third parties, as appropriate, to assist in assessing progress on social priorities

Involvement of Canadians

- Ensure effective mechanisms for Canadians to participate in developing social priorities and reviewing outcomes

Ensuring Fair and Transparent Practices

- Make eligibility criteria and service commitments for social programs publicly available

- Have in place appropriate mechanisms for citizens to appeal unfair administrative practices and bring complaints about access and service

- Report publicly on citizen's appeals and complaints, ensuring that confidentiality requirements are met

4. WORKING IN PARTNERSHIP FOR CANADIANS

Joint Planning and Collaboration

The Ministerial Council has demonstrated the benefits of joint planning and mutual help through which governments share knowledge and learn from each other.

Governments therefore agree to

- Undertake joint planning to share information on social trends, problems and priorities and to work together to identify priorities for collaborative action

- Collaborate on implementation of joint priorities when this would result in more effective and efficient service to Canadians, including as appropriate joint development of objectives and principles, clarification of roles and responsibilities, and flexible implementation to respect diverse needs and circumstances, complement existing measures and avoid duplication

Reciprocal Notice and Consultation

The actions of one government or order of government often have significant effects on other governments. In a manner consistent with the principles of our system of parliamentary government and the budget-making process, governments therefore agree to:

- Give one another advance notice prior to implementation of a major change in a social policy or program which will likely substantially affect another government

- Offer to consult prior to implementing new social policies and programs that are likely to substantially affect other governments or the social union more generally. Governments participating in these consultations will have the opportunity to identify potential duplication and to propose alternative approaches to achieve flexible and effective implementation

Equitable Treatment

For any new Canada-wide social initiatives, arrangements made with one province/territory will be made available to all provinces/territories in a manner consistent with their diverse circumstances.

Aboriginal Peoples

Governments will work with the Aboriginal peoples of Canada to find practical solutions to address their pressing needs.

5. THE FEDERAL SPENDING POWER—IMPROVING SOCIAL PROGRAMS FOR CANADIANS

Social Transfers to Provinces and Territories

The use of the federal spending power under the Constitution has been essential to the development of Canada's social union. An important use of the spending power by the Government of Canada has been to transfer money to the provincial and territorial governments. These transfers support the delivery of social programs and services by provinces and territories in order to promote equality of opportunity and mobility for all Canadians and to pursue Canada-wide objectives.

Conditional social transfers have enabled governments to introduce new and innovative social programs, such as Medicare, and to ensure that they are available to all Canadians. When the federal government uses such conditional transfers, whether cost-shared or block-funded, it should proceed in a cooperative manner that is respectful of the provincial and territorial governments and their priorities.

Funding Predictability

The Government of Canada will consult with provincial and territorial governments at least one year prior to renewal or significant funding changes in existing social transfers to provinces/territories, unless otherwise agreed, and will build due notice provisions into any new social transfers to provincial/territorial governments.

New Canada-wide Initiatives Supported by Transfers to Provinces and Territories

With respect to any new Canada-wide initiatives in health care, post-secondary education, social assistance and social services that are funded through intergovernmental transfers, whether block-funded or cost-shared, the Government of Canada will:

- Work collaboratively with all provincial and territorial governments to identify Canada-wide priorities and objectives

- Not introduce such new initiatives without the agreement of a majority of provincial governments

Each provincial and territorial government will determine the detailed program design and mix best suited to its own needs and circumstances to meet the agreed objectives.

A provincial/territorial government which, because of its existing programming, does not require the total transfer to fulfill the agreed objectives would be able to reinvest any funds not required for those objectives in the same or a related priority area.

The Government of Canada and the provincial/territorial governments will agree on an accountability framework for such new social initiatives and investments.

All provincial and territorial governments that meet or commit to meet the agreed Canada-wide objectives and agree to respect the accountability framework will receive their share of available funding.

Direct Federal Spending

Another use of the federal spending power is making transfers to individuals and to organizations in order to promote equality of opportunity, mobility, and other Canada-wide objectives.

When the federal government introduces new Canada-wide initiatives funded through direct transfers to individuals or organizations for health care, post-secondary education, social assistance and social services, it will, prior to implementation, give at least three months' notice and offer to consult. Governments participating in these consultations will have the opportunity to identify potential duplication and to propose alternative approaches to achieve flexible and effective implementation.

6. DISPUTE AVOIDANCE AND RESOLUTION

Governments are committed to working collaboratively to avoid and resolve intergovernmental disputes. Respecting existing legislative provisions, mechanisms to avoid and resolve disputes should:

- Be simple, timely, efficient, effective and transparent
- Allow maximum flexibility for governments to resolve disputes in a non-adversarial way
- Ensure that sectors design processes appropriate to their needs
- Provide for appropriate use of third parties for expert assistance and advice while ensuring democratic accountability by elected officials

Dispute avoidance and resolution will apply to commitments on mobility, intergovernmental transfers, interpretation of the Canada Health Act principles, and, as appropriate, on any new joint initiative.

Sector Ministers should be guided by the following process, as appropriate:

Dispute Avoidance

- Governments are committed to working together and avoiding disputes through information-sharing, joint planning, collaboration, advance notice and early consultation, and flexibility in implementation

Sector Negotiations

- Sector negotiations to resolve disputes will be based on joint fact-finding

- A written joint fact-finding report will be submitted to governments involved, who will have the opportunity to comment on the report before its completion

- Governments involved may seek assistance of a third party for fact-finding, advice, or mediation

- At the request of either party in a dispute, fact-finding or mediation reports will be made public

Review Provisions

- Any government can require a review of a decision or action one year after it enters into effect or when changing circumstances justify

Each government involved in a dispute may consult and seek advice from third parties, including interested or knowledgeable persons or groups, at all stages of the process.

Governments will report publicly on an annual basis on the nature of intergovernmental disputes and their resolution.

Role of the Ministerial Council

The Ministerial Council will support sector Ministers by collecting information on effective ways of implementing the agreement and avoiding disputes and receiving reports from jurisdictions on progress on commitments under the Social Union Framework Agreement.

7. REVIEW OF THE SOCIAL UNION FRAMEWORK AGREEMENT

By the end of the third year of the Framework Agreement, governments will jointly undertake a full review of the Agreement and its implementation and make appropriate adjustments to the Framework as required. This review will ensure significant opportunities for input and feed-back from Canadians and all interested parties, including social policy experts, private sector and voluntary organizations.

Source: Canadian Intergovernmental Conference Secretariat: Agreement Ref: 800-37/01 [online]. Available: http://www.scics.gc.ca/cinfo99/80003701_e.html [May 25 2004]. Reproduced with the permission of the Minister of Public Works and Government Services Canada, 2004, and courtesy of the Privy Council Office.

GLOSSARY

(Numbers in parentheses refer to the chapter(s) containing the main discussion of the term.)

A

Aboriginal peoples The descendants of the original inhabitants of North America. The Canadian Constitution recognizes three groups of Aboriginal people: Indians, Métis, and Inuit. (12)

accessibility The ease with which people can reach and use facilities, programs, services, or other resources. (8)

acclimatization stage The period of time during which recent immigrants are engaged in a variety of basic settlement tasks. Many of these tasks are completed with the assistance of government-sponsored programs and services. See also *adaptation stage* and *integration stage*. (13)

accommodation The act of modifying the environment so that a person with a disability is able to participate in activities that take place in that environment. (14)

accountability The demonstration or "proof" of how one uses resources and achieves results; the obligation to account to others; and/or the obligation to answer to, report or explain, or give reasons for one's actions. (6)

accreditation A process that an organization undertakes to demonstrate that it is achieving its goals and operating efficiently. To become accredited, an agency must allow a qualified, external accreditation body to set its performance standards, and then allow that same body to determine whether it is meeting those standards. (5)

active aging Participating in activities that maximize social, physical, and mental well-being throughout one's life. Active aging is seen as a way to ensure a good quality of life in later years and to extend healthy life expectancy. (11)

active programs Income security measures that help beneficiaries enter (or re-enter) the workforce or that give incentives to beneficiaries to choose work over benefits. Today's governments tend to see active programs as a way to foster self-sufficiency. Recent changes have made Employment Insurance, social assistance, and child benefit programs more active. See also *passive programs*. (9)

adaptation stage The period of time during which immigrants adjust psychologically, socioculturally, and economically to the ways of life in their new country. See also *acclimatization stage* and *integration stage*. (13)

adoption A legal process whereby an individual or couple takes a child into care and, in so doing, assumes the rights and duties of that child's birth parents. (10)

advocacy Speaking or acting on behalf of another person or group. This may include disseminating information in order to influence the opinions of others, and calling for changes in laws, regulations, and government policies. (5)

affordable housing Adequate and suitable shelter that can be purchased for 30 percent or less of one's before-tax household income. To be adequate, housing must be in good repair; to be suitable, it must be uncrowded. (9)

ageism Prejudice and discrimination against a person on the basis of age; usually used in reference to elderly people. (11)

aging in place Growing old while living in one's own home rather than in an institution. (11)

aging population A population is said to be aging when 10 percent or more of people are over sixty. Canada has an aging population, since over 13 percent of Canadians are elderly; this number is expected to reach 25 percent by 2041. (2, 11)

availability The number of resources in a community relative to the demand for those resources. Also, the extent to which resources in a community are coordinated and able to meet people's needs in a timely fashion. (8)

B

band (Indian) A group of First Nations people for whom lands have been set apart or whose money is held by the Crown. Many bands prefer to be known as First Nations. (12)

basic income program A proposed government scheme that would replace all existing income security programs (such as Employment Insurance, welfare, child benefits, and Old Age Security) with a single assistance program. Formerly referred to as a *guaranteed annual income*. (4)

best practices Activities or strategies that an organization identifies as successful or effective in some way. These practices are often based on the findings of program evaluations. (6)

bills Written proposals made to either the House of Commons or the Senate. These proposals may be in the form of public bills or private bills, but all recommend legislated change in a social, economic, political, or other system. (2)

block fund A lump sum of money given by the federal government to the provinces and territories. The sum given to each province or territory is calculated on a per capita basis and disregards the total costs of programs in each of those provinces or territories. (4)

board of directors A group of people elected to govern an organization's activities and to ensure that the agency follows its constitution and operates according to local bylaws and relevant government regulations. Also called a board of trustees. (5)

budgetary surpluses The amount by which government revenues exceed expenditures. (4)

bureaucratic model An organizational structure characterized by several divisions or departments, which are arranged in a hierarchical fashion; commonly associated with "big government." See also *collectivist-democratic model* and *learning organization model*. (6)

C

caregiver burden The negative physical and psychological consequences of caring for another person for an extended period of time. Caregiver burden tends to have objective consequences (such as physical health complaints) and subjective consequences (such as psychological distress). (11)

cash transfers Government funds that are targeted to individuals or families whose income or assets fall below a certain level. Examples include the Guaranteed Income Supplement, social assistance, and guaranteed income programs for people with severe disabilities. (1)

census family According to Statistics Canada, a "married couple (with or without children of either or both spouses), a couple living common-law (with or without children of either or both partners) or a lone parent of any marital status, with at least one child living in the same dwelling. A couple living common-law may be of opposite or same sex." (10)

child abuse An act against a child that harms or threatens that child's well-being. Child abuse includes physical or sexual assault, neglect or abandonment, emotional or psychological mistreatment, and witnessing family violence. Also called child maltreatment. (10)

children in care People under a specific age (varies according to provincial/territorial legislation) who come under the protection of a child welfare system. Children placed in care may continue living in their home under the supervision of a child protection worker or—in cases of extreme abuse or neglect—be placed in alternative care such as a foster home or a group facility. (10)

citizen participation The active involvement of community members in the planning, development, and/or administration of policies and programs that affect them. Citizen participation often takes a "grassroots" or "bottom-up" approach to change, whereby people initiate actions that they believe will improve conditions in their community, instead of waiting for plans and interventions to trickle down from professionals or government. (2)

clawbacks A government policy that requires high income–earning individuals to repay part or all of the cash benefits they receive from an income security program. Programs that utilize clawbacks include Employment Insurance and Old Age Security. (4)

code of ethics A written statement of ethical conduct that serves as a guide to professional groups in their practice. (7)

collaborations A type of working relationship that emphasizes a consensus model of decision-making and formal roles and responsibilities. Collaborations require all parties to contribute resources and to share equally the benefits and risks of any endeavour. An example of a collaborative agreement is *An Accord between the Government of Canada and the Voluntary Sector.* (5)

collectivist-democratic model An organizational structure dating back to the late 1970s that emphasizes power-sharing, group consensus, and a team approach to decision-making. See also *bureaucratic model* and *learning organization model.* (6)

colonization The encroachment upon, and subjugation of, one group by a more powerful group, usually for the purpose of exploiting the less powerful group's resources. The term *colonization* is often used in reference to the treatment by the Canadian government of Aboriginal peoples and their subsequent loss of resources, land, self-determination, family ties, and culture. (12)

commercial sector A subdivision of the private sector in which nongovernment businesses, corporations, and companies deliver programs and services for a profit. See also *voluntary sector.* (5)

community development A community-based process of helping citizens resolve local problems that directly affect them. The aim of community development is not to challenge or reform established social structures, but rather to work with existing structures to increase the problem-solving capacity of the community. (8)

community economic development A process whereby local people initiate and develop their own solutions to their community's economic (and social) challenges. The intended effect of such a process is to improve the quality of life of community members and build long-term community capacity. (8)

community living movement A collective, organized effort aimed at helping people with developmental disabilities make a smooth transition from institutional to community-based living. The movement supports the administration of antipsychotic drugs, and the provision of community-based services, as more appropriate approaches to disability than long-term institutionalization. (14)

community needs assessments A type of program evaluation used to determine the need for a particular program or service in a given community. The assessment usually involves gathering information from a variety of community sources to formulate a profile of local needs. (6)

community organization A process whereby a community identifies and prioritizes its needs, then obtains the resources and participates in activities to meet those needs. Such a process tends to generate cooperative and collaborative relationships in the community. (8)

community practice A social work field that focuses on motivating and helping community members to evaluate, plan, and coordinate their efforts to meet local health, social, and other needs. Sometimes referred to as developmental social work. (8)

community-based agencies Organizations that tend to be nonprofit, to be open to the general public, and to offer a range of programs and services in centrally located, noninstitutional facilities. (6)

compensation benefits Cash that is awarded to individuals who have suffered a loss as a result of an accident or another person's actions. Examples include workers' compensation and compensation awarded to victims of crime. (1)

conservatism A political ideology that promotes traditional values, moral (religious) standards, and conformity to the existing social order.

Conservatists encourage people to compete, work hard, and accumulate wealth and property, yet maintain close ties to family, religious groups, and other established social institutions. (1)

contracts Written, legally binding agreements between two or more organizations, in either the public or the private sector. Contracts issued by government usually specify how the contracted agency is allowed to use public money. (5)

cross-cultural practice models Frameworks used by social workers and other formal helpers to promote racial, cultural, social, and other differences as potentially enriching for both personal relationships and general society. (13)

cross-cultural training Education and skill-building that helps social workers and other formal helpers raise their level of cultural sensitivity. This type of training often involves a form of cultural immersion: participants are transported into ethnocultural communities, where they become sensitized to the cultural values of others and, at the same time, arrive at a better understanding of their own cultural values. (13)

D

debt The total sum of outstanding deficits. See also *deficits*. (4)

decentralization A process that involves one level of government transferring some or all of its functions, authority, and/or assets to a lower level of government, or to the private sector. Also called devolution. (4)

deficits The amount of money spent in excess of revenues. See also *debt*. (4)

deinstitutionalization movement A collective, organized effort that began in the 1960s and resulted in the closing of large institutions, the return of institutionalized people (such as people with mental disabilities) to their families and communities, and the expansion of community-based (noninstitutional) agencies and services. (6)

dementia A cluster of symptoms characterized by a chronic loss of cognitive and emotional abilities; these symptoms interfere with the activities of daily life. An example is Alzheimer's disease. (11)

"deserving" poor A social label that was once applied to people who were sick, aged, disabled, or otherwise incapable of supporting themselves yet were worthy of public aid. The term fell out of popular use by the mid-twentieth century. See also *"undeserving" poor*. (1)

direct relief Government aid given to the poor in the form of cash, vouchers for basic necessities, or essential resources such as food, fuel, and clothing. See also *indirect relief* and *public relief*. (3)

direct services Personal social services that involve face-to-face interactions with clients; these front-line services aim to prevent or reduce social or psychological problems among individuals, families, and/or small groups. See also *indirect services*. (6)

disability A health problem—or physical or mental condition—that restricts a person's ability to perform tasks that are normal for his or her age. (14)

disability community A collective of people with disabilities and the organizations that serve them. (14)

disability income system A range of income programs for people with disabilities. The system comprises earnings replacement programs (to replace income that has been lost due to an injury, illness, disability-related condition, or accident); income support programs (to provide income to people with disabilities who have little or no income); compensation for loss (to compensate people who have suffered pain and loss as a result of a disabling injury or accident); and compensation for disability-related costs (to offset the costs of having a disability). (14)

disability rights movement A collective, organized effort aimed at eliminating socially imposed restrictions on people with disabilities, ensuring their full citizenship, and creating equal access to mainstream resources and opportunities. (14)

E

ecological perspective A theory of disability that places a strong emphasis on the connections between impairment and a person's activity limitations; a person's dignity and human rights; and his or her participation in specific environments such as home, school, or work. Also called the social perspective. See also *impairment perspective* and *functional limitations perspective*. (14)

economic security A consistent standard of living that gives people the level of resources they need in order to participate fully, and with dignity, in social, economic, political, and cultural life. (9)

elder abuse The maltreatment of an older person within a relationship in which there is an expectation of trust (examples: the relationship between spouses, or between parent and child, or between caregiver and care recipient). Types of maltreatment include physical, sexual, or emotional abuse, financial exploitation, and neglect. (11)

empowerment The ability to help oneself and, ultimately, to manage one's own life effectively. A family that is empowered is able to (1) identify its needs and know where to go to get those needs met; (2) advocate on its own behalf so that it can access needed resources; and (3) have input into the programs and policies that directly affect it. Empowerment is often the goal of counselling services. (10)

enfranchisement A policy once followed by Canadian governments to persuade Aboriginal peoples to reject their heritage and fully assimilate into non-Aboriginal culture. Enfranchisement policies are no longer legal in Canada. (12)

English Poor Laws A series of British parliamentary acts that were initiated by Elizabeth I during the sixteenth and seventeenth centuries; their aim was to reduce poverty and begging in England. Many principles of these laws were adopted in early Canadian settlements—for example, in Nova Scotia and New Brunswick. (3)

ethnic group A segment of the population that shares similar racial, political, religious, ancestral, or cultural backgrounds. There are more than 200 ethnic groups in Canada. (13)

ethnic origin The ethnic or cultural group(s) to which a person's ancestors belonged. (13)

F

family casework A social work approach that emerged in the 1920s and 1930s to help families. The approach focuses on assisting the entire family (or several members of the family); bases interventions on sound knowledge of family relationships; and aims to reinforce the family unit by drawing on the family's strengths and the community's resources. (8)

family policy A guideline or plan developed and used by government to direct initiatives for families with children; a type of social policy. Examples include the National Children's Agenda, the Family Violence Initiative. (10)

family violence The abuse of power within a family, or in relationships of trust or dependency. Family violence encompasses a wide range of behaviours, including physical assault, emotional abuse, neglect, sexual assault, financial exploitation, and stalking. (10)

federalism A political system that divides legislative power between central (that is, federal) and regional (that is, provincial and territorial) governments. (2)

First Nations peoples Status and Non-Status Indian peoples in Canada. A term used by some First Nations in lieu of "Indian." See also *Indian*. (12)

fiscal crisis The negative economic impact of an accumulation of annual deficits, combined with a growing public debt. (4)

focus groups A group of people who have been invited to meet and give their views on—or generate ideas related to—a specific topic. Groups are often facilitated by a program planner. They tend to be useful for understanding attitudes, opinions, and behaviours of a selected population. (6)

food insecure When a person worries about not having enough money to buy food, is not eating the desired quality or variety of food, or does not have enough to eat (is hungry). (9)

formal help A type of service that is given either in the form of professional help (that is, help given by paid individuals who bring a recognized knowledge base, formal training, and relevant experience to their practice) or self-help (that is, mutual aid that is provided in formally organized but nonprofessional groups). See *professional help* and *self-help*. See also *informal help*. (7)

formal system An organization or group that operates according to set rules, roles, and procedures. (6)

formal volunteer work Tasks or activities performed by an unpaid worker in or on behalf of an organization; typically, these complement the professional services provided by the agency. See also *informal volunteer work*. (7)

functional limitations perspective A theory that defines disability largely in terms of how it limits a person's activities, as well as how people with disabilities and others perceive and react to those limitations. For other perspectives, see *impairment perspective* and *ecological perspective*. (14)

G

generalist A practitioner who is trained to apply a wide range of practice skills in a variety of contexts, and with any size of client system, including individuals, families, and small groups. (7)

gerontological social work A field of social work practice that focuses on the aging process and issues related to elderly people. Such issues include the health consequences of aging, social support, living arrangements, family care-giving, and financial well-being. (11)

globalization A process characterized by an "integration of international markets as a result of advances in communications and transportation, the liberalisation of trade, and the emergence of new competitors in the developing world" (Department of Finance, 2003h, 8). (2)

grants Money that a funding body (for example, a government department) gives to an individual or organization. Unlike contracts, grants are usually given with few restrictions as to how the money should be spent. (5)

grassroots approach Activities that are started by "average" people rather than by formal (such as government) systems; considered to be a "bottom-up" rather than "top-down" change strategy. (8)

guaranteed annual income A concept that suggests that all citizens have the right to a minimum income as the result of either paid work, or government subsidies, or a combination of the two. See also *basic income program*. (3)

H

harmonization The establishment of similar programs, services, and/or regulations in all countries within a single trading zone. (2)

healing According to Aboriginal theory, a process of restoring balance or harmony to one's overall health and well-being. (12)

holistic perspective Looking at the whole of something rather than just its individual parts; a holistic perspective of a person takes in all aspects of that person, including physical, emotional, social, and spiritual components, as well as connections to family, the community, the environment, and other entities. (12)

home and community care Programs that provide care in a person's home (rather than in a hospital or nursing home), that help people remain independent in their community for as long as possible, and that aim to prevent chronic health problems. (11)

(the) homeless A population that can be understood in terms of three subgroups: the "visible homeless" live on the street, in shelters, or in temporary housing situations; the "hidden homeless" are housed but may be living in substandard conditions or abandoned buildings, or drifting from one friend's house to another; people "at risk of homelessness" live in unstable conditions and may be forced to suddenly leave their home. (9)

homelessness A state of living in emergency shelters, on the street, or in temporary housing arrangements. (9)

horizontal equity Equal treatment by both the federal and regional levels of government regardless of where in Canada a person lives. See also *vertical equity.* (4)

human capacity A person's ability to perform tasks that are basic to survival and prosperity; human capacity is built through participation in learning and skill-building opportunities. (8)

human need A necessary condition or requirement for human health or welfare that, if not met, will result in serious physical, mental, or social harm. (1)

I

ideology A paradigm or belief system that shapes our perceptions of the world and that guides the ways we interact with that world. (1)

immigrant In Canada, someone who was born in another country and has been granted by Canadian immigration officials the legal right to live in this country. See also *refugees.* (13)

immigration service agencies Voluntary organizations whose specific purpose is to address the settlement needs of recent immigrants and refugees in Canada; usually found in communities with concentrated immigrant populations. (13)

impairment perspective The theory that disability is a biologically based illness or disease that originates in a person's body or mind, and that can be cured by specific interventions. For other perspectives, see *functional limitations perspective* and *ecological perspective.* (14)

income inequality The unequal distribution of wealth in a country, which creates an income gap between rich and poor citizens. (9)

income redistribution A government strategy that uses the tax system to shift income away from high- and moderate-income earners toward those with low incomes. (3)

income tests A type of financial test used by governments to determine eligibility for an income security program. Eligibility is based on an applicant's income rather than on personal needs or means of earning income. See also *needs tests* and *means tests.* (1)

income security programs Government-sponsored initiatives that provide pensions, tax reductions, or other financial aid to individuals and families. Recipients of income security benefits are generally limited in their ability to meet their needs due to old age, sickness, disability, or some other condition deemed beyond personal control. (1)

Indian The Indigenous peoples of Canada who are not Inuit or Métis. There are three categories of Indians in Canada: (1) a Status Indian is entitled to have his or her name included on the Indian Register (an official list maintained by the federal government), who is recognized as an Indian under the Indian Act, and who is entitled to certain rights and benefits under the law; (2) a Non-Status Indian is neither recognized as an Indian under the Indian Act nor registered, and is therefore not entitled to the same rights and benefits as are Status Indians; and (3) a Treaty Indian belongs to a First Nation that has signed a treaty with the Crown. See also *First Nations peoples*. (12)

indirect relief Government aid that was provided through publicly funded work projects during the Great Depression; the purpose of this aid was to get unemployed people back to work. See also *direct relief* and *public relief*. (3)

indirect services Activities in social agencies that do not usually involve personal contacts with clients but that can influence the type and quality of direct services. Examples include social administration, program development, and program evaluation. See also *direct services*. (6)

informal help A type of service that is provided by volunteers or "natural" (nonprofessional) helpers. This type of help includes unpaid care and support given through social agencies, as well as unstructured help given by family, friends, or co-workers. See also *formal help*. (7)

informal volunteer work Help given without monetary compensation to or by relatives, friends, and neighbours. See also *formal volunteer work*. (7)

institutional approach The view that the social welfare system is a normal and necessary institution in modern society that provides universal support to all citizens as a matter of right. See also *residual approach*. (1)

integration stage A period of time during which immigrants are encouraged to adapt to Canadian ways without giving up their cultures. See also *adaptation stage*. (13)

interdisciplinary field A profession, vocation, or specialized area of work whose knowledge base is influenced by two or more academic, artistic, or scientific disciplines. (1)

interest groups Organized (nongovernment) collectives that try to influence government policies for the benefit of their own members or on behalf of the general public. (2)

intergenerational programs Formal socialization opportunities that match people from different generations, usually for the purpose of enhancing social interaction and encouraging mutual learning. Example: Adopt-a-Grandparent program. (11)

intervention A strategy, technique, or method applied to help individuals, families, communities, or other social systems change. (8)

Inuit The Aboriginal peoples who inhabit the northern regions of Canada—primarily Nunavut, the Northwest Territories, and northern Labrador and Quebec. Inuit are not covered by the Indian Act. (12)

L

laissez-faire A French term that means "to leave alone"; usually used in reference to conservative governments of the sort that support minimal interference in the lives of citizens. (1)

learning organization model An organizational structure that emphasizes an ongoing expansion of knowledge in the workplace, collective learning among staff, and the nurturing of new ideas and creativity. See also *bureaucratic model* and *collectivist-democratic model*. (6)

liberalism A political ideology that emphasizes liberty, individualism, and competitive private enterprise and, at the same time, promotes equality and respect for human rights. See also *neoliberalism*. (1)

lone-parent families Families that are headed by one parent of any marital status, with at least one child living in the same dwelling. Women head the majority of lone-parent families. (10)

M

macro-level change An impact on social conditions or problems at the community level. Collective action is usually required for this level of change, since the conditions identified for change tend to be complex and entrenched in existing social, political, or cultural systems. See also *micro-level change* and *mezzo-level change*. (8)

mainstream approach A way of seeing and intervening in personal and social problems that reflects predominantly Euro-Canadian values, customs, and culture. For the most part, Canada's social welfare programs are based on the mainstream approach, which tends to isolate human problems (such as mental disorders) and to treat them as discrete entities that can be resolved through specific interventions (such as psychotherapy). See also *traditional approach*. (12)

mandatory retirement A policy or law that requires people to stop working when they reach sixty-five. Many people are against mandatory retirement policies on the basis that they discriminate against the elderly. (11)

means tests A type of financial test used by governments to determine eligibility for an income security program. Eligibility is based on the applicant's income and the value of his or her assets. See also *income tests* and *needs tests*. (1)

mental health The ability of people to interact with others and their environment in ways that maximize their use of mental capabilities, promote well-being, enhance personal self-control and life choices, lead to the achievement of personal goals, and improve quality of life. (11)

Métis People of mixed First Nations and European ancestry who identify themselves as distinct from Inuit and First Nations peoples. (12)

mezzo-level change An impact made at the organizational level of a society; that is, on formal systems that directly affect consumers, including social agencies and their programs, policies and procedures. This type of change is often triggered by influences external to the organization, such as a shifting economy or new funding patterns. Also called *organizational change*. See also *micro-level change* and *macro-level change*. (8)

micro-level change An impact made on a relatively small social system—such as an individual, family, or small group—that enables that system to access the resources and skills it requires to become self-sufficient. The change process at the micro-level is often referred to as direct service or clinical practice. See also *mezzo-level change* and *macro-level change*. (8)

mixed economy of welfare A myriad of service delivery systems, which are organized, funded, and managed in a variety of ways. These service delivery systems may be found in both the public and the private sector. (5)

multiculturalism Recognition of and respect for ethnic or cultural diversity; the promotion of equality, mutual respect, and acceptance among various ethnic groups. (13)

multidisciplinary teams A group of professionals or service providers from different agencies, service sectors, academic disciplines, and/or backgrounds; these people work together on behalf of a mutual client. Such teams are often employed to coordinate services for clients who have a variety of needs or concerns, or who require assistance from more than one type of helper or agency. In some cases, nonprofessionals (such as a client's friend or relative) are invited to participate on these teams. (7)

N

natural helping skills Abilities acquired through informal personal interactions rather than formal training, and that are recognized as benefiting people in need. Example: the ability to empathically listen to someone who is grieving the loss of a loved one. (7)

needs tests A financial test used by governments to determine eligibility for an income security program; eligibility is based on an applicant's personal needs and the level of income required to meet those needs. See also *income tests* and *means tests*. (1)

neoliberalism A modern version of liberalism, one that emphasizes small governments and fiscal responsibility. Underlying neoliberalism is the belief that a strong economy will provide many of the necessary resources to meet social welfare needs. See also *liberalism*. (1)

nonresidential centres Organizations that normally provide services on a drop-in, appointment, or outreach basis. These organizations cater to people who can look after many of their own needs, who require short-term help, who do not pose a threat to themselves or to the rest of society, and who otherwise do not need to be institutionalized in order to receive services. See also *residential centres*. (6)

O

open house concept A mental construct that emphasizes the full participation of people with disabilities in school, work, recreation, or other activity, and their enjoyment of the same rights and privileges as people who do not have disabilities. (14)

organizational change A fundamental shift in the way an organization operates, usually involving a significant restructuring of one or more aspects of an agency; a form of *mezzo-level change*. (8)

outcome measurement A type of program evaluation that assesses what a program actually achieves rather than what it intended to achieve, and that identifies any changes in behaviour, skills, attitudes, or knowledge of program participants. (6)

P

paraprofessional A trained worker who works in a profession but who is not a member of that profession. For example, individuals who perform social work duties, but who do not have a minimum of a bachelor of social work degree (or equivalent), may be considered paraprofessionals in the social work field. (7)

passive programs Income security measures that unconditionally give financial benefits to nonworking adults and that essentially leave it up to them to find their way into—or back into—the workforce. Today's governments tend to view passive programs as encouraging dependency on income security programs. See also *active programs*. (9)

personal social services Nonincome and intangible benefits that aim to enhance social functioning and general well-being for individuals, families, and small groups. Sometimes called "transfers-in-kind" since they are given to individuals and families in lieu of cash payments. Commonly referred to as social services or community social services. (1)

person-in-environment A social work perspective that acknowledges the complexity of interactions between people and their environment, and that recognizes that people both shape and are shaped by their environment. (7)

planned change process A step-by-step approach used by social workers to help people change. The process has five phases: (1) the intake phase; (2) the assessment phase; (3) the planning and contracting phase; (4) the intervention phase; and (5) the evaluation and termination phase. (8)

poorhouses Institutions built with public funds to house the poor and homeless; in colonial days, these facilities were used to "manage" the poor (that is, prevent them from roaming around the streets). Poorhouses were phased out in Canada in the early twentieth century. Also called almshouses. (3)

population health model A theoretical framework based on the belief that health is determined not only by biological conditions but also by a variety of nonmedical factors, including income, the quality of housing, the extent and nature of social support, education, and mobility or transportation. The population health model takes a more holistic approach to health than the medical model, which tends to focus on the treatment of disease in isolation from other life conditions. (11)

poverty (1) A subsistent standard of living caused by an income that is too low to allow for the purchase of adequate food, clothing, shelter, and/or other basic necessities; (2) a condition that excludes people from fully participating in social or community life. (9)

primary prevention Activities—usually targeted at large segments of the community—that aim to prevent the development of social problems by educating people, providing them with information, or promoting certain practices. Primary prevention activities include alcohol and drug education, AIDS-awareness strategies, and antiracism campaigns. See also *secondary prevention* and *tertiary prevention*. (6)

private sector A segment of society in which organizations are privately owned and operated (as opposed to being owned and operated by government). The private sector includes commercial (or profit-making) operations and voluntary (or nonprofit) operations. See also *public sector.* (5)

privatization The transfer of most or all assets or services from a government to the private sector (the private sector includes both for-profit and nonprofit organizations). (2)

professional help A formal service provided by paid individuals, who bring a recognized knowledge base, formal training, and relevant experience to their practice. Often, this type of help is guided by a code of ethics that is specific to the worker's profession. Professional helpers include social workers, psychiatrists, and psychologists. (7)

professions Vocations that have a code of ethics, the means to regulate and enforce set standards of behaviour among their members, and a theoretical body of knowledge that guides practice. The professions include social work, nursing, policing, law, and psychology. (7)

program evaluation A process of examining programs and services to determine whether they are needed and used, how effective they are, how well they are run, and/or whether their benefits justify their costs. (6)

program-planning A process carried out in social agencies to ensure that programs and services are designed to meet the needs of clients and that they reflect the community's broader goals. Planning involves a series of steps, which include setting goals and objectives, designing programs, and evaluating the plan's viability. (6)

programs and services Activities or projects that have a specific purpose, goal, and/or objectives. Services involve specific acts of giving assistance to others; programs may or may not have a service component. Example of a service: alcohol and drug counselling. Example of a program (without a service component): Social Development Partnerships Program. (1)

public housing Residential dwellings that are subsidized by public funds and designated for low-income individuals and families. In Canada, many public housing projects are financially supported by government yet managed by private organizations, such as nonprofit groups and housing authorities. (9)

public relief Government aid that is provided to people who are unable to support themselves through work or other means. A forerunner to *social assistance* or "welfare." See also *direct relief* and *indirect relief.* (3)

public sector A segment of society in which programs and services are funded fully by tax revenues and administered and delivered by governments. See also *private sector.* (5)

R

racism Prejudice or discrimination against one or more people that is based on the belief that race determines certain traits, behaviours, or abilities. Three types of racism have been identified: "individual racism" is evident in people's attitudes, beliefs, and behaviours; "systemic racism" is reflected in the policies and practices of organizations; and "cultural racism" reflects the dominant society's values and perceptions related to racial inferiority and superiority. (13)

refugees People who have been forced to flee persecution in their homeland and to take refuge in a foreign country. Refugees are often considered members of a country's immigrant population. (13)

reserves Tracts of land that have been set aside for the use of an Indian band. Many First Nations have replaced the term *reserve* with "First Nation community." (12)

residency requirement A federal-provincial-territorial policy that prohibits a provincial or territorial government from denying social assistance to anyone on the basis of how long the applicant has lived in a specific province or territory. The requirement was established under the Canada Assistance Act of 1966 and is currently a stipulation under the Canada Social Transfer. (4)

residential centres Organizations that provide living quarters, meals, and a range of services to people who require round-the-clock care. Formerly called "institutions." The types of residential facilities that exist in any given community are usually determined by the needs of that community's residents. See also *nonresidential centres*. (6)

residential school syndrome A cluster of symptoms that are experienced by Aboriginal people who have survived the Indian residential school system. Symptoms may include distressing memories or dreams of life at the school, and the avoidance of people, places, and events that bring back memories of living in the school. The syndrome does not apply to mainstream residential schools. (12)

residential school system A system of boarding schools that offer children both an education and a place to live. In Canada, the term is usually used in reference to an educational strategy initiated by the federal government in 1883. The system attempted to assimilate Aboriginal peoples into mainstream society by separating Aboriginal children from their parents and placing them in distant schools, where they were taught Euro-Canadian values and customs. The last residential school in Canada closed in 1996. (12)

residual approach The view that social welfare programs should be used sparingly and only as a last resort, when help from one's family, church, banks, and other private sources has been exhausted. See also *institutional approach*. (1)

respite services Formal programs that give caregivers a break from their caregiving duties. Example: daycare programs for elderly care recipients. (11)

retirement income system A range of income programs available to people in their senior or retirement years. In Canada, the system comprises three major programs: Old Age Security, Canada/Quebec Pension Plan, and private pension plans and savings. (11)

S

same-sex unions Couples comprising two male, or two female, adults who are married or living common law. (10)

scope of practice A guideline that delineates in which functions and activities the members of a profession may appropriately engage. (7)

secondary migration A move made by immigrants or refugees (usually during the early stages of settlement) from their original destination in Canada to a different community. (13)

secondary prevention Activities that focus on identifying a social problem in the early stages of development before it becomes serious or chronic, and then controlling or changing the conditions that caused the problem. Examples: victim assistance programs, respite services for family caregivers. See also *primary prevention* and *tertiary prevention*. (6)

self-governments Systems of laws, customs, and institutions established and administered by First Nations in cooperation with the federal government and (when applicable) with provincial governments. (12)

self-help A type of mutual aid provided in formally organized yet nonprofessional groups. These groups are run by members rather than professionals. Self-help groups have an organized structure for conducting meetings and are often affiliated with national organizations (for example, Alcoholics Anonymous). (7)

settlement practice Interventions, values, knowledge, and professional ethics adopted by settlement workers and applied to their work with recent immigrants and refugees. (13)

settlement programs A range of measures to help recent immigrants and refugees quickly become self-sufficient, contributing members of Canadian life. (13)

social action Collective and coordinated efforts that aim to eliminate a social problem, correct an injustice, or meet a human need. This approach usually involves influencing those with power (such as politicians) to change certain policies, laws, or procedures, and/or reforming social institutions that are deemed inadequate. (8)

social administration A social agency activity that involves developing or interpreting policies and procedures, planning and managing direct service activities, and ensuring that an agency meets its goals and objectives. (6)

social agency A formally structured organization whose main objective is to meet one or more human needs. (6)

social amelioration Actions taken to improve society through the relief of suffering or hardship. (2)

social assistance An income security program that gives cash to individuals and families who, for various reasons, are unable to adequately meet their needs and who have exhausted all other means of support. Commonly known as "welfare"; formerly referred to as *public relief*. (1)

social capital The product of cooperative relationships, social connections, shared trust, and the associated norms that enable community members to work together to achieve mutual goals. An important element of *social cohesion*. (8)

social casework A social work approach, which emerged during the late 1800s, that promotes a scientific, step-by-step approach to helping. (8)

social cohesion A condition in society whereby people feel both connected to the community in which they live and recognized as community members. Also called "social order." Related to *social capital*. (1)

social deficit A social phenomenon characterized by social and economic hardship, unmet human potential, and limited opportunities to fully participate in society. Canada's social deficit is largely attributed to globalization and heavy government cutbacks in social welfare programs. (4)

social democracy A political ideology that rejects individualism, private enterprise, and the competitive values of capitalism, and that encourages fellowship and cooperation. Social democrats generally see government as playing a prominent role in the social and economic lives of citizens. (1)

social group work A social work approach directed toward a small group of people who have similar needs or lifestyles, who are dealing with a common issue, and/or who are working toward a common goal. These groups usually have between three and ten members. (8)

social indicators Statistics that are collected and used to measure social conditions or levels of public well-being. (6)

social insurance Government-sponsored forced savings plans that require working individuals to contribute to a program, which then compensates them when they are not working. Benefits from these programs are based on the claimant's contributions. Examples include Employment Insurance and the Canada/Quebec Pension Plan. (1)

social investment The infusion of money and other resources into a particular social area for future gains. Example: increasing funds for early childhood programs to improve children's health and well-being, thereby enabling children to become productive, responsible, and contributing members of society as adults. (2)

social justice Equal access to resources, benefits, and opportunities; a society's recognition that all citizens matter and have a right to fair treatment; a social goal pursued by many democratic governments. (1)

social minimum A reasonable standard of living or quality of life that can be subjectively measured by social norms, or objectively measured by the average real gross domestic product (GDP) per person. (1)

social movement An organized, large-scale effort to achieve identified social goals; usually involves a large segment of the population that shares a similar ideology, vision, and objectives. Examples: labour reform movement, child welfare movement, women's liberation movement, disability rights movement, gay rights movement. (3)

social planning A community-based process committed to social development in a variety of areas, including health, safety, economic security, education, and urban renewal. (8)

social policy A plan or blueprint that guides a government's strategies for helping citizens meet a wide range of material and social needs. (1)

social problems Conditions in society that create some measurable degree of economic or social hardship, psychological or physical injury, or other negative consequence that people are concerned about and want changed. Social problems tend to affect a large segment of the population, and spark some kind of collective response aimed at correcting the situation. Examples: poverty, racism, family violence, unemployment, crime. (1)

social programs Systems consisting of services, benefits, or activities that are designed to improve human welfare or meet a social need. Canada has three social programs: social welfare, health care, and postsecondary education. (1)

social safety net A collection of government-sponsored health, social welfare, and emergency services designed to protect people from the negative consequences of natural disasters, personal crises, or medical problems. (1)

social security A range of income security programs and personal social services that help people meet their basic human needs from "cradle to grave." (1)

social service workers People who have been trained—usually at the college level—in basic aspects of social work. Also called human service workers. Social service workers are often viewed as *paraprofessionals* in the social work field if they do not possess a professional degree—that is, a minimum of a bachelor of social work degree. (7)

social union An initiative involving the federal, provincial (except Quebec), and territorial governments that has the primary objective of reforming

Canadian social policies and programs. The Federal-Provincial-Territorial Council on Social Policy Renewal was formed in 1996 to guide the social union initiative. (5)

social welfare A concept, field, and/or system that is concerned with individual and collective well-being; that helps people meet their basic social and economic needs; and that prevents, reduces, or alleviates social problems. (1)

social welfare programs Activities or projects supported by the social welfare system that have a specific purpose, goal, and/or objectives; programs may or may not have a service component. See also *programs and services*. (1)

social work A profession committed to helping people enhance their well-being, develop skills, and utilize resources for the purpose of resolving problems and/or meeting human needs. (1)

social workers People who are recognized as "social workers" according to the criteria established by a provincial/territorial social work association or college. Social workers are predominantly employed in the social welfare system and may work in the areas of direct services, program design, administration, program evaluation, policy-making, or social planning. (7)

specialist A practitioner who has been trained in a specific area of expertise and who directs his or her attention to a relatively narrow scope of human need or problem. Examples: family therapists, child protection workers, and psychiatric social workers. (7)

spousal violence Behaviours that are committed by one partner against the other, and that range from verbal threats to physical and sexual assaults. Also called partner violence. In Canada, most reported spousal violence incidents are committed by men against women. (10)

stigma A negative attitude toward, or stereotype of, an individual or group whose attributes or behaviours fall short of acceptable social norms. In social welfare, the fear of being negatively labelled or stigmatized can discourage a person from actively seeking the help he or she needs. Social assistance or "welfare" is possibly the most stigmatizing social welfare program. (8)

structural social work One of the many anti-oppressive social work models that focuses on changing systems (for example, social agencies or political structures) to improve social conditions. From the structural perspective, social problems are the result of social, economic, and/or political structures (for example, capitalism) rather than the failings of individuals. (8)

supportive housing A type of dwelling that offers both independent living space and a range of services, which may include a cafeteria, recreation area, on-site personal care, and support services. (11)

system of care A mix of services and resources that, when offered in a coordinated and integrated fashion, is responsive to the varying levels and changing needs of clients. (6)

T

targeted programs Government benefits that are restricted to certain populations that can meet some predetermined criteria of being in need. Also called selective programs. (1)

tax credits Government benefits that are delivered through the income tax system and calculated according to a taxpayer's income; reductions in the amount of income tax paid by low- or moderate-income earners. Examples: Canada Child Tax Benefit, and the Goods and Services Tax/Harmonized Sales Tax Credit. (1)

tertiary prevention Activities that aim to reduce the negative effects of personal or social problems—such as disability and dependence—that have become chronic or complex. Examples: child protection services, family therapy, and residential care for youth with emotional disorders. Tertiary prevention programs are often mandatory and supported by law. See also *primary prevention* and *secondary prevention.* (6)

traditional approach A way of seeing and intervening in personal and social problems that is based on Aboriginal theory; a process of healing that is shaped by a holistic perspective of human needs/problems, and emphasizes the participation of individuals in their own healing process. See also *mainstream approach.* (12)

traditional families Families comprising a mother, father, and one or more children. (10)

U

(the) underemployed People whose work does not pay enough to lift them out of poverty. The underemployed tend to be concentrated in part-time or nonstandard jobs, but many work full-time at minimum wage. (9)

"undeserving" poor A social label that once referred to able-bodied unemployed people who were capable of supporting themselves through paid labour and thus unworthy of public aid. The term fell out of popular use during the mid-twentieth century. See also *"deserving" poor.* (1)

universal programs Government benefits that are available to all Canadians as a matter of right regardless of economic status or need. Formerly called demogrants. (1)

V

vertical equity The reduction of income inequality between rich and poor people, and the assurance of equal opportunity for all Canadians. Vertical equity is largely achieved through governments' use of ***income redistribution***. See also *horizontal equity.* (4)

visible minorities "Persons, other than Aboriginal peoples, who are non-Caucasian in race or non-white in colour" (Canada's Employment Equity Act). Visible-minority groups include Chinese, Latin American, Black, and Filipino. (13)

voluntary sector A subdivision of the private sector within which non-government organizations deliver programs and services on a nonprofit basis. Also called the charitable, independent, or "third" sector. See also *commercial sector.* (5)

volunteers "Natural" helpers who donate their time and skills to assisting others without monetary compensation. (7)

vulnerable children Youngsters who tend to have learning or behaviour problems, and/or developmental delays that make it difficult for them to meet challenges, control their emotions, learn new skills, or get along with others. Vulnerability in children is often associated with inconsistent and nonpositive parenting. (10)

W

welfare state A country whose government is committed to correcting the problem of unequal distribution of wealth by redistributing income from high- to low-income groups and by ensuring that all citizens have equal access to health, social welfare, and other important resources. (1)

welfare wall A characteristic of welfare systems that inadvertently makes social assistance more financially attractive than employment. Governments try to break down the "wall" by providing incentives to work. For families with children, for example, subsidized childcare helps parents make the transition from welfare to work. (9)

welfare-to-work programs Provincial government initiatives that make it compulsory for able-bodied (that is, employable) welfare recipients to volunteer, work, or train in exchange for benefits. Also called "workfare" (slang). (4)

workhouses In colonial times, institutions built with public funds in which able-bodied unemployed people were compelled by law to work; people consigned to these facilities worked in exchange for basic provisions. (3)

working poor People whose earnings from employment are not enough to lift them out of poverty. (2)

Y

youth engagement The active involvement of youth in activities that they consider interesting and meaningful, and that provide an opportunity for learning and social connection. A method used to reduce risk-taking behaviours among youth. (10)

REFERENCES

(Numbers at the end of the reference refer to the chapter(s) containing the citation.)

Aboriginal Healing Foundation. (2002). *Annual Report 2002* [online]. Available: www.ahf.ca/english-pdf/annual_report_2002.pdf [May 16, 2004]. 12

Ad Hoc Federal-Provincial-Territorial Working Group. (2003 April). *Final Report of the Ad Hoc Federal-Provincial-Territorial Working Group Reviewing Spousal Abuse Policies and Legislation* [online]. Available: canada.justice.gc.ca/en/ps/fm/reports/spousal_e.pdf [May 20, 2004]. 10

Addario, L. (2001 June). *Implementing Canada's Commitments to Women: An Agenda for Action*. Canadian Feminist Alliance for International Action [online]. Available: www.fafia-afai.org/research/hrimple.html [February 2, 2004]. 2

Advocacy Centre for the Elderly. (2003). *Home* [online]. Available: www.advocacycentreelderly.org/index.htm [May 24, 2004]. 11

Agriculture and Agri-Food Canada. (1998 October 16). *Notes for an Address by Lyle Vanclief, P.C., M.P., Minister of Agriculture and Agri-Food, at the Launch of Canada's Action Plan for Food Security—Canada's Response to the World Food Summit, Toronto, October 16, 1998.* [online]. Available: www.agr.gc.ca/cb/min/index_e.php?s1=agmin&s2=dis-spe&s3=1998&page=s981016 [April 17, 2004]. 9

———. (2002 May). *Canada's Second Progress Report to the FAO Committee on World Food Security on the Implementation of Canada's Action Plan for Food Security in Response to the World Food Summit Plan of Action* [online]. Available: www.agr.gc.ca/misb/fsb/fsb-bsa_e.php?section=fsap&group=prog2&page=toc-tdm [June 15, 2004]. 9

———. (2003 June 10). *About Food Security* [online]. Available: www.agr.gc.ca/misb/fsb/fsb-bsa_e.php?page=index [June 15, 2004]. 9

Alberta Committee of Citizens with Disabilities. (n.d.). *Women with Disabilities: Fact Sheet*. Edmonton: Author. 14

Alberta Urban Municipalities Association. (2004). *Housing and Development Task Force Business Plan and Budget 2004-2006* [online]. Available: www.munilink.net/pdfs/housingbusinessplan2004-06.pdf [May 13, 2004]. 9

Alexander, M.L. (2001 June 11). *Democracy, Diversity, and Disability: Utilizing a Consultative Process to Advance the Disability Policy Agenda in Canada*. Background paper for the panel discussion: Society for Disability Studies 14th Annual Meeting: An International Conference Examining Emerging International Disability Studies Initiatives: Winnipeg, Manitoba: June 21–24, 2001 [online]. Available: www.ee.umanitoba.ca/~kinsner/sds2001/proceed/pdocs/docs/16.DOC [May 29, 2004]. 14

Ameyaw, S., and P. Simpson. (1994). *The CED Perspective*. Community Economic Development Centre. Burnaby: Simon Fraser University [online]. Available: www2.sfu.ca/cedc/resources/online/cedconline/sapsperspect.htm [March 7, 2004]. 8

Anderson, G., and W. Marr (1987). "Immigration and Social Policy." In S.A. Yelaja, ed., *Canadian Social Policy*, rev. ed., pp. 88–114. Waterloo: Wilfrid Laurier University Press. 13

Anderson, S., and J. Cavanagh. (2002 August 8). *Rethinking the NAFTA Record*. Institute for Policy Studies [online]. Available: www.ips-dc.org/projects/global_econ/rethinking%20nafta%20aug%202002.pdf [February 1, 2004]. 2

Annan, K. (1998 October 1). *A "Society for All Ages" Honours Traditional Leadership Role of Elders, Secretary General Says, Opening International Year of Older Persons*. United Nations Press Release [online]. Available: www.un.org/News/Press/docs/1998/19981001.sgsm6728.html [May 9, 2004]. 11

Arai, S. (2000 January). *Best Practices: A New Name for an Old Idea? Best Practices Discussion Paper 1*. Association of Ontario Health Centres [online]. Available: www.aohc.org/Articles/Discussion_Paper_11.doc [February 13, 2004]. 6

Arai, S. (1999 Fall). "Privatization and the Impact on Voluntary Associations: Tensions between Service Provision and Citizenship." *Journal of Leisurability* (26)4: [online]. Available: www.lin.ca/resource/html/Vol26/V26N4A2.htm [February 1, 2004]. 2

Armitage, A. (2003). *Social Welfare in Canada*, 4th ed. Don Mills: Oxford University Press. 3, 5

Arundel, C. (2003). *Falling Behind: Our Growing Income Gap*. Federation of Canadian Municipalities [online]. Available: www.fcm.ca/english/communications/igover.pdf [April 17, 2004]. 9

Asselin, R.B. (2001 January 18). *The Canadian Social Union: Questions About the Division of Powers and Fiscal Federalism*. Political and Social Affairs Division: Parliamentary Research Branch: Library of Parliament [online]. Available: www.parl.gc.ca/information/library/PRBpubs/prb0031-e.htm [February 4, 2004]. 4

Assembly of First Nations. (1999 April 22). *The Search for Wellness Results from the First Nations and Inuit Regional Health Surveys* [online]. Available: www.naho.ca/firstnations/english/pdf/rhs_wellness_1.pdf [May 9, 2004]. 12

Assembly of First Nations. (2000 September 28). *First Nations Suicide Rate*. Fact Sheet [online]. Available: www.afn.ca/Programs/Health/Factsheets/FS-Suicide-e.pdf [June 13, 2004]. 12

Au Coin, K. (2003a June). "Family Violence Against Older Adults." In H. Johnson and K. Au Coin, eds., *Family Violence in Canada: A Statistical Profile, 2003*, pp. 21–32. Statistics Canada/Canadian Centre for Justice Statistics: Catalogue no. 85-224-XIE [online]. Available: www.hc-sc.gc.ca/hppb/familyviolence/pdfs/2003famvioprofil_e.pdf [March 13, 2004]. 11

———. (2003b June). "Violence and Abuse Against Children and Youth by Family Members." In H. Johnson and K. Au Coin, eds., *Family Violence in Canada: A Statistical Profile, 2003*, pp. 33–45. Statistics Canada/Canadian Centre for Justice Statistics: Catalogue no. 85-224-XIE [online]. Available: www.hc-sc.gc.ca/hppb/familyviolence/pdfs/2003famvioprofil_e.pdf [April 29, 2004]. 10

Aycan, Z., and J.W. Berry. (1996). *Impact of Employment-Related Experiences on Immigrants' Psychological Well-Being and Adaptation to Canada* [online]. 11 Available: www.cpa.ca/cjbsnew/1996/ful_aycan.html [May 27, 2004]. 13

Ayed, N. (2000 March 2). "Reform MP Raises Ire of Justice Minister. *The Canadian Press* [online]. Available: www.slam.ca/CNEWSPolitics0003/03_reform_CP.html [April 28, 2004]. 10

B.C. Council for Families. (2001a). *About Nobody's Perfect* [online]. Available: www.bccf.bc.ca/programs/np_about.html [April 29, 2004]. 10

——. (2001b). *Couple Relationships: Links* [online]. Available: www.bccf.bc.ca/learn/coup_links.html [April 28, 2004]. 10

B.C. Public Interest Advocacy Centre. (2003 October 20). *Community Groups Prepare for Constitutional Challenge to Welfare Cut-Off* [online]. Available: www.bcpiac.com/pub/newsReleases/newsRel_Index.html [February 4, 2004]. 4

Babin, T. (2003 March 27). *Report Says Strong Economy Not Helping Most Albertans.* FFWD [online]. Available: www.ffwdweekly.com/Issues/2003/0327/news2.htm [February 4, 2004]. 4

Badets, J., and L. Howatson-Leo. (1999 Spring). "Recent Immigrants in the Workforce." *Canadian Social Trends*, 16–22. 13

Bailey, S. (2004a April 20). *Paul Martin Calls for New Beginning in Federal Relationship with Aboriginals.* Canadian Press [online]. Available: news.yahoo.com/news?tmpl=story&u=/cpress/20040419/ca_pr_on_na/aboriginal_overhaul_2 [May 16, 2004]. 12

——. (2004b February 19). *Workers Being "Fleeced" by Inflated Rates as EI Surplus Grows: Critics.* The Canadian Press. Childcare Resource and Research Unit: University of Toronto [online]. Available: www.childcarecanada.org/ccin/2004/ccin2_19_04A.html [April 17, 2004]. 9

Baines, C., P. Evans, and S. Neysmith. (1998). *Women's Caring: Feminist Perspectives on Social Welfare*, 2nd ed. Toronto: Oxford University Press. 11

Baker, M. (1997). "Women, Family Policies and the Moral Right." *Canadian Review of Social Policy* 40: 47–64. 10

Bakvis, H. (1997). "Getting the Giant to Kneel: A New Human Resources Delivery Network for Canada." In R. Ford and D. Zussman, eds., *Alternative Service Delivery: Sharing Governance in Canada,* p. 154. Toronto: Institute of Public Administration of Canada. 4

Balthazar, H. (1991). *Caring Communities: Proceedings of the Symposium on Social Supports*, Cat. No. 89-514E. Ottawa: Statistics Canada. 7

Banks, S., D. Crossman, D. Poel, and M. Stewart. (1997). "Partnerships among Health Professionals and Self-Help Group Members." *Canadian Journal of Occupational Therapy* 64(3): 259–69. [online]. Available: www.caot.ca/CJOT/CJOT64/Banks64_5_259-269.pdf [February 15, 2004]. 7

Banting, K. (1995). "Social Policy Challenges in a Global Society." In D. Morales-Gomez and M. Torres, eds., *Social Policy in a Global Society: Parallels and Lessons from the Canada–Latin America Experience*. Chapter 1 [online]. Available: network.idrc.ca/ev.php?ID=27520_201&ID2=DO_TOPIC [February 2, 2004]. 2

Banting, K.G. (1987). "Visions of the Welfare State." In S.B. Seward, ed., *The Future of Social Welfare Systems in Canada and the United Kingdom*, pp. 147–63. Proceedings of a Canada/UK Colloquium, October 17–18, 1986, Ottawa/Meech Lake. Halifax: Institute for Research on Public Policy. 3

Barker, R.L. (1991). *The Social Work Dictionary*, 2nd ed. Silver Spring: National Association of Social Workers. 1, 8

Barlow, M. (2001 February). *The Free Trade Area of the Americas and the Threat to Social Programs, Environmental Sustainability and Justice in Canada and the Americas*. Council of Canadians [online]. Available: www.canadians.org/documents/campaigns-ftaa-threat-barlow.pdf [January 31, 2004]. 2

Barnsley, J., and D. Ellis. (1992). *Research for Change: Participatory Action Research for Community Groups*. Vancouver: Women's Research Centre. 6

Battle, K. (2001 September). *Relentless Incrementalism: Deconstructing and Reconstructing Canadian Income Security Policy* [online]. Available: www.caledoninst.org/PDF/894598873.pdf [February 1, 2004]. 2, 6, 11

Battle, K., and M. Mendelson. (1997). *Child Benefit Reform in Canada: An Evaluation Framework and Future Directions*. Ottawa: Caledon Institute of Social Policy [online]. Available: www.caledoninst.org/Publications/PDF/255ENG%2Epdf [April 17, 2004]. 9

Battle, K., and S. Torjman. (2001 May). *The Post-Welfare State in Canada: Income Testing and Inclusion*. Caledon Institute of Social Policy [online]. Available: www.caledoninst.org/PDF/894598814.pdf [February 1, 2004]. 2

———. (2002 November). *Architecture for National Child Care* [online]. Available: www.johngodfrey.on.ca/pages/nca-architecture.htm [February 4, 2004]. 4, 10

Beiser, M. (1999). *Strangers at the Gate: The 'Boat People's' First Ten Years in Canada*. Toronto: University of Toronto Press. 13

Bellamy, D. (1965). "Social Welfare in Canada." *Encyclopedia of Social Work*, 15th ed., pp. 36–48. New York: National Association of Social Workers. 1, 3

Bellemare, D. (1993). "The History of Economic Insecurity." In *Family Security in Insecure Times*, pp. 57–86. Ottawa: National Forum on Family Security. 3

Bell-Lowther, E. and V. Radyo. (2002 September 18). *Evaluation of the Family Violence Initiative—Multiculturalism Program* [online]. Available: www.pch.gc.ca/progs/em-cr/eval/2002/2002_22/3_e.cfm [May 27, 2004]. 13

Berkowitz, B. (2003). *Conducting Focus Groups: Assessing Community Needs and Resources: Community Assessment, Agenda Setting, and Choice of Broad Strategies*. Community Tool Box: University of Kansas [online]. Available: ctb.ku.edu/tools/EN/sub_section_main_1018.htm [February 26, 2004]. 6

Betcherman, G. (1996). *Changing Workplace Strategies: Achieving Better Outcomes for Enterprises, Workers, and Society: Introduction*. HRDC [online]. Available: www.hrdc-drhc.gc.ca/sp-ps/arb-dgra/publications/research/change/intro_e.shtml [January 31, 2004]. 2

Beyene, D., C. Butcher, C, B. Joe, and T. Richmond. (1996). "Immigrant Service Agencies: A Fundamental Component of Anti-Racist Social Services." In C.E. James, ed., *Perspectives on Racism and the Human Services Sector,* pp. 172–82. Toronto: University of Toronto Press. 13

Biggs, B., and R. Bollman. (1991). "Urbanization in Canada." *Canadian Social Trends* 21 (Summer): 23–27. 3

Block, W. (1983). "Social Welfare in Canada: The Case for Selectivity." *Canadian Social Work Review '83*, 25–33. 1

Boadway, R. (1995). *The Canada Health and Social Transfer: Address to the Liberal Caucus*. Ottawa: House of Commons. 4

——. (2003 March). *Options for Fiscal Federalism: Royal Commission on Renewing and Strengthening Our Place in Canada* [online]. Available: www.gov.nf.ca/publicat/ royalcomm/research/Boadway.pdf [February 4, 2004]. 4

Boothroyd, P., and C. Davis. (1991). *The Meaning of Community Economic Development*. UBC Planning Papers, Canadian Planning Issues No 25. Vancouver: School of Community and Regional Planning. 8

Bourgon, J. (1999 December 3). *Serving in the Knowledge Age*. Canadian Centre for Management Development [online]. Available: www.ccmd-ccg.gc.ca/about/ newsroom/speeches/serving_e.html [February 12, 2004]. 6

Bowen, P., and A.J. McKechnie. (2001). *Volunteer Connections: New Strategies for Involving Older Adults*. Volunteer Canada [online]. Available: www.volunteer.ca/volunteer/pdf/OlderAdults-Eng.pdf [May 12, 2004]. 11

Boychuk, G. (2004 January). *The Canadian Social Model: The Logics of Policy Development*: CPRN Social Architecture Papers: Research Report F/36: Family Network. Canadian Policy Research Networks, Inc. [online]. Available: www.cprn.com/en/doc.cfm?doc=520# [March 13, 2004]. 2

Bracken, D., and C. Walmsley. (1992 Spring). "The Canadian Welfare State." *The Social Worker* 60(1): 21–24. 1

Brasfield, C.R. (2001 March). "Residential School Syndrome." *BC Medical Journal* 43(2): 78-81. [online]. Available: www.bcma.org/public/bc_medical_ journal/bcmj/march_2001/residentialschoolsyndrome.asp [May 16, 2004]. 12

Brewster, S., M. Buckley, P. Cox, and L. Griep. (2002 April). *Diversity Education: A Literature Review*. Alberta Community Development/Canadian Heritage/University of Calgary [online]. Available: www.ucalgary.ca/cdi/downloads/ CDILitReviewJan8.pdf [March 7, 2004]. 8

Brown, G.S. (2004). *The Ideological Roots of Socialism: A Collection of "ISMS."* Lecture Notes: University of Nevada, Las Vegas [online]. Available: www.unlv.edu/faculty/ gbrown/westernciv/wc201/wciv2c19/wciv2c19lsec2.html [January 19, 2004]. 1

Browne, P.L. (1996). *Love in a Cold World? The Voluntary Sector in an Age of Cuts.* Ottawa: Canadian Centre for Policy Alternatives. 5

Bruce, M. (1966). *The Coming of the Welfare State.* New York: Schocken Books. 8

Bryant, T., D. Raphael, I. Brown, T. Cogan, C. Dallaire, S. Laforest, P. McGowan, L. Richard, L. Thompson, and J. Young. (2002 November). *A Nation for All Ages? A Participatory Study of Canadian Seniors' Quality of Life in Seven Municipalities.* York University, Centre for Health Studies, School of Health Policy and Management, Toronto [online]. Available: www.utoronto.ca/seniors/seniorsfinalreport.pdf [May 12, 2004]. 11

Burghardt, S. (1987). "Community-Based Social Action." In A. Minahan, ed., *Encyclopedia of Social Work*, 18th ed., vol. 1, pp. 292–99. Washington: National Association of Social Workers. 8

Burke, M.A., J. Lindsay, I. McDowell, and G. Hill. (1997). "Dementia among Seniors." *Canadian Social Trends* (Summer): 24–27. 11

Burnet, J. (2004). "Multiculturalism." In J.A. Marsh, ed., *The Canadian Encyclopedia, 2004* [online]. Available: www.thecanadianencyclopedia.com/ PrinterFriendly.cfm?Params=A1ARTA0005511 [May 27, 2004]. 13

Bushie, B. (1993). *Community Holistic Circle Healing: A Community Approach* [online]. Available: www.iirp.org/library/vt/vt_bushie.html [May 25, 2004]. 12

Byfield, J. (2003 March 3). *The Charter—A Judicial Coup d'Etat: Citizens Centre REPORT.* CanadianGrassroots [online]. Available: www.canadiangrassroots.ca/ article.php?sid=7021 [February 1, 2004]. 2

CAILC (Canadian Association of Independent Living Centres). (n.d.). *An Introduction.* Ottawa: Author. 14

Cain R., and S. Todd. (2002 January). *Shifting Sands: The Changing Context of HIV/AIDS Social Services in Ontario.* Ontario HIV Treatment Network/McMaster University [online]. Available: www.socsci.mcmaster.ca/healthst/emplibrary/ shiftingsands.pdf [March 7, 2004]. 8

Calgary Herald. (1994 April 22). "Chretien Says He's Sorry for Remarks," A13. 8

Campaign 2000. (2001 November). *Family Security in Insecure Times: Tackling Canada's Social Deficit.* Child Poverty in Canada: Bulletin [online]. Available: www.campaign2000.ca/rc/01bulletin/Nov01Bulletin4p.pdf [April 17, 2004]. 9

———. (2002). *Meeting Your MP Campaign: Background Information* [online]. Available: www.campaign2000.ca/act/meetMP2002/meetyourMPbackground.pdf [April 17, 2004]. 9

———. (2003). *Honouring Our Promises: Meeting the Challenge to End Child and Family Poverty: 2003 Report Card on Child Poverty in Canada* [online]. Available: www.campaign2000.ca/rc/rc03/NOV03ReportCard.pdf [April 17, 2004]. 9

Canada Revenue Agency (2003 July). *Child Disability Benefit*: Fact Sheet [online]. Available: www.ccra-adrc.gc.ca/newsroom/factsheets/2003/july/cdb-e.html [May 29, 2004]. 14

Canada's Western Premiers Conference. (2003 June). *Federal/Provincial/Territorial Fiscal Relations in Transition: A Report to Canada's Western Premiers from the Finance Ministers of British Columbia, Alberta, Saskatchewan, Manitoba, Yukon, Northwest Territories, and Nunavut* [online]. Available: www.scics.gc.ca/cinfo03/850091004_ ae.pdf [February 4, 2004]. 4

Canadian Association for Community Living. (2004). *About Us* [online]. Available: www.cacl.ca/2004/English/aboutus/index.html [June 15, 2004]. 14

Canadian Association of Food Banks. (2003 October). *Hungercount 2003—Summary: Canada's Only Annual Survey of Food Banks & Emergency Food Programs: Something Has to Give: Food Banks Filling the Policy Gap in Canada.* Toronto: Canadian Association of Food Banks [online]. Available: www.cafb-acba.ca/pdfs/other_ documents/HC_summary_ENG.pdf [April 17, 2004]. 9

———. (2004). *About CAFB: Facts About Food Banks in Canada* [online]. Available: www.cafb-acba.ca/about_facts_e.cfm [April 17, 2004]. 9

Canadian Association of Gerontology. (2004). *Division of Aging and Seniors (DAS) Winter Update—2004* [online]. Available: www.cagacg.ca/english/225_e.php [June 13, 2004]. 11

Canadian Association of the Deaf. (2002 July 17). *Deaf Seniors* [online]. Available: www.cad.ca/english/resources/pp_deaf_seniors.htm [June 17, 2004]. 11

Canadian Centre for Justice. (2001 June). *Seniors in Canada.* Statistics Profile Series [online]. Available: www.statcan.ca/english/freepub/85F0033MIE/ 85F0033MIE01008.pdf [May 9, 2004]. 11

Canadian Centre for Management Development. (2000 June). *A Public Service Learning Organization: From Coast to Coast to Coast: Directions for the Future* [online]. Available: www.ccmd-ccg.gc.ca/ldc/2000/directions/dir_pg12_e.html [February 13, 2004]. 6

———. (2001a). *The Learning Organization Scorecard* [online]. Available: www.ccmd-ccg.gc.ca/ldc/2001/scorecard/score_page16_e.html [February 13, 2004]. 6

———. (2001b April). *A Proposed Continuous Learning Policy for the Public Service of Canada* [online]. Available: www.ccmd-ccg.gc.ca/ldc/pdf/continuous_learning_ policy.pdf [February 12, 2004]. 6

Canadian Centre for Policy Alternatives. (2003 April 17). *Stop Putting Debt Reduction, Tax Cuts over Equality: Alternative Provincial Budget* [online]. Available: www. policyalternatives.ca/manitoba/apb2003pr.html [February 4, 2004]. 4

Canadian Chamber of Commerce. (2003 November 3). *Federal Government's Economic and Fiscal Update* [online]. Available: www.chamber.ca/public_info/2003/economicupdate031103.pdf [February 4, 2004]. 4

Canadian Council for Public-Private Partnerships. (2004). *Definitions* [online]. Available: www.pppcouncil.ca/aboutPPP_definition.asp [February 1, 2004]. 2

Canadian Council for Refugees. (1998 February). *Best Settlement Practices: Settlement Services for Refugees and Immigrants in Canada* [online]. Available: www.web.net/~ccr/bpfinal.htm [May 27, 2004]. 13

———. (2000 May). *Canadian National Settlement Service Standards Framework* [online]. Available: www.web.net/~ccr/standards.PDF [May 27, 2004]. 13

———. (2003a June 19). *CCR Calls Attention to Refugee Youth in Canada* [online]. Available: www.web.net/~ccr/worldrefugeeday.htm [May 27, 2004]. 13

———. (2003b April 16). *Comments on Settlement and Integration to the Standing Committee on Citizenship and Immigration* [online]. Available: www.web.net/~ccr/settlementcomments.html [May 27, 2004]. 13

———. (2004). *Talking About Refugees and Immigrants: A Glossary Of Terms* [online]. Available: www.web.net/~ccr/glossary.htm [May 27, 2004]. 13

Canadian Council on Social Development (1969). *Social Policies for Canada, Part 1.* Ottawa: Author. 2, 3

———. (1990). *Canada's Social Programs Are in Trouble.* Ottawa: Author. 4

———. (1999 March 3). *CCSD Response to Recent Development of Welfare-to-Work Programs* [online]. Available: www.ccsd.ca/pubs/archive/wtw/pp.htm [April 17, 2004]. 9

———. (2000a). *Cultural Diversity: Immigrant Youth in Canada: Do Community Services Respond to the Needs of New Immigrants?* [online]. Available: www.ccsd.ca/subsites/cd/docs/iy/service.htm [February 12, 2004]. 8

———. (2000b). *Immigrant Youth in Canada: Highlights* [online]. Available: www.ccsd.ca/subsites/cd/docs/iy/hl.htm [May 27, 2004]. 13

———. (2002a November 4). *Child Hunger Increasing in Canada as Gap Widens Between Haves and Have-Nots, CCSD Report Concludes* [online]. Available: www.ccsd.ca/pubs/2002/pcc02/pr.htm [May 20, 2004]. 10

———. (2002b November). *Child Poverty: It's More Than Just a Numbers Game*: Op-Ed [online]. Available: www.ccsd.ca/pr/2002/oped-cp.htm [March 27, 2004]. 2

———. (2002c November 4). *Highlights: The Progress of Canada's Children 2002* [online]. Available: www.ccsd.ca/pubs/2002/pcc02/hl.htm [April 17, 2004]. 9

———. (2003a November 27). *Community Social Data Strategy: Urban Poverty Project* [online]. Available: www.ccsd.ca/subsites/socialdata/up.html [March 27, 2004]. 2

———. (2003b March 3). *Cultural Diversity: Frequently Asked Questions* [online]. Available: www.ccsd.ca/subsites/cd/about.htm [May 27, 2004]. 13

——. (2003c June 15). *Fact Sheet #5: The Funding Fall-Out: The Toll Exacted by the New Funding Regime* [online]. Available: www.ccsd.ca/pubs/2003/fm/fs5.htm [February 9, 2004]. 5

——. (2003d). *The Personal Security Index 2003: Backgrounder-Introduction* [online]. Available: www.ccsd.ca/pubs/2003/psi/backgrounders.pdf [April 17, 2004]. 9

Canadian Federation for the Humanities and Social Sciences. (2003 February 20). *Bulletin on the Federal Budget* [online]. Available: www.fedcan.ca/english/policyandadvocacy/briefsandstatements/pdf/budgetbulletin-e.pdf [February 9, 2004]. 5

Canadian Feminist Alliance for International Action. (2003 January). *Canada's Failure to Act: Women's Inequality Deepens* [online]. Available: www.fafia-afai.org/Bplus5/natFAFIAreport012103.pdf [May 29, 2004]. 14

Canadian Heritage. (2004a January 20). *Canadian Diversity: Respecting Our Differences* [online]. Available: www.pch.gc.ca/progs/multi/respect_e.cfm?nav=2 [May 27, 2004]. 13

——. (2004b January 20). *Multiculturalism: Health and Social Policy* [online]. Available: www.canadianheritage.gc.ca/progs/multi/reports/ann97-98/health_e.cfm [May 28, 2004]. 13

Canadian Institute for Health Information. (2004). *Summary Report: Improving the Health of Canadians.* [online]. Available: secure.cihi.ca/cihiweb/en/downloads/IHC2004_sum_e.pdf [May 13, 2004]. 12

Canadian Institute for Historical Microreproductions. (2004). *Canada in the Making, 1951–1981: Aboriginal Rights Movement* [online]. Available: www.canadiana.org/citm/themes/aboriginals/aboriginals12_e.html [May 13, 2004]. 12

Canadian Intergovernmental Conference Secretariat. (2002 October 16). *Federal-Provincial-Territorial Meeting of Ministers Responsible for Immigration: Ministers Agree to Work Together to Share the Benefits of Immigration.* News Release [online]. Available: www.scics.gc.ca/cinfo02/830766004_e.html [May 27, 2004]. 13

Canadian Mental Health Association. (2002 January). *Seniors' Mental Health and Home Care: A National Study.* A Report Prepared for the Canadian Mental Health Association [online]. Available: www.cmha.ca/english/shmcare/national_report.pdf [May 18, 2004]. 11

——. (2003 June). *Access to Mental Health Services: Issues, Barriers and Recommendations for Federal Action: A Brief to the Standing Senate Committee on Social Affairs, Science and Technology: Mental Health and Mental Illness: Phase One* [online]. Available: www.cmha.ca/english/research/images/kirbyjune03.pdf [March 7, 2004]. 8

——. (2004). *About CMHA* [online]. Available: www.cmha.ca/english/about/index.html [May 29, 2004]. 14

Canadian Policy Research Networks, Inc. (2003a November 26). *Unique Quebec Family Policy Model at Risk*. News Release. Ottawa: Canadian Policy Research Networks, Inc. [online]. Available: www.cprn.com/documents/25285_en.pdf [April 28, 2004]. 10

———. (2004 January 23). *Ambitious Project Tackles New Social Architecture for Canada*. News Release [online]. Available: www.cprn.com/en/doc.cfm?doc=513# [March 1, 2004]. 2

Canadian Public Health Association. (1996). *Canadian Public Health Association 1996 Discussion Paper on the Health Impact of Unemployment* [online]. Available: www.cpha.ca/english/policy/pstatem/unempl/page1.htm [April 17, 2004]. 9

Canadian Study of Health and Aging. (2002). *About the Study* [online]. Available: www.csha.ca/about_study.asp [May 12, 2004]. 11

Canadian Union of Public Employees. (2000). *Who's Pushing Privatization? Annual Report on Privatization 2000* [online]. Available: www.cupe.ca/arp/arpeng.pdf [June 13, 2004]. 9

Caregiver Resource Centre. (2004). *Housing Options for Seniors*. Don Mills Foundation for Seniors [online]. Available: www.dmfseniors.org/caregivers/housing_options.asp [May 13, 2004]. 11

Carniol, B. (2000). *Case Critical: Challenging Social Services in Canada*, 4th ed. Toronto: Between the Lines. 3, 5, 12

Carter, S. (1997 September). "Building Diversity Considerations into Social Planning." *Perception* 21(2): 7–8. 13

Cassidy, H.M. (1943). *Social Security and Reconstruction in Canada*. Toronto: Ryerson Press. 3

Castellano, M.B. (2002). *Aboriginal Family Trends: Extended Families, Nuclear Families, Families of the Heart*. Vanier Institute of the Family [online]. Available: www.vifamily.ca/library/cft/aboriginal.pdf [May 16, 2004]. 12

CASW (Canadian Association of Social Workers). (1983). *Canadian Association of Social Work Code of Ethics*. Ottawa: Author. 7

———. (1994a). *Annual Report 1993–94*. Ottawa: Author. 7

———. (1994b). *Social Work Code of Ethics*, Ottawa: Author. 7, 8

———. (1994c). "The Social Work Profession and the Aboriginal Peoples." *The Social Worker* 62(4): 158. 12

———. (1998 March). *CASW Statement on Preventive Practices and Health Promotion* [online]. Available: www.casw-acts.ca/Practice/RecPubsArt3.htm [March 7, 2004]. 8

———. (2000 March). *CASW National Scope of Practice Statement* [online]. Available: www.casw-acts.ca/Practice/RecPubsArt1.htm [February 15, 2004]. 7, 8

———. (2003a April). *Canadian Association of Social Workers Child Welfare Project: Creating Conditions for Good Practice* [online]. Available: www.casw-acts.ca/projects/Child%20Welfare%20Project_e.pdf [April 29, 2004]. 10

———. (2003b December 13). *CASW Presents the Social Work Profession* [online]. Available: www.casw-acts.ca/aboutcasw/caswpresents_e.htm [February 9, 2004]. 5

———. (2003c August 12). *Regulation of Social Work in Canada* [online]. Available: www.casw-acts.ca/canada/regulation_e.htm [February 15, 2004]. 7

———. (n.d.). *National Registry of Clinical and Non-Clinical Social Workers in Private Practice: Definition of Terms* [online]. Available: www.casw-acts.ca [February 15, 2004]. 7

CCOHS (Canadian Centre for Occupational Health and Safety). (2003 May). "Balancing Hurried Families and the Changing Workplace." *Health and Safety Report* 1(3) [online]. Available: www.healthandsafetyreport.com/archive-ezine.htm [February 1, 2004]. 2

Central Alberta Refugee Effort Committee. (2004). *Central Alberta Refugee Effort (CARE) Committee* [online]. Available: www.intentr.com/immigrantctr/care.htm [June 19, 2004]. 13

Centre for Addiction and Mental Health. (2004 April 5). *Population and Life Course Studies* [online]. Available: www.camh.net/fr/research/population_life_course.html [April 29, 2004]. 10

Centre for Research & Education in Human Services. (March 2000). *Enhancing Services and Supports for Immigrant Youth in Waterloo Region: Final Report* [online]. Available: www.settlement.org/downloads/Immigrant_Youth_Waterloo.pdf [May 27, 2004]. 13

Centre for Research and Information on Canada. (2001 November 6). *Portraits of Canada 2001* [online]. Available: www.cucweb.ca/pdf/portraits/portraits2001_highlights.pdf [May 27, 2004]. 13

———. (2002a March 20). *A Majority Says Racism Is a Big Problem in Canada but Canadians Are More Optimistic Than Ever about Reducing Prejudice.* Press Release [online]. Available: www.cucweb.ca/pdf/racism/racism_press_2002.pdf [May 27, 2004]. 13

———. (2003 August 13). *Canadians Favour Increased Power for Local Government: Federal Level of Government Is Least Favoured in Canada, the US and Mexico* [online]. Available: www.cric.ca/pdf_re/comparative_fed/comparative_fed_press_aug2003.pdf [February 9, 2004]. 5

Centre of Excellence for Youth Engagement. (2004). *Vision* [online]. Available: www.tgmag.ca/centres/vision_e.htm [April 29, 2004]. 10

Chappell, N. (1999). *Volunteering and Healthy Aging: What We Know.* Canadian Forum on Volunteering [online]. Available: www.volunteer.ca/volcan/eng/content/older-adults/canada_adults_report_printable.htm [February 15, 2004]. 7

———. (2000). [Cited in Volunteer Canada:] *Volunteering … A Booming Trend* [online]. Available: www.volunteerburnaby.ca/pdf/booming_trend.pdf [May 9, 2004]. 11

Charbonneau, D. (2000 December 19). "Share Country's Prosperity with Guaranteed Annual Income." Eye View, *Kamloops Daily News* [online]. Available: www.cariboo. bc.ca/dsd/cced/faculty/dcharbon/kdn/basic.htm [February 4, 2004]. 4

Charter Committee on Poverty Issues. (1998 November 13). *Submissions to the Committee on Economic, Social and Cultural Rights, United Nations* [online]. Available: www.equalityrights.org/ngoun98/ccpi.htm [February 4, 2004]. 4

Chaykowski, R.P. (2003 February 23). *Globalization and the Modernization of Canadian Labour Policy.* HRDC [online]. Available: labour.hrdc-drhc.gc.ca/psait_spila/ ntipt_ndlp/mmptc_gmclp/index.cfm/doc/english [February 1, 2004]. 2

Cheung, A.M., and S.W. Hwang. (2004 April 13). "Risk of Death among Homeless Women: A Cohort Study and Review of the Literature." *Canadian Medical Association Journal* 170(8) [online]. Available: www.cmaj.ca/cgi/content/ full/170/8/1243 [May 13, 2004]. 9

Christensen, C.P. (1996). "The Impact of Racism on the Education of Social Service Workers." In C.E. James, ed., *Perspectives on Racism and the Human Services Sector,* pp. 140–51. Toronto: University of Toronto Press. 13

———. (2001). "Immigrant Minorities in Canada." In J.C. Turner and F.J. Turner, eds., *Canadian Social Welfare,* 4th ed., pp. 180–209. Toronto: Pearson Education Canada. 13

Christie, N., and M. Gauvreau. (1996). *A Full-orbed Christianity: The Protestant Churches and Social Welfare in Canada 1900–1940.* Montreal: McGill-Queens University Press. 1, 3

Chung Yan, M. (1998). "Towards a Complete View of the Social Policy Process: An Integration of Policy Formulation and Implementation." *Canadian Review of Social Policy* 42: 37–53. 2

CIC (Citizenship and Immigration Canada). (1994). *Into the 21st Century: A Strategy for Immigration and Citizenship.* Ottawa-Hull: Minister of Supply and Services Canada. 13

———. (1995 December). *Growing Together—A Backgrounder on Immigration and Citizenship: The History of Immigration* [online]. Available: www.cic.gc.ca/ english/pub/grow/grow_00e.html [February 3, 2000]. 13

———. (1998). *Building on a Strong Foundation for the 21st Century: New Directions for Immigration and Refugee Policy and Legislation.* Ottawa: Minister of Public Works and Government Services Canada. 13

———. (1999a). *Canada ... The Place to Be: Annual Immigration Plan for the Year 2000.* Ottawa: Minister of Public Works and Government Services Canada. 13

———. (1999b). *You Asked About ... Immigration and Citizenship.* Ottawa: Minister of Public Works and Government Services Canada. 13

———. (2000 April 6). *Caplan Tables New Immigration and Refugee Protection Act*. News Release [online]. Available: www.cic.gc.ca/english/press/00/0009-pre.html [August 5, 2004]. 13

———. (2001 May). *Towards a More Balanced Geographic Distribution of Immigrants* [online]. Available: www.cic.gc.ca/english/research/papers/geographic/geographic-a.html [May 27, 2004]. 13

———. (2002a June 28). *Canada's Program for Women at Risk* [online]. Available: www.cic.gc.ca/english/refugees/women-1.html [May 27, 2004]. 13

———. (2002b March 8) *Immigration and Refugee Protection Act: Final Set of Proposed Regulations Prepublished* [online]. Available: www.cic.gc.ca/english/press/02/0203-pre.html [May 27, 2004]. 13

———. (2003a March 24). *Immigrant Settlement and Adaptation Program* [online]. Available: www.cic.gc.ca/english/newcomer/isap-fs.html [May 27, 2004]. 13

———. (2003b). *National Settlement Conference II: Settlement Accord* [online]. Available: integration-net.cic.gc.ca/inet/english/vsi-isb/conference2/working-travail/p03-01.htm [May 27, 2004]. 13

———. (2003c August 1). *A Newcomer's Introduction to Canada: Immigrant Serving Organizations* [online]. Available: www.cic.gc.ca/english/newcomer/guide/section-04.html#1 [May 27, 2004]. 13

———. (2004a January 13). *Financial Assistance and Loans* [online]. Available: www.cic.gc.ca/english/refugees/resettle-3.html [May 27, 2004]. 13

———. (2004b Winter). "The First Six Months in Canada: The Importance of Family and Friends." *The Monitor* [online]. Available: www.cic.gc.ca/english/monitor/issue04/06-feature.html [May 28, 2004]. 13

———. (2004c January 13). *Resettling Refugees in Canada* [online]. Available: www.cic.gc.ca/english/refugees/resettle-1.html [May 27, 2004]. 13

City of Moncton. (2001). *Support to Community Organizations* [online]. Available: www.moncton.org/search/english/CITYLIVING/yourcommunity/supportpolicy.htm [February 29, 2004]. 6

Citizens for Public Justice. (2003 September). *Closing the Gap: Eliminating the Social Deficit, Creating a Stronger Canada* [online]. Available: www.cpj.ca/budget/03/brief03.pdf [February 4, 2004]. 4

Clutterbuck, P. (1997). "A National Municipal Social Infrastructure Strategy." *Canadian Review of Social Policy* 40 (Winter): 69–75. 5

———. (2001 November 8). *Social Inclusion and Community Participation*. Presentation paper to A New Way of Thinking? Towards a Vision of Social Inclusion. Social Inclusion Conference, Ottawa, November 8–9, 2001. Canadian Council on Social Development/Laidlaw Foundation [online]. Available: www.ccsd.ca/subsites/inclusion/bp/pc.htm [March 7, 2004]. 8

Clutterbuck, P., and M. Novick. (2003 April). *Building Inclusive Communities: Cross-Canada Perspectives and Strategies* . Federation of Canadian Municipalities and the Laidlaw Foundation [online]. Available: www.fcm.ca/newfcm/Java/inclusive.pdf [March 4, 2004]. 2, 5

CMHC (Canada Mortgage and Housing Corporation). (2003). *Canadian Housing Observer*. Canada: Canada Mortage and Housing Corporation. 9

———. (2004a May 21). *Affordable Housing Conditions Improve across Canada. Newsroom* [online]. Available: www.cmhc-schl.gc.ca/en/News/nere/2004/2004 -05-21-0800.cfm [June 13, 2004]. 9

———. (2004b). *Improving Quality & Affordability: More Affordable Housing for Canadians* [online]. Available: www.cmhc-schl.gc.ca/en/imquaf/afho/afho_021.cfm [April 17, 2004]. 9

Code, R. (2003 June). "Shelters for Abused Women and Their Children." In H. Johnson and K. Au Coin, eds., *Family Violence in Canada: A Statistical Profile, 2003*, pp. 46–51. Statistics Canada/Canadian Centre for Justice Statistics: Catalogue no. 85-224-XIE [online]. Available: www.hc-sc.gc.ca/hppb/ familyviolence/pdfs/2003famvioprofil_e.pdf [April 29, 2004]. 10

Collins, K. (1976 January–February). "Three Decades of Social Security in Canada." *Canadian Welfare* 51(7): 5–9. 3

Collins, S.B. (1998). "The Challenge of Equity in Canadian Social Welfare Policy. *Canadian Review of Social Policy* 42: 1–14. 4

Community Economic Development Centre. (1995). *A Working Definition of CED*. Burnaby: Simon Fraser University [online]. Available: www2.sfu.ca/cedc/ resources/online/cedconline/ceddefn.htm [March 7, 2004]. 8

Compton, B. (1980). *Introduction to Social Welfare and Social Work: Structure, Function, and Process*. Homewood: Dorsey Press. 1

Conceptual Framework Subcommittee of the Residential Services Advisory Committee. (2002 January). *Working with Community to Support Children, Youth and Families* [online]. Available: www.mcf.gov.bc.ca/change/pdfs/working_with_ community.pdf [March 13, 2004]. 6, 8

Conference Board of Canada. (2000). *Performance and Potential 2000–2001: Seeking "Made in Canada" Solutions*. Ottawa: Author. 2, 5

Conn, D.K. (2003 September 19). "An Overview of Common Mental Disorders Among Seniors." In National Advisory Council on Aging, *Writings in Gerontology: Mental Health and Aging* (18) [online]. Available: www.hc-sc.gc.ca/seniors-aines/ naca/writings_gerontology/writ18/writ18_2_e.htm [May 19, 2004]. 11

Connaway, R.S., and M.E. Gentry. (1988). *Social Work Practice*. Englewood Cliffs: Prentice-Hall. 8

Copps, S. (2003 September 8). *Canadian Heritage Performance Report for the Period Ending March 31, 2003*. Treasury Board of Canada [online]. Available: www.tbs-sct.gc. ca/rma/dpr/02-03/CanHer-PC/CanHer-PC03D01_e.asp [May 27, 2004]. 13

Cossette, L., and E. Duclos. (2002 December). *A Profile of Disability in Canada, 2001*. Statistics Canada [online]. Available: www.statcan.ca/english/freepub/89-577-XIE/pdf/89-577-XIE01001.pdf [May 22, 2004]. 11, 14

Council of Canadians with Disabilities. (2004). *Frequently Asked Questions* [online]. Available: www.ccdonline.ca/FAQs/index.htm [May 29, 2004]. 14

Courchene, T. (2003 February 19). "Securing Dominion over the Provinces." *National Post* [online]. Available: www.canada.com/national/features/budget_2003/story.html?id=C0B5712B-2200-4834-92E9-C31D80950CFB [February 4, 2004]. 5

Courchene, T.J. (1987). *Social Policy in the 1990s: Agenda for Reform: Policy Study No. 3*. C.D. Howe Institute. Scarborough: Prentice-Hall. 2

Coyle, G.L. (1959). "Some Basic Assumptions about Social Group Work." In M. Murphy, ed., *The Social Group Work Method in Social Work Education*, Curriculum Study XI, pp. 91–100. New York: Council on Social Work Education. 8

Cranswick, K. (2002). *Caring for an Aging Society*. General Social Survey Cycle 16. Statistics Canada [online]. Available: www.statcan.ca/english/freepub/89-582-XIE/ [May 12, 2004]. 11

Crompton, S., and A. Kemeny. (1999). "In Sickness and in Health: The Well-Being of Married Seniors." *Canadian Social Trends* (Winter): 22–27. 11

Cross, S. (1985 Spring). "Professionalism: The Occupational Hazard of Social Work. 1920–1960." *The Social Worker* 53(1): 29–33. 7

Daniels, A. and B. Ewart. (2002). "Transforming Ontario's Social Assistance Delivery System." *Canadian Government Executive, Issue 1:* 26–28 [online]. Available: www.accenture.ca/content/en/industries/govt/cpbt.pdf [February 9, 2004]. 5

Day, S., and G. Brodsky. (1998). *Women and the Equality Deficit: The Impact of Restructuring Canada's Social Programs*. Ottawa: Status of Women Canada. 1

De Long, J.B. (1998 November). *Canada in The 21st Century: I. Scene Setting: Global Trends: 1980–2015 and Beyond*: Industry Canada Research Publications [online]. Available: strategis.ic.gc.ca/epic/internet/ineas-aes.nsf/vwGeneratedInterE/ra01741e.html [January 31, 2004]. 2

deGroot-Maggetti, G. (2003a March). *Federal Budget 2003: Rethinking Canadian Economic and Social Policy*. Citizens for Public Justice [online]. Available: www.cpj.ca/budget/03/budget2.html [January 31, 2004]. 2

———. (2003b September). *The Size and Costs of Reduced Social Transfers*. Citizens for Public Justice [online]. Available: www.cpj.ca/pjrc/research/03_transfrs.pdf [February 4, 2004]. 4

Department of Finance. (2000 October 18). *Economic Statement and Budget Update: Overview* [online]. Available: www.fin.gc.ca/ec2000/pdf/overe.pdf [March 28, 2004]. 4

——. (2001). *Budget 2001: Annex 4: Fiscal Performance of Canada's Federal-Provincial-Territorial Government Sector: Highlights* [online]. Available: www.fin.gc.ca/budget01/bp/bpan4e.htm [February 4, 2004]. 4

——. (2003a February 18). *Budget 2003: Annex 5: Fiscal Performance of Canada's Federal-Provincial-Territorial Government Sector* [online]. Available: www.fin.gc.ca/budget03/bp/bpa5e.htm [February 4, 2004]. 4

——. (2003b). *The Budget in Brief 2003* [online]. Available: www.fin.gc.ca/budget03/brief/briefe.htm [February 9, 2004]. 5

——. (2003c February 18). *Budget 2003: Overview* [online]. Available: www.fin.gc.ca/budget03/PDF/overe.pdf [February 4, 2004]. 4, 11

——. (2003d). *Budget 2003: Investing in Canada's Health Care System* [online]. Available: www.fin.gc.ca/budget03/booklets/bkheae.htm [February 4, 2004]. 4

——. (2003e October). *Canada Health and Social Transfer: What Is the Canada Health and Social Transfer?* [online]. Available: www.fin.gc.ca/FEDPROV/chse.html [February 4, 2004]. 4

——. (2003f November 2). *The Economic and Fiscal Update: Annex 1: Canadian Economic and Fiscal Progress: The Last Ten Years* [online]. Available: www.fin.gc.ca/ec2003/eca1e.html [May 9, 2004]. 11

——. (2003g October). *Federal Transfers to Provinces and Territories* [online]. Available: www.fin.gc.ca/FEDPROV/FTPTe.html [February 9, 2004]. 5

——. (2003h December 8). *Glossary: Globalization* [online]. Available: www.fin.gc.ca/gloss/gloss-g_e.html#glob [January 31, 2004]. 2

——. (2003i June 10). *Glossary: Surplus* [online]. Available: www.fin.gc.ca/gloss/gloss-s_e.html [February 4, 2004]. 4

——. (2003j October 8). *Backgrounder: Social Workers' Services.* News Release [online]. Available: www.fin.gc.ca/news03/data/03-046_1e.html [February 15, 2004]. 7

——. (2003k October). *Tax Transfers: What Is a Tax Transfer?* [online]. Available: www.fin.gc.ca/FEDPROV/taxe.html [February 4, 2004]. 5

——. (2004). *Budget in Brief 2004* [online]. Available: www.fin.gc.ca/budget04/pdf/briefe.pdf [May 29, 2004]. 14

Department of Foreign Affairs and International Trade. (2003 September 26). *World Trade Organization (WTO): Canada and the WTO* [online]. Available: www.dfait-maeci.gc.ca/tna-nac/WTO-CO-en.asp [February 1, 2004]. 2

Department of Justice Canada. (2004 April 30). *Part V.1. Canada Health Transfer, Canada Social Transfer and Health Reform Transfer* [online]. Available: lois.justice.gc.ca/en/F-8/58471.html [August 1, 2004]. 4

Department of Justice Canada/Canadian Heritage. (2002 April 30). *Inclusion for All: A Canadian Roadmap to Social Cohesion: Insights from Structured Conversations* [online]. Available: canada.justice.gc.ca/en/ps/rs/rep/comsocohe.pdf [February 4, 2004]. 4

Dirks, G.E. (2004). "Immigration Policy." In J.A. Marsh, ed., *The Canadian Encyclopedia, 2004* [online]. Available: www.thecanadianencyclopedia.com/ PrinterFriendly.cfm?Params=A1ARTA0003961 [May 27, 2004]. 13

Djao, A.W. (1983). *Inequality and Social Policy*. Toronto: John Wiley and Sons. 1, 3

Dobelstein, A.W. (1978). "Introduction: Social Resources, Human Need, and the Field of Social Work." In A. Fink, ed., *The Field of Social Work*, 7th ed., pp. 3–21. New York: Holt, Rinehart and Winston. 1

Doe, T., and S. Kimpson. (1999 March). *Enabling Income: CPP Disability Benefits and Women with Disabilities*. Ottawa: Status of Women Canada. 14

Dorais, M. (2002). "Immigration and Integration through a Social Cohesion Perspective." *Horizons* 5(2): 4–5 [online]. Available: policyresearch.gc.ca/ v5n2_e.pdf [May 27, 2004]. 13

Drover, G. (1983 Winter). "Beyond the Welfare State: Brief to the Royal Commission on the Economic Union and Development Prospects for Canada." *The Social Work*, 51(4): 141–44. 3

Dunn, M. (1992 Fall–Winter). "One Heart—Many Voices: Canada's National Native Organization." *Perception* 15(4)/16(1): 24–27. 12

Durst, D. (2002 October 3). *Self-Government and the Growth of First Nations Child and Family Services* [online]. Available: www.iigr.ca/conferences/archive/pdfs3/ Durst.pdf [May 16, 2004]. 12

Economic Council of Canada. (1968). *Fifth Annual Review*. Ottawa: Author. 3

Edmonton Mennonite Centre for Newcomers. (2004). *Securing Hopeful Futures: An Early Intervention Program of the Edmonton Centre for Survivors of Torture and Trauma* [online]. Available: www.emcn.ab.ca/Securing_EIP.htm [February 12, 2004]. 6

Eichler, M., and M. Lavigne. (2003). "Women's Movement." In J.A. Marsh, ed., *The Canadian Encyclopedia, 2003* [online]. Available: www.thecanadianencyclopedia. com/index.cfm?PgNm=TCE&Params=A1ARTA0008684 [January 22, 2004]. 3

EKOS Research Associates Inc. (2002a December 17). *Fall 2002 Survey of First Nations People Living On-Reserve*. Indian and Northern Affairs Canada [online]. Available: www.ainc-inac.gc.ca/pr/pub/srv/srv03_e.pdf [June 13, 2004]. 12

———. (2002b March). *Positioning the Voluntary Sector in Canada: What the Elite and the General Public Say: Final Report* [online]. Available: www.vsi-isbc.ca/eng/aware- ness/pdf/awareness_opinion_report.pdf [February 10, 2004]. 5

———. (2002c May). *Public Attitudes towards Family Violence: A Syndicated Study, Final Report* [online]. Available: www.ekos.com/media/files/family31may02.pdf [April 29, 2004]. 10

Elias, B. and D. Demas. (2001 March). *First Nations People with a Disability Needs Assessment Survey Findings: A Profile of Manitoba First Nations People with a Disability* [online]. Available: www.umanitoba.ca/centres/centre_aboriginal_ health_research/researchreports/Disability_Report.pdf [May 29, 2004]. 14

Elliott L. (2003 October 1). "Federal Social Spending Will Depend on What Canada Can Afford: Martin." *CNEWS* [online]. Available: cnews.canoe.ca/CNEWS/Politics/Liberal/2003/10/21/232429-cp.html [February 4, 2004]. 4

Epstein, L. (1980). *Helping People: The Task-Centered Approach*. St. Louis: C.V. Mosby. 8

Evans, G. (2003). *Canada: Administrative and Civil Service Reform*. World Bank Group [online]. Available: www1.worldbank.org/publicsector/civilservice/rsCanada.pdf [February 1, 2004]. 2, 4

Farris-Manning, C., and M. Zandstra. (2003 April). *Children in Care in Canada: A Summary of Current Issues and Trends with Recommendations for Future Research*. Child Welfare League of Canada [online]. Available: www.nationalchildrensalliance. com/nca/pubs/2003/Children_in_Care_March_2003.pdf [April 29, 2004]. 10

Fawcett, S.B. (2003). *Some Lessons Learned on Community Organization and Change*: Models for Promoting Community Health and Development: Gateways to the Tools: Our Model for Community Change and Improvement. The Community Tool Box: University of Kansas [online]. Available: ctb.ku.edu/tools/en/sub_section_main_1386.htm [March 13, 2004]. 1

Federal-Provincial-Territorial Ministers Responsible for Social Services. (1999 December 6). *In Unison: A Canadian Approach to Disability Issues: A Vision Paper* [online]. Available: socialunion.gc.ca/pwd/unison/unison_e.html [May 28, 2004]. 14

——. (2000a). *In Unison 2000: Disability Supports* [online]. Available: www.socialunion. gc.ca/In_Unison2000/iu02100e.html [May 29, 2004]. 14

——. (2000b). *In Unison 2000: Next Steps* [online]. Available: [May 29, 2004]. 14

Federal-Provincial-Territorial Ministers Responsible for the Status of Women. (2002). *Assessing Violence against Women: A Statistical Profile* [online]. Available: www. swc-cfc.gc.ca/pubs/0662331664/200212_0662331664_e.pdf [April 29, 2004]. 10, 13

Federation of Canadian Municipalities. (2000 October 11). *A National Affordable Housing Strategy* [online]. Available: www.fcm.ca/english/national/strategy2-e.pdf [April 18, 2004]. 9

——. (2001 August 14). *FCM Urges Housing Ministers to Act on Canada's Affordable Housing Crisis*. Meeting of Federal, Provincial and Territorial Housing Ministers [online]. Available: www.fcm.ca/english/communications/aug15.htm [April 18, 2004]. 9

Fietz, M. (2002 Fall). "The Voluntary Sector in Canada: Special Interest Group or Human Interest Group?" *Let's Talk Families* 13(6). Family Service Canada [online]. Available: www.familyservicecanada.org/_files/newsletters_families/parlons_famille_fall2002_e.pdf [February 9, 2004]. 5

Fife, R. (2003 July 5). "Canada Tumbles to 8th Place on UN List." *Vancouver Sun*: A3. 4

Finn, E. (1985). *The Great Deficit Hoax*. Ottawa: Canadian Centre for Policy Alternatives. 4

First Nations Child and Family Caring Society of Canada. (2002 November). *Affirming and Promoting Indigenous Knowledge and Research* [online]. Available: www.cecw-cepb.ca/DocsEng/FNCFCSNov2002.pdf [May 9, 2004]. 12

———. (2003 October 14). *Sub Committee on Children and Youth at Risk of the Standing Committee of Human Resources Development and the Status of Persons with Disabilities Aboriginal Children and Youth Resident on Reserve* [online]. Available: www.fncfcs.com/docs/UnitedNations.pdf [May 16, 2004]. 12

First Nations University of Canada. (2004). *About School of Indian Social Work* [online]. Available: www.sifc.edu/Indian%20Social%20Work/Indian%20Social%20Work.htm [May 16, 2004]. 12

Fischer, J. (1978). *Effective Casework Practice: An Eclectic Approach.* New York: McGraw-Hill. 8

Forsey, E. (1974). *The Canadian Labour Movement, 1812–1902.* Historical Booklet, No. 27. Ottawa: Canadian Historical Association. 3

Foucault, M. (1965). *Madness and Civilization.* London: Random House. 12

Fraser, M.J. (2003 March 5). *International Women's Day 2004.* United Food and Commercial Workers Union [online]. Available: www.ufcw.ca/cgi-bin/full_story.cgi?story_id=1186&from_page=6 [April 18, 2004]. 9

Frenette, M. and G. Picot. (2003 March). *Life after Welfare: The Economic Well Being of Welfare Leavers in Canada During the 1990s.* Statistics Canada: Analytic Studies: Research Paper Series: Catalogue no. 11F0019MIE: No. 192 [online]. Available: www.statcan.ca/english/research/11F0019MIE/11F0019MIE2003192.pdf [April 18, 2004]. 9

Frenzel, A. (1987). "Unemployment." In S.A. Yelaja, ed., *Canadian Social Policy,* rev. ed., pp. 115–38. Waterloo: Wilfrid Laurier University Press. 1

Friedlander, W.A., and R.Z. Apte. (1980). *Introduction to Social Welfare,* 5th ed. Englewood Cliffs: Prentice-Hall. 3

Friendly, M. (2000 August). *Child Care and Canadian Federalism in the 1990s: Canary in a Coal Mine: The Federal/Provincial Climate after 1995.* Child Care Resource and Research Unit, Child Care Canada [online]. Available: www.childcarecanada.org/resources/CRRUpubs/canary/canary7_2.html [February 4, 2004]. 4

Friends of Seniors. (2003). *Programs* [online]. Available: www.friendsofseniors.org/programs.html [June 17, 2004]. 11

Friendship-Keller, R. (1988 January). *Factsheet: Program Planning for Organizations.* Ontario Ministry of Agriculture and Food [online]. Available: www.gov.on.ca/OMAFRA/english/rural/facts/96-007.htm [February 12, 2004]. 6

Galper, J.H. (1975). *The Politics of Social Services.* Englewood Cliffs: Prentice-Hall. 1

George, V., and P. Wilding. (1985). *Ideology and Social Welfare.* London and New York: Routledge. 1

Ginsler, E. (1988, September). "Social Planning Councils." *Perception* 2(2), 52–53. 8

Goss Gilroy Inc. (2000 August). *Evaluation Framework for the Host Program Citizenship and Immigration Canada.* Cited in Community Bridging Programs Research Project. March 2003, p. 9 [online]. Available: www.amssa.org/programs/iicc/CB%20Research%20Report%2031-03-03-%20Web_copy.pdf [May 27, 2004]. 13

Gottlieb, B.H. (1983). *Social Support Strategies.* Beverly Hills: Sage. 7

Government of Alberta. (1996 October). *Towards a Learning Organization in the Alberta Public Service: A Corporate Learning Strategy* [online]. Available: www.pao.gov.ab.ca/learning/learningstrat/learnorg/learning-org-in-aps.htm [August 7, 2004]. 6

——. (2002 May 22). *Low-Income Review Presents a Vision for the Future.* News Release [online]. Available: www.gov.ab.ca/acn/200205/12391.html [March 24, 2004]. 8

——. (2004). *What Benefits Are Provided?* Alberta Children's Services [online]. Available: www.child.gov.ab.ca/whatwedo/disabilities/page.cfm?pg=What%20supports%20are%20available%3F [May 29, 2004]. 14

Government of British Columbia. (2000). Ministry Responsible for Multiculturalism and Immigration. *What Is Multiculturalism? The Myths and Facts* [online]. Available: www/mrmi.gov.bc.ca/publications/index3.html [May 11, 2000]. 13

Government of Canada. (1970). *Income Security for Canadians.* Ottawa: Department of National Health and Welfare. 3

——. (1988 July). *Canadian Multiculturalism Act.* Ottawa: Minister of Supply and Services Canada. 13

——. (1994a). *Creating a Healthy Fiscal Climate: The Economic and Fiscal Update.* Ottawa: Department of Finance. 4

——. (1994b). *Improving Social Security in Canada—From Unemployment Insurance to Employment Insurance: A Supplementary Paper.* Hull-Ottawa: Ministry of Supply and Services Canada, Human Resources Development Canada. 4

——. (1994c). *Improving Social Security in Canada: A Discussion Paper.* Hull-Ottawa: Minister of Supply and Services Canada. 4

——. (1994d). *Improving Social Security in Canada—Guaranteed Annual Income: A Supplementary Paper.* Hull-Ottawa: Minister of Supply and Services Canada. 3

——. (1994e). *Improving Social Security in Canada—Reforming the Canada Assistance Plan: A Supplementary Paper.* Hull-Ottawa: Minister of Supply and Services Canada. 3

——. (1995). *Budget in Brief.* Ottawa: Department of Finance. 4, 5

——. (1997a September 23). *Background Information on the National Children's Agenda: Announced in the Speech from the Throne* [online]. Available: www.socialunion.ca/nca/nca1_e.html [April 29, 2004]. 10

——. (1997b). *Expanding Aboriginal Head Start to On-Reserve Children* [online]. Available: socialunion.gc.ca/nca/nca4_e.html [May 16, 2004]. 12

——. (1999a). *The Fiscal Balance in Canada, August 1999.* Ottawa: Department of Finance. 4

——. (1999b February 4). *A Framework to Improve the Social Union for Canadians: An Agreement between the Government of Canada and the Governments of the Provinces and Territories* [online]. Available: socialunion.gc.ca/news/020499_e.html [May 16, 2004]. 12

——. (1999c December 16). *Meeting of the Federal-Provincial-Territorial Ministerial Council on Social Policy Renewal*. News Releases [online]. Available: socialunion.gc.ca/news/161299_e.html [January 27, 2000] 12

——. (2000a). *Budget 2000: Improving the Quality of Life of Canadians and Their Children*. Ottawa: Department of Finance. 4

——. (2000b). *The Budget Speech 2000*. Ottawa: Department of Finance. 9

——. (2000c). *Canada's Participation in the International Year of Older Persons (IYOP)—1999* [online]. Available: iyop-aipa.ic.gc.ca/english/raising.htm [April 4, 2000]. 11

——. (2000d February 11). *Government of Canada to Amend Legislation to Modernize Benefits and Obligations* [online]. Available: canada.justice.gc.ca/en/news/nr/2000/doc_25019.html [April 28, 2004]. 10

——. (2001a November). *Federal/Provincial/Territorial Early Childhood Development Agreement Report on Government of Canada Activities and Expenditures 2000–2001: Part 1* [online]. Available: socialunion.gc.ca/ecd/ecd_part1.pdf [May 16, 2004]. 12

——. (2001b November). *Federal/Provincial/Territorial Early Childhood Development Agreement Report on Government of Canada Activities and Expenditures 2000–2001: Part 2* [online]. Available: socialunion.gc.ca/ecd/ecd_part2.pdf [May 16, 2004]. 12

——. (2002a November). *Backgrounder: Government of Canada's initiatives—Helping to Give Canadian Children the Best Possible Start in Life* [online]. Available: socialunion.gc.ca/ecd/2002/back-e.htm [April 29, 2004]. 10

——. (2002b). *Bridging the Gap: Government of Canada Programs and Services of Interest to Canadians with Disabilities* [online]. Available: www.sdc.gc.ca/en/hip/odi/documents/bridgingTheGap/bridgingTheGap.pdf [May 29, 2004]. 14

——. (2002c December 10). *Canadian Rural Partnership: Introduction* [online]. Available: www.rural.gc.ca/crpfacts_e.phtml [March 7, 2004]. 8

——. (2002d November). *The Well-Being of Canada's Young Children: Government of Canada Report 2002*, Federal/Provincial/Territorial Early Childhood Development Agreement [online]. Available: socialunion.gc.ca/ecd/2002/reportb-e.pdf [May 16, 2004]. 10

——. (2003a November). *Federal/Provincial/Territorial Early Childhood Development Agreement: Early Childhood Development Activities and Expenditures: Government of Canada Report 2002–2003* [online]. Available: socialunion.gc.ca/ecd/2003/RH64-20-2003-AE.pdf [May 25, 2004]. 12

——. (2003b November). *Government of Canada Response to "Listening to Canadians: A First View of the Future of the Canada Pension Plan Disability Program": The Fifth*

Report of the Standing Committee on Human Resources Development and the Status of Persons with Disabilities [online]. Available: www.dsc.gc.ca/en/isp/pub/cpp/disability/5threport/5threport.pdf [June 19, 2004]. 14

———. (2003c April 4). *Indian Residential Schools Resolution Canada: Frequently Asked Questions* [online]. Available: www.irsr-rqpi.gc.ca/english/news_questions.html [May 16, 2004]. 12

———. (2003d). *Job Futures: Community and Social Service Workers (NOC 4212)* [online]. Available: www.jobfutures.ca/noc/4212p1.shtml [February 15, 2004]. 7

———. (2003e). *Job Futures: Social Workers (NOC 4152)* [online]. Available: www.jobfutures.ca/noc/4152p1.shtml [February 15, 2004]. 7

———. (2003f December). *Multilateral Framework for Labour Market Agreements for Persons with Disabilities* [online]. Available: socialunion.gc.ca/pwd/priorityareas.html [June 19, 2004]. 14

———. (2003g March). *Multilateral Framework on Early Learning and Child Care* [online]. Available: socialunion.gc.ca/ecd-framework_e.htm [April 29, 2004]. 10

———. (2003h November). *The Well-Being of Canada's Young Children: Government of Canada Report 2003.* [online]. Available: socialunion.gc.ca/ecd/2003/RH64-20-2003E.pdf [April 29, 2004]. 10, 14

———. (2004a April). *A Canada Fit for Children: Canada's Plan of Action in Response to the May 2002 United Nations Special Session on Children* [online]. Available: www11.sdc.gc.ca/en/cs/sp/socpol/publications/2002-002483/canadafite.pdf [May 17, 2004]. 9, 10

———. (2004b). *Description of Reinvestments: Provincial, Territorial and First Nations Reinvestments and Investments.* The National Child Benefit [online]. Available: www.nationalchildbenefit.ca/ncb/progdesc.shtml [April 25, 2004]. 9

———. (2004c March 16). *Employability Assistance for People with Disabilities* [online]. Available: www.sdc.gc.ca/en/hip/odi/08_eapd.shtml [May 29, 2004]. 14

———. (2004d). *How Does the NCB Work?* The National Child Benefit [online]. Available: www.nationalchildbenefit.ca/ncb/thenational2.shtml [April 25, 2004]. 9

———. (2004e January 12). *National Homelessness Initiative: About the Initiative* [online]. Available: www21.hrdc-drhc.gc.ca/initiative/index_e.asp [February 10, 2004]. 5

———. (2004f July 14). *Seniors Policies and Programs Database* [online]. Available: www.sppd.gc.ca/sppd-bdppa/english/details.jsp?PROGRAM_ID=204 [July 30, 2004]. 1

———. (2004g). *Social Union: Main Menu* [online]. Available: www.socialunion.ca/menu_e.html [April 29, 2004]. 10

———. (2004h February 2). *Speech from the Throne* [online]. Available: www.pm.gc.ca/grfx/docs/sft_fe2004_e.pdf [April 29, 2004]. 12

——. (2004i). *A Unique Partnership of the Government of Canada, Provinces and Territories and First Nations.* The National Child Benefit [online]. Available: www.nationalchildbenefit.ca/ncb/thenational1.shtml [April 18, 2004]. 9

Government of Canada/Government of Mexico. (2003 April 29). *A Guide for the Development of a Comprehensive System of Support to Promote Active Ageing* [online]. Available: www.hc-sc.gc.ca/seniors-aines/pubs/paho/paho_1_e.htm [May 9, 2004]. 11

Government of Canada/Voluntary Sector Initiative. (1999 August). *Working Together: A Government of Canada/Voluntary Sector Joint Initiative: Report of the Joint Tables* [online]. Available: www.vsr-trsb.net/publications/pco-e.pdf [February 9, 2004]. 5

Government of Manitoba. (2004). *Children's Special Services.* Family Services and Housing [online]. Available: www.gov.mb.ca/fs/pwd/css.html [May 29, 2004]. 14

Government of New Brunswick. (2003a November 26). *Adoption Project to Become Permanent.* Press Release: Family and Community Services [online]. Available: www.gnb.ca/cnb/news/fcs/2003e1123fc.htm [April 28, 2004]. 10

——. (2003b November 4). *Continued Success for Special Adoption Project*: Family and Community Services [online]. Available: www.gnb.ca/cnb/news/fcs/2003e1017fc.htm [May 18, 2004]. 10

Government of Newfoundland and Labrador. (2000 December 13). *Single Parent Employment Program.* News Release by Julie Bettney, Minister of Human Resources and Employment [online]. Available: www.gov.nf.ca/releases/2000/hre/1213n03.htm [April 28, 2004]. 10

——. (2004). *Social Cohesion and the Strategic Social Plan: Diuscussion Paper.* Community Accounts for the Province of Newfoundland and Labrador [online]. Available: www.communityaccounts.ca/communityaccounts/referencedocuments/cohesion.pdf [August 2, 2004]. 4

Gower, D. (1992 Autumn). "Historical Unemployment Rate: A Note on Canadian Unemployment Since 1921." *Perspectives* 4(3). Statistics Canada [online]. Available: www.statcan.ca/english/studies/75-001/archive/1992/pear1992004003s3a03.pdf [February 1, 2004]. 2

Grady, P., R. Howse, and J. Maxwell. (1995). *Redefining Social Security.* Kingston: School of Policy Studies, Queen's University. 4, 5

Gray, G. (1990). "Social Policy by Stealth." *Policy Options* (March): 17–29. 4

Gregg, A.R. (2003 December 29). "Bumpy Ride." *Macleans.ca* [online]. Available: www.macleans.ca/topstories/polls/article.jsp?content=20031229_72597_72597 [March 27, 2004]. 2

Guest, D. (1980). *The Emergence of Social Security in Canada.* Vancouver: University of British Columbia Press. 3

——. (1988). "Social Security." *The Canadian Encyclopedia,* 2nd ed., vol. 3, pp. 2032–34. Edmonton: Hurtig Publishers. 3

——. (1997). *The Emergence of Social Security in Canada,* 3rd ed. Vancouver: University of British Columbia Press. 1, 3, 6

———. (2003). "Social Security." In J.A. Marsh, ed., *The Canadian Encyclopedia, 2003* [online]. Available: www.thecanadianencyclopedia.com/index.cfm?PgNm= TCE&Params=A1ARTA0007530 [January 22, 2004]. 2, 3, 8

Hall, M., L. Greenberg, and L. McKeown. (2000). *Talking about Charities: Canadians' Opinions on Charities and Issues Affecting Charities.* Edmonton: Muttart Foundation [online]. Available: www.muttart.org/download/talkingaboutcharities.pdf [February 12, 2004]. 6

Hall, M., T. Knighton, P. Reed, P. Bussiere, D. McRae, and P. Bowen. (1998 August). *Caring Canadians, Involved Canadians: Highlights from the 1997 National Survey of Giving, Volunteering and Participating.* Ottawa: Statistics Canada. 7

Hall, M., L. McKeown, and K. Roberts. (2001 August). *Caring Canadians, Involved Canadians: Highlights from the 2000 National Survey of Giving, Volunteering and Participating.* Ottawa: Statistics Canada [online]. Available: www.givingand volunteering.ca/pdf/n-2000-hr-ca.pdf [February 15, 2004]. 7

Hall, M.H., A. Andrukow, C. Barr, K. Brock, M. deWit, D. Embuldeniya, L. Jolin, D. Lasby, B. Levesque, E. Malinsky, S. Stowe, and Y. Vaillancourt. (2003a). *The Capacity to Serve: A Qualitative Study of the Challenges Facing Canada's Nonprofit and Voluntary Organizations.* Canadian Centre for Philanthropy [Online]. Available: www.vsi-isbc.ca/eng/Knowledge/pdf/capacity_to_serve.pdf [February 9, 2004]. 5, 6, 7, 8

Hall, M.H., S.D. Phillips, C. Meillat, and D. Pickering. (2003b). *Assessing Performance: Evaluation Practices and Perspectives in Canada's Voluntary Sector.* Canadian Centre for Philanthropy/Centre for Voluntary Sector Research and Development [online]. Available: www.nonprofitscan.ca/pdf/Vserp_Report.pdf [February 12, 2004]. 6

Halseth, G. and A. Booth. (1998 November). *Paper #2: Community Participation in the New Forest Economy Discussion Paper on Concepts: Community Development.* British Columbia Resource Communities Project: University of Northern British Columbia. [online]. Available: web.unbc.ca/~quarles/frbc/commdev.htm [March 7, 2004]. 8

Handel, G. (1982). *Social Welfare in Western Society.* New York: Random House. 1

Hanley, J. (2000). *Social Work Practice and Government Policy on Cultural Diversity— The Case of Ontario and Quebec.* Paper presented at the International Federation of Social Workers and International Association of Schools of Social Work Joint Conference Proceedings, Montreal, July 29–August 2, 2000 [online]. Available: www.mun.ca/cassw-ar/papers2/Hanley.pdf [May 27, 2004]. 13

Hanselmann, C. (2001 September). *Urban Aboriginal People in Western Canada: Realities and Policies.* Canada West Foundation [online]. Available: www. aboriginal-edmonton.com/PDF/CanWestUrbanRpt.pdf [May 9, 2004]. 12

Hanvey, L. (2002a November). *Children with Disabilities and Their Families in Canada.* A Discussion Paper Commissioned by the National Children's Alliance for the First National Roundtable on Children with Disabilities [online]. Available: www.national childrensalliance.com/nca/pubs/2002/hanvey02.pdf [May 29, 2004]. 14

———. (2002b June). *Middle Childhood: Building on the Early Years: A Discussion Paper*. National Children's Alliance [online]. Available: www.nationalchildrensalliance. com/nca/pubs/2002/hanvey.pdf [April 29, 2004]. 10

Hardy, S., and A.M. Mawhiney. (2002). "Diversity in Canadian Social Work Practice." In F.J. Turner, ed., *Social Work Practice: A Canadian Perspective*, 2nd ed., pp. 57–68 Toronto: Prentice-Hall. 13

Hareven, T.K. (1969 April). "An Ambiguous Alliance: Some Aspects of American Influences on Canadian Social Welfare." *Social History: A Canadian Review* 3: 82–98. 1

Hayden, J. (1997). *Neo-Conservatism and Child Care Services in Alberta: A Case Study: Five Phases of Policy Directions: Overt Policies*. Child Care Resource and Research Unit, Child Care Canada [online]. Available: www.childcarecanada.org/ resources/CRRUpubs/op9/9op3.html#top [February 4, 2004]. 4

Health Canada. (1993 December). *Family Violence and Substance Abuse: Information from the National Clearinghouse on Family Violence* [online]. Available: www.hc-sc. gc.ca/hppb/familyviolence/pdfs/fvsubab.pdf [May 24, 2004]. 10

———. (1996a). *Family Violence in Aboriginal Communities: An Aboriginal Perspective*. Ottawa: National Clearinghouse on Family Violence. 12

———. (1996b). *Guide to Project Evaluation: A Participatory Approach*. Chapter 6, "Collecting Evaluation Data." Ottawa: Health Canada, Population Health Directorate [online]. Available: www.hc-sc.gc.ca/hppb/phdd/resources/guide/ collecting.htm [February 26, 2004]. 6

———. (1998a). *The Family Violence Initiative: 1997/1998 Annual Report*. Ottawa: National Clearinghouse on Family Violence. 10

———. (1998b). "The Future of Caregiving." *Seniors Info Exchange* 7(3) (Winter 1997–98). 11

———. (1998c). *National Native Alcohol and Drug Abuse Program General Review 1998: Final Report* [online]. Available: www.hc-sc.gc.ca/fnihb/cp/nnadap/publications/ nnadap_general_review.pdf [May 16, 2004]. 12

———. (1999a December 15). *Introduction: National Framework on Aging* [online]. Available: www.hc-sc.gc.ca/seniors-aines/pubs/nfa-cnv/en/nfa3_e.htm [April 29, 2004]. 11

———. (1999b December 15). *National Framework on Aging* [online]. Available: www.hc-sc.gc.ca/seniors-aines/pubs/nfa-cnv/nfaguide.htm [April 29, 2004]. 11

———. (1999c). *Parenting Today's Teens: A Survey and Review of Resources* [online]. Available: www.hc-sc.gc.ca/dca-dea/publications/pdf/teens_e.pdf [April 29, 2004]. 10

———. (2002a May 14). *Accountability*. Audit and Accountability Bureau [online]. Available: www.hc-sc.gc.ca/aab-bvr/english/accountability_e.htm [February 12, 2004]. 6

———. (2002b). *Canada's Aging Population*. Division of Aging and Seniors [online]. Available: www.hc-sc.gc.ca/seniors-aines/pubs/fed_paper/pdfs/fedpager_e.pdf [May 9, 2004]. 11

——. (2002c September 2). *National Plan of Action for Children: History* [online]. Available: www.hc-sc.gc.ca/dca-dea/npa-pan/main_e.html [April 28, 2004]. 10

——. (2002d August 20). *Who Are Canada's Seniors?* Division of Aging and Seniors [online]. Available: www.hc-sc.gc.ca/seniors-aines/pubs/fed_paper/fedreport1_01_e.htm [February 1, 2004]. 2

——. (2003a March 4). *About Us*. Division of Aging and Seniors [online]. Available: www.hc-sc.gc.ca/seniors-aines/index_pages/aboutus_e.htm [May 9, 2004]. 11

——. (2003b September 30). *The National Advisory Council on Aging: Working for Canada's Seniors Today and Tomorrow*. Division of Aging and Seniors [online]. Available: www.hc-sc.gc.ca/seniors-aines/naca/whois_naca_e.htm#WhoAre [May 19, 2004]. 11

——. (2003c Spring/Summer). *Newsletter—National Clearinghouse on Family Violence,* Issue 8 [online]. Available: www.hc-sc.gc.ca/hppb/familyviolence/pdfs/newsletter-issue8_e.pdf [May 27, 2004]. 13

——. (2003d May 27). *Renewal of Canada's Drug Strategy to Help Reduce the Supply and Demand for Drugs*. News Release [online]. Available: www.hc-sc.gc.ca/english/media/releases/2003/2003_34.htm [February 2, 2004]. 2

——. (2003e February 25). *Second World Assembly on Ageing, Madrid: April 8–12, 2002: FAQ* [online]. Available: www.hc-sc.gc.ca/seniors-aines/waa/faq_e.htm [May 9, 2004]. 11

——. (2004 May 29). *Still Quite New for Immigrant Children*. Community Action Plan for Children Projects Directory Online [online]. Available: www.ssjs.hc-sc.gc.ca/capc/details.htm?ProNum=289&language=undefined [May 27, 2004]. 13

Health Systems Research Unit. (1997). *Review of Best Practices in Mental Health Reform*. Federal/Provincial/Territorial Advisory Network on Mental Health. Clarke Institute of Psychiatry. Ottawa: Health Canada [online]. Available: www.hc-sc.gc.ca/hppb/mentalhealth/pubs/bp_review/pdf/e_bp-rev.pdf [February 15, 2004]. 7

HealthyWay Magazine. (1997a June 16). "Self-Help Groups: Discover the Healing Power of Sharing and Caring" [online]. Available: www.nb.sympatico.ca/Contents/Health/healthyway/archive/feature_sel2.html [February 15, 2004]. 7

——. (1997b June 16). "You're Not Alone if You're Online: Tips for Healing on the Internet" [online]. Available: www.nb.sympatico.ca/Contents/Health/healthyway/archive/feature_sel1.html [February 15, 2004]. 7

HeartWood Institute. (2004). *About Us* [online]. Available: www.heartwood.ns.ca/about.shtml [April 29, 2004]. 10

Heclo, H. (1981). "Toward a New Welfare State?" In P. Flora and A.J. Heidenheimer, eds., *The Development of Welfare States in Europe and America,* pp. 383–406. New Brunswick and London: Transaction Books. 3

Heimann, C. (2003 September 17). *Perceptions of a Problem: Report on Hunger: Trending Update*. Totum Research Inc. [online]. Available: www.cafb-acba.ca/pdfs/other_documents/Totum2003_ENG.pdf [April 18, 2004]. 9

Heisz, A. and L. McLeod. (2004 April). *Trends and Conditions in Census Metropolitan Areas: Low-Income in Census Metropolitan Areas, 1980–2000.* Statistics Canada [online]. Available: www.statcan.ca/english/research/89-613-MIE/2004001/89-613 -MIE2004001.pdf [May 22, 2004]. 9

HelpAge International. (2002 September). *Ageing and Development,* Issue 12 [online]. Available: www.helpage.org/images/pdfs/AandD/ad12eng.pdf [May 9, 2004]. 11

Henslin, J.M. (2003). *Social Problems,* 6th ed. Upper Saddle River: Prentice Hall. 1

Herberg, C., and E.N. Herberg. (2001). "Canada's Ethno-Racial Diversity: Policies and Programs in Canadian Social Welfare." In J.C. Turner and F.J. Turner, eds., *Canadian Social Welfare,* 4th ed., pp. 167–79. Toronto: Pearson Education. 13

Herd, D. (2002). "Rhetoric and Retrenchment: 'Common Sense' Welfare Reform in Ontario." *Benefits* 34(10)2: 105–10 [online]. Available: www.utoronto.ca/ facsocwk/sane/doc/herd_rhetoric.pdf [April 18, 2004]. 9

Herman, R.D. and D.O. Renz. (1998). "What Is Not-for-Profit Organization Effectiveness?" *The Not-For-Profit CEO Monthly Letter* 5(6): 4–6, [online]. Available: www.bloch.umkc.edu/mwcnl/research/whatis.pdf [February 12, 2004]. 6

Hess, M. (1993). *An Overview of Canadian Social Policy.* Ottawa: Canadian Council on Social Development. 3

Hick, S. (1998). *Canada's Unique Social History* [online]. Available: www.socialpolicy.ca/ cush/index.htm [January 22, 2004]. 3

———. (2004). *Social Welfare in Canada: Understanding Income Security: An Introduction.* Toronto: Thompson Educational Publishing [online]. Available: socialpolicy.ca/swc/ book_g.htm [May 9, 2004]. 11

Hightower, H.C., J. Hightower, and M.J. Smith. (2003). *Out of Sight, Out of Mind: The Plight of Seniors and Homelessness.* Seniors Housing Information Program [online]. Available: www.seniorshousing.bc.ca/OutofsightOutofmind.pdf [May 9, 2004]. 11

Hikel, R. (1997). "Alternative Service Delivery and the Prospects for Success: Political Leadership and Performance Measurement. In R. Ford and D. Zussman, eds., *Alternative Service Delivery: Sharing Governance in Canada,* pp. 74–84. Toronto: Institute of Public Administration of Canada. 5

Hoffart, I. and M. Cooper. (2002 December 1). *System Reform:Meeting the Challenges of Service Fragmentation, Duplication, and Shortages in the Child and Youth Not-for-Profit Sector.* Report Submitted to the Calgary Joint Funding Review Initiative: Phase II [online]. Available: www.calgary.ca/docgallery/bu/community/fcss_ service_reform_paper.pdf [February 12, 2004]. 8

Hogg, G. (2001). "Keep Children Safe Within Their Families." Interview by Peter Grierson, *CBC Island Radio,* October 10, 2001 [online]. Available: www.mcf.gov. bc.ca/media_site/breaking_news_archives/breaking_news_101001_cbc.htm [March 23, 2004]. 6

Holcroft, C. (2000). "Now Is the Time for an Activist Approach." *Pundit Magazine* [online]. Available: www.punditmag.com/articles/activistapproach.html [February 4, 2004]. 4

Holosko, M.J., L. White, and M.D. Feit. (1996). "Gerontological Social Work Practice in the 1990s and Beyond." In Holosko and Feit, eds., *Social Work Practice with the Elderly,* 2nd ed., pp. 395–402. Toronto: Canadian Scholars' Press. 11

Horn, M. (1984). *The Great Depression of the 1930s in Canada.* Historical Booklet, No. 39. Ottawa: Canadian Historical Association. 3

Horner, J.S. (2002 January). "Innovative Projects Aim to Prevent Family Violence." *Let's Talk Families* 13(4): 7. Canadian Paediatric Society [online]. Available: www.familyservicecanada.org/_files/newsletters_families/parlons_famille_janv200 2_e.pdf [April 28, 2004]. 10

Hossli. W. (2000 October). *Competition in the Voluntary Sector: The Case of Community-based Trainers in Alberta.* Muttart Foundation [online]. Available: www.onestep.on.ca/whatsnew/pdfs/Competition.pdf [February 10, 2004]. 5

Hourston, S. (2000). *Wellness and Disability Initiative: Health and Homelessness.* [online]. Available: www.bccpd.bc.ca/trmarapou/health/html [June 1, 2000]. 9

Howlett, D. (1992, May/June). "The Arithmetic, Chemistry, and Art of Coalition Projects." *Action Canada Dossier* 37: 7–9. Action Canada Network. 3

HRDC (Human Resources Development Canada). (1994). *Annual Report, 1993–1994.* Ottawa: Author. 4

———. (1998a). *Canada and New Brunswick Sign New Agreement to Assist People with Disabilities* [online]. Available: www.hrdc-drhc.gc.ca/common/news/ dept9851.shtml [June 28, 2000]. 14

———. (1998b). *The Government of Canada's Record on Disability Issues* [online]. Available: www.hrdc-drhc.gc.ca/common/news/9821b4.html [June 28, 2000]. 14

———. (1999a November). *Lessons Learned: Reconnecting Social Assistance Recipients to the Labour Market.* Catalogue No. SP-AH123T-11-99E [online]. Available: www11.hrdc-drhc.gc.ca/pls/edd/RSARLM.lhtml [April 18, 2004]. 9

———. (1999b July). Office for Disability Issues. *Future Directions: The Challenges Facing Persons with Disabilities* [online]. Available: www.hrdc-drhc.gc.ca/ socpol/reports/disability/sect3e.shtml [June 8, 2000]. 14

———. (2000 March). *Reconnecting Social Assistance Recipients to the Labour Market: Lessons Learned: Final Report*: Evaluation and Data Development Strategic Policy: Human Resources Development Canada, Catalogue #SPAH123E-03-00 [online]. Available: www11.hrdc-drhc.gc.ca/pls/edd/SARLM.lhtml [April 18, 2004]. 9

———. (2001). "The Proportion of Vulnerable Children Does Not Change, but Some of the Children Do." *Applied Research Bulletin: Winter/Spring 2001* 7(1): 4–5 [online]. Available: www11.sdc.gc.ca/en/cs/sp/arb/publications/bulletins/ 2001-000004/2001-000004.pdf [May 18, 2004]. 10

——. (2002a December). *Advancing the Inclusion of Persons with Disabilities*: A Government of Canada Report [online]. Available: gateway.cotr.bc.ca/Downloads/AdvnIncDisabil.pdf [May 29, 2004]. 14

——. (2002b March). *Child Welfare in Canada 2000: British Columbia: Administration and Service Delivery* [online]. Available: www.hrdc-drhc.gc.ca/sp-ps/socialp-psociale/cfs/rpt2000/rpt2000e_12.shtml [February 15, 2004]. 7

——. (2002c October 23). *The History of Canada's Public Pensions: 1867–1914 Old Age and Poverty: Researcher's Summary.* Civilization.ca [online]. Available: www.civilization.ca/hist/pensions/cpp-m1867summary_e.html [January 19, 2004]. 1

——. (2002d September 10). *The History of Canada's Public Pensions: 1968–1989: Reaching More Canadians: Political Events.* Civilization.ca [online]. Available: www.civilization.ca/hist/pensions/cpp-a68-pe_e.html [January 22, 2004]. 3, 4

——. (2003a). *Defining Disability: A Complex Issue.* Office for Disability Issues [online]. Available: dsp-psd.communication.gc.ca/Collection/RH37-4-3-2003E.pdf [May 29, 2004]. 14

——. (2003b March). *Evaluation of the National Homelessness Initiative: Implementation and Early Outcomes of the HRDC-based Components: Final Report.* Strategic Evaluations, Evaluation and Data Development: Strategic Policy: Catalogue No. RH63-2/203-03-03E [online]. Available: www21.hrdc-drhc.gc.ca/initiative/evaluationreport/index_e.asp [April 18, 2004]. 9

——. (2003c July 3). *Understanding Homelessness: Reviewing the Numbers* [online]. Available: www21.hrdc-drhc.gc.ca/homelessness/h02_e.asp [April 18, 2004]. 9

——. (2003d). *Disability in Canada: A 2001 Profile* [online]. Available: www.sdc.gc.ca/en/hip/odi/documents/PALS/PALS.pdf [May 29, 2004]. 14

——. (2004a January 12). *About the Initiative.* National Homelessness Initiative [online]. Available: www21.hrdc-drhc.gc.ca/initiative/index_e.asp [April 18, 2004]. 9

——. (2004b March 26). *Employment Assistance Services* [online]. Available: www.hrsdc.gc.ca/en/epb/sid/cia/grants/eas/desc_eas.shtml [April 18, 2004]. 9

——. (2004c). *First Nations and Inuit Child Care Initiative* [online]. Available: www17.hrdc-drhc.gc.ca/ARO-BRA/ARO.cfm?Menu=childcaremenu2_e.cfm&File=Child_Care/fnicc_e.cfm&SubMenu=Child. Available: [May 16, 2004]. 12

Hum, D. (1985). "Social Security Reform During the 1970s." In J.S. Ismael, ed., *Canadian Social Welfare Policy*, pp. 29–47. Kingston and Montreal: McGill-Queen's University Press. 3

Hurley, M.C. (2002 October 10). *Bill C-7: The First Nations Governance Act.* Law and Government, Division Library of Parliament, Legislative Summaries [online]. Available: www.parl.gc.ca/common/Bills_ls.asp?Parl=37&Ses=2&ls=C7 [May 16, 2004]. 12

Ibbitson, J. (2003 February 19). "Federal Budget: Big Government Is Back in Town." *Globe and Mail:* A1 [online]. Available: www.globeandmail.com/servlet/Article News/TPStory/LAC/20030219/UIBBIN/TPColumnists/ [February 4, 2004]. 4

IMPACS (Institute for Media, Policy and Civil Society). (2002 March). *Let Charities Speak: Report of the Charities and Advocacy Dialogue* [online]. Available: www.ginsler.com/documents/let_charities_speak.pdf [February 10, 2004]. 8

INAC (Indian and Northern Affairs Canada). (1990). *The Canadian Indian.* Hull-Ottawa: Minister of Supply and Services Canada. 12

———. (1993 May). *The International Year of the World's Indigenous People.* Information Sheet No. 58. Ottawa: Author. 12

———. (1998 November). *The International Decade of the World's Indigenous People* [online]. Available: www.ainc-inac.gc.ca/pr/info/info123_e.html [March 13, 2004]. 12

———. (2001 October). *First Nations Child and Family Services* [online]. Available: www.ainc-inac.gc.ca/nr/iss/fnf_e.html [May 16, 2004]. 12

———. (2002a October 9). *First Nations Governance and Independent Claims Body Legislation Reinstated* [online]. Available: www.ainc-inac.gc.ca/nr/prs/s-d2002/2-02204_e.html [May 9, 2004]. 12

———. (2002b August). *Evaluation of Self-Government Negotiations Funding Support Program* [online]. Available: www.ainc-inac.gc.ca/pr/pub/ae/ev/00-20_e.pdf [May 16, 2004]. 12

———. (2002c October). *Words First: An Evolving Terminology Relating to Aboriginal Peoples in Canada: Aboriginal Self-Government.* Communications Branch, Indian and Northern Affairs Canada [online]. Available: www.ainc-inac.gc.ca/pr/pub/wf/trmrslt_e.asp?term=3 [May 13, 2004]. 12

———. (2003 July). *Individuals Responsible for Indian and Northern Affairs in Canada, 1755 to 2003* [online]. Available: www.ainc-inac.gc.ca/pr/info/irp_e.html [May 13, 2004]. 12

Industry Canada. (2001a March). *Overview of Canada's Service Economy: The Service Economy at a Glance* [online]. Available: strategis.ic.gc.ca/pics/sc/service-eng.pdf [January 31, 2004]. 2

———. (2001b June). *Public Private Partnerships: A Canadian Guide.* Service Industries [online]. Available: strategis.ic.gc.ca/epic/internet/inpupr-bdpr.nsf/vwapj/guide-e.pdf/$FILE/guide-e.pdf [February 9, 2004]. 5

———. (2003). *Conference Overview: Industry Canada Presents a Conference on Service Industries and Knowledge-Based Economy* [online]. Available: strategis.ic.gc.ca/SSG/ra01866e.html [November 10, 2003]. 2

Information Centre on Aboriginal Health. (2004). *Programs and Services* [online]. Available: www.icah.ca/content/en/programs/ [June 13, 2004]. 12

Institute for the Prevention of Child Abuse. (1994). *Stop the Hurt.* Toronto: Rotary Club of Toronto (Don Valley). 1

Institute on Goverance. (2004). *Learning Tools: Goverance Basics: What Is Governance? Getting to a Definition* [online]. Available: www.iog.ca/boardgovernance/html/gov_wha.html [February 12, 2004]. 6

Interfaith Social Assistance Reform Coalition. (2001). *ISARC: We're Growing Up!* Copyright 2001–2006 [online]. Available: www.isarc.ca/aboutus_grow.htm [February 9, 2004]. 5

International Federation of Social Workers. (2000 July). *Definition of Social Work.* International Federation of Social Workers [online]. Available: www.ifsw.org/Publications/4.6e.pub.html [February 15, 2004]. 7

International Labour Organization. (2001 October 15–19). *The Impact of Decentralization and Privatization on Municipal Services: Joint Meeting on the Impact of Decentralization and Privatization on Municipal Services* [online]. Available: www.ilo.org/public/english/dialogue/sector/techmeet/jmms01/jmmsr.pdf 2001 [February 4, 2004]. 4

International Reform Monitor. (2004 March). "Social Policy, Labour Market Policy and Industrial Relations" [online]. Available: www.reformmonitor.org/pdf-cache/doc_stq_fp-id-104.pdf [March 31, 2004]. 2, 10

Irving, A. (1987). "Federal–Provincial Issues in Social Policy." In S.A. Yelaja, ed., *Canadian Social Policy,* rev. ed., pp. 326–49. Waterloo: Wilfrid Laurier University Press. 2

Jackson, A. (2001 June 18). *Globalization and Progressive Social Policy.* Canadian Council on Social Development [online]. Available: www.ccsd.ca/pubs/2001/ajglob.htm [January 31, 2004]. 2

———. (2003a December). *Paul Martin's Economic Record: Living Standards of Working Families and Prospects for Future Prosperity: Alternative Federal Budget: Technical Paper #2: Summary.* Canadian Centre for Policy Alternatives [online]. Available: www.policyalternatives.ca/afb/afb2004martinecorecordsum.html [April 18, 2004]. 9

———. (2003b February 24). *The U-Turn Budget?* Canadian Labour Congress [online]. Available: action.web.ca/home/clccomm/en_op-ed.shtml?sh_itm=495c1c61877f69c11dc45680d80c8728 [February 4, 2004]. 4

Jackson, A., and M. Sanger. (2003). *When Worlds Collide: Implications of International Trade and Investment Agreements for Non-Profit Social Services.* Canadian Centre for Policy Alternatives and Canadian Council on Social Development [online]. Available: www.policyalternatives.ca/publications/wwc.pdf [January 31, 2004]. 2

Jaco, R.M. (2001). "Social Agencies and Human Service Organizations." In J.C. Turner and F.J. Turner, eds., *Canadian Social Welfare,* 4th ed., pp. 362–87. Toronto: Pearson Education Canada. 5, 6, 8

Jacobs, E., F. Storey, and F. Poirier. (1992 October 19). *Liberating Our Children, Liberating Our Nations.* Report of the Aboriginal Committee Community Panel Child Protection Legislation Review in British Columbia [online]. Available: www.turtleisland.org/healing/liberate.doc [May 13, 2004]. 12

JamiesonHartGraves Consulting. (2002 March 28). *Aboriginal Women's Program Family Violence Initiative Learning Circle March 16 and 17, 2002 Report* [online]. Available: www.pch.gc.ca/progs/pa-app/progs/ppfa-awp/LC_report.pdf [May 16, 2004]. 12

Janzen, C., and O. Harris. (1997). *Family Treatment in Social Work Practice,* 3rd ed. Itasca: F.E. Peacock. 8

Jedwab, J. (2003). *Diversity Popular among Canadians as Federal Government Proclaims National Multiculturalism Day* [online]. Available: www.acs-aec.ca/Polls/Poll45.pdf [May 27, 2004]. 13

Jenson, J. (1998 November 27). *Mapping Social Cohesion: The State of Canadian Research.* Canadian Policy Research Networks, Inc. [online]. Available: cprn.com/en/doc.cfm?doc=180# Study No. F/03 [August 2, 2004]. 4

———. (2003a May 12). *Canadian Economic and Social Policy: North American or Mid-Atlantic?* Canadian Policy Research Networks, Inc. [online]. Available: www.cprn.org/en/doc.cfm?doc=356 [January 31, 2004]. 2

———. (2003b February 7). *Redesigning the "Welfare Mix" for Families: Policy Challenges.* Canadian Policy Research Networks, Inc [online]. Available: www.cprn.org/en/doc.cfm?doc=157 [April 18, 2004]. 9

———. (2003c November 21). *Social Citizenship, Governance and Social Policy.* Canada Research Chair in Citizenship and Governance. [online]. Available: www.cccg.umontreal.ca/PDF/Korea_paper_1_.pdf [April 18, 2004]. 9

Jill Florence Lackey & Associates. (2004). *What Is a Needs Assessment?* [online]. Available: my.execpc.com/~lackassc/page3.html [February 26, 2004]. 6

Johansen, R. (1996). *Poverty, Virtue, and Grace.* Acton Institute for the Study of Religion and Liberty [online]. Available: www.acton.org/publicat/books/remedy/first.html [February 13, 2004]. 1

Johnson, A.W. (1987). "Social Policy in Canada: The Past as It Conditions the Present." In S.B. Seward, ed., *The Future of Social Welfare Systems in Canada and the United Kingdom: Proceedings of a Canada/UK Colloquium, October 17–18, 1986, Ottawa/Meech Lake.* pp. 29–70. Halifax: Institute for Research on Public Policy. 3

Johnson, L.C., R.W. McClelland, and C.D. Austin. (2000). *Social Work Practice: A Generalist Approach,* Can. ed. Scarborough: Prentice-Hall Canada. 7, 8

Johnson, L.C., C.L. Schwartz, and D.S. Tate. (1997). *Social Welfare: A Response to Human Need,* 4th ed. Needham Heights: Allyn & Bacon. 1, 7

Johnston, P. (1983). *Native Children and the Child Welfare System.* Toronto: Canadian Council on Social Development in association with James Lorimer and Company. 12

Jones, C., L. Clark, J. Grusec, R. Hart, G. Plickert, and L. Tepperman. (2002 March). *Poverty, Social Capital, Parenting and Child Outcomes in Canada, Final Report.* Applied Research Branch, Strategic Policy, Human Resources Development Canada, Catalogue #SP-557-01-03E [online]. Available: dsp-psd.communication.gc.ca/Collection/RH63-1-557-01-03E.pdf [April 18, 2004]. 9

Justice as Healing (Newsletter of Aboriginal Concepts of Justice). (1995 Winter). *Report of the Hollow Water First Nations Community Holistic Circle Healing (C.H.C.H.): Appendix 3.* Cited in Native Law Centre of Canada [online]. Available: www.usask.ca/nativelaw/publications/jah/seeds.html [May 25, 2004]. 12

Kahn, S. (1995). "Community Organization." In R.L. Edwards, ed., *Encyclopedia of Social Work,* 19th ed., vol. 1, pp. 569–76. Washington, D.C.: National Association of Social Workers. 8

Keung, N. (2004 May 10). "Ethnic Mini-Cities on Rise: StatsCan." *Toronto Star* [online]. Available: www.thestar.com/NASApp/cs/ContentServer?pagename= thestar/Layout/Article_Type1&c=Article&cid=1078873816531&call_pageid= 968332188492&col=968793972154 [May 27, 2004]. 13

Kirkwood, T. and A. Pangarkar. (2003). "Workplace Learning—Beyond the Classroom." *CMA Management* (May): 10–12 [online]. Available: www.workopolis. com/content/partners/cma/pdf/may2003-article7.pdf [February 12, 2004]. 6

Kirmayer, G., M. Brass, and C.L. Tait. (2000). "The Mental Health of Aboriginal Peoples: Transformations of Identity and Community." *Canadian Journal of Psychiatry* 45: 607–16 [online]. Available: www.cpa-apc.org/Publications/ Archives/CJP/2000/Sep/InReview.asp [May 16, 2004]. 12

Klein, S. and A. Long. (2003 June). *A Bad Time to Be Poor: An Analysis of British Columbia's New Welfare Policies.* Canadian Centre for Policy Alternatives [online]. Available: www.policyalternatives.ca/bc/welfare.pdf [February 9, 2004]. 5

Knutson, R.D., and R.F. Ochoa. (2003). *Convergence, Harmonization, and Compatibility under NAFTA: A 2003 Status Report.* Farm Foundation [online]. Available: www.farmfoundation.org/farmpolicy/knutson-ochoa.pdf [January 31, 2004]. 2

Kroeger, A. (1996). "Changing Course: The Federal Government's Program Review of 1994–95." In A. Armit and J. Bourgault, eds., *Hard Choices or No Choices: Assessing Program Review,* pp. 21–28. Toronto: Institute of Public Administration of Canada. 4

Kuiken, J. (2001 Fall). "Presidents Report." *The Advocate* 16(3): 8–9 [online]. Available: www.acsw.ab.ca/publications/advocate_fall_2001.PDF [March 23, 2004]. 7

Laidlaw Foundation. (2002). *Laidlaw Foundation's Youth Engagement Program Grants 2002* [online]. Available: www.laidlawfdn.org/files/2002_youth_engagement.pdf [May 24, 2004]. 10

Lane, P., Jr., M. Bopp, J. Bopp, and J. Norris. (2002). *Mapping the Healing Journey: The Final Report of a First Nation Research Project on Healing in Canadian Aboriginal Communities.* Solicitor General Canada and the Aboriginal Healing Foundation [online]. Available: www.psepc-sppcc.gc.ca/publications/abor_corrections/ pdf/apc2002_e.pdf [May 16, 2004]. 12

Lapierre-Adamcyk, E. (2002 June). *Family Transformation and Labour Market.* Family Transformation and Social Cohesion [online]. Available: www.ssc.uwo.ca/sociology/ ftsc/Family%20Transformations%20and%20Labour%20Market.pdf [February 1, 2004]. 2

LaRoque, E.D. (1994 March). "Violence in Aboriginal Communities." Reprinted from *The Path to Healing: Royal Commissions on Aboriginal Peoples.* Health Canada [online]. Available: www.hc-sc.gc.ca/hppb/familyviolence/pdfs/vac.pdf [May 9, 2004]. 12

Latimer, J. (1998). *The Consequences of Child Maltreatment: A Reference Guide for Health Practitioners.* Health Canada: Family Violence Prevention Unit [online]. Available: www.hc-sc.gc.ca/hppb/familyviolence/html/nfntsconsequencevio_e.html [April 29, 2004]. 10

Lautenschlager, J. (1992). *Volunteering: A Traditional Canadian Value.* Voluntary Action Program, Canadian Heritage [online]. Available: www.nald.ca/fulltext/heritage/ComPartnE/Tradval1.htm [January 22, 2004]. 3

Lawton, V. (2000 February 8). "Same-Sex Legislation Is Expected This Week." *Toronto Star* [online]. Available: www.egale.ca/index.asp?item=190&version=EN [April 28, 2004]. 10

Lazar, H. (2000 August). *The Social Union Framework Agreement: Lost Opportunity or New Beginning?* School of Policy Studies, Queens University, Working Paper 3 [online]. Available: www.queensu.ca/sps/WorkingPapers/files/sps_wp_03.pdf [February 2, 2004]. 2

Lecomte, R. (2001). "Distinguishing Features of Social Work Education in Canada." In J.C. Turner and F.J. Turner, eds., *Canadian Social Welfare,* 4th ed., pp. 498–504. Toronto: Pearson Education Canada. 7

Legislative Review Committee. (2003 March). *Report on the Review of the Protection for Persons in Care Act* [online]. Available: www.cd.gov.ab.ca/helping_albertans/persons_in_care/Leg_review/CommitteeReport_March2003.pdf [May 12, 2004]. 11

Lerner, S. (2003). *Proceedings and Final Report: Working Conference on Strategies to Ensure Economic Security for All Canadians* [online]. Available: www.ccsd.ca/events/2003/lerner.pdf [March 7, 2004]. 8

LeRoy, S. and J. Clemens (2003 September 25). *Ending Welfare as We Know It: Lessons from Canada.* National Center for Policy Analysis: Brief Analysis: No. 457 [online]. Available: www.ncpa.org/pub/ba/ba457/ [February 1, 2004]. 2, 4

Lewington, J. (2002 March 13). "Urban Centres Blossom." *Globe and Mail* [online]. Available: www.globeandmail.com/special/census/2001/stories/20020313-pe-urban.html [February 1, 2004]. 2

Liberal Party of Canada. (2004a). *Platform: Chapter 2: Strengthening Our Social Foundations* [online]. Available: www.liberal.ca/platform_e_3.aspx [August 4, 2004]. 10 11

——. (2004b June 1). *Seniors, the Disabled, and Family Caregivers Get a $2.5 Billion Boost* [online]. Available: www.liberal.ca/news_e.aspx?site=news&news=580 [June 13, 2004]. 11

Liberal Task Force on Seniors. (2004 February). *Liberal Task Force Report* [online]. Available: www.liberal.parl.gc.ca/seniors/documents/seniors_report_en.pdf [May 9, 2004]. 11

Lipman, E.L., M.H. Boyle, M.D. Dooley, and D.R. Offerd. (1998 October). *Children and Lone Mother Families: An Investigation of Factors Influencing Child Well-Being.* Ottawa: Applied Research Branch, Strategic Policy, Human Resources Development Canada. 10

Lutherwood. (2004). *Residential Services* [online]. Available: www.lutherwoodcoda.com/MentalHealth/residential.asp [April 29, 2004]. 10

MacDonald, A. and R. Adachi. (2001). *Regulation of Social Work Practice in Canada: Canadian Social Work Forum 2001.* CASW [online]. Available: www.casw-acts.ca/SW-Forum/CdnSWForum-Regulation.htm [February 15, 2004]. 7

MacMurchy, H. (1932). *Sterilization? Birth Control?* Toronto: Macmillan. 14

Manitoba Family Services and Housing. (2004). *Child Related Income Support Program* [online]. Available: www.gov.mb.ca/fs/assistance/crisp.html [January 19, 2004]. 1

Marcoux, L. (2002). "Communication and Social Cohesion in a Post-September 11th World." *Horizons* 5(2): 14 [online]. Available: policyresearch.gc.ca/v5n2_e.pdf [May 27, 2004]. 13

Marsh, J.H. (Ed.) (various authors) (2003). *The Canadian Encyclopedia* [online]. Available www.thecanadianencyclopedia.com [January 19, 2004]. 1

Marsh, L. (1943). "Report on Social Security for Canada." In M. Bliss, ed., *The Social History of Canada*, 1975 reprint. Toronto: University of Toronto Press. 3

Marsh, L. (1950). *The Welfare State: Is It a Threat to Canada?* Proceedings on the Canadian Conference on Social Work, 1950. Ottawa: Canadian Conference on Social Work. 3

Mawhiney, A.M. (2001). "First Nations in Canada." In J.C. Turner and F.J. Turner, eds., *Canadian Social Welfare,* 4th ed., pp. 153–66. Toronto: Pearson Education Canada. 12

Max-Neef, M.A. (1991). *Human Scale Development: Conception, Application and Further Reflections.* The Apex Press. 1

Maxwell, J. (2003a September 19). *Policy Skills and Social Policy.* Canadian Policy Research Networks, Inc. [online]. Available: www.cprn.com/en/doc.cfm?doc=389 [January 19, 2004]. 1

———. (2003b May 2). *What Is Social Cohesion, and Why Do We Care?* Canadian Policy Research Networks, Inc. [online]. Available: www.cprn.com/en/doc.cfm?doc=210 [January 19, 2004]. 1, 2

McCarthy, S. (1995, March 1). "Cuts Keep Programs Alive: Martin." *Toronto Star:* A10. 4

———. (2002 September 30). "PM Plans More Cash for Health." *Globe and Mail* [online]. Available: www.globeandmail.com/servlet/ArticleNews/front/RTGAM/20020930/wlibs0929/Front/homeBN/breakingnews [February 4, 2004]. 4

McClosky, D. (1998). "Newcomers: Immigrant Families Adapting to Life in Canada." *Transition* 28(3): 2. 13

McDonald, G. (2001). "Evaluation in Social Welfare." In J.C. Turner and F.J. Turner, eds., *Canadian Social Welfare*, 4th ed., pp. 435–42. Toronto: Pearson Education Canada. 6

McDougall, B. (2001 June 21). *Free Trade: Ten Years On. Canadian Institute of International Affairs* [online]. Available: www.ciia.org/speech7.htm [January 31, 2004]. 2

McGill University, School of Social Work, Greater Victoria Survey Committee. (1931). *Problems in Family Welfare, Relief and Child Development.* Montreal: Author. 8

McGilly, F. (1998). *An Introduction to Canada's Public Social Services: Understanding Income and Health Programs,* 2nd ed. Don Mills: Oxford University Press. 3

McIntyre, L., S. Connor, and J. Warren. (1998 October). *A Glimpse of Child Hunger in Canada.* Hull: Applied Research Branch, Strategic Policy, Human Resources Development Canada. 9

McKenzie, B and V. Morrissette (2003 April). "Social Work Practice with Canadians of Aboriginal Background: Guidelines for Respectful Social Work." *Envision: The Manitoba Journal of Child Welfare* 2(1). 12

McKeown, L. (2003). *Fact Sheets: Volunteering in Canada.* Canadian Centre for Philanthropy [online]. Available: www.givingandvolunteering.ca/fact-sheets/2000_CA_volunteering_in_canada.asp [February 15, 2004]. 7

McMahon, M.O. (1994). *Advanced Generalist Practice with an International Perspective.* Englewood Cliffs: Prentice Hall. 7

McMullen, K., and R. Brisbois. (2003 December). *Coping with Change: Human Resource Management in Canada's Non-Profit Sector.* CPRN Research Series on Human Resources in the Non-profit Sector No/4. Canadian Policy Research Networks [online]. Available: www.cprn.com/documents/25445_en.pdf [February 13, 2004]. 6

McNamera, C. (1998). *Basic Guide to Program Evaluation.* Management Assistance Program for Nonprofits [online]. Available: www.mapnp.org/library/evaluatn/fnl_eval.htm [February 12, 2004]. 6

McQuaig, L. (1995). *Shooting the Hippo: Death by Deficit and Other Canadian Myths.* Toronto: Penguin. 4

Meinhard, A., and M. Foster. (2002). *Responses of Canada's Voluntary Organizations to Shifts in Social Policy: A Provincial Perspective.* Centre for Voluntary Sector Studies. ISTR Conference Working Papers, Volume III, Cape Town Conference [online]. Available: www.jhu.edu/~istr/conferences/capetown/volume/meinhard.pdf [February 1, 2004]. 2

Melchers, R. (1999). "Local Governance of Social Welfare: Local Reform in Ontario in the Nineties." *Canadian Review of Social Policy* 43: 29–57. 5, 9

Mendelsohn, M. (2002 November 21). "Five Facets of the Collective Canadian Mindset." *Opinion Canada* 4(42). Centre for Research and Information on Canada [online]. Available: www.cric.ca/en_html/opinion/opv4n42.html [February 9, 2004]. 5

Mendelson. M. (1993). *Social Policy in Real Time*. Ottawa: Caledon Institute of Social Policy. 2, 4

Meston, J. (1993). *Child Abuse and Neglect Prevention Programs*. Ottawa: Vanier Institute of the Family. 10

Michaud, S., C. Cotton, and K. Bishop. (2004 February). *Exploration of Methodological Issues in the Development of the Market Basket Measure of Low Income for Human Resources Development Canada*. Statistics Canada [online]. Available: www.statcan.ca/ english/research/75F0002MIE/75F0002MIE2004001.pdf [May 22, 2004]. 9

Michels, K. (1996 July). *Creating a Capacity for Change in Health Promotion and the Non-Profit Sector: A Discussion Paper on Healthy Organizational Change*. Ontario Prevention Clearinghouse [online]. Available: www.opc.on.ca/english/our_ programs/hlth_promo/resources/healthy/healthy_chng.htm [March 7, 2004]. 8

Milan, A. (2000). "One Hundred Years of Families." *Canadian Social Trends* (Spring): 2–12. 10

Ministerial Council on Social Policy Reform and Renewal. (1996). *Premiers Release Report of the Ministerial Council on Social Policy Reform and Renewal: Report to Premiers*. Government of Newfoundland and Labrador [online]. Available: www.gov.nf.ca/exec/premier/social/ENGLISH.HTM [March 1, 2004]. 2

Mishra, R. (1981). *Society and Social Policy: Theories and Practice of Welfare,* 2nd ed. London and Basingstoke: Macmillan Press. 3

———. (2001). "The Political Bases of Canadian Social Welfare. In J.C. Turner and F.J. Turner, eds., *Canadian Social Welfare,* 4th ed., pp. 54–66. Toronto: Pearson Education Canada. 2

MLA Committee to Review Low-Income Programs. (2001 November). *Low-Income Programs Review—What We Heard*. Alberta Human Resources and Employment [online]. Available: www3.gov.ab.ca/hre/lir/pdf/WhatWeHeard.pdf [February 12, 2004]. 8

Montgomery, J.E. (1977). "The Housing Patterns of Older People." In R.A. Kalish, ed., *The Later Years*, pp. 253–61. Belmont: Wadsworth Publishing. 11

Morel, S. (2002 September). *The Insertion Model or the Workfare Model? The Transformation of Social Assistance within Quebec and Canada*. Status of Women Canada [online]. Available www.swc-cfc.gc.ca/pubs/0662323467/ 200209_0662323467_e.pdf [January 19, 2004]. 3

Morgan, J.S. (1961). "Social Welfare Services in Canada." In M. Oliver, ed., *Social Purpose for Canada*, pp. 130–67. Toronto: University of Toronto Press. 3

Moscovitch, A. (2003). "Welfare State." In J.A. Marsh, ed., *The Canadian Encyclopedia, 2003* [online]. Available: www.thecanadianencyclopedia.com/PrinterFriendly. cfm?Params=A1ARTA0008518 [January 22, 2004]. 3

Moscovitch, A., and G. Drover. (1987). "Social Expenditures and the Welfare State: The Canadian Experience in Historical Perspective." In A. Moscovitch and

J. Albert, eds., *The Benevolent State: The Growth of Welfare in Canada,* pp. 13–43. Toronto: Garamond Press. 3

Moylum, M. (2000). *What Kind of Canada Do We Want in the 21st century?* 2.2: Culture, Cultural Goods, Trade and Globalization. Pearson-Shoyama Institute [online]. Available: www.pearson-shoyama.ca/whatkind/2-2.html [May 27, 2004]. 13

Muegge, J. and N. Ross. (1996 November). *Volunteers: The Heart of Community Organizations.* Ministry of Agriculture and Food: Government of Ontario [online]. Available: www.gov.on.ca/OMAFRA/english/rural/facts/96-017.htm [February 15, 2004]. 7

Mullaly, B. (1997). *Structural Social Work.* Toronto: Oxford University Press. 8

National Aboriginal Health Organization. (2004). *Briefing Note Re: Speech from the Throne, February 2004* [online]. Available: www.naho.ca/firstnations/english/pdf/ BN_speech_from_throne_2004.pdf [May 29, 2004]. 14

National Advisory Council on Aging. (1993). *The NACA Position on Canada's Oldest Seniors: Maintaining the Quality of Their Lives,* Document No. 13. Ottawa: Author. 11

———. (1995). *The NACA Position on Community Services in Health Care for Seniors: Progress and Challenges* [online]. Available: www.hc-sc.gc.ca/seniors-aines/naca/ position/16_community_services/pdf/position16_e.pdf [May 13, 2004]. 11

———. (2003). *Seniors in Canada 2003: Interim Report Card* [online]. Available: www.hc-sc.gc.ca/seniors-aines/naca/report_card2003/pdf/ Interim%20Report%20card%202003_e.pdf [May 9, 2004]. 11

National Anti-Poverty Organization. (2002 October 17). *International Day for the Eradication of Poverty: Governments Targeting Poor People Instead of Poverty.* Media Room. [online]. Available: www.napo-onap.ca/media_room.htm [March 9, 2004]. 9

———. (2003 October). *Brief to House of Commons Standing Committee on Finance* [online]. Available: www.napo-onap.ca/House%20of%20Commons.htm [February 4, 2004]. 4

———. (2004). *History* [online]. Available: www.napo-onap.ca/history.htm [March 7, 2004]. 8

National Children's Agenda. (1999 May 7). *Federal-Provincial-Territorial Council on Social Policy Renewal: Saskatoon, Saskatchewan: Federal, Provincial and Territorial Governments Launch Dialogue Process for National Children's Agenda.* News Release [online]. Available: socialunion.gc.ca/news/99may7e.html [April 29, 2004]. 10

National Clearinghouse on Family Violence. (2002). *Family Violence and People with Intellectual Disabilities.* Health Canada [online]. Available: www.hc-sc.gc.ca/ hppb/familyviolence/pdfs/fvintellectu_e.pdf [May 29, 2004]. 14

National Council of Welfare. (1990). *Pension Reform.* Ottawa: Author. 4

———. (1995). *The 1995 Budget and Block Funding.* Ottawa: Author. 4

———. (1997 Autumn). *Another Look at Welfare Reform.* Ottawa: Author. 9

———. (1999a Summer). *A Pension Primer.* Ottawa: Author. 11

———. (1999b Autumn). *Poverty Profile, 1997.* Ottawa: Author. 11

———. (2001 Winter) *The Cost of Poverty: Vol. 115.* Ottawa: National Council of Welfare. 9

———. (2002a Summer). *Poverty Profile 1999* [online]. Available: www.ncwcnbes.net/ htmdocument/reportpovertypro99/Introduction.html [February 1, 2004]. 2, 9

———. (2002b October). *The Social Union Framework Agreement (SUFA): Third Year Review: A Submission by the National Council of Welfare* [online]. Available: www.ncwcnbes.net/htmdocument/principales/Sufa.HTM [February 4, 2004]. 4

———. (2002c June 7 and 8). *Summary Report: National Council of Welfare's Welfare-to-Work Roundtable* [online]. Available: www.ncwcnbes.net/htmdocument/princi-pales/RoundtableWtoW.htm [February 4, 2004]. 4

———. (2003a October 20). *Recommendations on the Creation of the Canada Social Transfer: Presentation to the Liberal Caucus Social Policy Committee* [online]. Available: www.ncwcnbes.net/htmdocument/principales/ Oct2003-NCWPresentationtoLiberalCaucusSocialPolicyCommittee.pdf [February 4, 2004]. 4, 5

———. (2003b Spring). *Welfare Incomes 2002. Vol. 119.* Ottawa: Author. 1, 4, 9

———. (2004 Spring). *Income for Living? Vol. 120* [online]. Available: www. ncwcnbes.net/htmdocument/reportIFL/IFL_e.pdf [May 13, 2004]. 9

National Native Addictions Partnership Foundation Inc. (2000 December). *NNADAP Renewal Framework* [online]. Available: www.nnapf.org/ implementation%20framework%20final.pdf [May 16, 2004]. 12

National Union of Public and General Employees. (2000 May). *Workfare: A Low-Wage Strategy for the Canadian Economy.* National Union Research [online]. Available: www.nupge.ca/publications/Workfare%20complete.pdf [February 9, 2004]. 5

National Youth in Care Network. (1998). *The Real Deal: Rights, Resources and Opportunities for Youth in and from Care in Ontario: Types of Care and Placements* [online]. Available: www.hri.ca/realdeal/care.htm [April 29, 2004]. 10

New Brunswick Association for Community Living. (1992). *A Social Policy Framework for People with a Mental Handicap in New Brunswick.* Fredericton: Author. 14

New Democratic Party. (2004). *Fair Trade Not Free Trade: NDP on Trade and Globalization* [online]. Available: www.ndpontrade.parl.gc.ca/Alternatives.htm [February 1, 2004]. 2

Nicholson, W. (2001 September). *The Design of Summative Evaluations for the Employment Benefits and Support Measures (EBSM).* "Section: A. Defining the 'Participant' in Employment Benefits and Supports Measures (EBSM) Evaluations." Government of Canada, Catalogue #SP-AH168-09-01E [online]. Available: www11.hrdc-drhc.gc.ca/pls/edd/EBSM3_249003.htm [April 18, 2004]. 9

Nonprofit Quarterly. (2001 Fall). "Collaboration: A Generosity of Spirit." *Building Strategic Relationships* 8(3) [online]. Available: www.nonprofitquarterly.org/ print/346.html [February 10, 2004]. 5

Norvell, W. (2003 July 10). "We Are the Poor: Coming to Terms with Middle-Class Poverty." *Eye Weekly* [online]. Available: www.eye.net/eye/issue/issue_07.10.03/city/poor.html [April 18, 2004]. 9

O'Donnell, V and H. Tait. (2003 September). *Aboriginal Peoples Survey 2001—Initial Findings: Well-Being of the Non-Reserve Aboriginal Population: Health.* Statistics Canada [online]. Available: www.statcan.ca/english/freepub/89-589-XIE/pdf/89-589-XIE03001.pdf [May 25, 2004]. 12

O'Hara, K. (1997 November 28). *Reflexion—Securing the Social Union: Next Steps.* Canadian Policy Research Networks, Inc. [online]. Available: www.cprn.com/en/doc.cfm?doc=25 [March 13, 2004]. 2, 5

O'Sullivan, E. (1996). *Homelessness and Social Policy in the Republic of Ireland.* Occasional Paper Series No. 5. Dublin: Trinity College: Department of Social Studies. 9

OASW (Ontario Association of Social Workers). (2000 December). *The Professional Membership Association and the Regulatory Body: We Need Them Both* [online]. Available: www.oasw.org/eng/regbody.htm [February 15, 2004]. 7

OCISO (Ottawa Community Immigrant Services Organization). (2004). *Home* [online]. Available: www.ociso.org/index.htm [May 27, 2004]. 13

OCSWSSW (Ontario College of Social Workers and Social Service Workers). (2003). *About OCSWSSW* [online]. Available: www.ocswssw.org/sections/about_ocsw/generalinfo.html [February 15, 2004]. 7

Oderkirk, J. (1996). "Canada and Quebec Pension Plans." *Canadian Social Trends* (Spring): 8–15. 3

OECD (Organization for Economic Co-operation and Development). (1997). *Societal Cohesion and the Globalising Economy: What Does the Future Hold?* [online]. Available: www.oecd.org/dataoecd/38/19/17724730.pdf [August 2, 2004]. 4

———. (2001). *The Well-Being of Nations: The Role of Human and Social Capital.* Paris: Author. 2

Office of the Prime Minister. (2004 February 2). *Speech from the Throne* [online]. Available: www.pm.gc.ca/eng/sft-ddt.asp [February 9, 2004]. 4, 7

Olasky, M. (1995). *The Tragedy of American Compassion.* [online]. Available: www.olasky.com/Archives/toac.html [February 15, 2004]. 1

Ontario Metis Aboriginal Association. (2004). *Community Action Plan for Children* [online]. Available: www.omaa.org/page_20_Community_action_plan_for_children.htm [May 9, 2004]. 12

Ontario Ministry of Community and Social Services. (2000 February 7). *24 Straight Months of People Moving Off Welfare* [online]. Available: www.gov.on.ca/CSS/page/news/feb700.html [June 6, 2004]. 9

Osterkamp, L. (1991). "Family Caregivers: America's Primary Long-Term Care Resource." In H. Cox, ed., *Aging,* 7th ed., pp. 180–83. Guilford: Dushkin Publishing. 11

Overton, J. (1991 Winter). "Dissenting Opinions." *Perception* 15(1): 17–21. 2

PAGVS (Panel on Accountability and Governance in the Voluntary Sector). (1999 February). *Building on Strength: Improving Governance and Accountability in Canada's Voluntary Sector* [online]. Available: www.vsr-trsb.net/pagvs/Building_on_ Strength.htm [February 10, 2004]. 5, 6

Pal, L.A., ed. (1998). *How Ottawa Spends, 1998–99—Balancing Act: The Post-Deficit Mandate*, pp. 1–30. Toronto: Oxford University Press. 1

Panitch, M. (1998). "Forty Years On! Lessons from Our History." *Entourage* 11(4): 9–16. 14

Pape, B. (1990 December). *Self-Help/Mutual Aid*. Canadian Mental Health Association, Social Action Series [online]. Available: www.cmha.ca/english/sas/ selfhelp.htm [June 8, 2004]. 7

Paquet, G., and R. Shepherd. (1996). "The Program Review Process: A Reconstruction." In G. Swimmer, ed., *How Ottawa Spends, 1996–97: Life under the Knife* (pp. 39–72). Ottawa: Carleton University Press. 4

Parents Together. (2004). *Introduction* [online]. Available: www.parentstogether.ca [May 22, 2004]. 10

Parsons, T. (1960). *Structure and Process in Modern Societies*. New York: Free Press of Glencoe. 6

Patterson, E.P., II. (1987). "Native Peoples and Social Policy." In S.A. Yelaja, ed., *Canadian Social Policy*, rev. ed.: pp. 175–94. Waterloo: Wilfrid Laurier University Press. 12

Patterson, J. (2003 June). "Spousal Violence." In H. Johnson and K. Au Coin, eds., *Family Violence in Canada: A Statistical Profile, 2003*, pp. 4–20. Statistics Canada/Canadian Centre for Justice Statistics: Catalogue no. 85-224-XIE [online]. Available: www.hc-sc.gc.ca/hppb/familyviolence/pdfs/2003famvioprofil_e.pdf [April 29, 2004]. 10

Patterson, S.L., J.L Memmott, E.M. Brennan, and C.B. Germain. (1992 September). "Patterns of Natural Helping in Rural Areas: Implications for Social Work Research." *Social Work Research and Abstracts* 28(3): 22–28. 7

Peters, J. (2002 December 19). *A Fine Balance: Canadian Unions Confront Globalization*. Canadian Centre for Policy Alternatives [online]. Available: www.policyalternatives.ca/whatsnew/afinebalancepr.html [February 1, 2004]. 2

Peters, Y. (2003 February). *Federally Sentenced Women with Mental Disabilities: A Dark Corner in Canadian Human Rights*. "Part 1: Overview of Disability Discrimination." DisAbled Women's Action Network (DAWN) Canada [online]. Available: www.elizabethfry.ca/submissn/dawn/4.htm [May 29, 2004]. 14

Phillips, S., B.R. Little, and L. Goodine. (2002) *Caregiving Volunteers: A Coming Crisis?* Canadian Centre for Philanthropy [online]. Available: www.nonprofitscan.ca/ pdf/SR/Phillips-SR2-English-Web.pdf [May 13, 2004]. 11

Phillips, W. (1996 January). *A Comparison of Online, E-Mail, and In-Person Self-Help Groups Using Adult Children of Alcoholics as a Model.* New Jersey [online]. Available: www.rider.edu/~suler/psycyber/acoa.html#studying [February 15, 2004]. 7

Philp, M., and R. Mackie. (1998 April 17). "Beer Gibe Earns Harris a Blast." *Globe and Mail:* A1. 8

Picard, A. (2003). "Charities." In J.A. Marsh, ed., *The Canadian Encyclopedia, 2003* [online]. Available: www.thecanadianencyclopedia.com/PrinterFriendly.cfm?Params=A1ARTA0009235 [January 22, 2004]. 5

Picot, G., R. Morissette, and J. Myles. (2003 January). *Low-Income Intensity During the 1990s.* Statistics Canada, Analytical Studies Branch: Catalogue #11F0019MIE—No. 172 [online]. Available: www.statcan.ca/english/research/11F0019MIE/11F0019MIE2003172.pdf [April 18, 2004]. 9

Pillar-Voluntary Sector Network. (2003). *Pillar FAQ* [online]. Available: www.pillarv.com/_dox/media/pillar%20faq%20sheet.pdf [February 9, 2004]. 5

Podnieks, E., K. Pillemer, J.P. Nicholson, T. Shillington, and A. Frizzel. (1990). *National Survey on Abuse of the Elderly in Canada.* Toronto: Ryerson Polytechnical Institute. 11

Pold, H. (2001 Summer). "Trends in Part-time Work." *Perspectives: Statistics Canada* [online]. Available: www.statcan.ca/english/studies/75-001/archive/2001/pear2001013002s2a04.pdf [January 31, 2004]. 2

Porter, B. (1998 September 18). *Social Rights and the Question of a Social Charter: Presentation to the Symposium on the Social Union.* Canadian Centre for Policy Alternatives [online]. Available: www.equalityrights.org/cera/docs/social.htm [February 4, 2004]. 4

Poulin, G. (2003–2004 Winter). "Hidden Harm: The Abuse of Seniors." *Expression* 17(1). National Advisory Council on Aging [online]. Available: www.hc-sc.gc.ca/seniors-aines/naca/expression/17-1/pdf/exp17-1_e.pdf [May 9, 2004]. 11

Prairie Research Associates, Inc. (2000 March). *Reconnecting Social Assistance Recipients to the Labour Market: Lessons Learned:* Final Report: Evaluation and Data Development: Strategic Policy: Human Resources Development Canada [online]. Available: www11.hrdc-drhc.gc.ca/pls/edd/SARLM.lhtml [March 7, 2004]. 4

Prasil, S. (1993). "Seniors 75+: Lifestyles." *Canadian Social Trends* (Autumn): 26–29. 11

Pratt, A. (2002). *Treaty Implementation: Presenting the Issues, Discussing the Options.* Harold Cardinal and Associates for the Assembly of First Nations [online]. Available: www.afn.ca/Programs/Treaties%20and%20Lands/Doc/Treaty%20Implementation-March%202002.pdf [May 16, 2004]. 12

Premiers' Council on Canadian Health Awareness. (2002 August). *Strengthening Home and Community Care across Canada: A Collaborative Strategy: Report to the Annual Premiers' Conference* [online]. Available: www.premiersforhealth.ca/pdf/homecare_eng.pdf [May 9, 2004]. 11

Prime Minister's Caucus Task Force on Urban Issues. (2002 April). *Canada's Urban Strategy, a Vision for the 21st Century: Interim Report* [online]. Available: www.liberal.parl.gc.ca/urb/Vision_English.pdf [February 1, 2004]. 2

Prince, M.J. (1987). "How Ottawa Decides Social Policy: Recent Changes in Philosophy, Structure, and Process." In J.S. Ismael, ed., *The Canadian Welfare State: Evolution and Transition*, pp. 247–73. Edmonton: University of Alberta Press. 1

——. (2001 June). *Governing in an Integrated Fashion: Lessons from the Disability Domain.* Canadian Policy Research Networks, Inc. [online]. Available: www.cprn.org/en/doc.cfm?doc=172 [April 28, 2004]. 10, 14

Privy Council Office. (1999 June 15). *The Voluntary Sector—Society's Vital Third Pillar* [online]. Available: www.pco-bcp.gc.ca/volunteer/backgrounder3_e.htm [February 17, 2004]. 5

——. (2003a July 8). *Cabinet Directive on Lawmaking.* Government of Canada [online]. Available: www.pco-bcp.gc.ca/default.asp?Page=Publications&Language=E&doc=legislation/lmgcabinetdirective_e.htm [February 1, 2004]. 2

——. (2003b January 10). *Intergovernmental Relations by Sector: Health and Social Programs* [online]. Available: www.pco-bcp.gc.ca/aia/default.asp?Language=E&page=relations&sub=healthandsocialprograms [April 18, 2004]. 9

——. (2003c November 24). *Urban Aboriginal Strategy* [online]. Available: www.pco-bcp.gc.ca/interloc/default.asp?Language=E&Page=strategy [May 9, 2004]. 2, 12

Proctor, E.K., and L.E. Davis. (1994 May). "The Challenge of Racial Difference: Skills for Clinical Practice." *Social Work* 39(3): 314–23. 13

Pross, P. (1995). "Pressure Groups and Lobbying." In M.S. Whittington and G. Williams, eds., *Canadian Politics: Critical Approaches*, 2nd ed., pp. 425–53. Scarborough: Nelson Thomson Learning. 2

Province of Quebec (2001). *Federal Transfer Programs to the Provinces: Background Paper for Public Consultation* [online]. Available: www.desequilibrefiscal.gouv.qc.ca/en/pdf/federal_transfer.pdf [February 1, 2004]. 2

Public Safety and Emergency Preparedness Canada. (2003 November). *Cost-Benefit Analysis of a Community Healing Process.* Research Summary: Corrections Research and Development. Vol. 8, No. 6 [online]. Available: www.psepc-sppcc.gc.ca/publications/corrections/pdf/200311_e.pdf [May 25, 2004]. 12

Quarter, J. (1992). *Canada's Social Economy: Co-operatives, Non-Profits, and Other Community Enterprises.* Toronto: James Lorimer. 5

"Quebec Rejects Social Union Deal" (1999 February 1–15). *Canadian News Facts*, p. 5815. Toronto: MPL Communications. 3, 5

Rankin, L.P., and J. Vickers. (2001). *Women's Movements and State Feminism: Integrating Diversity into Public Policy.* Status of Women Canada [online]. Available: www.swc-cfc.gc.ca/pubs/0662657756/200105_0662657756_1_e.html [January 31, 2004]. 2

Raphael, D. (2003 Spring–Summer). "When Social Policy Is Health Policy: Why Increasing Poverty and Low Income Threatens Canadians' Health and Health Care System." *Canadian Review of Social Policy* 51 [online]. Available: dawn.thot.net/docs/dennisraphael1.doc [April 18, 2004]. 9

RCAP (Royal Commission on Aboriginal Peoples). (1996a). *Highlights from the Report of the Royal Commission on Aboriginal Peoples: Looking Forward, Looking Back* [online]. Available: www.ainc-inac.gc.ca/ch/rcap/rpt/lk_e.html [March 13, 2004]. 12

———. (1996b). *Volume 1: Looking Forward, Looking Back.* "Appendix A: The Commission's Terms of Reference" [online]. Available: www.ainc-inac.gc.ca/ch/rcap/sg/cga1_e.pdf [March 13, 2004]. 12

———. (1996c). *Volume 1: Looking Forward, Looking Back.* "Part 2: False Assumptions and a Failed Relationship. Chapter 9: The Indian Act. Section 8: The Indian Act and Indians: Children of the State" [online]. Available: www.ainc-inac.gc.ca/ch/rcap/sg/sg24_e.html#79 [March 13, 2004]. 12

———. (1996d). *Volume 3: Gathering Strength.* "Chapter 3: Health and Healing, Part B" [online]. Available: www.ainc-inac.gc.ca/ch/rcap/sg/ci3b_e.pdf [May 13, 2004]. 12, 14

Reay-Young, R. (2001). "Support Groups for Relatives of People Living with a Serious Mental Illness: An Overview." *International Journal of Psychosocial Rehabilitation* 5: 147–68 [online]. Available: www.psychosocial.com/psr/supgroup.html [February 15, 2004]. 7, 11

Rehman, L. and J. Gahagan. (2003 December). *Everyone Has a Right to a Home: A Community Needs Assessment of Harm Reduction Supports for the "Hard to House" in the Halifax Regional Municipality (HRM)* [online]. Available: www.region.halifax.ns.ca/planning/Homelessness/HarmReductionDec2003.pdf [April 18, 2004]. 9

Reichwein, B.P. (2002 December). *Benchmarks in Alberta's Public Welfare Services: History Rooted in Benevolence, Harshness, Punitiveness and Stinginess.* Edmonton: Alberta College of Social Workers [online]. Available: www.canadiansocialresearch.net/Alberta_welfare_history.pdf [April 18, 2004]. 9

Results–Resultats Canada. (2004 January). *Homelessness in Canada: The Need for a Federal Housing Program.* Action Sheet [online]. Available: www.results-resultats.ca/actions/2004-01-en.html [April 18, 2004]. 9

Rice, J.J., and M.J. Prince. (1993). "Life of Brian: A Social Policy Legacy." *Perception* 17(2): 6, 8, 30–33. 4

———. (2000). *Changing Politics of Canadian Social Policy.* Toronto: University of Toronto Press. 3, 4, 5

Richards, J. (1997). *Retooling the Welfare State: What's Right, What's Wrong, What Needs to Be Done?* Policy Study No. 31. Ottawa: C.D. Howe Institute. 1

Richmond, T. and J. Shields. (2003 June). *NGO Restructuring: Constraints and Consequences: Presentation to the 11th Biennial Social Welfare Policy Conference.*

"Evolution of Social Services Delivery." University of Ottawa [online]. Available: www.ocasi.org/downloads/NGO_Restructuring.pdf [February 9, 2004]. 5, 6, 7

Roberts, L. (2001 December). *Caught in the Middle: What Small, Non-Profit Organizations Need to Survive and Flourish: Voluntary Sector Initiative Report* [online]. Available: www.vsi-isbc.ca/eng/pdf/reports_caught.pdf [February 15, 2004]. 7

Robinson, T.R. (1999 July 29). *Social Security: Historical Statistics of Canada: Section C.* Statistics Canada [online]. Available: www.statcan.ca/english/freepub/ 11-516-XIE/sectionc/sectionc.htm [March 13, 2004]. 3

Roeher Institute. (1996). *Disability, Community, and Society: Exploring the Links.* North York: Author. 14

Rogow, S.M. (2002). *The Disability Rights Movement: The Canadian Experience.* International Conference on Autism, May 2002, Kamloops, B.C. International Special Education [online]. Available: www.internationalsped.com/magazines_ articles/The%20Disability%20Rights%20Movement%20Ed.1.pdf [May 29, 2004]. 14

Romanow, R.J. (2002 November). *Building on Values: The Future of Health Care in Canada: Final Report* [online]. Available: www.hc-sc.gc.ca/english/pdf/ care/romanow_e.pdf [February 4, 2004]. 4

Romeder, J.M. (1990). *The Self-Help Way: Mutual Aid and Health.* Ottawa: Canadian Council on Social Development. 7

Rondeau, G. (2001). *Challenges That Confront Social Education in Canada: Canadian Social Work Forum 2001.* CASW [online]. Available: www.casw-acts.ca/SW-Forum/ CdnSWForum-Challenges.htm [February 15, 2004]. 7

Rose, D., V. Preston, V., and I. Dyck. (2002). "Women, Gender and Immigration: Perspectives and Challenges." *Horizons* 5(2): 12–13 [online]. Available: policy research.gc.ca/v5n2_e.pdf [May 27, 2004]. 13

Rosell, S.A. (1999). "The Learning Organization." In S.A. Rosell, ed., *Renewing Governance: Governing by Learning in the Information Age,* pp. 60–85. Don Mills: Oxford University Press. 5

Rosenberg, M. (2002). Cited in *Inclusion for All: A Canadian Roadmap to Social Cohesion: Insights from Structured Conversations.* Department of Justice Canada [online]. Available: canada.justice.gc.ca/en/ps/rs/rep/comsocohe.pdf [January 19, 2004]. 1

Ross, D. (1995 Winter). "Who Will Speak for Canada's Children?" *Perception* 19(2): 2–3. 4

Ross, D.P. (1987). "Income Security." In S.A. Yelaja, ed., *Canadian Social Policy,* rev. ed., pp. 27–46. Waterloo: Wilfrid Laurier University Press. 3

Ross, D.P., K. Scott, and M.A. Kelly. (1996 November). *Overview: Children in Canada in the 1990s.* Hull: Human Resources Development Canada. 10

Ross, M.G. (1967). *Community Organization: Theory, Principles, and Practice,* 2nd ed. New York: Harper & Row. 8

Rothman, J. (1979). "Three Models of Community Organization Practice, Their Mixing and Phasing." In F.M. Cox, J.L. Erlich, J. Rothman, and J.E. Tropman, eds., *Strategies of Community Organization: A Book of Readings,* 3rd ed., pp. 25–45. Itasca: F.E. Peacock. 8

Rothman, L. (2003 November 7). *Sustaining the Momentum: Brief to the Standing Committee on Finance for the 2003 Pre-Budget Consultations.* Campaign 2000 [online]. Available: www.campaign2000.ca/res/briefs/pre_budgetNOV03.pdf [February 4, 2004]. 4

Roy, J. (n.d.). *Acknowledging Racism.* Canadian Race Relations Foundation [online]. Available: www.crr.ca/EN/MediaCentre/FactSheets/ eMedCen_FacShtAcknowledgeRacism.pdf [May 27, 2004]. 13

Royal Commission on the Economic Union and Development Prospects for Canada. (1985). Report: Vols. 1, 2, and 3. Ottawa: Ministry of Supply and Services Canada. 4

Ruff, N.J. (2003). "Provincial Government." In J.A. Marsh, ed., *The Canadian Encyclopedia, 2003* [online]. Available: www.thecanadianencyclopedia.com/ index.cfm?PgNm=TCE&TCE_Version=A&SectionId=644444&mState=1 [February 2, 2004]. 2

Sainsbury, E. (1977). *The Personal Social Services.* London: Pitman Publishing. 1

"Same-Sex Bill Passes Second Reading." (2000 February 22). *Vancouver Sun*: A8. 10

Saskatchewan Education. (1999 February). "Family and Community Involvement." *On Course.* Planning, Evaluation and Children's Services Branch of Saskatchewan Education [online]. Available: www.sasked.gov.sk.ca/branches/cap_ building_acct/otherdocs/oncourse/1999-02.pdf [May 18, 2004]. 10

Sauber, R. (1983). *The Human Services Delivery System.* New York: Columbia University. 5

Saunders, R. (2003 November). *Defining Vulnerability in the Labour Market.* Canadian Policy Research Networks Inc. [online]. Available: www.cprn.com/en/ doc.cfm?doc=468 [April 18, 2004]. 9

———. (2004 January). *Passion and Commitment under Stress: Human Resource Issues in Canada's Non-Profit Sector: A Synthesis Report: CPRN Research Series on Human Resources in the Non-profit Sector No. 5.* Canadian Policy Research Networks Inc. [online]. Available: www.cprn.org/en/doc.cfm?doc=504# [February 10, 2004]. 5, 7

Schizophrenia Society of Canada. (1999 December). "About the Schizophrenia Society of Canada." *Learning about Schizophrenia: Rays of Hope*, Chapter 16 [online]. Available: www.schizophrenia.ca/famref/szref17.pdf [February 12, 2004]. 8

Scott, K. (1996 Winter). "Insight: Investing in Canada's Children." *Perception* 20(3) [online]. Available: www.ccsd.ca/perception/203/per_ins.htm [April 28, 2004]. 10

Scott, K. (2003). *Funding Matters: The Impact of Canada's New Funding Regime on Nonprofit and Voluntary Organizations.* [online]. Available: www.ccsd.ca/pubs/2003/fm/ [February 9, 2004]. 5

Seguin, R. (2004 April 3). "Cash Overtakes Coercion in Quebec Welfare System." *Globe and Mail Online.* Available: www.theglobeandmail.com/servlet/ArticleNews/TPPrint/LAC/20040403/WELFARE03/TPNational/ [May 13, 2004]. 9

Seidle, F.L. (2002 December). *The Federal Role in Canada's Cities: Overview of Issues and Proposed Actions.* Discussion Paper F/27: "Family Network." Canadian Policy Research Networks [online]. Available: www.cprn.com/en/doc.cfm?doc=158# [February 9, 2004]. 5

Self-Help Resource Centre (Ontario). (2002). "Fact Sheet: Self-Help 101" [online]. Available: www.selfhelp.on.ca/shaw2002Factsheet.pdf February 15, 2004]. 7

——. (2003). *Self-Help Facts and Definitions* [online]. Available: www.selfhelp.on.ca/cgi-bin/resource/webdata_shrc.pl?fid=1055121535&query=Format%3Dfactsheet%26pagenum%3D1%26cgifunction%3Dsearch%26submit%3Dsearch&cgifunction=form [February 15, 2004]. 7

Self-Help Groups. (1999 Summer). *Expression* 12(4). Ottawa: National Advisory Council on Aging. 7

Senate of Canada. (2002). *The Senate of Canada Annual Report 2001–2002* [online]. Available: www.parl.gc.ca/information/about/process/Senate/AnnualRep/2002/pdf/AR-0102-COMP-e.pdf [February 2, 2004]. 2

Senge, P. (1990). *The Fifth Discipline: The Art and Practice of the Learning Organization.* New York: Doubleday Currency. 6

Shepherdson, D. (1995 April). *Meeting the Challenge: Managing Change in the Nineties: Management Practices No. 9.* Canadian Centre for Management Development and Conference Board of Canada [online]. Available: www.ccmd-ccg.gc.ca/Research/publications/pdfs/p48e.pdf [March 7, 2004]. 8

Siena, K.P. (2003), *Before the Welfare State: Poverty, Public Medicine and the English Poor Law in Eighteenth-Century London and pre-Confederation Toronto.* Comparative Program on Health and Society, 2002–03 Working Paper Series, Trent University [online]. Available: www.utoronto.ca/cphs/WORKINGPAPERS/CPHS2002_Kevin_Siena.pdf [February 12, 2004]. 6

Simich, L., M. Beiser, F. Mawani, and J. O'Hare. (2001 August). *Paved with Good Intentions: Paths of Secondary Migration of Government-Assisted Refugees in Ontario* [online]. Available: settlement.org/downloads/Paved_With_Good_Intentions.pdf [May 27, 2004]. 13

Smith, E. (2004 March). *Nowhere to Turn? Responding to Partner Violence against Immigrant and Visible Minority Women: Voices of Frontline Workers.* Canadian Council on Social Development [online]. Available: www.ccsd.ca/pubs/2004/nowhere/voices.pdf [May 27, 2004]. 13

Smith, M. (2000). "Interest Groups and Social Movements." In M.S. Whittington and G. Williams, eds., *Canadian Politics in the 21st Century,* pp. 173–91. Scarborough: Nelson Thomson Learning. 3

Smye, V. and B. Mussell. (2001 July). *Aboriginal Mental Health: "What Works Best": A Discussion Paper* [online]. Available: www.mheccu.ubc.ca/publications/amh/discussion-paper.pdf [June 13, 2004]. 12

Sobol, M. (2000). *Adoption Trends and a Political Agenda for Ontario.* Adoption Council of Canada [online]. Available: www.adoption.ca/sobol.htm [April 28, 2004]. 10

"Social Democrat." (2004). *Wikipedia, The Free Encyclopedia* . [online]. Available: en.wikipedia.org/wiki/Social_Democrat [2004 January 19]. 1

Social Development Canada. (2004a March 3). *Canada's Retirement Income System— Simply Stated* [online]. Available: www.sdc.gc.ca/en/isp/common/ris/simple.shtml [May 9, 2004]. 11

———. (2004b May 10). *Social Development Partnership Program—Frequently Asked Questions* [online]. Available: www.hrsdc.gc.ca/en/hip/sd/03_SDPP_FAQ.shtml [May 29, 2004]. 14

Social Planning Council of Metropolitan Toronto. (1997). *Policy Statement on Provincial Devolution of Responsibilities to Municipalities and Communities* [online]. Available: www.worldchat.com/public/tab/polstmnt.htm [March 16, 2004]. 8

Social Planning Council of Ottawa-Carleton. (2001 August 15). *Advancing the Community by Strengthening the Voluntary Sector: Report on the 2001 Community Consultation* [online]. Available: www.spcottawa.on.ca/PDFs/Publications/Advancing%20the%20Voluntary%20Sector.pdf [February 23, 2004]. 5

Social Planning Council of Winnipeg. (2004). *About Us* [online]. Available: www.spcw.mb.ca/about.html [March 7, 2004]. 8

Social Research and Demonstration Corporation. (2004). *About SRDC* [online]. Available: www.srdc.org/english/about/about.htm [July 30, 2004]. 1

Specken, J. and T. Geyer. (2000 November). *Seniors and Volunteerism: The Impact of Volunteering on Senior Volunteers and on Services for Seniors.* Society for the Retired and Semi-Retired [online]. Available: www.srsr-seniors.com/pdf/Seniors%20and%20Volunteer.pdf [February 26, 2004]. 7

Spicker, P. (2004). *An Introduction to Social Policy.* Robert Gordon University [online]. Available: www2.rgu.ac.uk/publicpolicy/introduction/contents.htm [January 19, 2004]. 1, 4

Splane, R. (1965). *Social Welfare in Ontario, 1791–1893.* Toronto: University of Toronto Press. 2

Splane, R. (1987). "Further Reflections: 1975–1986." In S.A. Yelaja, ed., *Canadian Social Policy,* rev. ed., pp. 245–65. Waterloo: Wilfrid Laurier University Press. 2

Standing Committee on Finance. (1997 December). *Keeping the Balance: Security and Opportunity for Canadians* [online]. Available: www.parl.gc.ca/InfoComDoc/36/1/FINA/Studies/Reports/FINARP02-E.htm [February 4, 2004]. 4

Standing Committee on Human Resources Development and the Status of Persons with Disabilities. (2000). *Interim Report* [online]. Available: www.parl.gc.ca/InfoComDoc/36/1/SC/R/studies/reports [April 27, 2004]. 5, 10

Standing Senate Committee on Aboriginal Peoples. (2003 October). *Urban Aboriginal Youth: An Action Plan for Change: Final Report* [online]. Available: www.turtleisland.org/news/absenuayrpt.pdf [May 16, 2004]. 12

Stasiulis, D., and Y. Abu-Laban. (2004). "Unequal Relations and the Struggle for Equality: Race and Ethnicity in Canadian Politics. In M. Whittington and G. Williams, eds., *Canadian Politics in the 21st Century*, 6th ed., pp. 371–97. Scarborough: Thomson Nelson. 13

Statistics Canada. (1995). *A Portrait of Persons with Disabilities.* Cat. No. 89-542E. Ottawa: Minister of Industry, Science and Technology. 14

———. (1997 Spring). "Canadian Children in the 1990s: Selected Findings of the National Longitudinal Survey of Children and Youth." *Canadian Social Trends.* Catalogue No. 11-008-XPE [online]. Available: www.statcan.ca/english/kits/pdf/social/kids1.pdf [April 29, 2004]. 10

———. (2000). *Women in Canada.* Catalogue 89-503-XPE. Ottawa: Author. 2

———. (2001 August 15). "Food Insecurity in Canadian Households." *The Daily* [online]. Available: www.statcan.ca/Daily/English/010815/d010815a.htm [April 18, 2004]. 9

———. (2002a November 5). *2001 Census Analysis Series: Collective Dwellings.* Catalogue: 96F0030XIE2001004 [online]. Available: www12.statcan.ca/english/census01/Products/Analytic/companion/coll/pdf/96F0030XIE2001004.pdf [February 12, 2004]. 6

———. (2002b November 6). *2001 Census: Families and Households Profile: Canada* [online]. Available: www12.statcan.ca/english/census01/products/analytic/companion/fam/canada.cfm [May 9, 2004]. 11

———. (2002c November 6). *2001 Census: Profile of Canadian Families and Households: Diversification Continues: Canada* [online]. Available: www12.statcan.ca/english/census01/products/analytic/companion/fam/canada.cfm [February 1, 2004]. 2

———. (2002d August 27). "Health of the Off-Reserve Aboriginal Population, 2000/01." *The Daily* [online]. Available: www.statcan.ca/Daily/English/020827/d020827a.htm [May 9, 2004]. 12

———. (2002e October 22). *Profile of Canadian Families and Households: Diversification Continues.* Catalogue No. 96F0030XIE2001003 [online]. Available: www12.statcan.ca/english/census01/Products/Analytic/companion/fam/pdf/96F0030XIE2001003.pdf [April 28, 2004]. 10

——. (2003a). *2001 Census: Analysis Series: Aboriginal Peoples of Canada: A Demographic Profile* [online]. Available: www12.statcan.ca/english/census01/Products/Analytic/companion/abor/pdf/96F0030XIE2001007.pdf [May 13, 2004]. 12

——. (2003b January). *2001 Census: Analysis Series: Canada's Ethnocultural Portrait: The Changing Mosaic* [online]. Available: collection.nlc-bnc.ca/100/200/301/statcan/2001_census_analysis_96f0030-e/96F0030XIE2001008.pdf [May 27, 2004]. 13

——. (2003c November 25). *Appendix A: Glossary of Terms, 2001 Census Technical Report: Families*. Catalogue No. 92-381-XIE [online]. Available: www12.statcan.ca/english/census01/Products/Reference/tech_rep/family/app_a.cfm [April 28, 2004]. 10

——. (2003d May 13). *Canada: Overview: Analyzing Family Income* [online]. Available: www12.statcan.ca/english/census01/products/analytic/companion/inc/canada.cfm [April 18, 2004]. 1, 9

——. (2003e May 13). "Census of Population: Income of Individuals, Families and Households: Religion, 2001." *The Daily* [online]. Available: www.statcan.ca/Daily/English/030513/d030513a.htm [April 18, 2004]. 9

——. (2003f February 11). "Census of Population: Labour Force Activity, Occupation, Industry, Class of Worker, Place of Work, Mode of Transportation, Language of Work and Unpaid Work." *The Daily* [online]. Available: www.statcan.ca/Daily/English/030211/d030211a.htm [May 27, 2004]. 13

——. (2003g March). *Earnings of Canadians: Making a Living in the New Economy*. 2001 Census: Analysis Series [online]. Available: www12.statcan.ca/english/census01/Products/Analytic/companion/earn/pdf/96F0030XIE2001013.pdf [June 15, 2004]. 13

——. (2003h September). *Ethnic Diversity Survey: Portrait of a Multicultural Society* [online]. Available: www.statcan.ca/english/freepub/89-593-XIE/pdf/89-593-XIE03001.pdf [May 27, 2004]. 13

——. (2003i September 29). *Residential Care Facilities*. [online]. Available: www.statcan.ca/english/sdds/3210.htm [February 12, 2004]. 6

——. (2004a March 12). *Analyzing Family Income* [online]. Available: www12.statcan.ca/english/census01/products/analytic/companion/inc/canada.cfm [May 9, 2004]. 11

——. (2004b January 13). "Federal Government Finance: Assets and Liabilities." *The Daily* [online]. Available: www.statcan.ca/Daily/English/040113/d040113c.htm [February 23, 2004]. 4

——. (2004c January). *Latest Release from the Labour Force Survey* [online]. Available: www.statcan.ca/english/Subjects/Labour/LFS/lfs-en.htm [February 23, 2004]. 2

——. (2004d February). *Latest Release from the Labour Force Survey* [online]. Available: www.statcan.ca/english/Subjects/Labour/LFS/lfs.pdf [March 25, 2004]. 2

———. (2004f March 12). "Labour Force Survey." *The Daily* [online]. Available: www.statcan.ca/Daily/English/040312/d040312a.htm [April 18, 2004]. 9

———. (2004g March 26). "Study: Moving Out of Low-Paid Work: 1996 to 2001." *The Daily* [online]. Available: www.statcan.ca/Daily/English/040326/ d040326d.htm [May 13, 2004]. 9

Statistics Canada/Canadian Centre for Justice Statistics. (2001 June). *Family Violence in Canada: A Statistical Profile 2001* [online]. Available: collection.nlc-bnc.ca/ 100/201/301/statcan/family_violence/0000185-224amend01_07_16-XIE.pdf [May 16, 2004]. 12

Status of Disabled Persons Secretariat. (1994). *Disability Policy and Programs in Canada: A Brief Overview.* Ottawa: Human Resources Development Canada. 14

Stephenson, M., G. Rondeau, J.C. Michaud, and S. Fiddler. (2000). *In Critical Demand: Social Work in Canada, Vol. 1, Final Report.* Social Work Sector Steering Committee [online]. Available: www.socialworkincanada.org/pdf/vol1_en/ toc_en.pdf [February 10, 2004]. 5, 7, 11, 12

Stevenson, K. (1999). "Family Characteristics of Problem Kids." *Canadian Social Trends* (Winter): 2–6. 10

Stewart, J. (2002 September 10). *Speaking Notes for the Honourable Jane Stewart, Minister of Human Resources Development Canada: To the International Social Security Association: Vancouver, B.C.* [online]. Available: www.hrdc-drhc.gc.ca/common/ speeches/minhrdc/20020910.html [January 31, 2004]. 2

Strong-Boag, V. (1979 Spring). "Wages for Housework: Mothers' Allowances and the Beginnings of Social Security in Canada." *Journal of Canadian Studies* 14(1): 24–34. 3, 8

Struthers, J. (1983). *No Fault of Their Own: Unemployment and the Canadian Welfare State, 1914–1941.* Toronto: University of Toronto Press. 3

Stutt, T., and E. Adelberg. (1998 March). "Can Ottawa Eliminate Canada's Social Deficit?" *Perception* 21(4): 5–7. 4

Sudbury, F. and M. Rook. (2003 November 20). "Needs-Based Access to Residential Care: Changing Policy, Practice and Outcomes on Southern Vancouver Island." *Stride* [online]. Available: www.stridemagazine.com/2003_11%20November/ article_03.shtml [February 12, 2004]. 6

Sussman, S. (1998 April). "The First Asylums in Canada: A Response to Neglectful Community Care and Current Trends." *Canadian Journal of Psychiatry* 43(3) (Review Paper): 260–64 [online]. Available: www.cpa-apc.org/Publications/ Archives/CJP/1998/April/apr98_revpap1.htm [February 12, 2004]. 6

Swanson, S.M. (1999). *Abuse and Neglect of Older Adults: Information from the National Clearinghouse on Family Violence.* Health Canada [online]. Available: www.hc-sc.gc.ca/ hppb/familyviolence/pdfs/abuseneg98en.pdf [May 13, 2004]. 11

Swimmer, G., ed. (1996). "An Introduction to Life under the Knife." *How Ottawa Spends, 1996–97: Life Under the Knife,* 1–37. Ottawa: Carleton University Press. 4

Tator, C. (1996). "Anti-Racism and the Human-Service Delivery System." In C.E. James, ed., *Perspectives on Racism and the Human Services Sector,* pp. 152–70. Toronto: University of Toronto Press. 13

Taylor, G. (1969). *The Problem of Poverty, 1660–1834.* Seminar Studies in History, Kings College School. Wimbledon, UK: Longmans, Green, and Company. 3

THCU (The Health Communication Unit). (2001 April). *Introduction to Health Promotion Program Planning, Version 3.0.* Centre for Health Promotion, University of Toronto [online]. Available: www.thcu.ca/infoandresources/publications/Planning.wkbk.content.apr01.format.aug03.pdf [February 12, 2004]. 6

Thompson, A.H., A. W. Howard, and Y. Jin. (2001). "A Social Problem Index for Canada." *Canadian Journal of Psychiatry* 46: 45–51 [online]. Available: www.cpa-apc.org/Publications/Archives/CJP/2001/Feb/Feb2001.asp [January 19, 2004]. 1

Thompson, J. (n.d.). "Healthy Lifestyles and Aging." *Expression* 10(2). Ottawa: National Advisory Council on Aging [online]. Available: www.hc-sc.gc.ca/seniors-aines/naca/expression/10-2/pdf/ex10-2e.pdf [May 9, 2004]. 11

Thorburn, H.G. (2003). "Pressure Group." In J.A. Marsh. ed., *The Canadian Encyclopedia, 2003* [online]. Available: www.thecanadianencyclopedia.com/PrinterFriendly.cfm?Params=A1ARTA0006467 [February 1, 2004]. 2

Thursz, D. (1977). "Social Action." In J.B. Turner, ed., *Encyclopedia of Social Work,* 17th ed., Vol. 2, pp. 1274–80. Washington, D.C.: National Association of Social Workers. 8

Tobis. D. (2000). *Moving from Residential Institutions to Community-Based Social Services in Central and Eastern Europe and the Former Soviet Union.* Washington, D.C.: The World Bank [online]. Available: lnweb18.worldbank.org/eca/eca.nsf/Attachments/Moving+from+Residential+Institutions+to+Community-Based+Social+Services/$File/14490.pdf [February 12, 2004]. 6

Torjman, S. (1995). *Milestone or Millstone: The Legacy of the Social Service Review.* Ottawa: Caledon Institute of Social Policy. 4

———. (1996 October). *The Disability Income System in Canada.* Ottawa: Caledon Institute of Social Policy. 14

———. (1997 November). *Welfare Warfare.* Ottawa: Caledon Institute of Social Policy. 8

———. (1998 October). *Investing in the Whole Community: Strategies for a Caring Society.* Ottawa: Caledon Institute for Social Policy [online]. Available: www.caledoninst.org/Publications/PDF/full107%2Epdf [March 24, 2004]. 8

———. (2002 September). *The Bases Are Loaded: Presentation to the Groundswell Conference.* Caledon Institute of Social Policy [online]. Available: www.caledoninst.org/Abstracts/553820282.htm [January 31, 2004]. 2

Townson, M. (2003 March). *Women in Non-Standard Jobs: The Public Policy Challenge.* Status of Women Canada [online]. Available: www.swc-cfc.gc.ca/pubs/0662334809/200303_0662334809_e.pdf [February 1, 2004]. 2

Trainor, C. (2003 June). *Family Violence in Canada: A Statistical Profile 2002.* Statistics Canada Catalogue No.85-224-XIE [online]. Available: www.statcan.ca/english/freepub/85-224-XIE/85-224-XIE00002.pdf [April 29, 2004]. 10

Trattner, W.I. (1989). *From Poor Law to Welfare State,* 4th ed. New York: Free Press. 3

Treasury Board of Canada Secretariat. (1995 November). *Stretching the Tax Dollar Series—The Federal Government as "Partner": Six Steps to Successful Collaboration* [online]. Available: www.tbs-sct.gc.ca/pubs_pol/opepubs/tb_o3/fgpe2_e.asp [February 10, 2004]. 5

———. (2000 April 11). *SUFA Template: Guide to Federal Government Reporting* [online]. Available: www.tbs-sct.gc.ca/rma/account/sufa-ecus/temp-mod_e.asp [February 12, 2004]. 6

———. (2003a February 26). *Estimates for the Government of Canada and Other Supporting Documents: 2004–2005 Estimates: Part I: The Government Expenditure Plan* [online]. Available: www.tbs-sct.gc.ca/est-pre/20042005/001_e.pdf [March 28, 2004]. 4

———. (2003b December 10). *Host Program* [online]. Available: www.tbs-sct.gc.ca/rma/eppi-ibdrp/hrdb-rhbd/h020_e.asp [May 27, 2004]. 13

———. (2003c October 30). *Canada's Performance 2003—Highlights* [online]. Available: www.tbs-sct.gc.ca/report/govrev/03/cp-rc-b_e.asp [August 9, 2004]. 9

Trempe, R., S. Davis, and R. Kunin. (1997). Advisory Group, Citizenship and Immigration Canada. *Not Just Numbers: A Canadian Framework for Future Immigration.* Ottawa: Minister of Public Works and Government Services Canada. 13

Trocmé, N., B. MacLaurin, B. Fallon, J. Daciuk, D. Billingsley, M. Tourigny, M. Mayer, J. Wright, K. Barter, G. Burford, J. Hornick, R. Sullivan, and B. McKenzie. (2001). *Canadian Incidence Study of Reported Child Abuse and Neglect: Final Report.* Health Canada [online]. Available: www.hc-sc.gc.ca/pphb-dgspsp/publicat/cisfr-ecirf/pdf/cis_e.pdf [April 29, 2004]. 10

Tropp, E. (1977). "Social Group Work: The Developmental Approach." In J.B. Turner, ed., *Encyclopedia of Social Work,* 17th ed., Vol. 2, pp. 1321–28. Washington, D.C.: National Association of Social Workers. 8

Tsoukalas, S. and A. MacKenzie. (2003). *Personal Security Index, 2003: A Reflection of How Canadians Feel Five Years Later.* Canadian Council on Social Development [online]. Available: www.ccsd.ca/pubs/2003/psi/psi03.pdf [April 18, 2004]. 9

Turner, J.C. (2001). "The Historical Base." In J.C. Turner and F.J. Turner, eds., *Canadian Social Welfare,* 4th ed., pp. 80–95. Toronto: Pearson Education Canada. 4

Tyjnych, J. (2003 August). *The Basis of Adoption Legislation in Canada.* Adoption Council of Canada newsletter [online]. Available: www.adoption.ca/legislation/030909legbasis.htm [April 28, 2004]. 10

United Nations. (1999 November 29). *Families: Victims of Poverty and Homelessness.* United Nations, International Day of Families. Division for Social Policy and

Development [online]. Available: www.un.org/esa/socdev/family/IntObs/IDF/Backgrounders/Backg96.htm [April 28, 2004]. 10

——. (2003a January 15). *Ageing: Implications of an Ageing Society* [online]. Available: www.un.org/esa/socdev/ageing/ageimpl.htm [May 9, 2004]. 11

——. (2003b January 15). *Vienna International Plan of Action on Ageing*. UN/Division for Social Policy and Development [online]. Available: www.un.org/esa/socdev/ageing/ageipaa.htm [May 9, 2004]. 11

University of Manitoba. (2004). *Learning Opportunities: Elizabeth Hill Counselling Centre* [online]. Available: www.elizabethhill.ca/learning.html [February 15, 2004]. 7

Urban Poverty Consortium of Waterloo Region. (2000 November 20). *Let's Talk about Poverty: Poverty Fact Sheet #6* [online]. Available: www.waterlooregion.org/poverty/talk/6.html [April 18, 2004]. 9

Vanier Institute of the Family. (1992). *Canadian Families in Transition: The Implications and Challenges of Change*. Ottawa: Author. 10

Vargo, F. (2004). "Disability." In J.A. Marsh, ed., *The Canadian Encyclopedia, 2004* [online]. Available: www.thecanadianencyclopedia.com/PrinterFriendly.cfm?Params=A1ARTA0002310 [May 29, 2004]. 14

Vida, S., R.C. Monks, and P. Des Rosiers. (2002). "Prevalence and Correlates of Elder Abuse and Neglect in a Geriatric Psychiatry Service." *Canadian Journal of Psychiatry* 47: 459–67 [online]. Available: www.cpa-apc.org/Publications/Archives/CJP/2002/june/originalResearchVida.asp [May 12, 2004]. 11

Voluntary Sector Initiative. (2004a February 23). *About the VSI: Background: The Capacity Joint Table* [online]. Available: www.vsi-isbc.ca/eng/about/cjt_general.cfm [February 23, 2004]. 5

——. (2004b). *Working and Volunteering: National Volunteerism Initiative Environmental Scan on Volunteering in Canada* [online]. Available: www.vsi-isbc.ca/eng/hr/environmental_scan_summary.cfm [February 15, 2004]. 7

Voluntary Sector Steering Group. (2002). *Building a Stronger Voluntary Sector: How the VSI Is Making a Difference. Voluntary Sector Steering Group Report to the Voluntary Sector in Canada*. Voluntary Sector Initiative [online]. Available: www.vsi-isbc.ca/eng/about/pdf/building.pdf [March 7, 2004]. 5

Volunteer Canada. (2000a). *Canadian Code for Volunteer Involvement* [online]. Available: www.volunteer.ca/volunteer/pdf/CodeEng.pdf [February 15, 2004]. 7

——. (2000b) *Volunteering … A Booming Trend* [online]. Available: www.volunteerburnaby.ca/pdf/booming_trend.pdf [May 9, 2004]. 11

——. (2001). *Rethinking Volunteer Engagement: International Year of Volunteers 2001* [online]. Available: www.volunteer.ca/volunteer/pdf/RethinkingEng.pdf [February 15, 2004]. 7

——. (2004a). *Canada Volunteerism Initiative* [online]. Available: www.volunteer.ca/volcan/eng/content/canvol-init/canvol-init.php [February 15, 2004]. 7

——. (2004b). *Older Adult Volunteerism* [online]. Available: www.volunteer.ca/volcan/eng/volincan/older-adults.php?display=2,0,8 [May 23, 2004]. 11

——. (2004c). *Trends in Volunteerism* [online]. Available: www.volunteer.ca/volcan/eng/volincan/trendsinvol.php?display=2,0,9 [February 15, 2004]. 7

Wachtel, A. (1997). *The "State of the Art" in Child Abuse Prevention, 1997.* Ottawa: National Clearinghouse on Family Violence. 10

Walkem, A. and H. Bruce. (2002). *Calling Forth Our Future: Options for the Exercise of Indigenous Peoples' Authority in Child Welfare.* Union of B.C. Indian Chiefs [online]. Available: www.ubcic.bc.ca/docs/UBCIC_OurFuture.pdf [May 9, 2004]. 12

Walker, B.E. (2003). *News and What's New: Same-Sex Marriage* [online]. Available: www.bwalkerlaw.com/news/samesex.html [February 1, 2004]. 2

Wallace, E. (1950). "The Origin of the Social Welfare State in Canada: 1867–1900." *Canadian Journal of Economics and Political Science* 16(3): 383–93. 2

Ward, L. (2002 June 14). "The First Nations Goverance Act." CBC News [online]. Available: www.cbc.ca/news/indepth/firstnations/indianact.html [May 13, 2004]. 12

Watson, W. (2001 March). *Has Neo-Conservatism Failed?* Institute for Research on Public Policy [online]. Available: www.irpp.org/po/archive/po0301.htm [January 19, 2004]. 1

Watt, S., and A. Soifer. (1996). "Conducting Psycho-Social Assessments with the Elderly." In M.J. Holosko and M.D. Feit, eds., *Social Work Practice with the Elderly,* 2nd ed.: pp. 37–53. Toronto: Canadian Scholars' Press. 11

Weinfeld, M. (1999). "The Challenge of Ethnic Match: Minority Origin Professionals in Health and Social Services." In H. Troper and M. Weinfeld, eds., *Ethnicity, Politics, and Public Policy: Case Studies in Canadian Diversity,* pp. 117–41. Toronto: University of Toronto Press. 13

Weinfeld, M., and A. Wilkinson. (1999). "Immigration, Diversity, and Minority Communities." In P.S. Li, ed., *Race and Ethnic Relations in Canada,* pp. 55–87. Don Mills: Oxford University Press. 13

Whalen, J.M. (2002). "Last Resort for the Poor: The Saint John Almshouse, 1843–1900." *Saint John, New Brunswick: Saint John Vintage* [online]. Available: new-brunswick.net/Saint_John/almshouse.html [February 12, 2004]. 6

Wharf, B. (1986). "Social Welfare and the Political System." In J.C. Turner and F.J. Turner, eds., *Canadian Social Welfare,* 2nd ed., pp. 103–18. Don Mills: Collier Macmillan Canada. 2

——. (1992 Spring/Summer). "From Coordination to Social Reform." *Perception* 16(2-3): 41–46, 54. 5

Whelan, S. (2000 April). *Productivity and Innovation: A Competitive and Prosperous Canada.* Report of the Standing Committee on Industry, Parliament of Canada [online]. Available: www.parl.gc.ca/InfoComDoc/36/2/INDU/Studies/Reports/indy20-e.html [January 31, 2004]. 2

Whitehorn, A. (2003a). "New Democratic Party." In J.A. Marsh, ed., *The Canadian Encyclopedia, 2003* [online]. Available: www.thecanadianencyclopedia.com/index.cfm?PgNm=TCE&Params=A1ARTA0005699 [January 19, 2004]. 1

———. (2003b). "Social Democracy." In J.A. Marsh, ed., *The Canadian Encyclopedia, 2003* [online]. Available: www.thecanadianencyclopedia.com/index.cfm?PgNm=TCE&Params=A1ARTA0007520 [January 19, 2004]. 1

Wilensky, H., and C. Lebeaux. (1965). *Industrial Society and Social Welfare.* New York: Free Press. 1

Woodall, C. (2004). "Focal Point: Silent Voices in Distress." *Diversity Now* [online]. Available: www.diversitynow.ca/features/focalpoint/silentvoices.shtml [May 27, 2004]. 13

Woolcock, M. (2001 Spring). "The Place of Social Capital in Understanding Social and Economic Outcomes." *Canadian Journal of Policy Research/Revue canadienne de recherche sur les politiques* 2(1). Ottawa: Government of Canada's Policy Research Secretariat. 8

World Bank Group. (2001 April 6). *In-Kind Transfers* [online]. Available: www.worldbank.org/poverty/safety/inkind/index.htm [January 19, 2004]. 1

World Health Organization. (2001a). *Global Movement for Active Ageing—Background Information.* Department of Noncommunicable Disease Prevention and Health Promotion [online]. Available: www.who.int/hpr/globalmovement/background.htm [May 9, 2004]. 11

———. (2001b). *ICF Introduction* [online]. Available: www.who.int/classification/icf/intros/ICF-Eng-Intro.pdf [May 29, 2004]. 14

———. (2002). *The Toronto Declaration on the Global Prevention of Elder Abuse* [online]. Available: www.who.int/hpr/ageing/TorontoDeclarationEnglish.pdf [May 9, 2004]. 11

World Summit for Social Development. (2000 February 10). *Overall Review and Appraisal of the Implementation of the Outcome of the World Summit for Social Development: Draft Agreed Conclusions* [online]. Available: www.icsw.org/copenhagen_implementation/csd38rev1.htm [September 10, 2000]. 5

Yalnizyan, A. (1994). "Securing Society: Creating Canadian Social Policy. In A. Yalnizyan, T.R. Ide, and A.J. Cordell, eds., *Shifting Time: Social Policy and the Future of Work,* pp. 17–71. Toronto: Between the Lines. 3

Young, W.R. (2002 May 9). *Current Disability Issues in Canada: A Background Paper.* Canada Pension Plan (CPP) Disability: Consultations with Canadians [online]. Available: www.parl.gc.ca/cppd/issues/disability_issues_8_e.asp [May 29, 2004]. 14

Zastrow, C. (2004). *Introduction to Social Work and Social Welfare*, 8th ed. Belmont: Brooks-Cole/Thomson Learning. 3, 8, 9, 11

INDEX